Data and Evidence in Linguistics

The question of what types of data and evidence can be used is one of the most important topics in linguistics. This book is the first to present comprehensively the methodological problems associated with linguistic data and evidence. Its originality is twofold. First, the authors' approach accounts for a series of unexplained characteristics of linguistic theorising: the uncertainty and diversity of data, the role of evidence in the evaluation of hypotheses, the problem-solving strategies as well as the emergence and resolution of inconsistencies. Second, the findings are obtained by the application of a new model of plausible argumentation which is also of relevance from a general argumentation-theoretical point of view. All concepts and theses are systematically introduced and illustrated by a number of examples from different linguistic theories, and a detailed case-study section shows how the proposed model can be applied to specific linguistic problems.

ANDRÁS KERTÉSZ is Professor of German Linguistics and Director of the Centre for Linguistics and Philosophy at the University of Debrecen. He is also Head of the Research Group for Theoretical Linguistics of the Hungarian Academy of Sciences.

CSILLA RÁKOSI is Senior Research Fellow in the Research Group for Theoretical Linguistics of the Hungarian Academy of Sciences.

Data and Evidence in Linguistics

A Plausible Argumentation Model

András Kertész and Csilla Rákosi

CAMBRIDGE
UNIVERSITY PRESS

CAMBRIDGE UNIVERSITY PRESS
Cambridge, New York, Melbourne, Madrid, Cape Town,
Singapore, São Paulo, Delhi, Tokyo, Mexico City

Cambridge University Press
The Edinburgh Building, Cambridge CB2 8RU, UK

Published in the United States of America by Cambridge University Press,
New York

www.cambridge.org
Information on this title: www.cambridge.org/9781107009240

First published 2012

Printed in the United Kingdom at the University Press, Cambridge

A catalogue record for this publication is available from the British Library

Library of Congress Cataloguing in Publication data
Kertész, András.
Data and evidence in linguistics : a plausible argumentation model / András Kertész,
Csilla Rákosi.
p. cm.
Includes bibliographical references and index.
ISBN 978-1-107-00924-0 (hardback)
1. Linguistic analysis (Linguistics) 2. Linguistics – Research – Methodology.
3. Corpora (Linguistics) 4. Computational linguistics. I. Rákosi, Csilla. II. Title.
P126.K43 2012
410.1 – dc23 2011043831

ISBN 978-1-107-00924-0 Hardback

Contents

List of figures and table

Figures

Table

Preface

This book is the latest product of a long-term metalinguistic research programme whose earlier stages have been hallmarked by a series of monographs (e.g. Kertész 1991, 1993, 2004a, b; Rákosi 2005). The idea that linguistic theorising is built on plausible argumentation was put forward in Kertész (1993) and was integrated with other components of the programme in Kertész (2004a). The elaboration of the p-model of plausible argumentation, around which the present book centres, is the accomplishment of the task set out in Part V of Kertész (2004a); thus, it is the direct continuation of this line of the programme.

The implementation of the plan was prepared at two levels in parallel, which have been conjoined in the present book. On the one hand, we elaborated different aspects of the p-model with the help of detailed case studies (Kertész & Rákosi 2005a, b, 2006, 2009a, b). On the other hand, on the basis of thorough and multifaceted analyses of the current literature on linguistic data and evidence, we arrived at conclusions that – besides the findings of Kertész (1993) and (2004a) – clearly motivate the application of the p-model of plausible argumentation to linguistic theorising (Kertész & Rákosi 2008a, b, c, 2009c).

The present book is a research monograph written primarily for linguists. However, it also raises problems of current research in argumentation theory and the philosophy of science. Therefore, as a secondary target group, it also addresses philosophers of science and argumentation theorists. Moreover, since it includes a series of examples which are intended to be simple and illuminating, and which illustrate the methodology of linguistic problem solving, it can also be used as a textbook recommended for students in these fields.

Accordingly, the chapters have been organised in a way which facilitates different readings. The main text should be read by all target groups. The subsections entitled 'Motivation and background' may be skipped by linguists (but consulted if they are interested in the details of the theoretical considerations behind the concepts) and should be read by philosophers of science and argumentation theorists. The examples may be skipped by the latter, but should be read by linguists. Nevertheless, all readers are advised to go through the detailed case study in Part IV which exemplifies how our approach works in practice.

Work on the present book was supported by the Research Group for Theoretical Linguistics of the Hungarian Academy of Sciences at the Universities of Debrecen, Pécs and Szeged. It was also supported by the projects TÁMOP 4.2.1./B-09/1/KONV-2010–0007 and OTKA K 77823. We are very grateful to two anonymous referees for their insightful comments, constructive criticism and useful suggestions. We are also indebted to George Seel for improving our English. Our special thanks are due to Helen Barton at Cambridge University Press for her constant encouragement and help without which the book could not have been published. Finally, we thank the publishers for permission to include revised versions of the following articles in the present book: A. Kertész & Cs. Rákosi, 'Daten und Evidenz in linguistischen Theorien: ein Forschungsüberblick', in A. Kertész & Cs. Rákosi (eds.), *New Approaches to Linguistic Evidence. Pilot Studies/Neue Ansätze zu linguistischer Evidenz. Pilotstudien* (Frankfurt am Main: Lang, 2008), 21–60; A. Kertész & Cs. Rákosi, 'On current approaches to linguistic data and evidence', *Sprachtheorie und germanistische Linguistik* 19(2) (2009), 127–72; Cs. Rákosi, 'Metatheoretical reconstruction of psycholinguistic experiments 1', *Sprachtheorie und germanistische Linguistik* 20(1) (2011), 55–93; Cs. Rákosi, 'Metatheoretical reconstruction of psycholinguistic experiments 2', *Sprachtheorie und germanistische Linguistik* 20(2) (2011), 159–87.

András Kertész
Csilla Rákosi

Abbreviations and central concepts

Symbols

$\sim p$	the negation of statement p
$\|p\|_S$	the plausibility value of statement p on the basis of source S
$0 < \|p\|_S < 1$	statement p is plausible on the basis of source S
$0 \leq \|p\|_S < 1$	statement p is of neutral plausibility or plausible on the basis of source S
$0 < \|p\|_S \leq 1$	statement p is plausible or true with certainty on the basis of source S
$0 \leq \|p\|_S \leq 1$	statement p has a plausibility value on the basis of source S
p & q	the conjunction of statements p and q
$p \rightarrow p'$	transformation of premise p into statement p'
$[p]$	statement p is a latent background assumption
$\min \{a_1, \ldots, a_n\}$	the minimum (lowest value) of $a_1, \ldots, a_n$
$\max \{a_1, \ldots, a_n\}$	the maximum (highest value) of $a_1, \ldots, a_n$
$\sqrt[n]{a_1 \cdot \ldots a_n}$	geometric mean of $a_1, \ldots, a_n$
$\frac{a_1 + \ldots + a_n}{n}$	arithmetic mean of $a_1, \ldots, a_n$

1 Introduction

The problem of linguistic data and evidence is in the air. A tiny spark suffices to kindle interest in it. In fact, new publications on the nature of linguistic data and evidence appear and conferences are held almost continuously. Adherents of different linguistic schools conduct – sometimes extremely heated – debates with each other on this topic. The question of which data count as evidence is one of the most important topics in linguistics, which has a direct and profound impact on the *fundamentals* of this discipline. This is, of course, by no means accidental. It is easy to see that the evaluation of the workability of conflicting theories depends heavily on what kinds of data can be regarded as evidence that either supports or refutes (in some sense) their hypotheses.

In their volume *What counts as evidence in linguistics*?, Penke and Rosenbach formulate the problem as follows:

> While thirty years ago linguists were still debating whether linguistics ought to be an 'empirical science' . . . , today we can safely say that this issue has been settled by and large and that nowadays most linguists will probably agree that linguistics is indeed an empirical science. What is being discussed is . . . not *whether* empirical evidence may or should be used, but rather, *what type of* empirical evidence, and *how* it is to be used. (Penke & Rosenbach 2004a: 480; emphasis as in the original)

Thus, the current debate on data and evidence centres around the following *methodological problem*, which is of great significance for the everyday research practice in linguistics, and which we will treat as the *Central Problem* of the debate:

(CP) (a) What types of data/evidence can be used,
and
(b) how does data/evidence work in linguistic theories?

We aim to contribute to the current debate on data and evidence from a perspective which has not been developed so far, although it is, in our opinion substantial.[1] The *basic idea* of the book is based on three considerations.

First, tackling and solving (CP) *presupposes* the clarification of a series of further problems: 'What is a datum?', 'What is evidence?', 'What is the structure of data/evidence?', 'What is the function of data/evidence in linguistic theories?' etc. Most of the current literature does not raise these issues, while the few attempts which touch on them are fragmentary and controversial.

Second, due to the nature of linguistic theorising, there is a close but hidden relationship between the *structure and function of data and evidence* on the one hand and the *argumentation structure of theories* on the other. Thus, so as to understand the former, it is indispensable – among other things – to reveal this relationship.

Third, the main shortcoming of the literature dealing with (CP) is that mechanically adopted metatheoretical prejudices overlap with the naïve reflection of the linguists on their everyday research practice. Therefore, in order to propose an adequate solution to the problems in connection with data and evidence, it seems to be necessary to develop a novel, coherent and sophisticated *metatheoretical* framework.

On the basis of these three considerations, we reformulate (CP) as the *Main Problem* of this book:

(MP) (a) What is the *structure* of linguistic data/evidence
and
(b) which *functions* do they fulfil in linguistic theories
if
(c) (a) and (b) are tackled by an argumentation-theoretic model of linguistic theorising?

(MP) will be divided into subproblems, addressed by different parts of the book. The solutions of these subproblems will lead, step by step, to the solution of (MP).

In Part I, we will provide a critical analysis of the current literature and reveal the solutions to (CP) which different approaches to linguistic data and evidence seem to have proposed. Thereby, we will raise several questions which the approaches to be discussed have left open. The open questions, along with the fact that the proposed solutions to (CP) are contradictory, will motivate the raising of (MP)(a) and (b) as well as the characteristics of the metascientific model referred to in (MP)(c).

The task of Part II will be the elaboration of this model – which will be called *the p-model of plausible argumentation* – and the exemplification of its workability by way of linguistic examples.

Part III, entitled 'Data and evidence', shows how the two notions which the book centres on can be defined with the help of the p-model.

The function of Part IV is to exemplify the workability of the p-model. It presents a detailed case study which illustrates how the p-model can be applied to the practice of linguistic theorising. In this way it elucidates that the p-model is indeed capable of bridging the gap between linguistic research practice and metatheoretical reflection on this practice.

Finally, in Part V, we will summarise those conclusions on the basis of which we will obtain a possible solution to (MP).

Part I

The state of the art

2 The problem $(P)_I$

In accordance with the structure of the book as outlined in Chapter 1, we begin with an analysis of the current literature discussing (CP). This analysis is expected to answer two questions. First, we will survey which solutions have been proposed for (CP) by the different approaches in the current discussion on linguistic data and evidence. The second question is motivated by our assumption that the problem of linguistic data and evidence may be solved by the elaboration of an appropriate metatheoretical model. Therefore, we have to clarify which metascientific background assumptions the proposals put forward in the literature as putative solutions to (CP) rely on.

Accordingly, the first subproblem of (MP) can be formulated as follows:

$(P)_I$ (a) What solutions have been proposed to (CP) in the current literature?
(b) What metascientific background assumptions can be revealed in the particular views?

Part I aims at

(a) the presentation and systematisation of views belonging to a significant – and from the point of view of the development of linguistics *relevant and progressive* – trend of the current debate on linguistic data and evidence;
(b) the critical analysis of these views on the basis of this systematisation;
(c) the solution of $(P)_I$ on the basis of systematisation and critical analysis, and
(d) the identification of the questions which the analysed views have left open and which motivate raising (MP), as well as the elaboration of a new metatheoretical model.

We cannot go into a detailed and thorough investigation of the historical roots of the contemporary debate on data/evidence nor can we provide an exhaustive analysis of the empiricalness debates in different fields of linguistics. We will solely highlight that trend which immediately motivates the problems raised in a certain part[1] of the most recent literature.

Chapter 3 will be devoted to the pre-history of the current debate on linguistic data and evidence. We will reveal the most important stages in the emergence of the *standard view of linguistic data and evidence*. This view presupposes the dichotomy of introspective and corpus data, as well as *the standard view of the analytical philosophy of science*.

In Chapter 4, on the basis of the latest literature, we will show that the *practice* of linguistic research – that is, *object*-scientific inquiry – has clearly departed from the standard view of linguistic data.

In Chapter 5, we will examine whether, and if so, in what way and to what extent, *meta*scientific reflection follows linguistic practice in this respect. We will scrutinise the solutions to (CP) proposed by the current literature on linguistic data and evidence. However new the trend of the current debate about data/evidence we mentioned may be, it is enormously complex and multifaceted. It comprises several sub-tendencies, some of which partially overlap, while others run in opposite directions. We will focus solely on those approaches that can be regarded as *progressive* in so far as they explicitly question, at least partly, the standard view of linguistic data and evidence. Accordingly, we will not go into the case studies published in the literature but will discuss the following state-of-the-art articles (occasionally referring to further relevant publications as well): Borsley (2005a), Geeraerts (2006), Kepser & Reis (2005a), Lehmann (2004), Penke & Rosenbach (2004a); we will also refer to Schütze (1996).

In our answer to the question in $(P)_I(a)$ we point out that none of the proposed solutions to (CP) is satisfactory. They are *progressive* insofar as they try to go beyond the shortcomings of the standard view of linguistic data in a problem-sensitive way. Nevertheless, contrary to this intention, they remain fragmentary at several important points and also include elements of the standard view of linguistic data. Although they recognise the untenability of the standard view of the analytical philosophy of science, they *still contain its remnants*. Therefore, they do not provide us with the systematic and elaborated metascientific framework that is needed for the sophisticated and comprehensive treatment of the problems raised. In this way, we will obtain the answer to $(P)_I(b)$.

Accordingly, Chapter 6 will summarise the double-facedness revealed in the writings examined, and will also draw some far-reaching conclusions.

3 Historical background

3.1 Overview

In the present chapter we provide a concise overview of the historical antecedents of the current debate on linguistic data/evidence. First, we will summarise those tenets which shaped the methodological foundations of mainstream linguistics in the twentieth century and call them 'the standard view of the analytical philosophy of science'. Second, our analysis will reveal that the two predominant camps in linguistics from the middle of the 1950s to the end of the 1990s, corpus linguists and generative linguists, heavily rely on methodological assumptions which are in perfect accord with the standard view of the analytical philosophy of science. We will call the set of these assumptions 'the standard view of linguistic data and evidence'. It is this view which has been dominant over the past decades, right up to the turn of the last millennium, and which new approaches to linguistic data and evidence seriously question.

3.2 The problem of evidence in the philosophy of science

In order to solve $(P)_I$, we have to refer to the well-known circumstance that *the standard view of the analytical philosophy of science* played a decisive role in the emergence of the norms against which scientific theories have been evaluated for several decades in the twentieth century. Basically, the standard view of the analytical philosophy of science involved two approaches: logical empiricism initiated by the Vienna Circle and Popper's critical rationalism.[1] The reason these approaches have been subsumed under the standard view is that despite their differences they shared similar assumptions on a number of important issues.

First of all, both of them accepted Reichenbach's (1938) distinction between the 'context of discovery' and the 'context of justification'. The 'context of discovery' covers the creative, cognitive, social, historical etc. aspects of scientific discovery, theory formation and problem solving, while 'the context of justification' involves the logical reconstruction and the evaluation of the results of the discovery process, i.e. scientific theories. Both trends focused solely on the *justification* of scientific theories, excluding the process of discovery, theory formation and problem solving from their field of interest.

Another central idea of the standard view of the analytical philosophy of science was that *empirical* theories must consist of statements which can be tested on the basis of a special subset of data, namely, *evidence*.[2] According to this idea – to put it in a very simplified manner, as a first approximation – the intuition underlying the notion of evidence was the following:

(E) Evidence
- (a) is objective;
- (b) serves as a neutral arbiter among rival hypotheses/theories;
- (c) is expected to justify (verify, falsify, confirm) hypotheses/theories;
- (d) is immediately given;
- (e) is primary to the theory;
- (f) is reliable.

The properties mentioned in (E) motivate the central role of evidence; they can be regarded as the common intuitive core of the different approaches to evidence within the standard view of the analytical philosophy of science.[3] Nevertheless, the interpretation of these properties is highly problematic. Therefore, in twentieth-century philosophy of science the discussions concerning the nature of evidence aimed at their explication, and also attempted to decide which of them were really relevant. In the course of the controversies, each of (E)(a)–(f) has been seriously questioned and each of them has been explicated in a variety of ways often incompatible with each other.[4] In certain cases, however, suggestions were put forward that seem to have been widely accepted.[5] During the debates quandaries and paradoxes were continuously raised (see primarily Goodman 1983 [1955]; for a detailed discussion of Goodmans' and others' paradoxes see Stegmüller 1970).

According to *inductivists* such as Carnap, the function of evidence is the *verification* of the hypotheses. Later, still within inductivism, it was also explicated in terms of *confirmation*, according to which evidence strengthens the hypothesis, or makes it more probable, without, however, proving its truth.[6] Thus, confirmation includes verification as an extreme case. Popper's *hypothetico-deductive* view highlighted the *falsificatory* function of evidence in the sense that, although it cannot verify a hypothesis, it is capable of falsifying (i.e., refuting) it.[7] Although these three explications – each of which has several versions – were developed in different periods of the analytical philosophy of science and were the focus of heated debates, they are logically related:

If *E* is evidence for some hypothesis *H*, then *E* makes it more likely that *H* is true: in such circumstances, *E confirms H*. On the other hand, if *E* is evidence against *H*, then *E* makes it less likely that *H* is true: *E disconfirms H*. *Verification* is the limiting case of confirmation: a piece of evidence verifies a hypothesis in this sense just in case it conclusively establishes that hypothesis as true. At the other end of the spectrum, *falsification* is the limiting case of disconfirmation: a piece of evidence falsifies a hypothesis just in case it conclusively establishes that the hypothesis is false. It is at least somewhat controversial whether full-fledged verification or falsification in this sense ever occurs. (Kelly 2006; emphasis as in the original)

In close connection with the distinction of the context of discovery and the context of justification, the norms of the standard view of the analytical philosophy of science require that the structure of scientific theories be *deductive*. It has to be emphasised that inductivists impose this requirement on theories, too. From this it follows that with rational reconstruction, the relevance of empirical evidence does not stem from the role it plays in the discovery process, in the generation of hypotheses, or in the creation of the theory but solely from its role as a means of justification. Therefore, as we have seen, the function of evidence is the verification/confirmation, or, according to falsificationism, the potential falsification, of hypotheses/theories which have been obtained by whatever methods.

For the sake of later reference, we summarise the basic tenets of the standard view of the analytical philosophy of science from the point of view of the present book as follows:

(SVAPS)

(a) Only theories conforming to the norms of *rationality* can be regarded as scientific.
(b) Philosophy of science aims at the *justification* of scientific theories with the help of the rational reconstruction of theories.
(c) There is a clear distinction between the 'context of discovery' and the 'context of justification'. This distinction is motivated by the consideration that neither the creative, intuitive, cognitive processes present during scientific theorising, nor the historical and sociological factors that may influence the researcher can be revealed and controlled. Therefore, rational reconstruction deems them irrelevant. It is solely certain characteristics of the *final product* of the discovery process (i.e. the logical structure and the empirical foundation of closed scientific theories) that significance can be assigned to during the justification of theories.
(d) The analytical philosophy of science involves two dominant trends, namely inductivism (verificationism/confirmationism) and hypothetico-deductivism.
(e) *Evidence*, as characterised in (E), is attributed special significance in the justification of hypotheses and theories. That is, hypotheses of empirical theories have to be verified/confirmed by evidence, or they have to be falsifiable by evidence.[8]
(f) Empirical scientific theories are *deductive (axiomatic) systems*.[9]

(SVAPS) is the metatheoretical background against which the standpoints in the debate on data/evidence will be evaluated in Part I of the book.

3.3 Debates on empiricalness in theoretical linguistics and the standard view of linguistic data (SVLD)

Dominant linguistic theories in the twentieth century – although in different ways and to a different extent – adapted their methodological norms from the standard view of the analytical philosophy of science (SVAPS).[10] The emergence of generative linguistics gave rise to a series of closely related and inextricably intertwined methodological debates. Each of these debates centred around particular aspects of the *problem of the empiricalness* of linguistic theories. However, from debate to debate, this problem was tackled from different perspectives, explicated differently, and reduced to different subproblems. In order to motivate the problem the present book will focus on, we need to refer briefly to *four* of them.

As it is well known, the methodology of American structuralism was predominantly taxonomic and inductive. Chomsky launched a fierce attack against this in the 1950s–60s, contrasting it with the hypothetico-deductive method of the standard view of the analytical philosophy of science (SVAPS). With the application of the latter he intended to follow the norms prescribed for theories in the natural sciences (Chomsky 1975 [1957], 1965).[11] Thus, in the 1950s–60s a debate evolved around the central methodological question which was – to put it in a simplified way – whether linguistics as an empirical discipline should rely primarily on *inductive* generalisations or on the *deductive* testing of hypotheses (Allan 2003, 2007).

In the 1970s, new themes emerged and became the object of fierce discussions in the debate on the problem of the empiricalness of theoretical linguistics. Instead of the confrontation of the two main trends within (SVAPS), the debate focused on the antagonism between (SVAPS) and hermeneutics. Linguists following the hypothetico-deductive branch of the standard view of the analytical philosophy of science (SVAPS) regarded generative linguistics as an explanatory empirical theory similar to theories in natural sciences,[12] while hermeneutics saw it as a non-empirical, normative, interpretative enterprise (see e.g. Allan 2003, 2007; Penke & Rosenbach 2004a; Wunderlich 1976; Perry 1980 etc.). By the late 1970s the debate had become fruitless, since the participants defended their views with reference to rigidly and mechanically applied abstract methodological principles. At the same time, they disregarded aspects relevant for the practising linguist as well as the arguments of the opposition camp (see Kertész 1991, 2004a; Kepser & Reis 2005a; Penke & Rosenbach 2004a etc.).

From the middle of the 1970s – simultaneously with the gradual dying down of this controversy – a new phase of the debate on empiricalness unfolded as a consequence of several independent but converging developments in linguistics. The question by then was not whether hermeneutics or the hypothetico-deductive approach within the standard view of the analytical philosophy of science was more appropriate for capturing the structure of linguistic theories. Rather, once again, the conflict between inductive and deductive methodology already seen in the 1950s and 1960s moved to the centre of attention, but this time from another point of view (for an overview see e.g. McEnery & Wilson 1996: 1ff.; Lemnitzer & Zinsmeister 2006: 7ff.). One[13] – but in no way the only – development was the appearance and rapid spread of electronic data-processing. This led to the emergence of a tendency which turned against the use of introspective data preferred by generative linguists and contributed significantly to the development of *corpus linguistics*. The *Brown Corpus of Standard American English*, put forward by W. N. Francis and H. Kučera in the early 1960s, was a seminal turning point. Of similar importance was the *Survey of English Usage* associated with the name of Quirk, as well as the neo-Firthian COBUILD-project launched at the University of Birmingham by J. Sinclair and others. Generative linguists, however, considered the collection and analysis of great amounts of data stemming from language use trivial and irrelevant. Chomsky sharply questioned the relevance of induction at every stage of theory formation. Neither in the 'discovery' of theories (that is as a technique of data collection) nor in the 'justification' of theories did he attribute special significance to induction.[14] As opposed to this, researchers in favour of corpus data argued for the indispensability of induction and the strict methodological rules concerning the handling of inductive data. They did not consider data based on the linguist's introspection as empirical.[15]

This means that with respect to the treatment of the data/evidence problem, basically two camps emerged: on the one hand, the advocates of corpus data and on the other hand generativists in favour of introspective data.[16] Despite the considerable differences, however, the views share a series of assumptions which we call *the standard view of linguistic data* (SVLD):

(SVLD)

(a) Not all linguistic theories can be considered as empirical but only those which rely on the *appropriate type of data*. Only *certain data types* may be regarded as relevant and legitimate: in the generativist view it is introspective data, while according to corpus linguists it is primarily corpus data.[17]
(b) It is solely the *origin of the data* that decides what counts as the appropriate type of data.
(c) Both camps regard their *own data-handling procedure as unproblematic*. They believe that a few general methodological rules are sufficient for controlling the reliability of the data.
(d) They deem the relationship between the data and the hypotheses of the theory *unidirectional*, and *determined by general, strict methodological rules*. They explicate it either as *induction* from data to hypotheses, or as *deduction* from hypotheses to data.[18]

(e) *Evidence* is considered as an empirical datum playing a pivotal role. Its significance lies in the features captured in (E). The most important of these is that it is assumed to constitute a directly controllable special subset of data, that is, it is qualified as reliable without reference to any theory. Thus, it is treated as an unquestionable fact suitable for the justification (verification, confirmation or falsification) of hypotheses.

The theses summarised in (SVLD)(a)–(e) witness that during the period we have overviewed, linguists took for granted the following background assumptions:

(a) The structure of data is simple; their origin determines what data types are legitimate. The treatment of data is unproblematic; a few general methodological rules are sufficient. The use of data in linguistic theories is unproblematic as well; as certainly true evidence, they allow for the justification (verification, confirmation or falsification) of theories.
(b) It is the standard view of the analytical philosophy of science that serves as a methodological background.

In connection with these assumptions, we highlight four points. First, they had been regarded for decades as the firm methodological foundation of linguistic theorising. Second, they reveal that the standard view of linguistic data and evidence (SVLD) is motivated basically not by linguistic but by general meta-scientific (philosophical) considerations. Third, they also show that (SVLD) is applied in some cases in an unreflected and unsystematic manner. For example, induction is often (also) regarded as a tool of hypothesis generation. Fourth, they constitute the point of departure for our solution to $(P)_I$ to be summarised in Chapter 6.

In the 1980s and 1990s, the two camps' position was still strong. Both of the two opposing views disregarded criticism by the other party. They seemed to coexist side by side without cooperation and without any chance of rapprochement. This could have resulted in the infertility, or even the termination of the empiricalness debate. However, the exact opposite of this happened. From the second half of the 1990s the methodological debates on data and evidence were gradually extended, and were enriched with new elements. Today they affect several different research fields and branches of linguistics. They concern not only the origin of linguistic data but questions regarding their function, structure, and the criteria for their acceptability, too. Previously, such questions had been neglected and had remained unreflected. In particular, at the turn of the millennium new works were published that changed the focus of the problem once again. As we have mentioned, in the 1970s the central problem was the confrontation between hermeneutics and the hypothetico-deductive branch of the analytical philosophy of science. In the 1980s and 1990s, this opposition was reduced to the dichotomy of introspective and corpus data. Today, however, the following questions are focused on: what *types of data* may be used, what data may count as *evidence*, and what *function* can be attributed to them in different fields of linguistic theorising?

This is the central problem of the fourth debate which has been conducted currently. It is this problem that we raised as (CP) in Chapter 1.[19] The latest stage of the debate on data/evidence – in which each element of the standard view of linguistic data and evidence (SVLD), along with the two background assumptions just discussed were questioned – unfolded, in the first place, in the following publications:

(a) Schütze (1996) is the seminal work which motivated the reappraisal of the problem of the structure and function of linguistic data in theoretical linguistics in the years immediately before the turn of the millennium.
(b) *Studies in Language* devoted a thematic issue to the problem of data/evidence based on the materials of the congress of the Deutsche Gesellschaft für Sprachwissenschaft in 2003. The papers in this issue provide us with a systematic overview of the main aspects of the data/evidence problem in several different fields of linguistics by confronting alternative positions (Penke & Rosenbach 2004b).[20]
(c) The journal *Lingua* published a similar thematic issue on the problem of data in theoretical linguistics (Borsley 2005b).
(d) At the University of Tübingen there has been a research project in progress since 1999, investigating the problem of linguistic data (Reis *et al.* 1998). The main results were presented at the conference on 'Linguistic Evidence, Empirical, Theoretical, and Computational Perspectives' in 2004 and published in Kepser & Reis (2005b).
(e) The continuation of this enterprise was published as Featherston & Winkler (2009) and Winkler & Featherston (2009). The two collections of papers contain the proceedings of the international conference 'Linguistic Evidence 2008'.
(f) *The Linguistic Review* devoted a thematic issue to the methodological problems in linguistics. One of its sections addressed the problem of data. The most relevant papers of this volume are those of Lehmann (2004), Mereu (2004) and Simone (2004).
(g) In 2005, the Institut für Deutsche Sprache Mannheim also devoted a conference to the problem; the conference lectures were published in Kallmeyer & Zifonun (2007).
(h) Kristiansen *et al.* (2006) discusses the problem of the empirical base of cognitive linguistics, highlighting the problem of data.
(i) There are also two further sub-branches of the data/evidence debate in linguistics. First, in 2007 *Corpus Linguistics and Linguistic Theory* published a special issue entitled *Grammar without grammaticality* (see Stefanowitsch & Gries 2007). Second, *Theoretical Linguistics* published a special issue entitled *Data in generative grammar* (see Sternefeld 2007). Since we

discussed them separately in Kertész & Rákosi (2008b, c), we will refer to them in this book only sporadically.

(j) In the Forum Section of *Zeitschrift für Sprachwissenschaft* 28 (2009) discussion papers were published on the topic 'Linguistic data: Elicitation – Evaluation – Theoretical implications'.

3.4 Conclusions

The latest literature listed above expressly calls attention to the importance of raising the problem of data and evidence in linguistics.[21] It also emphasises that the current situation is not simply the automatic continuation of former debates, but rather an attempt to address new and more relevant issues.[22] The problem of linguistic data and evidence is not restricted to a single field of linguistics, but has been acknowledged as relevant by a series of very different approaches and research areas in contemporary linguistic research.

At the same time, however, it is inseparably intertwined with metascientific background assumptions without the consideration of which it cannot be solved. Lehmann, for example, formulates this point as follows:

> Questions about the nature of data, corpora and documentation, the role they play in our scientific inquiry as well as in practice are raised in other disciplines, too; their combination, however, is typical of linguistics. They are closely related to the question of *what kind of inquiry linguistics is*, and seem to presuppose the clarification of the latter. In reality, this relationship is not a unidirectional relation of precondition, because *the essence of a discipline is determined by decisions on its subject and methodology.* (Lehmann 2007: 9; our translation; emphasis added)[23]

Accordingly, if we want to draw a realistic picture of the current stage of the debate on data/evidence, then there is no avoiding the examination of the role *metascientific considerations* play in the solutions that have been proposed to the problems raised. Thus, we will try to find an answer not only to $(P)_I(a)$ but to $(P)_I(b)$ as well.

Nevertheless, before presenting our solution to $(P)_I(a)$ and (b), we will give a concise overview of some tendencies which illustrate how practising linguists gradually depart from the standard view of linguistic data and evidence (SVLD) while pursuing their research activities – without, however, declaring the abandonment of these views.

4 The partial rejection of (SVLD) in the practice of *object*-scientific research

4.1 Overview

The aim of this chapter is to reveal a series of tendencies which suggest that the *practice* of linguistic research – that is, *object*-scientific inquiry – has clearly departed from the standard view of linguistic data (SVLD). The first tendency we mention is that novel methods and data types entered the scene which differ from those applied so far. Second, in order to support their hypotheses, some generative linguists make use of research results which, instead of being restricted to introspection as the sole data source, also take into consideration corpora or experiments. Third, an increasing number of factors have been identified that may influence the reliability of the data, thus witnessing that even the preferred data types are regarded as problematic. Fourth, not infrequently, the methodological rules which are assumed to govern the relation between data and theory by one of the versions of (SVLD), are violated. Finally, there is also a tendency towards the temporary rejection of counterexamples, which means that the way evidence is handled is not in accord with (SVLD).

From these new developments in object-scientific research, we will conclude that present-day linguistic practice implicitly tends to abandon the tenets of the standard view of linguistic data and evidence.

4.2 New tendencies in object-scientific research

The barren methodological debates of the 1980s and 1990s did not reflect on several tendencies related to the problem of data and evidence undoubtedly *present in everyday linguistic research*. These converging tendencies suggest that there is a wide gap between the *practice* of linguistic theorising and the metascientific *principles* summarised in the standard view of linguistic data and evidence (SVLD). Relying on the literature mentioned, below we give a brief overview of the tendencies which bear witness to the development that the practice of linguistic research tries to follow the methodological stances described in (SVLD) less and less rigidly, and that there is an increasing demand on the differentiation of the data to be made use of in linguistic research.

(i) *Ad (SVLD)(a)*. New methods and data types appeared that question the categorisation described in (SVLD)(a). Approaches using probabilistic methods, for example, allowed a new interpretation of grammatical competence (see Penke & Rosenbach 2004a: 495ff.). Computer modelling also constitutes a new method which in principle should be rejected both by generative linguists accepting linguistic intuition as data and by linguists working with corpora consisting of linguistic utterances. The use of such data, however, may be fruitful, since they have been applied successfully in testing learning models which are not directly testable at the present state of neurology (see Penke & Rosenbach 2004a: 491).

Schütze (2009) characterises the World Wide Web as a corpus which is, from several points of view, the best available. It is not only the largest one but it grows continuously and always remains up-to-date. It considerably increases the chances of finding examples which are relevant to the current research but which would not otherwise come to the linguist's mind. Despite this, the reliability of data originating from this source is often called into question and is usually checked against the linguistic intuition of the researcher or of native speakers. That is, data from the internet are rather a mixture of corpus and intuitive data.

Various kinds of experimental data constitute a data type which cannot be placed within a dichotomy of corpus data vs introspective data. As Schlesewsky (2009: 170) emphasises, questionnaires, priming experiments, eye movement studies or experiments conducting neuro-anatomic measurements put participants into an artificial situation and try to make them produce 'interpretable' reactions to a complex cognitive stimulus by eliminating as many external factors which might influence the results as possible.[1] From this we may conclude that experimental data based on participants' responses to the stimuli are substantially different from both corpus data and introspective data: they are neither results of spontaneous language use like the former, nor are they regarded as representative of a homogeneous speech community as is the case with introspective data. Moreover, experimental data are in most cases more complex and involve the results of measurements related to manifestations of linguistic behaviour.

(ii) *Ad (SVLD)(b)*. In order to support their hypotheses, some generative linguists – disregarding (SVLD)(b) – make use of research results which are not solely based on the analysis of introspective data, but arise from some kind of corpus or experiment. Linguists aiming at the identification of the principles of universal grammar, for example, found the results of typological, historical linguistic, neuro- and psycholinguistic research useful, and therefore integrated these in their investigations (see Penke & Rosenbach 2004a: 494f.). As Schlesewsky (2009: 174f.) remarks in connection with experimental data, in contrast to earlier practice, these new data types are more and more frequently regarded as equivalent or even superior to the traditionally accepted introspective data insofar as they no longer serve as mere illustrations of one's theoretical point of view but they may function as counterexamples whose explanation leads to the revision of the theory. At the same time, those working with corpus data rely on their linguistic intuition as well. First, the comparison of the meanings of constructions containing the linguistic structure at issue is an indispensable component of data analysis (see Borsley 2005a: 1477). Second, when processing corpora we have to distinguish sentences containing slips of the tongue and other defective utterances from grammatical sentences. To make such decisions, linguists fall back on their own linguistic intuition (see Schütze 1996: 2; Lehmann 2004: 200, 207).

(iii) *Ad (SVLD)(c)*. A further important development resulting from the deepening of linguistic research is that the researchers – breaking with (SVLD)(c) – no longer regard even the types of data they themselves prefer as unproblematic, since they identify more and more factors that may influence the reliability of data. The complexity of the data used and the number of the factors to be controlled are constantly increasing, while researchers often find themselves unable to control all factors involved. However, they do not try to overcome such problems with the help of general methodological principles, but strive to reveal those *specific* factors that influence the reliability of certain data types as accurately as possible. Let us mention a few examples.

As for corpora, for example, both 'positive' and 'negative evidence' raise serious problems that are either unsolvable with the methodologies at the researchers' disposal or their solution is fraught with difficulties. Although 'positive evidence' may support a hypothesis, it is often difficult to decide how to differentiate relevant data from insignificant, isolated, unreliable, dubious information. Controlling the reliability of data inevitably leads to further searches for data and to the increased complexity of the theory – but there are obvious practical limitations to this process. 'Negative evidence' (that is, the absence of a certain form or construction) may provide one's hypotheses only with weaker supportive force. Moreover, it does not necessarily reveal whether the absence of a certain form or construction can be regarded as systematic, or is only accidental resulting from the contingency of certain circumstances (e.g. one did not examine the necessary amount of data, or one failed to notice the existence of a rare but existing and recordable form or construction). With 'quantitative data' the question is not simply whether a given phenomenon occurs or not, but the extent to which it does (i.e. whether its occurrence is statistically significant; see Penke & Rosenbach 2004a: 486; see also point (iv)). It has also been realised that the choice of the statistical method applied in corpus linguistic research is a factor which has a significant impact on the range and reliability of the results that can be achieved. For example, Arppe (2009: 1ff.) states that linguistic phenomena whose complexity requires the use of a wide range of variables from different levels of linguistic analysis cannot be accounted for properly by focusing on only one level or one single feature. He suggests that for a satisfactory explanation of all relevant features as well as their interactions multivariate (multicausal) models are needed which might be capable of incorporating all of the variables into the analysis at the same time.

Questionnaires and interviews also raise a number of serious methodological problems which are well known from sociology. An example is the 'observer's paradox' which means that linguists usually want to find out how speakers naturally behave when they are not being observed, but this can only be discovered if the linguist observes them. One typical manifestation of this paradox is that informants often judge non-standard forms as bad, and distance themselves from them during the experiment, while, as a rule, they still use such forms actively (Penke & Rosenbach 2004a: 490; Schütze 1996: 61).

Experimental settings often involve a similar problem as well. So as to control the parameters that potentially influence the result, experiments may construct artificial situations which therefore yield less natural data. There is a relatively new insight among linguists working with experimental data that measurements – in contrast to the established view – do not mirror linguistic stimuli directly (see Schlesewsky 2009: 170). Instead, the output of the stimulus processing includes – besides linguistic manipulation – several external factors such as the task environment, the capacity of memory or of the attention etc. whose impact on the results is not clear and which cannot yet be accounted for by any cognitive model. Moreover, the standards which could govern the experimental procedure and the evaluation of the results are missing. While in the natural sciences experimental data are controlled by the replication of the experiment, this is relatively rarely practised by linguists.

Schütze (1996: 3f.) refers to similar problems discussed in the literature in connection with judgement data. First, besides the artificial nature of the elicitation situation, 'the subject is being asked for a sort of behavior that, at least on the face of it, is entirely different from everyday conversation'. Metalinguistic tasks often relate to 'areas of linguistic knowledge that rarely occur in regular speech' (Schütze 1996: 91). This raises the question of whether and to what extent results obtained from research based on grammaticality/acceptability judgements[2] as data can be generalised to the whole of linguistic behaviour. Second, grammaticality judgements are no longer regarded as directly mirroring grammaticalness and linguistic competence but as products of metalinguistic performance. As such, they are interpreted as complex phenomena produced by a series of different cognitive skills. Thus, linguistic competence is only one of the contributing factors which are not directly accessible and whose role cannot be clarified without revealing the structure of the whole process of producing acceptability judgements, that is, without having any idea about the range of skills which contribute to this process and about the peculiarities of the contribution they make.

Schütze (1996: chapters 4–5) provides an overview of the *subject-related* and *task-related factors* which, according to the literature, may distort the reliability of grammaticality judgements. Within the first group, field dependence (fusing aspects of the world and experiencing it globally vs differentiating information and experiences into components), handedness (which is supposed to be a good indicator of linguistic structures in the brain), age, sex and general cognitive endowment belong to the organismic related factors, while linguistic training, literacy and education, amount of exposure to a language, accumulated world knowledge etc. belong to the experiential factors. The second group consists of two subgroups, too. Procedural factors involve the instructions (that is, how the procedure of judging is explained to the subjects), the order of presentation of the sentences presented for judgement, repetition (the effect of repeated exposure to sentences on judgements of their grammaticality, and the interaction of repetition with other manipulations), mental state (the effect of objective vs subjective self-awareness), judgement strategy (focusing on syntactic and semantic structure vs looking at pragmatic use), modality (spoken vs written presentation of the stimuli) and register (clarity, awkwardness, slanginess, floweriness), and speed of judgement. Stimulus factors are, for example, context, meaning, parsability, frequency, lexical content, morphology and spelling, and rhetorical structure.

The problems related to judgement data also highlighted the need to change the data-handling techniques of generative linguistics and motivated the search for new, more reliable and useable data types. Schütze (1996: 55ff.) mentions several proposals such as asking subjects to supplement their judgement with an explanation; asking subjects under what conditions, if any, the sentence at issue could be grammatical; requesting subjects to create rank orderings of sentences by grammaticality; asking for comparison of the types of violation in bad sentences; eliciting paraphrases for ambiguous sentences; using rating scales, or measurements of event-related brain potentials. Featherston (2009b) compares the advantages and disadvantages and problematic points of three methods for gathering judgements, including the standard seven-point scale, magnitude estimation and his own method, which he calls 'thermometer judgements'.

(iv) *Ad (SVLD)(d).* Breaking with (SVLD)(d), representatives of different approaches violate the methodological rules concerning the relation of data and theory required by one of the versions of the standard view of the analytical philosophy of science (SVAPS). First, among the linguists dealing with corpus data there are some who actually accept Popperian falsificationism, though they still assign induction an important – but not exclusive – role (see e.g. Geeraerts 2006: 24). Second, more and more researchers have realised that the Popperian model is too strict.

One of the strategies applied by linguists working with corpus data was *the weakening of the criterion of falsifiability*. Beside the 'strong' version of the principle (according to which a single counterexample is sufficient to falsify a hypothesis), in research practice there emerged a 'weak' version as well, stating that rules of language have to be interpreted not as strict prescriptions but as statistical tendencies. Thus, statistically rare occurrences are not sufficient to falsify a hypothesis. As Penke & Rosenbach (2004a: 483) remark, it is not clear, however, how to distinguish exactly such rare occurrences from counterexamples that do falsify the hypothesis.

Another strategy, employed primarily by generativists, is *the temporary ignoring of counterexamples*. According to Chomsky (2002: 98ff.), this may be a rational decision in certain cases, because at a later stage of the development of the theory the tools might be available that allow for the resolution of the given inconsistency (Penke & Rosenbach 2004a: 484).[3] In such cases, it would have been premature to reject the theory/hypothesis in question right at the outset.

(v) *Ad (SVLD)(e)*. The temporary ignoring of counterexamples means a tentative departure from (SVLD)(e) as well, since one does not consider the counterexample as falsifying evidence, and the inconsistency is resolved through the – temporary – rejection of the given datum, and not that of the hypothesis at hand.

The insight mentioned in (iv), according to which both induction and deduction play a role in the process of theory formation also indicates the departure from (SVLD)(e) and at the same time from the rigid distinction between the 'context of discovery' and the 'context of justification' (see Geeraerts 2006: 24f.).

4.3 Conclusions

We may draw the conclusion that in the ongoing changes in *research practice* the intention to *break with the views described in (SVLD)* is clearly present. The question, therefore, is whether the changes in *research practice* are accompanied by changes in *metascientific reflection*, and if so, in what way, and to what extent.

In the next chapter, we will summarise the views on linguistic data presented in the current literature cited in Section 3.3. Although – as we will see – there are considerable differences between these views, they share some relevant factors. The latter make it possible to present their proposals related to (CP) on the basis of uniform criteria by highlighting the convergences and pointing out the divergences, too.

5 The partial rejection of (SVLD) in *meta*scientific reflection

5.1 Overview

We tackle the issue raised at the end of Chapter 4, namely, whether the changes in *research practice* are accompanied by changes in *metascientific reflection*, and if so, in what way, and to what extent. By analysing *current approaches* to linguistic data and evidence from seven different points of view, we obtain the answer that they clearly intend to break with the standard view of linguistic data and evidence, but, corresponding to the seven points of view mentioned, they leave open the following questions: (OQ1) Under what conditions is the diversity of data legitimate and how can data belonging to different data types be combined? (OQ2) What role do sources play in the judgement of the reliability of data? (OQ3) How can the complexity of data be accounted for? (OQ4) How can the uncertainty of data be treated? (OQ5) What is the relationship between data and theories? (OQ6) On the basis of what criteria can it be decided whether a contradiction may be tolerated, and what strategies should we adopt for inconsistency resolution? (OQ7) What data can serve as evidence in linguistic theories, if, on the one hand, evidence has to be capable of supporting or weakening hypotheses, and, on the other, data cannot be regarded as true with certainty?

The state-of-the-art analysis of the literature presented in Sections 5.2–5.8 unveils the intrinsic *double-facedness* of the views surveyed. On the one hand, they still *contain several components* of the standard view of the analytical philosophy of science (SVAPS) and the standard view of linguistic data and evidence (SVLD). On the other hand, however, they also include ideas which are not compatible with (SVAPS) and (SVLD) and which clearly indicate the *need to depart* from the latter. Moreover, the literature goes at several points clearly beyond the old methodology by raising sophisticated, insightful and progressive suggestions.

5.2 The diversity and the combinability of data

Metatheoretical reflection on the nature of linguistic data – along the lines of the tendencies described in Section 4.2 (i) and (ii) – first of all has to supersede the dichotomy of introspective data vs corpus data that dominated the previous stage of the debate on empiricalness. It should take into account the development that a number of *new data types and new methods of data-handling* have appeared, mainly due to the deepening of linguistic research and the cooperation between linguistics and certain fields of cognitive science, sociology and computer science. Kepser & Reis (2005a: 1) mention, for example, the following types of data: introspective data, corpus data, data from (psycho)linguistic experiments, synchronic vs diachronic data, typological data, neurolinguistic data, data from first and second language acquisition, data from language disorders etc. Kepser & Reis (2005a), Penke & Rosenbach (2004a), Borsley (2005a) and Schütze (1996) consider all kinds of information in connection with some aspect of linguistic behaviour as *potential data*.[1]

Haspelmath (2009) argues that although all data types are deficient and problematic, they are relevant and usable in different fields of linguistic research. His typology covers physiological data, acceptability judgements, judgements of meaning, translation, psycholinguistic tests, stimulated narratives, ordinary spontaneous corpora, and non-verbal data.

Lehmann's view, however, is different. Though he suggests a typology which allows us to grasp the diversity of linguistic data, his approach does not constitute a complete break with the standard view of linguistic data and evidence (SVLD). While he attempts to delineate a much more refined typology than the mere contrasting of introspective vs corpus data, he rejects the legitimacy of the former in the spirit of (SVLD):

> this use of introspection is a *misuse* of the concept and associated ethos of empirical science. . . . introspection is necessary and useful as a heuristic tool in linguistic work, but is *not part of empirical methodology*, and the data thus produced have *no status in empirical research* besides illustrating what the linguist theorises. (Lehmann 2004: 196; emphasis added)

Geeraerts (2006: 27) shares a similar view, because he regards only experimental methods applied in psychology, methods of data collection used in sociology, and corpus analysis as legitimate and rejects the use of introspective data.

Summary. As we have seen, the standpoints mentioned go significantly beyond the dichotomy of corpus vs introspective data. Some representatives of current literature seem to consider all data types listed above (at least under certain conditions) as legitimate. Nevertheless, one of the otherwise most refined approaches – which undoubtedly elaborates a far more flexible taxonomy of data than most other attempts – fiercely rejects introspective data and in this respect remains close to the view described in (SVLD)(a) and (b). The following question remains open:

(OQ1) Under what conditions is the diversity of data legitimate and how can data belonging to different data types be combined?

5.3 The role of the sources in the reliability of data

According to the literature, in exploring the properties of the individual data types, among other relevant factors, one has to consider those stemming from the *diversity of their sources*. Penke & Rosenbach (2004a: 488ff.) distinguish two main groups of data on the basis of their sources. *Spontaneous speech data* are naturally occurring linguistic phenomena which, recorded in corpora, may serve as the subject of linguistic analysis. Corpora may be collected by the linguist herself with the specific aim of studying a certain linguistic structure, but she may also use public collections of data with no specific focus on a certain linguistic construction. *Elicited data* are gained by experiment or observation in a situation created and controlled by the linguist. Penke and Rosenbach are of the opinion that the two types of data have different advantages and disadvantages. The quality of spontaneous data is obviously influenced by the representativeness of the corpus and the systematicity of the way it has been collected. The reliability of elicited data crucially depends on the method of data recording, and the experimental technique used.

Lehmann (2004: 196ff.) applies a similar typology when – after rejecting introspection – he distinguishes two 'serious ways' of data collection: *data discovered* and *data produced by the researcher*. However, he clearly prefers the former group. He claims that at least in two respects data discovered better meet the very requirement of empiricalness which declares, among other things, that the properties of the objects under investigation shall be independent of the researcher (see Lehmann 2004: 192). First, since in the case of research based on corpus data there is less possibility for manipulation of the data, it ensures a higher objectivity than research relying on other types of data. Second, he believes that corpora not produced by the linguist are varied, full of surprises, and therefore they serve as sources of ingenious insights undermining preliminary expectations (Lehmann 2004: 201). Among the data produced by the researcher, Lehmann considers only data obtained from linguistic behaviour elicited by non-linguistic stimuli or controlled by the combination of different techniques as legitimate. He regards, for example, translation from one language to another as well as work with data elicited by metalinguistic procedures as a non-empirical, hermeneutic method (see Lehmann 2004: 201ff.), because he considers the factors influencing the choice of relevant data, the reliability of the data and the evaluation of the results to be uncontrollable. Thus, he assumes, such data are acceptable only when they are used together with other data types. However, while he exposes the weaknesses even of data discovered with an extraordinarily keen eye and accuracy, in judging them he is more permissive than in the case of data produced, although there is close similarity between the problems in the two cases (see e.g. Lehmann 2004: 200).[2]

Summary. As regards the role which data sources play, there has been a considerable change in attitude compared to the standard view of linguistic data and evidence (SVLD). Whereas (SVLD)(b) saw it as a crucial factor, in the literature we have surveyed it is simply *one of* the relevant factors. Further, while representatives of the standard view of linguistic data and evidence (SVLD) considered only one data source as legitimate, now *a wide variety of sources* is acknowledged. Nevertheless, in the papers examined here, this significant and progressive change is not accompanied by systematic investigations into the nature of data sources but happens in a rather inconsequential way. The following question is still unanswered:

(OQ2) What role do sources play in the judgement of the reliability of data?

5.4 The complexity of linguistic data

The views summarised in the standard view of linguistic data and evidence (SVLD) are regarded as insufficient by the authors mentioned not only because they narrow down the range of data, but – as (SVLD)(c) clearly demonstrates – they also neglect another factor of crucial importance: the *complexity of data*.

Kepser and Reis trace this complexity back to the fact that the object of linguistic inquiry is not directly accessible, but has to be reconstructed from the directly observable manifestations of linguistic behaviour (Kepser & Reis 2005a: 1).

In accordance with this, Penke & Rosenbach (2004a: 487ff.), too, distinguish between data reflecting knowledge of language *directly* and *indirectly*. They believe that corpus and intuitive data reflect aspects of knowledge of language in a more direct way than results from experiments which yield information, for example, about the properties of a certain linguistic construction only indirectly. The authors provide us with a detailed overview of the problems resulting from the complexity of data types described in Section 4.2 (iii); however, they do not attempt to systematise and generalise them.

Lehmann (2004) identifies considerably more aspects of the structure of linguistic data, proposing a sophisticated and comprehensive system of criteria:

- In his view linguistic data are *semiotic representations*, that is, representations of particular aspects of speech events. This means that data are not given at the outset, but are – at least to a certain extent – produced by the researcher. Although they refer to some entity independent of the researcher, the identification of even the most elementary linguistic datum is based on *abstraction* and *semiotic processes*.

- *Primary data* are representations of speech events with spatiotemporal coordinates. *Secondary data* do not possess historical identity, that is, cannot be linked to a certain place and time, and are therefore more abstract. Secondary data include types of primary data that, in turn, may be regarded as tokens. Metalinguistic statements also constitute secondary data, which describe different properties of speech events or capture generalisations; for example, sentences preceded by an asterisk marking ungrammaticality, or 'negative data' stating that a certain linguistic construction does not exist. Such data, Lehmann claims, are semiotic objects of a higher order in the sense that they contain the combination of meta- and object-language.
- He also differentiates between *raw data* (*non-symbolic representations*) and *processed data* (*symbolic representations*). Raw data are iconic representations of speech events such as a tape recording. Linguists, however, almost never work with raw data, but process them by converting them into symbolic representations that highlight special properties of the speech event, and downplay features deemed irrelevant in the given inquiry. This, however, inevitably leads to the reduction and distortion of the speech event. Transcripts of linguistic utterances or phrase structure trees in syntax are good examples of symbolic representations.
- *Original recordings* are based directly on the speech event, while *derived representations* are based on other representations, that is, on other data. For example, a recording of a conversation, for linguist *A* constitutes the data on the basis of which he carries out acoustic phonetic investigations. Linguist *B*, being a segmental phonologist, will consider the symbolic representation of the recording transcribed with the help of the IPA as data. Linguist *C* – who is a post-generative phonologist – complements this with symbols marking suprasegmental relations. Linguist *D* is a conversation analyst who uses one of the transcription systems of conversation analysis to produce a certain transcription of the conversation recorded that includes, among others, turn-taking. Linguist *E* is a grammarian who considers the latter as data which may help him elaborate a fragment of the grammar of the spoken version of a Swabian dialect near Tübingen. Linguist *F* considers the hypotheses of this grammar as data which he relies on in order to point out the differences between written and spoken language. The list of examples could be continued, and this perfectly illustrates at least two important issues. First, that something that constitutes the *result* of data analysis for one linguist, may serve as *data* for the other. Second, that defining the domain of the data does not depend on their inherent characteristics, but rather, on the particular interest, purpose, tools, conceptual framework and problems of the research at issue.

Summary. The authors seem to agree that (SVLD)(c) has to be given up, because it crucially hinders the efficient handling of the problems described in

Section 4.2 (iii). Therefore, they are of the opinion that one of the inevitable tasks of the metatheoretical reflection on data consists in revealing their *structure*. At the same time, the attempts to capture the complexity of data make use of very different categorisations which are of different depths. Hence, the following question is still open:

(OQ3) How can the complexity of data be accounted for?

5.5 The treatment of the uncertainty of data

Current literature – breaking with the views summarised in (SVLD)(a)–(c), and more or less in accordance with the state of the art outlined in Section 4.2 (iii) – seems to hold that the acceptability of data can be judged on the basis of a complex process which has to consider the *source* and the *structure* of data along with *certain properties of the theory* at issue as well.

According to Kepser and Reis, the decision regarding the acceptability of the data is not to be restricted to the examination of a certain datum or data type. It has to consider *all* available data/data types and in addition further, partly non-linguistic factors as well. In this respect the authors significantly go beyond the monolithic character of (SVLD)(b):

> the linguist's central task of building theories about the above-mentioned linguistic objects is invariably bound up with several empirical tasks as well: (i) collecting/selecting a representative as well as reliable database *from one or more data types*, (ii) *evaluating* the various data types as to how they reflect linguistic competence (recall that even so-called primary data from introspection as well as authentic language production are complex performance data involving different nonlinguistic factors), (iii) assessing the relationship between the various data types such that comparison between studies of the same issue *based on different data types* is possible, and potential conflicts in results can in principle be resolved. (Kepser & Reis 2005a: 1; emphasis added)

Penke and Rosenbach are content to notice that data collection must be *systematic*, although the examples they mention clearly indicate that this criterion is not sufficient.

Borsley raises the problem of the reliability of data, too, but he leaves it open.[3] Nevertheless, it is noteworthy that he – referring to Chomsky – does not deem, for example, grammaticality judgements incontestable. He assumes that the reliability of grammaticality judgements is influenced by several factors which, nevertheless, cannot be controlled completely (see Borsley 2005a: 1476f.).

Geeraerts thinks that the pluralism of methods and, accordingly, of data types is useful because they can supplement each other and thus provide more reliable results than when they are applied in isolation.[4] However, he also maintains that it is necessary to establish a *common, strict methodology* which the methods have to be based on. One of the most important tasks linguistics has to solve is therefore the development of a *theory-neutral empirical basis*. He assumes that the hypotheses of linguistic theories should be formulated in such a way that they can be confronted with 'observations' (see Geeraerts 2006: 23ff.). In order to achieve this, a theory-independent observation language is needed in his view in which the data can be described and into which the hypotheses of the theory can be translated. However, with this claim he falls back on the acceptance of the standard view of the analytical philosophy of science (SVAPS).[5]

On the basis of the typology we summarised in Section 5.4, Lehmann (2004: 204ff.) formulates the generalisation that linguistic data are normally not speech events taking place in space and time, but rather, are representations located on different levels of abstraction and supplemented by different kinds of information. From this claim he concludes that data inevitably exhibit problem- and theory-dependent characteristics. First, they represent only certain aspects of the object of investigation, and second – since they are constructed through a series of intermediate stages – they simplify and distort the original. Nevertheless, he believes that the methodology which allows us to gain reliable data is available. In this respect he seems to agree with Geeraerts:

> In general, for a datum to be accepted as such in the discipline, there must be operational procedures of relating secondary to primary data, and primary data to the ultimate substrate. Such procedures are part of the methodology of that discipline, viz. of the methods that *allow* scientists to *control* the relationship between the theory and the data . . . If there are no such operational procedures, then firstly there is no basis on which *the datum can be taken for granted*, which means that it is not a datum in the sense of our definition; and secondly, there is no way of relating a theory to a perceptible epistemic object, which means it is *not an empirical theory*. (Lehmann 2004: 185f.; emphasis added)

Therefore, he presumes that with the help of raw data the correctness of the representation can be checked.[6] This assumption does not go beyond the views summarised in the standard view of linguistic data and evidence (SVLD). In this respect, Lehmann seems to advocate the standard view of the analytical philosophy of science (SVAPS) and assume that general methodological rules are capable of guaranteeing that data can be treated as firm facts. However, here one level of metareflection comes into conflict with another. As for the analysis of the internal structure of data, several of Lehmann's claims indicate that data – since they are representations – cannot be considered as 'facts' which are 'true' with certainty and are given at the outset.[7] Rather, they are merely points of departure which need further refinement or which may turn out to be insufficient, not reliable enough or even useless (see e.g. Lehmann 2004: 207). But, referring to the operational procedures as mentioned in the last quotation points in the opposite direction. The obtaining of perceptible and thus maximally reliable data is required not only as a norm but is supposed to be an objective which can easily be achieved.

Schütze (1996: 1) does not believe that the methodological principles prevalent in the natural sciences, in sociology or psychology are infallible, although he, too, rejects theories obtained on the basis of uncontrolled data that have not been supported by experiments (see Schütze 1996: 4f.). He points out that the evaluation of the reliability of data is a highly complex task *which cannot be separated from the process of theory formation*. The factors influencing the reliability of data can be controlled or even eliminated only if the properties of their *sources* are systematically revealed – that is if hypotheses are put forward concerning the structure and functioning of data sources. Accordingly, the hypotheses concerning the reliability of data are *part* of the theory at issue.[8] Schütze's strategy is fruitful since it encourages one to look actively for the unquestioned background assumptions which may turn out to be wrong and can decrease the reliability of data. This also means that the detection of the factors influencing the reliability of data, the formulation of hypotheses and their confrontation with the data *cannot be separated*.

While there seems to be a consensus about the necessity of developing new standards of data collection and data evaluation, there is disagreement among researchers about the *content* of the criteria to be applied. While Schütze (1996) identifies, as we have seen in Section 4.2, a series of subject-related and task-related factors which might distort the results of experiments which elicit introspective judgements from the participants, Featherston (2009a) expresses the opinion that the distorting effect of subject-related factors such as social, educational, professional, dialect background, age, sex, or speed of response required is negligible, and it is only some task-related factors in connection with the content, length, complexity and comprehensibility of the stimulus material which have to be controlled carefully.[9] Fanselow (2009: 133ff.) takes an extreme position when he states that the practice of using uncontrolled introspective data in generative linguistics is fully legitimate and the research results based on them are not burdened with the effects of the application of 'marginally acceptable' or 'unclear facts'. Moreover, he deems experimental data or corpus data in most cases useless in connection with questions regarding linguistic competence and proposes to restrict their application to 'specific problematic cases'. He suggests that the use of acceptability experiments is not only superfluous but impossible, too, because of the practical limits of data collection.[10] Acceptability judgements, in contrast, he labels as 'self-psychical facts' which can only be distorted by the influence of the theory preferred by the linguist. Fanselow takes the view that their use requires only the application of a few well-known maxims of caution such as the systematic variation of lexical material or care in the construction and evaluation of minimal pairs.

Summary. As we have seen, most authors recognise the significance of the problems related to the acceptability of data and try to find appropriate criteria. This clearly signals the refinement of metascientific reflection in current linguistic literature. However, there are obvious differences between the criteria proposed. None of the authors outlines a coherent solution to the problem of the acceptability of linguistic data which would really be able to capture the difficulties mentioned. Above all, the means which could capture the uncertainties the complexity of data inevitably yields are missing. None of the standpoints is able to resolve the *tension* between two poles. One is the recognition that the factors influencing the reliability of data cannot be controlled completely. The other is the intention inherited from the standard view of the analytical philosophy of science (SVAPS) that data should provide a firm basis for testing the hypotheses of the theory (see also Sections 5.6 and 5.8). Therefore, the following question has to be raised:

(OQ4) How can the uncertainty of data be treated?

5.6 The relationship between data and theory

In the metatheoretical literature of the fourth stage of the data/evidence debate in linguistics, the views concerning the relation between data and theory are still dominated by models based on induction and deduction.[11] Nevertheless – in accordance with the tendencies mentioned in Section 4.2 (iv) – the authors also formulate ideas which go beyond (SVLD)(d). First, it is claimed that during scientific theorising, the relation between data and theory *cannot* be reduced simply to the *linear* application of the deductive or inductive method, but is, rather, *cyclic* in nature:

> Empirical research involves an *empirical cycle* in which several rounds of data gathering, testing of hypotheses, and interpretation of the results follow each other... Just like it is misguided to think that empirical, data-driven research automatically gives you all the answers, it is misguided to think that it immediately gives you the final answer. (Geeraerts 2006: 24f.; emphasis added)

Second, some authors assume that the selection of data is *problem- and theory-dependent*.[12] Featherston, for instance, suggests a close connection between the complexity of data and the complexity of their application in the process of linguistic theorising:

> it became clear that linguistic data is always complex and requires filtering, interpretation, and location within a wider model to yield its full evidential value. The developing different wings of grammar research therefore need each other; neither all-data nor all-theory can have as much value as a judicious combination of the two. (Featherston 2009a: 127)

Haspelmath (2009) is of the opinion that in principle, all data types which have been applied in linguistics so far are relevant for linguistic inquiry. Nevertheless, peculiarities of the problem under investigation impose strict limits on their application. In possession of the currently available linguistic data it is possible, for example, to raise questions in relation to the rules of language use of a given language and to the rule types of the languages in the world. The study of questions pertaining to the mental grammar of a speaker, to the biological basis of mental grammar, or to the origin of the limitations which can be revealed in the rules of the world's languages, however, leads only to highly speculative answers on the basis of the data currently available. Therefore, answers to these questions would clearly require the application of new data types.

This theory- and problem-dependence is, however, also incompatible with the linear relation between data and theory. Namely, if the selection of data is significantly influenced by the properties of the particular problem to be solved[13] as well as by the conceptual and methodological background of the theory,[14] then the relationship between data and theory cannot be reduced to the confrontation of the hypotheses with experience – that is, to the justification of the hypotheses by data independent of the theory.

Featherston places great emphasis on the equal importance of hypothesis generation and hypothesis testing and assigns data a vital role in both of them, without, however, raising the question of how data which serve as the starting point of hypothesis generation can be interpreted without a theoretical framework:

> When we gather data more broadly, the data patterns gain an independent existence as evidence in themselves: we can print out the results as bar charts and hang them on the wall. Linguists interested in grammar architectures can look at wider sets of data and ask themselves what sort of system could produce the data patterns that they find. This is datadriven linguistics, and while it can usefully be theoretically informed, it need not be constrained by theory. The work done on the relationship between data and theory within the SFB 441 has demonstrated the value of this approach (e.g. Featherston 2005). (Featherston 2009a: 130)

Lehmann (2004: 191) raises the issue of the relation between theory and data on the basis of more refined guidelines than other authors. He attributes three functions to data. First: during theory formation (this corresponds to the 'context of discovery' in the sense of the analytical philosophy of science), data work as the *basis of induction* in the process of finding the hypotheses. Second: they are the means of *testing hypotheses* obtained by deduction (this seems to correspond to the 'context of justification'). Finally, with respect to the presentation of the theory, they play the role of evidence serving the *persuasion* of the reader in the course of argumentation. However, he does not clarify the relation of these functions to each other. This leads, of course, to considerable difficulties.

One problem arises from the circumstance that, as we have just mentioned, due to the role they play in the discovery of hypotheses, he assumes data to be inevitably *theory- and problem-dependent*:

> Whether anybody regards any of the representations . . . as linguistic data *depends on his purposes* and on his conviction that the representation can be related back to primary data by standard methodological procedures. *There is*, alas, *no clear-cut distinction between data and constructs; a representation is, by definition, a construct.* (Lehmann 2004: 208; emphasis added)

In spite of this, as we have seen in Section 5.5, Lehmann also assumes that data can fulfil their second function, that is, the testing of hypotheses, only if the effects of the relativistic elements associated with them are sorted out and the return to the least theory- and problem-dependent kind of data, namely, *raw data*, is secured.[15]

However, he expressly asserts that although the recursion to raw data may make the data more reliable, it cannot guarantee their certainty.[16] On the basis of this, Lehman puts forward the desideratum that data should be – at least to a certain extent – *independent of the researcher*.[17] This is in contrast to the hypothesis of the theory- and problem-dependence of data. He does not ask the question of why and to what extent this partial theory-independence could be sufficient for the fulfilment of the control function of data.

The fact that the relation between the three functions of data has not been clarified raises a second problem as well. Namely, Lehmann associates a particular criterion with the argumentative function of data which is at variance with the criteria connected to the previous two functions:

> Something is not a datum by virtue of corresponding to some elementary observation . . . On the contrary, it may be highly abstract. It may nevertheless function as a datum in some research that *assigns it the role of unquestionable evidence in the argumentation*. (Lehmann 2004: 181; emphasis added)

This formulation characterises data as the unquestionable basis of theory formation. However, this unquestionability is not traced back to some kind of objective criterion but seems, rather, to be interpreted relativistically by being associated with the argumentative role data may play in the theory at issue. If this is so, then it should follow that data are *theory-dependent* – and this leads to a contradiction (see also Section 5.8).

Summary. The views we have surveyed witness the difficulties resulting from the *incompatibility* of the theory- and problem-dependence, the complexity and the uncertainty of the data with the norms of the standard view of the analytical philosophy of science (SVAPS). The latter prescribes the rigid distinction between the 'context of discovery' and the 'context of justification', and requires, therefore, a unidirectional relation between the data and the theory. The views we have discussed, however, assume this relation – as a result of the acceptance and legitimisation of object-scientific practice – to be much more complicated. Nevertheless, since they have no alternative metatheoretical framework at their disposal, these views remain incomplete and problematic in several respects. The relationship between data and linguistic theories, that is, the function of data in linguistic theories, remains unclarified. Therefore, the following question remains open:

(OQ5) What is the relationship between data and theories?

5.7 Data and the treatment of inconsistencies

Another relevant property of linguistic data is that they may be *the source of contradictions*. The most trivial manifestation of this is that linguists are continuously confronted with 'exceptions' or 'counterexamples' whenever they put forward hypotheses.

Referring to Chomsky (2002: 98ff.), Penke & Rosenbach (2004a: 484) emphasise that in linguistic theorising there are situations in which the immediate resolution of a contradiction triggered by data does not appear to be necessary. The fact that there are data contradicting the hypotheses does not necessarily have to lead to the rejection of the theory. It may be reasonable to ignore them till, in a later stage of the research, the tools become available that allow for the theory to explain their behaviour:

> According to Chomsky it is legitimate to ignore certain data to gain a deeper understanding of the principles governing the system under investigation . . . In all these cases, the apparent counter-evidence was not taken to refute a theory, but stimulated further research that resulted in the discovery of principles so far unknown, thus enhancing our understanding of the phenomena under study. (Penke & Rosenbach 2004a: 484)

However, they contrast this strategy without comment with the standpoint of corpus linguists and others opposing generative grammar who reject this way of ignoring data which contradict the hypotheses.[18] Moreover, Penke and Rosenbach do not attempt to clarify the relation between the above strategy, on the one hand, and the 'strong' and 'weak' versions of falsification we mentioned in Section 4.2 (iv), on the other.

In another context, Kepser & Reis (2005a: 3), too, emphasise that contradictions resulting from the diversity of data may be fruitful.[19] Different data types may lead to contradictory hypotheses, but these contradictions may be resolved and thus play a progressive role in the inquiry.[20]

Nevertheless, the substantial problem is that, in spite of these important diagnoses, the authors mentioned do not attempt to reveal *the strategies of inconsistency resolution* related to data.

As regards the latter, Schütze (1996: 4) notes that in linguistics the techniques of inconsistency resolution which have been applied in the natural sciences are absent, but he neither clarifies what techniques he has in mind nor supports this claim with references.

With respect to corpora, Geeraerts assumes that it is statistical methods that might provide the means of inconsistency resolution.[21] His suggestion, just like the previous ones, touches on important aspects of the treatment of contradictions, but does not break radically with the views summarised in the standard view of linguistic data and evidence (SVLD). Rather, it seeks more refined solutions within the boundaries of the standard view of the analytical philosophy of science (SVAPS). In a series of cases he accepts Popperian falsificationism without critique, although he questions its applicability in certain situations. In particular, if one finds a small number of occurrences of a certain linguistic phenomenon in a corpus, then it might be the case that these are marginal data which cannot be considered as falsifying or confirming evidence. In such cases, possible alternatives should be examined by comparing them with the help of statistical methods. But this procedure leaves a series of questions unanswered. First, it does not resolve, for instance, those situations in which there is a conflict between two hypotheses supported by different types of data approximately to the same degree. Second, it cannot be applied to every type of data. Third, in contrast to Schütze, who mentions only the criteria for selecting the 'more reliable' hypothesis (see Schütze 1996: 4), Geeraerts seems to assume that statistical methods are entirely objective and yield unambiguous results. However, it is well known that the choice of the test applied and the interpretation of its results depends – at least to a certain extent – on the researcher's decision; another test may lead to another result, thus generating inconsistency. It is also often the case that the repetition of the experiment with the same or with similar materials leads to the opposite outcome. Statistical methods do not yield ultimate results, either; they may only increase the reliability of one's conclusions gained from the examination of data.[22] With respect to experiments, Geeraerts refers to *experimentum crucis*[23] – but of course he can do so only in the spirit of the analytical philosophy of science.

Summary. It is an important and progressive insight of the literature analysed that inconsistencies arising from the use of different types of data are natural parts of linguistic theorising. This insight signals the departure from the standard view of the analytical philosophy of science (SVAPS) and the convergence with new tendencies in the philosophy of science. Inconsistency in science is one of the most important topics of contemporary philosophy of science (see Meheus 2002). Therefore, the development that the issue of inconsistency is raised in the works we examined is a very progressive step towards making the methodology of linguistics more up-to-date. Nevertheless, there are only a few works which systematically discuss the role inconsistency plays in linguistic theorising (Moravcsik 1993, 2006, 2010; Kertész 2004a, b; Kertész & Rákosi 2006, 2009a, c). Nevertheless, there is no agreement on the answer to the following questions: what are the principles which one should apply to decide when a certain contradiction can be tolerated and when it cannot? How can inconsistencies be resolved? The views of the authors cited are incomplete. Thus, they are not capable of deciding between the strategies outlined in Section 4.2 (iv) or of putting forward new methods. This means that the treatment of inconsistency must also be considered an open question:

(OQ6) On the basis of what criteria can it be decided whether a contradiction may be tolerated, and what strategies should we adopt for inconsistency resolution?

5.8 Linguistic evidence

The latest literature does not explicate the notion of 'linguistic evidence'. The publications mentioned in Section 3.3 clearly indicate the *confusion* characterising the use of this notion as well as a tendency which allows us to highlight certain of its relevant aspects. From the circumstance that none of the authors define the notion of evidence, it need not, of course, necessarily follow that there is confusion around its interpretation. It would also be possible that its meaning is clear and familiar to everyone. However, if we carefully examine the way the authors use this term, it will turn out that it is applied in different senses and incoherently.

In Penke & Rosenbach (2004a) the terms 'data' and 'evidence' occur *synonymously* at several places. For example, when data types are discussed, on page 485 we find the expression 'qualitative vs quantitative *data*' whereas on the next page 'qualitative vs quantitative *evidence*' (emphasis added). They classify direct and indirect evidence as data types, too, but – interpreting and relating the two categories in an entirely different way – they also claim that one of the functions of data is to serve as evidence for hypotheses.[24] In this way – following the intentions of the standard view of the analytical philosophy of science (SVAPS) – they interpret evidence as *a special, designated and secure subset* of data whose task is the testing of hypotheses. However, they think that there are no general methodological criteria on the basis of which it can be decided which data are capable of serving this function, because theory- and problem-dependent aspects have to be considered, too. Thus, in this respect, they go beyond (SVAPS).[25] They also refer to potential conflicts between the problem- and the theory-dependence of data. Namely, it may happen that at a certain point of research particular types of data seem to be relevant which the methodology of the theory either does not acknowledge or even forbids. They think that in such cases it is the 'open-mindedness' of the linguist that may further the research. By this they mean that, in order to find an effective solution to the problem at issue, linguists are often ready to consider and to treat as evidence such data which their theory does not permit. However, the methodological norms on the basis of which the control of the data's reliability could be associated with a certain phase within the process of theorising remain unclear. They do not reveal the relations which hold between the hypotheses of the theory, its methodological background assumptions, the criteria of the acceptability of data, and the process of object-theoretical activity. Although Penke and Rosenbach touch on the problem that the confrontation of the hypotheses with the data may lead to the revision of methodological principles – for example, to the modification of the range of the acknowledged data types – they do not integrate the mutual influence of data and the hypotheses of the theory into the process of theorising.

The standpoint of Kepser and Reis is similar. They hold that the selection of evidence from among the set of data is a complex and far from trivial task. This task cannot be carried out solely on the basis of general methodological norms, independently of concrete linguistic research (Kepser & Reis 2005a: 1). The question of what counts as evidence can be answered only with respect to the particularities of the theory at issue and those of a concrete problem. Namely, the latter factors decide whether certain data or a certain data type can be regarded as *adequate* and *relevant*, that is, if it is capable of *supporting* or *refuting* some hypothesis of the theory:[26]

> it is not so much the origin of evidence that counts. What is more important is adequacy and the status of the data as true 'evidence'. Adequacy means that the data put forward to support a certain claim actually do so. (Kepser & Reis 2005a: 3)

Since they think that the adequacy of the data can be decided only on an individual level, with respect to the particular problem at issue, they do not go into the problem of adequacy. At the same time, they emphasise that certain data can serve as 'true evidence' if they are *reliable* and *reproducible*:

> Whether certain data can be regarded as *true evidence* touches the key questions of reliability and reproducibility of data. Reliability encompasses reproducibility, but requires more. A proper analysis and control of the factors that influence the constitution of the data are necessary as well. With *reproducibility and reliability secured*, data can be fruitfully used *as evidence* for strengthening or refuting hypotheses. (Kepser & Reis 2005a: 3; emphasis added)

In this way they assume that an empirical basis can be established which makes it possible to treat certain data as 'true evidence'. This means, however, that Kepser and Reis' view is *double-faced* in a similar way to Penke and Rosenbach's. They admit the uncertainty and fallibility of data rooted in their complexity, but at the same time, in accordance with the standard view of the analytical philosophy of science (SVAPS), they try to select those data which are expected to secure a firm and theory-independent base for testing the theory. Kepser and Reis seem to assume that theory formation has to be *preceded* by the selection of reliable and reproducible evidence and that the process of theory formation is to be regarded as linear. Nevertheless, this procedure is not able to provide such a firm empirical basis for theory formation. In particular, so as to select the components of the basis – that is to control the linguistic and non-linguistic factors that may influence the reliability of the data – one or more further empirical theories would be needed; these further theories, however, rely on data whose own reliability can be controlled only with the help of further theories, and so on ad infinitum.

Moreover, as Lehmann shows with the help of several examples, unlike, for example, in physics or other natural sciences, in certain kinds of linguistic research data are *not reproducible*, but rather, individual and unique:

Much linguistic research is devoted to data that are *not reproducible*, be it for contingent reasons, because the factual preconditions for their production can no longer be met, be it for theoretical reasons, because they do not have the status of tokens but that of types. (Lehmann 2004: 197)

As regards Lehmann's view, first, as we have seen in Section 5.6, he maintains that one function of data is that they play 'the role of unquestionable evidence in the argumentation' (Lehmann 2004: 181). In this way, he reverses the relation between data and evidence: it is not the case that evidence has to be selected from the set of data, but rather, being evidence is the precondition of becoming a datum. It is worth noting that in the above quotation Lehman relates the question of whether something is evidence to the *argumentation* at issue. This implies that it is not the abstract logical structure of the theory that is focused on, but its *argumentation structure*. This claim might have led to a radical turn in the reconstruction of linguistic theories. However, Lehmann did not draw this conclusion, as the following quotation witnesses:

As to the user of the data, we may distinguish between *the researcher who takes them for granted* and *the addressee of the research*. Starting with the researcher, we can distinguish between the research itself and the report on the research delivered to the consumer. In the research itself, the data are used either as the basis for induction or as the test of theorems that were deduced. *In the report, the data play the argumentative role of evidence for the theory*. (Lehmann 2004: 191; emphasis added)

Second, it is easy to see that the above quotation is incompatible with the second quotation by Lehmann in Section 5.6 (p. 33 above). This claims that if the representation of a certain speech event plays the role of unquestionable evidence in the argumentation, then it functions as a datum in the research at issue. In contrast, in the former quotation evidence is merely a *rhetorical tool* serving to persuade the reader.

Third, in accordance with the standard view of the analytical philosophy of science (SVAPS), Lehmann seems to assume that with respect to theories it is their logical structure that is relevant, whereas argumentation structure may play a role only in the presentation of the theory. However, this stance is not compatible with the clause in the first sentence of the last quotation which says that the linguist takes the data *for granted* – we might also say that they are considered as 'unquestionable evidence'. This means that Lehmann raises but leaves unexplicated the relation between the logical structure of linguistic theories and linguistic argumentation. In this respect, he still holds a position akin to the standard view of linguistic data and evidence (SVLD) in that – similarly to Geeraerts and Kepser & Reis – he considers evidence as a firm empirical basis independent of theories.

Summary. We may conclude that in characterising the notion of evidence the literature is far from unanimous. On the one hand, the view summarised in (SVLD)(e) still prevails, as well as a series of methodological principles borrowed from the standard view of the analytical philosophy of science (SVAPS) – above all, the assumption that a certain group of data can be selected that works as a firm basis during the testing of the hypotheses. On the other hand, all the different standpoints we discussed clearly include components which are no longer compatible with (SVAPS). For example, the theory- and problem-dependence of data has been realised, as well as the insight that the relation between the hypotheses and data which may be more or less uncertain is much more sophisticated than (SVAPS) assumes: namely, that the data do not confirm or falsify the hypotheses once and for all. However, the methodological principles which could provide the metatheoretical explication of the new insights are completely missing. Thus, the following question remains to be answered:

(OQ7) What data can serve as evidence in linguistic theories, if, on the one hand, evidence has to be capable of supporting or weakening hypotheses, and, on the other hand, data cannot be regarded as true with certainty?

5.9 Conclusions

The above state-of-the-art analysis of the literature has revealed two facts, among others. *On the one hand*, in the views we have surveyed, components of the standard view of the analytical philosophy of science (SVAPS) and the standard view of linguistic data and evidence (SVLD) are still present. *On the other hand*, the same approaches include sophisticated, insightful and progressive suggestions as well, ideas which are not compatible with (SVAPS) and (SVLD) and which clearly indicate the need to depart from the latter. In their proposals for (CP), they *differentiate, relativise* and *weaken* the requirements linguistic data and evidence are expected to meet.

Differentiation means that the authors do not seek to define the notion of 'linguistic datum' on the basis of the properties of just one data type. Rather, they acknowledge the pluralism of linguistic data in that it is not just one type of data that may be legitimate. They strive to put forward a rich system of criteria which allows us to reveal the internal structure of different data types and to elaborate the typology of data as applied in different linguistic theories. They consider linguistic data to be complex entities whose reliability is influenced by the peculiarities of their structure and source.

Relativisation means that the evaluation of the applicability of linguistic data is not assumed to be epistemologically independent of the linguistic theory at issue, but rather, data and evidence are regarded as problem- and theory-dependent.

By *weakening* we mean that these approaches treat not only statements which capture directly given linguistic utterances with spatiotemporal coordinates as empirical data, but abstractions from utterances at different levels, too, which therefore unavoidably idealise and reduce the speech events in certain ways. Moreover, they permit different versions of falsifiability, and they also touch on the temporary tolerability of inconsistencies arising from the application of different data types.

Consequently, as a general conclusion, the only claim we are allowed to make is that the *demand* for a departure from the standard view of linguistic data and evidence (SVLD) and the standard view of the analytical philosophy of science (SVAPS) can be identified in these views, but there is no dominating tendency fundamentally overruling them. (SVLD) is not replaced by a radically new perspective, but rather, by a *double-faced* tendency. This tendency comprises a series of different views which have in common, first, that they are still close to (SVLD) and (SVAPS) in several respects, and second, that they try to go beyond the latter by putting forward relevant new suggestions, although in several respects they do this inconsistently.

6 The solution to $(P)_I$

On the basis of the conclusions summarised in Section 5.9, the following solution to $(P)_I(a)$ presents itself:

$(SP)_I$

(a) (i) On the one hand, in accordance with the standard view of the analytical philosophy of science (SVAPS) and the standard view of linguistic data and evidence (SVLD), 'linguistic evidence' is still interpreted as a specific subset of data which is not revisable within the theory at issue. It is supposed to comprise statements which are true with certainty and whose main task is to test the hypotheses of the theory.

(ii) On the other hand, in opposition to the tenets summarised in the standard view of linguistic data and evidence (SVLD), the new proposals surveyed raise a series of innovative ideas. These progressive insights are, however, not shared by all authors; and even if they are accepted by several of them, this acceptance takes different forms, so that they cannot be generalised. Despite this, we can highlight the following insights which appear in one or more contributions and are – in comparison to the standard view of the analytical philosophy of science (SVAPS) and the standard view of linguistic data and evidence (SVLD) – of a clearly innovative nature in that they conform to the process of differentiation, relativisation and weakening:

- The pluralism of linguistic data is acknowledged instead of preferring just one type of data. The combination of several data types within a given piece of research is considered to be a desideratum.
- The origin of data is not held to be decisive; rather, it is treated as only one relevant factor among others, such as the structure, the complexity, the directness, the abstractness of data etc.
- All data types are assumed to be problematic; therefore, it seems indispensable to clarify their structure and function.
- The relationship between data and theory is assumed to be cyclic rather than linear.
- Linguistic data are considered to be theory- and problem-dependent. It is admitted that data treated as evidence very often do not support or refute the hypotheses unanimously. They are not certain and may also generate contradictions.

Nevertheless, neither the relation between $(SP)_I(a)(i)$ and (ii), nor the criteria which might facilitate the application of the assumptions summarised in

(ii) have been tackled. In consequence of the double-facedness of the views summarised in $(SP)_I$(a), the following questions could not be answered:

(OQ1) Under what conditions is the diversity of data legitimate and how can data belonging to different data types be combined?
(OQ2) What role do sources play in the judgement of the reliability of data?
(OQ3) How can the complexity of data be accounted for?
(OQ4) How can the uncertainty of data be treated?
(OQ5) What is the relationship between data and theories?
(OQ6) On the basis of what criteria can it be decided whether a contradiction may be tolerated, and what strategies should we adopt for inconsistency resolution?
(OQ7) What data can serve as evidence in linguistic theories, if, on the one hand, evidence has to be capable of supporting or weakening hypotheses, and, on the other, data cannot be regarded as true with certainty?

We will show in Part V how our own approach to linguistic data and evidence answers these questions.

Although our survey in Sections 5.2–5.8 revealed that current approaches try to elaborate a considerably more sophisticated account of linguistic data and evidence, it also highlighted a fundamental difficulty of a *metatheoretical* nature: namely, (CP) presupposes raising and solving (MP)(a)–(b). The latter, however, cannot be solved without systematic metascientific reflection, while it is still unclear what role metatheoretical reflection can play in linguistic theorising.

Thus, the latest literature focusing on the problem of linguistic data/evidence shows *a second kind of double-facedness*, which characterises the role attributed to metascientific reflection. On the one hand, the authors realise the necessity of metascientific reflection. On the other hand, the way metascientific reflection is carried out is inconsequent and remains fragmentary. Reflecting on the practice of linguistic research, they admit the untenability of the standard view of linguistic data and evidence (SVLD) and appreciate that linguistic inquiry works very differently from what the mechanical adaptation of the standard view of the analytical philosophy of science (SVAPS) to linguistics suggests. At the same time, they do not realise that the untenability of (SVAPS) indicates the need to look for alternative metascientific points of departure. Therefore, they fall back on the tenets of the analytical philosophy of science in the form of explicit declarations or implicit background assumptions again and again. By doing this, however, they generate apparent contradictions between the tenets of the analytical philosophy of science they make use of and the conclusions they draw from the practice of linguistic theorising.

Thus, as the result of our analyses we obtain the following *solution to* $(P)_I$*(b)* which reflects the second double-facedness just mentioned:

$(SP)_I$

(b) (i) The views we have investigated *realise* the need for metascientific reflection on the structure and function of linguistic data and evidence.

(ii) This, however, does not go beyond the linguist's naïve (self-)reflection on research practice. Although the continuous, partly implicit, partly explicit confrontation of the standard view of the analytical philosophy of science (SVAPS) and the standard view of linguistic data and evidence (SVLD) with everyday research experience suggests the unacceptability of the former, the necessity to develop alternative metascientific tools has *not been realised*.

Nevertheless, the finding that – as we have shown in our analyses and summarised in $(SP)_I$(b)(ii) – there is a wide gap between everyday research practice and the tenets of the analytical philosophy of science is not unique to linguistics but a problem of general relevance legitimising the elaboration of *new* metascientific approaches to data and evidence. As Peter Achinstein writes in the introductory chapter of his seminal book:

> standard philosophical theories about evidence are (and ought to be) *ignored* by scientists. They ought to be ignored because they propose concepts of evidence that are based on assumptions *incompatible with* ones scientists make when they speak of, and offer, evidence for hypotheses. (Achinstein 2001: 3; emphasis added)

The two kinds of double-facedness we have summarised in $(SP)_I$(a) and $(SP)_I$(b) convincingly motivate the raising of (MP) and the systematic development of a metascientific approach which transgresses the limits of the standard view of the analytical philosophy of science (SVAPS) and resolves the two discrepancies by elaborating a model that is well founded from a metascientific point of view and, at the same time, takes into account the practice of linguistic theorising. In addition, as the above quotation illustrates, such a novel approach seems to be legitimised by general metascientific considerations independent of the peculiarities of linguistics.

Part II

The p-model

7 The problem $(P)_{II}$

The starting point of Part II of the book is the result of Part I: namely, the insight that the double-facedness revealed in the above literature – as summarised in $(SP)_{I}$ (a)–(b) – emerges from the circumstance that the role of the *metascientific reflection* in the process of linguistic problem solving is still unclear. In current literature, the authors maintain *extreme positions* with respect to the role of metascientific reflection. Similarly to the debate of the 1970s, some of the authors are still inclined to adopt established metatheoretical views that are incompatible with the practice of linguistic theorising (e.g. Lehmann 2004, Geeraerts 2006). Others, however, intend to deal with this issue in the 'absence of purely abstract discussions of methodologies', since, according to their view, 'it is only with respect to concrete problems that the quality of the method and of the various types of evidence brought to bear on them can be evaluated' (Kepser & Reis 2005a: 4).

We believe that we have to choose the middle course between the two extremes. On the one hand, the structure of linguistic data/evidence and their function in theories have to be considered a *metascientific problem* that cannot be solved without the application of metascientific tools. The necessity of this is formulated by Gehweiler, for example, in her review of Kepser & Reis (2005b) in the following way:

> Most papers in the volume 'Linguistic Evidence' address issues concerning linguistic evidence in relation to specific linguistic problems, using and combining various data types (experimental data and corpus data are perhaps the most frequently used data types here). The volume shows that the question of how to gain linguistic evidence is (or should be) important for all linguists and that linguists can only gain when they use more than one data type. Evidence involving more than one type of data provides a different, but definitely a more comprehensive perspective on a given linguistic phenomenon – whether it confirms one's hypothesis, or whether it contradicts it. There are only few papers that explicitly address methodological and theoretical questions concerning linguistic evidence (e.g. Featherston, Kempen/Harbusch and Schütze), but as linguistic evidence is quite a new topic of linguistic discussion *it may well be hoped that we will get more linguistic evidence-theory and -methodology in the near future*. (Gehweiler 2006; emphasis added)

On the other hand, however, in order to avoid the barrenness of the former debates, metascientific reflection must not be confined to the mechanical adoption of prefabricated views. Therefore, we have to open *a new chapter* in metascientific reflection. Investigations into the nature of linguistic data and evidence cannot be narrowed down to the issues raised by the standard view of the analytical philosophy of science in connection with the concepts of 'evidence', 'confirmation' or 'justification' etc. Our aim can only be to obtain a deeper understanding of the practice of linguistic research, which cannot be achieved without systematic metascientific reflection. We must *go substantially beyond* the views of the analytical philosophy of science and make use of only those elements of the latter which can be retained.

Consequently, a prerequisite for finding a *novel* solution to the problems which were raised with respect to linguistic data and evidence – which is expected to avoid each of the above mentioned extremes – is the elaboration of a model of linguistic theorising that is

(a) *autonomous*, insofar as it reflects the practice of linguistic theorising instead of relying on metatheoretical principles alien to linguistics and unreflectedly adopted from other disciplines;
(b) *sophisticated*, insofar as it is in accord with tendencies of the philosophy of science that are relevant from the point of view of (MP);
(c) *systematic*, insofar as it elaborates a conceptual system which is capable of solving the problems raised; and
(d) *comprehensive*, insofar as it tries to answer (MP) by elaborating a model encompassing the whole process of linguistic theorising.[1]

Therefore, the task of Part II is to prepare the solution of (MP) by solving the metascientific problem which $(SP)_I$ (a) and $(SP)_I$ (b) boil down to:

$(P)_{II}$ What kind of metatheoretical model allows us to define the notions of 'data' and 'evidence' in linguistics?

The central hypothesis of this part of the book is that $(P)_{II}$ can be solved with the help of a model of plausible argumentation which we call – as mentioned in Chapter 1 – the *p-model*. In the chapters of Part II, we will systematically build up the p-model, and in Part III, we will show how the p-model can be used to redefine the notions of 'data' and 'evidence'.

In this part, we will proceed as follows. In order to show the motivation behind the introduction of the constitutive features of the p-model, in Chapter 8 we will give a short overview of some relevant tendencies in the philosophy of science. In Chapter 9, the concepts of 'plausible statement' and 'plausible inference' will be introduced. Relying on these definitions, in Chapter 10 we will outline our model of plausible argumentation which is in accordance with the metascientific tendencies presented in Chapter 8. Finally, in Chapter 11 we will summarise our solution to $(P)_{II}$.

8 Historical background

8.1 Overview

The chapter elaborates the motivation for the *p-model* which is meant to provide our solution to the problem $(P)_{II}$. As we have seen, current debates on the nature of data and evidence in linguistics have highlighted, among other things, *the uncertainty*, *the variety* and *the combinability* of linguistic data and evidence. It is these characteristics which the p-model is intended to capture. Independently of linguistics, the latest philosophical and epistemological literature reached similar findings with respect to the notions of 'data' and 'evidence'. Moreover, new developments in logic and argumentation theory seem to focus on, among others things, different kinds of inferences whose main common characteristic is that they go beyond purely formal considerations and take into account the uncertainty of premises, too. Due to these motivations, the basic properties of the p-model fit into current trends in the philosophy of science, logic and argumentation theory.

8.2 The liberalisation of the concepts of 'data' and 'evidence' in the philosophy of science

Significant changes have occurred in the philosophy of science over the past decades. The standard view of the analytical philosophy of science has become outdated. Although its importance from the point of view of the *history* of the philosophy of science is, of course, indisputable, it no longer belongs to the mainstream trends. Therefore, the position of linguistics is highly *anachronistic* since it still greatly relies on a number of obsolete elements that have already been eliminated from among the tools of the philosophers of science (see Kertész 2004a: 17ff.; Kertész & Rákosi 2005b, 2009c).

The former dominance of the analytical philosophy of science has been replaced by a variety of new trends, none of which have become dominant. This *pluralism* legitimises the elaboration of a metascientific model that is, on the one hand, in accordance with general tendencies, and, on the other hand, facilitates the solution of current metascientific problems without dogmatism, in a flexible manner.

The interpretation of the concepts of 'scientific theory', 'inference', 'linguistic theorising', 'datum' and 'evidence' has also become pluralistic by now. There are several approaches that clearly indicate the strong *liberalisation* of previous views.[1] Without intending to be exhaustive, in order to document this development in a concise, illustrative manner, we will refer to three metascientific approaches, which – although decades have elapsed between their publication – exhibit the elements of a strong tendency in the philosophy of science (see also Section 8.3):

(a) *Data as truth-candidates*. Although our model has been partly motivated by Nicholas Rescher's work, we have not adopted his categories and theorems in an unaltered form. Rescher does not introduce the concept of 'evidence', however, he discusses the concept of 'datum' in detail. He interprets the latter in the following way, which perfectly fits into the aforementioned process of liberalisation:

- In Rescher's view, data are not 'facts' that can be grasped directly and whose truth is guaranteed by experience. Nor do they provide a secure basis for the formulation of theories. He denies that data are true at the outset and superior to other knowledge such as the protocol statements of the logical positivists.[2]
- The raw data used by the theories have to be processed so that they can come into contact with other statements of the theory:

> experience . . . only provides the 'raw' data for knowledge. . . . The 'raw' data are . . . *only part of the total data* and are by no means fixed and sacred but subject to a cyclic process of *reappraisal and revision*. (Rescher 1979: 73f.; emphasis added)

- A *raw datum* is unprocessed in the sense that it does not have a plausibility value. It becomes a datum if one processes it, that is, one assigns it a plausibility value by weighing up its acceptability on the basis of the peculiarities of its source.[3] Accordingly, by *datum*, Rescher means a raw datum that has been assigned a plausibility value.[4]
- The data undergo processing in the *cyclic and prismatic process of retrospective re-evaluation*.[5]
- One cannot deem data true with certainty, but one can only state that they are more or less reliable *truth-candidates*. They consist of two components: first, an information content, and, second, a plausibility value.[6]
- Consequently, Rescher's concept of data covers the *background assumptions* and other *hypotheses* used in the theory (Rescher 1973: 53ff., 1976: 8) as well. Therefore, it significantly differs from the view of the analytical philosophy of science that restricts data to intersubjectively observable spatiotemporal events.

In sum: unlike the standard view of the analytical philosophy of science, Rescher's system does not consider data to be certainly true bases for the construction of scientific theorising. In contrast, data are basically *uncertain*, *fallible* and *revisable*.

(b) *The method of reflective equilibrium.* The idea of 'reflective equilibrium' has been put forward by Goodman (1983 [1955]), even though the notion was not introduced by him but by Rawls (1971). Whereas nowadays it is primarily used in ethics, Goodman's aim was to establish logic, and within this, to justify inductive and deductive inference rules by seeking for reflective equilibrium between rules of inference and instances (particular cases) of inferential reasoning judged to be correct. Therefore, concerning its origin, this method is of a purely epistemological and metascientific nature.[7] Its basic characteristics – which are radically different from the concept of 'evidence' in the analytical philosophy of science – are the following (see Daniels 2003):

- The aim of the method of reflective equilibrium is to create *coherence* among one's judgements on particular instances or cases and the rules and regularities assumed to lie behind them, as well as the theoretical considerations which motivate the acceptance of the latter.
- Coherence can be achieved in the course of a *cyclic* epistemological process that retrospectively revises and refines one's beliefs in the light of subsequent pieces of information until at least a temporary coherence is created between them.
- During this process, one continuously *reflects* on the beliefs at one's disposal and the relations between them. One attempts to reveal the system of relations between the beliefs, thereby making their relationships or incompatibility explicit. Reflectivity is, therefore, a constitutive component of this mechanism.
- The coherentist view related to reflective equilibrium is in sharp contrast with the standard view of the analytical philosophy of science in another respect as well. It *does not acknowledge such privileged beliefs* that could be considered to be given and true with certainty at the outset – such as 'evidence' in the sense of the standard view. It is the whole of the process of reflective equilibrium that decides what beliefs are accepted at a certain stage of scientific theorising.
- Consequently, *every* belief can be revised.
- *Inference rules* can be justified (see Daniels 2003) by bringing them into reflective equilibrium with instances of inferences considered to be generally accepted.
- Not only can inference rules be corrected in the light of the practice of drawing inferences, but *the practice of inferring* is also corrected by bringing them into reflective equilibrium with the inference rules that have been

provisionally accepted. This means a complete revision and a retrospective re-evaluation of every component of one's knowledge.

Pullum (2007) has proposed the application of the method of reflective equilibrium in linguistics, even though he has not worked out his model in detail (see also Sections 10.5–6).

(c) *The equivalence of evidence and knowledge*. In his seminal book, Timothy Williamson elaborates on a seemingly simple idea, namely, that a given person's or community's evidence is equivalent to the totality of the knowledge that is at the disposal of the given person or community (Williamson 2000: 185). He indicates this equivalence with the formula $E = K$, where E stands for evidence, and K for knowledge. The main characteristics of this thesis are as follows:

- He does not treat 'knowledge' as 'true belief', but as a mental state, a factive attitude towards a proposition, and considers it to be a basic concept (see Williamson 2000: 21f., 29ff.). Consequently, evidence is also propositional.
- If evidence is identical with the entire knowledge one has, then it follows from this that it is not restricted exclusively to observable experiences. In addition to this, evidence includes the knowledge gained with the help of inferences and *theoretical knowledge*, as well (Williamson 2000: 190–200, 221). It is obvious that this consequence of the thesis $E = K$ radically liberalises the concept of evidence, and is in sharp contrast with the standard view of the analytical philosophy of science.
- It allows for the *context-dependence, uncertainty and fallibility* of evidence (see Williamson 2000: 189, 205, 213ff.).
- Another important consequence of this thesis is that evidence also involves what one knows about one's experience through *introspection*. Williamson's theory is, therefore, in sharp contrast with such notions of evidence that reject introspection as a source of data and evidence by claiming that it is not observable intersubjectively (see Kelly 2006, Williamson 2000: 194ff.).

Besides these three models of data and evidence,[8] there are several other approaches in the current epistemology and philosophy of science, a good number of which have retained substantial elements of the standard view of the analytical philosophy of science. Nonetheless, there is a striking *convergence* among the attempts at the liberalisation of the concept of evidence. The three models mentioned share, among others, the following common properties:

- The standard view of the analytical philosophy of science assumes that there is a special set of statements that provide the basis for the assertion of other statements. This stance manifests itself, for example, in the tenet of the standard view according to which evidence has to be considered as a directly given and irrevisable fact and in the requirement that it demands a deductive structure of scientific theories. As opposed to this, a common feature in

Rescher's and Goodman's epistemology is that the acceptability of the statements depends on how coherent they are with other pieces of knowledge at one's disposal. In this respect, Williamson occupies an intermediate position. Although he does not consider evidence to be an unquestionable fact that is given at the outset and forms the basis of other knowledge, he represents some kind of 'modest foundationalism', although from an entirely different perspective:

$E = K$ suggests a very modest foundationalism, on which all one's knowledge serves as the foundation for all one's justified beliefs. (Williamson 2000: 186)

- Another common feature in Rescher's and Goodman's approaches is the cyclic and reflective process of the constant re-evaluation of data, which may repeatedly return to groups of data.
- All the three approaches strongly liberalise the concept of 'datum' insofar as they consider not only statements about intersubjective observations concerning spatiotemporal events in the sense of the standard view to be data, but theoretical knowledge as well.

In the next section, we will supplement this overview with further considerations which are also relevant for the elaboration of the p-model.

8.3 Trends in logic and argumentation theory

It is no accident that we consider *plausible inferences* to be the starting point of the model intended to answer $(P)_{II}$.[9] This decision is motivated by the following considerations with respect to current trends in logic and argumentation theory.

First, over the past three or four decades, logic, argumentation theory, AI-research, pragmatics and psychology have become open to the study of inferences that are different from deductive inference schemata. Plausible inferences have become the centre of attention in part of the literature. The role of such inferences in both everyday and scientific knowledge has become more and more evident:

Plausible reasoning is pervasive in daily life as well as in scientific activity. While inductive reasoning and probabilistic thinking have been the object of much interest among psychologists for a long time, the frequent case where people process uncertain premises and draw an uncertain conclusion . . . has remained relatively neglected. This is so despite the recognition of its importance by logicians and mathematicians . . . (Rescher, 1976) and by philosophers . . . and the development of non-monotonic reasoning formalisms in Artificial Intelligence. (Politzer & Bourmaud 2002: 346)

Walton (2001) provides a highly valuable contribution both to the history and the interpretation of the concept of 'plausible inference'/'plausible reasoning'. He traces its origin back to Plato, Aristotle and Carneades, and considers Rescher's work as well. Walton characterises its importance as follows:

> Plausible reasoning applies to cases where there is some evidence, but where there is doubt whether this evidence is veridical or conclusive. Something could appear to be true now, but when tested later, it may turn out to actually have been false. Or, at any rate, it may now appear to be false, on the balance of the evidence. Plausible reasoning is especially useful in cases where there is some unsettled issue or controversy, so that opinions on both sides of the issue are feasible. Plausible reasoning is best judged as relative to the given evidence in the case and even, or especially when that evidence is yet incomplete. Thus typically, in a kind of case in which plausible reasoning is most useful, there are two opposed theses, both are alternatives with some weight of evidence behind them, and the total evidential situation is incomplete . . . The choice between alternatives is made on a balance of considerations. Neither alternative can be proved, but neither can be disproved. It is a decision between carrying the search for more evidence forward, or because of costs and practical exigencies, making a guess now. (Walton 2001: 164)

Second, in Section 5.9 we emphasised that in recent linguistic literature, the substantial uncertainty of linguistic data and evidence has been realised; therefore, the notions of data and evidence have been relativised, weakened and differentiated. Now, it is exactly *the capturing of this uncertainty* that models of plausible inference and argumentation aim at: they try to account for inferences and argumentation processes which do not start from pieces of information which are true with certainty, but from statements that are *uncertain* to some extent, and lead to consequences of the latter that are similarly *uncertain*.

Third, in accordance with these new developments, we outlined different aspects of a possible argumentation theoretical model of linguistic theorising in a number of monographs and papers (Kertész 1993, 2004a; Rákosi 2005; Kertész & Rákosi 2005a, b, 2006, 2009a, b). The basic idea of the model is that metascientific reflection must not be restricted to the analysis of the logical structure of theories, but should rather capture their argumentation structure. The elaboration of this model has been motivated by the following considerations:[10]

- The structure of linguistic theories cannot be separated from the *heuristic process* of raising and solving problems.
- Accordingly, we consider linguistic theorising[11] to be *processes of plausible argumentation.*
- The central elements of this argumentation process are *plausible inferences.*
- In accordance with this, we have to dismiss the claim of the standard view of the analytical philosophy of science that makes a distinction between the context of discovery and the context of justification.[12]
- Therefore, we cannot restrict our investigations to the logical reconstruction of theories. Instead, we have to focus on the *whole of* the *argumentation process*. This involves the construction, the application and the testing of hypotheses alike, which are regarded as inseparably intertwined.

8.4 Conclusions

As a consequence of relating our findings as summarised in Chapter 6 to the motivations just discussed, from the next chapter on we will develop the p-model. Our aim is to present a coherent conceptual system, which delineates a new and effective model of plausible argumentation. Its basic idea is that linguistic theorising is an argumentation process that leads to plausible results, because it relies on pieces of information that are basically not true with certainty but only partially supported, plausible. The central notions of the p-model systematically related to each other are *plausible statement*, *plausible inference* and *plausible argumentation*. These concepts allow us to model the characteristics of linguistic data and evidence enumerated in $(SP)_I$(a)(ii) in such a way that the contradiction in $(SP)_I$(b) does not emerge. Thus, the p-model offers *novel answers* to (OQ1)–(OQ7).

Our endeavour to propose answers to (OQ1)–(OQ7) is closely related to the target groups of the book. As mentioned in the Preface, the primary target group are practising linguists, and the secondary group are philosophers of science and argumentation theorists. Since the p-model's workability requires that it meets the standards of the philosophy of science and argumentation theory, in elaborating it we will make use of more recent, post-positivist but already mainstream metatheoretical works, e.g. the literature on plausible inferences. Accordingly, the result is intended to be a contribution to the philosophy of linguistics meeting the requirements of current philosophy of science and argumentation theory as well as the specific interests of the working linguist.

Our line of reasoning in Part II is complex and abstract. To facilitate its understanding, the introduction of the basic concepts of the p-model – in accordance with what we have already said in the Preface – will be supplemented by two embedded text types. On the one hand, the basic concepts introduced in the main text will be elucidated by simple *examples* set into frames. These examples stem partly from everyday situations, but most of them are taken from the linguistic literature. The former aim to illustrate the coherence of the model; the latter highlight its applicability to linguistics. On the other hand, the definitions of the concepts introduced will be followed by passages entitled 'Motivation and background'. They are intended to illuminate the basic idea of the definitions.

9 Plausible inferences

9.1 Overview

The aim of the chapter is to make the first steps towards the development of the p-model. We introduce and elaborate on two central notions: plausible statement and plausible inference. Our starting point is the notion of *plausible statement*. The basic idea is that hypotheses are not truths whose certainty can be secured by experience or by other hypotheses. Rather, they are merely more or less *plausible* insofar as they are considered to be acceptable *to some extent* on the basis of suitable *sources* that support them. Such sources may be, for example, sense perception, introspection, the use of special tools, methods, procedures, corpora, events, theories, our memory, conjectures, presumptions, certain methodological principles (e.g. simplicity, uniformity etc.), experts, witnesses, historical documents, or even inferences. Plausibility is *gradual* and *strongly source-dependent*. A statement may be very plausible according to one source, and less plausible with respect to others, depending on the *reliability* of the sources at issue. It may also happen that some sources make the statement in question implausible by supporting another that is incompatible with it.

The second part of the chapter deals with *plausible inferences*. The latter are capable of making their conclusion *plausible* – but not true with certainty – on the basis of the content and plausibility value of their premises. In such inferences the connection between the premises and the conclusion cannot be reduced to the relationship between their logical structures, as is the case with deductive inferences, but always rests on *a semantic relation*: for example, causality, analogy, similarity, sign, necessary or sufficient condition, part–whole relation etc. Section 9.5 introduces the notion of 'plausible inference' gradually, by presenting and characterising its three types. Sections 9.6–9.9 discuss three highly important features of plausible inference: their fallibility, their dynamism and their p-context-dependence, and, in addition, their heuristic function which is of utmost significance for linguistic theorising.

9.2 The concept of 'inference' and 'deductive inference'

It is important to emphasise that our claim, according to which the argumentation structure (rather than the logical structure) of theories is relevant from the point of view of metascientific reflection, does not imply that we underestimate or contest the role of logic in reconstructing scientific theories. We believe, however, that we have to reconsider the role of logic, basically in the following respects. First, it plays a role not only in the evaluation of the final result of theorising:

> it is just false that initial thinking in the context of generation has no controls, no constraints. Thus, discovery includes justification. (Nickles 1980: 10)

> A good deal of evaluation and justification occurs during the reasoning to the theory . . . (Nickles 1980: 13)

Second, the reverse of this is also true; the evaluation of theories cannot be restricted to the means of logic and it cannot refer only to the final result of theorising:

> justification includes discovery, especially if justification is extended to include low level evaluation and plausibility assessment on one side and the interpretation and understanding of 'justified' results on the other . . . (Nickles 1980: 10)

> the period of testing an available theory is full of discovery episodes. The psychological processes involved in the search for testable consequences or the search for difficulties in a theory belong to the context of discovery in Reichenbach's sense . . . (Nickles 1980: 13)

Third, we consistently and exclusively interpret the term 'logic' as a *formal system functioning as a norm*. In other words, we consider only deductive systems to be logic. The 'practice of argumentation' is, however, not formal, but takes the *content* of statements into account, too. It is context-sensitive and is not necessarily deductive. It is not logic, but *heuristics*.

Accordingly, the goal of the definitions proposed below is *not to work out a formal system*. Rather, the task of the tools used in the definitions consists of making our metalanguage as clear as possible, thereby making the linguistic applications of the p-model controllable.

One of the most important characteristics of plausible inferences is that – in contrast to deductive inferences – *they do not constitute a calculus*. One reason for this is that plausible inferences take into consideration non-formalisable characteristics of statements as well. Therefore, we want to emphasise the following principles in advance, which will be set forth in detail later:

- The theory of plausible inferences is *no logic*. Nor can it be interpreted as a more comprehensive formal system (in whatever sense) than logic. That is, it cannot be regarded as a logic in a broader sense which would lay down the formal criteria for the inheritance of plausibility instead of truth.
- Plausibility values, as well as the prefixes 'it is plausible that', 'it is true with certainty that' etc. do not belong to the logical structure of statements.

- The logical structure, semantic structure and plausibility value belong to different dimensions of the statements' representation.
- Thus, there is no direct connection between the truth values of logic relevant for the logical structure of statements and the prefixes 'true with certainty' or 'false with certainty'. The latter represent limiting cases of plausibility/implausibility, while the former are used hypothetically and allow for the representation of certain relations among statements: for example, whether a set of statements can hold simultaneously or if one (set of) statement(s) implies another etc.
- To deem an inference a plausible inference, it is not sufficient to reveal its formal characteristics (logical structure). The plausibility value and semantic structure of the premises also have to be taken into consideration (see Section 9.5). Therefore, the theory of plausible inferences cannot arrive at that level of generality and abstraction which logic does with the use of inference schemata. This does not mean that there are no plausible inference patterns; their status is, however, completely different from that of the inference schemata of logic (see Sections 9.5–9.6).

At the same time, however, the notion of 'inference' as used in logic is *indispensable* as a *point of reference* for the explication of the concepts 'inference' and 'plausible inference'. Nevertheless, logic is not a monolithic discipline but involves a multitude of different systems ('logics'). These systems are partly rivals of each other, and partly behave complementarily. Despite this, at a sufficiently high level of abstraction, there is a *common ground* that is acknowledged by all systems. The different systems can be interpreted as different specifications of the components of this common ground[1] which we summarise as follows:

(1) (a) An inference consists of
 (i) two sets of statements (the premises and the conclusion), and
 (ii) the consequence relation between the premises and the conclusion.
 (b) The goal of logic is to define the scope of *logically correct (valid) inferences*.
 (c) Inferences are logically valid, if it is *the logical structure* of the premises and of the conclusion that ensures that *if* the premises are true, then the conclusion will be necessarily true, too.[2] In such cases, we say that there holds a *logical consequence relation* between the premises and the conclusion.
 (d) Logic treats inferences *structurally* in that it neglects meaning components that are deemed irrelevant to the logical structure and *formalises* the factors considered as relevant.[3]
 (e) At the same time, logic requires the strongest linkage between the premises and the conclusion insofar as it narrows down the scope of its interest to cases when the premises – *provided* that they are true – are capable of *guaranteeing the truth of the conclusion*. Inferences that guarantee the truth of the conclusion *hypothetically* are called *deductive inferences*.

Although (1) is presupposed and used by the p-model as well, no concept of inference can be generalised from it that could also comprise plausible inferences. In order to capture the latter as well, we have to define inferences not as complexes consisting of a set of statements and a relation between them. Rather, we have to interpret them as *tools for extending the set of information at one's disposal*. We will regard inferences as tools allowing for the attribution of certain characteristics (such as truth value, provability, hypothetical truth, plausibility, possibility, necessity, probability etc.) to a statement p on the basis of a set of statements Q and their relevant characteristics, provided that the statement p satisfies certain criteria. Accordingly, we propose the following general definition of the concept of inference:

(2) By **inference**, we mean a mapping from a set of statements (*premises*) with certain characteristics (*relevant characteristics*) to a statement (*conclusion*) with certain characteristics in the following way:
(a) The amount of the information at one's disposal is extended by a characteristic of the conclusion. This characteristic is a function of the characteristics of the premises and the relation between the characteristics of the premises and the conclusion.
(b) If any premise or any characteristic of the premises is omitted or modified, then no mapping is possible between the remaining set of premises and their characteristics, on the one hand, and the conclusion and its characteristics, on the other, in such a way that this mapping takes into consideration the remaining set of characteristics.

Motivation and background

(2)(a) is expected to exclude cases in which the inference-candidate in question does not extend the set of (explicit) information available. This happens, for example, if the conclusion is identical to one of the premises. (2)(b) prohibits cases where the set of the premises contains superfluous, irrelevant elements. These properties of (2) are rejected by most logical systems. The reason for this discrepancy lies in the different aims of the two approaches. Logical systems are intended to check whether a given statement follows deductively from a set of statements. This means two things. First, regarding the existence of the logical consequence relation, it is considered to be irrelevant whether its checking is transparent or requires a complicated, multistage process. Second, logic does not deal with the question of how and why inferences are created. Logic does not provide us with methodologies but with systems of criteria. Its concept of inference presupposes logically omnipotent users striving for maximal formalisation, idealisation, normativity and generality. It ignores our cognitive and situative limits as well as our aims and needs. That is, it is not a theory of everyday, scientific or professional arguments or argumentations but that of deductively valid inferences. Harman captures the essence of this difference as follows:

> It is one thing to say 'A, B, and C imply D'. It is quite another thing to say, 'If you believe A, B, and C, you should or may infer D'. The first of these remarks is a remark about implication. The second is a remark about inference. The first says nothing special about belief or any other psychological state, unless one of A, B, or C has psychological content, nor does the first remark say anything normative about what one 'should' or 'may' do [Goldman 1986].
>
> The first remark may be true without the second being true. It may require considerable logical talent, even genius, to see that the implication holds. A person without such genius or talent may believe A, B, and C without having any reason at all to believe D.
>
> Furthermore, a person who believes A, B, and C and realises that A, B, and C imply D may also believe for very good reason that D is false. Such a person may now have a reason to stop believing one of A, B, and C rather than a reason to believe D.
>
> Moreover, even someone who believes A, B, and C, who realises that A, B, and C imply D, and who has no reason to think that D is false, may have no reason to infer D. Such a person may be completely uninterested in whether D is true or false and no reason to be interested.
>
> Many trivial things follow from one's beliefs without one having any reason to infer them. One has no reasons to clutter one's mind with trivialities just because they follow from other things one believes.
>
> These and related examples indicate that the connection between inference and implication is fairly complex. (Harman 2002: 173f.)

From this it does not follow that the theory of argumentation and inferences belongs to psychology and can be developed as a purely descriptive theory. Instead, a theory of inferences should elaborate norms and criteria which make it possible to differentiate between 'correct' (rational, applicable, cognitively real,[4] reliable, leading to well-founded conclusions etc.) and 'defective' (irrational, inapplicable, unreliable, leading to unfounded consequences etc.) inferences. The above quotation also makes clear that the theory of inferences is only part of the theory of argumentation. The question of which inferences have to or ought to be drawn in a given context cannot be decided solely with reference to the characteristics of the premises and the conclusion; rather, one has to take into consideration the totality of the given information state.

It is important to remark that we do not ascribe cognitive reality to (2) or to the definitions of deductive, demonstrative and plausible inferences interpreted as special cases of (2) later in this chapter. That is, we do not claim that these definitions capture the way in which inferences are in fact produced.

Relevant characteristics can be divided into two groups:

(3) (a) Relevant characteristics which indicate that there is a relation between the premises and the conclusion connected to the given characteristic are called **primary characteristics**.

(b) **Secondary characteristics** capture some characteristic of the conclusion on the basis of the related characteristics of the premises as well as on the basis of the primary characteristics.

From (3)(a) it follows that primary characteristics make it possible to set down semantic, logical etc. criteria.

Motivation and background

Primary characteristics in the sense of (3)(a) contribute not simply to checking the correctness of inferences in the sense of (2); that is, besides laying down the criteria relating to the latter, they may play a role in the production of inferences as well. Namely, they capture patterns with the help of which the conclusion of a given set of premises can be found. These patterns are not necessarily formal; they often concern semantic factors or relations. This also means that the logical structure of inferences must not be regarded as the sole or even decisive factor of inference patterns. With secondary characteristics in the sense of (3)(b), the p-model has to stipulate how the characteristics of the conclusion can be obtained from the corresponding characteristics of the premises.

We get different types of inferences by fixing the relevant characteristics, narrowing down the possibilities left open by (2), in other words, as *specifications* of (2).

Deductive inferences can be interpreted as specifications of (2) as follows:

(4) By **deductive inference**, we mean an inference in the sense of (2) in which

(a) the set of the premises is consistent;

(b) between the premises and the conclusion there is a logical consequence relation; that is, on the basis of the logical structure of the premises and the conclusion it can be established that the conclusion is true, *provided* that the premises are also true;

(c) the premises are deemed to be hypothetically true.

In the case of deductive inferences, the logical structure of the premises and of the conclusion count as primary characteristics in the sense of (3)(a). Although the information content of the conclusion of deductive inferences does not go beyond that of the premises, they are capable of making implicit information explicit. Therefore, deductive inferences are capable of *extending hypothetically* the amount of the information at one's disposal (see (2)(a)): they show which further statements would be true *if* the premises were also true. To put it otherwise, the premises possess the secondary characteristic in the sense of (3)(b) that they are hypothetically – that is, *irrespective of the sources at issue*[5] – true. Consequently, the conclusion has the secondary characteristic of being hypothetically – that is, under the assumption of the truth of the premises – true.

Motivation and background

(4) is more restrictive than the standard logical interpretation of deductive inferences usually tacitly presupposed in the logical literature. It contains elements that are not required by (1) but are indispensable if we want to interpret inferences as tools for the extension of the information given. First, (4)(a) precludes the deduction of any arbitrary statement from a contradictory pair of statements. Second, although 'A, therefore A' fulfils (1), it cannot be regarded as a deductive inference in the sense of (4), since it violates (2)(a). This divergence is due to the circumstance that this inference does not provide us with new information in any sense, since it is not even the case that it would make any implicit information explicit. Third, (2)(b) requires that the set of the premises contains only statements needed to establish the consequence relation. Without this stipulation, all consistent extensions of the set of the premises would fulfil this function, because there is a logical consequence relation between such extensions and the conclusion as well.

Deductive inferences in the sense of (4) possess only one primary characteristic in the sense of (3)(a), which is related to the logical structure of the premises and the conclusion. Therefore, logical inference schemata can be supposed to contribute to the production of the inferences as well. Nevertheless, deductive inferences are used to hypothetically extend the set of information at hand when the consequence relation is transparent. From this it follows that logic as a device for interpreting inferences in terms of (1) (that is, as a tool for checking the consequence relation) is remarkably stronger and richer than as a device for producing inferences or as a device for checking inferences, which aim at hypothetically extending the set of information at one's disposal along the lines of (4). In the latter sense, the task of logic is usually confined to revealing some simple and frequently used inference schemata (such as *modus ponens*, *modus tollens*, chain rule etc.) and to the checking of the consistency of the set of the premises.

(4) preserves the intention of logic according to which the criterion of the correctness of inferences can be narrowed down to a single aspect of the relation between the premises and the conclusion. Namely, it focuses on the question

of whether the conclusion necessarily follows from the premises for structural, formal reasons, *provided* that they are true. Three aspects of this intention are especially significant with respect to the present study.

First, in order to reveal the logical structure of statements – that is, to determine the depth of the logical analysis and to choose or to construct the logical system to be used – logic has to take into consideration certain aspects of the *meaning* of the statements. Logic is, however, a formal discipline; accordingly, by fixing the meaning of the logical constants, it tries to *formalise* these semantic components.

Second, it may happen that the relationship between a given set of statements and a further statement cannot be evaluated unanimously because according to one analysis there is a consequence relation between them, while according to another, this is not the case. This means that logic is not a monolithic and terminated discipline, but a continuously developing field, encompassing a wide range of different systems.

Third, in most cases (that is, in everyday and in research situations alike), not only does one want to know what *might* follow from the information at hand (provided that it is true), but one may also be interested in what can '*in fact*' be said about a statement on the basis of the – not necessarily certainly true but more or less insecure, merely plausible – information at one's disposal in the given situation. With the help of logic, we can only give a partial answer to this question. Therefore, in the next section we will define the notion of plausible statements, and in Sections 9.4–9.5, we will discuss inferences which take into consideration the *plausibility value* of the premises as well.

9.3 The notion of 'plausible statement'

Both in everyday and research situations, most of the statements at one's disposal cannot be regarded as certainly true. They may be supported by certain considerations, which, however, do not make them perfectly reliable. Moreover, statements based on these statements are only more or less uncertain pieces of information, too. This inherent and unavoidable uncertainty of the information at one's disposal cannot be tackled with formal means (for example, with the tools of logic). What is needed is a method that allows for the representation of the uncertainty of the information and makes it possible to take this partial reliability into consideration as a relevant factor. Therefore, the p-model – following Rescher (1976) – interprets statements not as propositions but as *plausible statements*. Plausible statements are 'truth-candidates' (see Rescher 1976: 8), that is, they are statements whose reliability is not guaranteed but only partially supported by the *source* from which they originate; thus, they can be regarded as acceptable only to a certain extent.

Example 1

According to Rescher (1976: 6), the range of the sources that may be applied to determine the plausibility value of statements is considerably wide. For example:

- individuals' accounts: expert opinions, diaries, testimonies of eyewitnesses etc.;
- depersonalised historical sources: oral tradition, rumour, newspapers, common knowledge etc.;
- one's own observations: sense perception, memory, etc.;
- intellectual resources: guess, conjecture, inference, assumption, postulation, theories, papers, books, etc.;
- methodological principles: simplicity, uniformity etc.

Of course, there are considerable differences among different fields on the range of the usable sources. Thus, for example, renowned newspapers might be reliable sources for political history but they are useless in the natural sciences.

The plausibility value of a statement indicates to what extent its information content is supported, is made reliable by the given source, and as a result, to what extent one is ready to accept it. Nevertheless, not all sources of information can be used to determine the plausibility value of statements:

(5) A source is *suitable* for determining the plausibility of a given statement if it does not provide information for and against it at the same time.

(5) means that on the basis of a suitable source, one cannot make contradictory judgements about the statement at issue. That is, a suitable source either allows us to judge the given statement unequivocally or it does not offer any relevant and reliable information related to it. If this is not the case, then one may try to divide it into smaller sources each of which judges the statement in question unequivocally – that is, an unsuitable source has to be subdivided into a set of suitable sources.

Example 2

If during an experiment native speakers do not judge the grammaticality of an utterance unanimously and there is no statistically significant difference between the positive and the negative judgements, then this experiment cannot be regarded as a suitable source in the sense of (5) in connection with statements about the grammaticality of this utterance. By referring to this experiment, one cannot assign a plausibility value to the statement which says that the given utterance is acceptable in the given language (see e.g. Schütze 1996; Featherston 2007). If, however, dialectological factors or age-group characteristics can be identified which make it possible to separate the opposing judgements, then the participants of the experiment can be divided into two groups both of which can be regarded as reliable sources – although supporting opposite judgements.

If one finds that a suitable source speaks for the statement *p*, then one may judge *p* plausible, or, in the extreme case, true with certainty on the basis of this source. Of course, it may happen that a source votes not for but against the statement *p*, insofar as it opposes it to some extent. In the p-model, this means that this source supports *p*'s negation (~*p*). In such cases, we say that we have to deem *p* *implausible* on the basis of this source. Thus, we obtain:

(6) (a) **Statement *p* is true with certainty on the basis of the source *S*** if *S* is suitable in the sense of (5) and *p* can be regarded as certain and completely acceptable on the basis of *S*.

(b) **Statement *p* is plausible on the basis of source *S*** if *S* is suitable in the sense of (5) and *p* can be regarded as reliable to some extent on the basis of *S* so that it cannot be regarded as true with certainty but it can be accepted as a truth-candidate.

(c) **Statement *p* is implausible on the basis of source *S*** if on the basis of *S*, ~*p* is plausible on the basis of *S*.

(d) **Statement *p* is false with certainty on the basis of source *S*** if on the basis of *S*, ~*p* is true with certainty on the basis of *S*.

(e) **Statement *p* is of neutral plausibility on the basis of source *S*** if *S* is suitable in the sense of (5) but none of the above cases hold.

Neutral plausibility means that on the basis of the given source, one judges *p* neither plausible, nor implausible, nor true with certainty, nor false with certainty, and this source does not judge it equivocally, either. This may be the case if *S* is irrelevant from the point of view of the evaluation of *p*, or if it is relevant but provides reliable information neither for nor against *p* in the given situation (because of, for example, practical limits). In such cases, one has no reason to accept or to reject *p* but one may still retain the possibility of its future acceptance or rejection: after extending *S* to a set of sources by further sources, it may become possible to deem *p* plausible or implausible.

Examples 3(1)–(2)

(1) If a psycholinguistic experiment seems to be reliable to a certain extent (but not totally), then one can evaluate hypotheses supported by it as plausible in the sense of (6)(b). It may also happen that an experiment

does not support but refutes a hypothesis. In such cases one has to deem this statement implausible in the sense of (6)(c) on the basis of the experiment as a source. Nevertheless, one cannot consider the result of an experiment to be suitable for making a hypothesis plausible in the sense of (6)(b) or implausible in the sense of (6)(c), if there is a reasonable suspicion that the measuring instrument was not precise enough.

(2) There are several aspects of the cognitive mechanisms of metaphor processing and usage which cannot be judged for lack of an appropriate theoretical (neurological, linguistic etc.) and experimental basis. The plausibility of statements related to these aspects has to be assumed to be neutral in the sense of (6)(e). Although linguistic, neurological etc. theories at our disposal can usually be regarded as reliable sources, they do not provide usable information or are even irrelevant for certain aspects of metaphor processing and usage (see e.g. the criticism of Dodge & Lakoff 2005 in Rohrer 2006). Since they do not provide contradictory judgements on hypotheses regarding this topic, they are suitable in the sense of (5); despite this, they do not allow us to deem such hypotheses plausible or implausible because of their lack of reliability.

Motivation and background

From the above definition of plausibility, it is clear that plausibility cannot be identified with objective or subjective probability. Low plausibility value does not mean that one assigns the given statement low probability, that is, one deems it improbable. Rather, low plausibility indicates that one is in possession of pieces of information that are, to a small degree but expressly, in favour of it, support it slightly, make it reliable to a certain extent. For instance, if one formulates a conjecture on the strength of three linguistic data but one has not yet tested its acceptability, then this hypothesis may be considered slightly plausible. Clearly, this does not mean that one deems this conjecture improbable.[6]

A further important property of this concept of plausibility is that – in contrast to probability – one cannot judge the plausibility of a statement's negation on the basis of the plausibility value of the statement at issue. Thus, for example, it may be the case that one deems a conjecture plausible (that is, reliable) to some extent on the strength of three linguistic data and one is aware that this hypothesis requires further testing. Therefore, its usage needs special caution, and it may receive only a low plausibility value. It is clear, however, that from this it does not follow that a high plausibility value should be assigned to the statement that the conjecture is faulty.[7]

Basically, sources can be divided into two groups:

(7) (a) A source is called a **direct source** with respect to a statement if a statement is assigned a plausibility value on the basis of the reliability of the given source.[8]

(b) With **indirect sources**, the plausibility value of the given statement is determined on the basis of the plausibility of other statements – that is, with the help of an inference.[9]

In the case of direct sources, the reliability of the statement at issue is judged on the basis of the reliability of its source according to (7)(a). Thus, (6) can be specified as follows:

(8) (a) **Statement *p* is true with certainty on the basis of the direct source *S*** if *S* is suitable in the sense of (5), supports *p* and is considered as a completely reliable source in judging *p*.

(b) **Statement *p* is plausible on the basis of the direct source *S*** if *S* is suitable in the sense of (5), supports *p* and is a source of *p* which is to some extent but not completely reliable.

(c) **Statement *p* is implausible on the basis of the direct source *S*** if on the basis of *S*, ~*p* is plausible.

(d) **Statement *p* is false with certainty on the basis of the direct source *S*** if on the basis of *S*, ~*p* is true with certainty.

(e) **Statement *p* is of neutral plausibility on the basis of the direct source *S*** if *S* is suitable in the sense of (5) but none of the above cases hold.

Examples 4(1)–(2)

(1) Head's (1978) paper summarises his investigations covering more than one hundred languages. This work can be regarded as a direct source for judging the plausibility of the following linguistic universal:

(U) *In languages in which variation of person in pronominal reference is used to show degrees of respect or social distance, the third person indicates greater social distance when used in reference to either the addressee or the speaker than do the pronouns of the second and first person, respectively.* (Head 1978: 191)

This source definitely supports *U*, since Head did not find any counterexample. It cannot be regarded, however, as a perfectly reliable source, because *U* – just like other universals – should apply to every language, to every historical stage of the languages and to languages coming into being in future; these, of course, could not be tested exhaustively by Head's investigations. Therefore, *U* is not true with certainty on the basis of Head's paper as a direct source in the sense of (8)(a) but only plausible along the lines of (8)(b).

Simon (1997), however, is a source which speaks against U, that is, it supports its implausibility in the sense of (8)(c). According to this paper, around the year 1800 in German, the second person pronoun *Ihr* indicated a greater social distance than the personal pronouns of the third person *er* and *sie* did.

(2) The definitions provided in (8) make it possible to re-evaluate the tenability of the two standpoints within the standard view of linguistic data and evidence (SVLD) (see Section 3.3).

Both standpoints consider the origin of data to be decisive. The generativist tradition holds that linguists' own linguistic competence is basically a perfectly reliable source for judging the grammaticality of sentences. Corpus linguists, however, deem representative electronic corpora to be basically completely reliable sources. The latter consider the occurrence in a corpus as the criterion of acceptability, while in the case of the former, judgements of linguistic intuition can fulfil this function. There are, however, also views that break with the standard view insofar as they no longer consider corpora or linguistic intuition perfectly reliable or even unreliable:

(a) Let source S be the linguistic intuition of the linguist X and p the statement 'Construction Y is grammatical in the given language.' p can be considered to be plausible on the basis of source S if X judges sentences containing Y expressly correct. At the same time, however, S cannot be regarded as a perfectly reliable source guaranteeing the truth of p. There are various reasons for this. First, X's judgements do not cover and even cannot cover every instance of Y. Thus, it is possible that only certain occurrences of Y are grammatical in the given language. Second, the linguistic intuition of X may be influenced and rendered unreliable by the theory X relies on. Thus, she may be mistaken about the analysis of the sentences at issue and state incorrectly that they contain the construction Y, or she may misjudge its grammaticality (more exactly: she may judge the grammaticality of the sentence differently than many or most speakers of the given language do and state that her judgement is the sole correct one). Third, it might happen that other native speakers judge the sentences containing the given construction differently, etc. Factors mentioned by Schütze (1996) and Featherston (2007) which weaken the reliability of grammaticality judgements are arguments for the thesis that the linguistic intuition of native speakers cannot be regarded as a perfectly reliable source, either. Moreover, in some cases it may turn out to be unreliable. Views according to which new methods are needed to make linguistic intuition an appropriately reliable source are gaining more and more ground; see Kertész & Rákosi (2008b) and Sections 4.2 and 5.3 above.

(b) Let source *S* be a corpus on the basis of which the statement *p*, 'Construction *Y* is grammatical in the given language', should be deemed implausible because it does not contain any sentence with this construction ('negative evidence'). One cannot treat *p* as false with certainty on the basis of *S*, since it may be the case that *Y* is a rare phenomenon in the given language but it can be found in a larger corpus. Moreover, occurrence in a corpus does not guarantee the certainty of the statement in question because corpora may contain slips of tongue and sentences that are not correct for some other reason. Therefore, corpora are only more or less reliable sources. They are often capable of contributing to the explanation of a linguistic phenomenon only in combination with other data types. See Kertész & Rákosi (2008c) for a detailed analysis of these issues.

(6) can be easily applied to indirect sources in the sense of (7)(b) as well. In this case, one does not assign a plausibility value to the given statement on the basis of the reliability of the source but on the basis of the plausibility values and other relevant characteristics of the premises, as well as the system of relations between the premises and the conclusion:

(9) (a) **Statement *p* is true with certainty on the basis of inference *I* as indirect source** if the premises of *I* and the relevant characteristics of the premises and of *p* completely support *p*.

(b) **Statement *p* is plausible on the basis of inference *I* as indirect source** if the premises of *I* and the relevant characteristics of the premises and of *p* partially support *p*.

(c) **Statement *p* is implausible on the basis of inference *I* as indirect source** if on the basis of *I*, ~*p* is plausible.

(d) **Statement *p* is false with certainty on the basis of inference *I* as indirect source** if on the basis of *I*, ~*p* is true with certainty.

(e) **Statement *p* is of neutral plausibility on the basis of inference *I* as indirect source** if none of the above cases hold.

(9) treats the plausibility value of the premises and the conclusion as secondary characteristics in the sense of (3)(b).

Plausibility can not only be defined categorically. It can also be interpreted in such a way that it expresses the *degree* of plausibility that can be assigned to statements on the strength of single sources. The plausibility of a statement on the basis of a given source may lie between *two extremes*. If the source supports it perfectly, then the plausibility value of this statement will be maximal according to this source. This maximal plausibility value will be represented as 1. The minimum value of plausibility is 0; this is assigned to a statement if it is of neutral plausibility on the basis of the given source. Most statements are only partially supported by their source; therefore, they are between these two poles, and gain a plausibility value between 0 and 1:

(10) **The plausibility value of statement *p* on the basis of source *S* is such that:**
(a) $|p|_S = 1$, if *p* is true with certainty on the basis of *S*;
(b) $0 < |p|_S < 1$, if *p* is plausible on the basis of *S*;[10]
(c) $|p|_S = 0$, if *p* is of neutral plausibility on the basis of *S*.

From the above definitions it clearly follows that plausibility is not an inherent characteristic of statements but is *source-dependent*. Statements may acquire a plausibility value from manifold sources, and different sources may lead to different evaluations of a statement's plausibility. Moreover, the reliability of the sources may be judged differently in different fields of research or theories.[11] Therefore, plausibility values do not represent general categories which are applicable to all research fields.

Examples 5(1)–(2)

(1) In empirical theories one may apply, for example, the following plausibility rankings:

$|h|_S = 0.2$ (*h* has a very low plausibility according to *S*), if *S* is an untested conjecture – in this case, *S* is a conjecture as an intellectual source;
$|h|_S = 0.4$ (*h* has a rather low plausibility according to *S*), if *h* stems from a thought experiment – in this case, *S* is a thought experiment as an intellectual source;
$|h|_S = 0.6$ (*h* has a rather high plausibility according to *S*), if *h* has been checked with the help of some well-known, generally accepted experimental procedure – in this case, *S* is an experiment;
$|h|_S = 0.8$ (*h* has a high plausibility according to *S*) if *h* is a central, generally accepted hypothesis of the given theory – in this case, *S* is the theory with its successful applications;
$|h|_S = 1$ (*h* can be regarded as true with certainty on the basis of *S*), if *h* is a mathematical theorem – that is, *S* is a mathematical theory.

This plausibility ranking is, of course, only *an example*, that is, an evaluation applicable in certain research fields but not applicable in others. As we have already mentioned, *there are* plausibility rankings that are based on the consensus of some subgroup of the scientific community. These rankings are, however, often called into question by adherents of rival theories – as the debates over data and evidence clearly show. In other contexts, for example, untested conjectures may be assigned no plausibility value; similarly, there are theories which do not deem thought experiments to be reliable sources. There are linguists who consider only corpus data to be reliable; other linguists, in addition to corpus data, also accept experimental data, introspective data, data obtained by computer simulations etc. Within the latter group, there may be differences in their preference for various data types. Such preferences might also be influenced by the peculiarities of the linguistic phenomenon investigated (that is, the use of corpus data may be more appropriate in some cases than in others etc.). From this it follows that striving for overall valid plausibility rankings or general rules regarding the assignment of the initial plausibility values is hopeless and unrealistic, and it would represent a falling back into the dogmatism of the standard view of linguistic data and evidence (SVLD).

(2) The testimony of a passer-by behind whose back a traffic accident occurred (source *S*) is suitable in the sense of (5) but it does not count as a reliable source by judging the statement *p*, 'The motorcyclist crossed the double white lines.' Therefore, *p* is of neutral plausibility on the basis of *S*: $|p|_S = 0$. This value means that *S* was capable of providing any support neither for nor against the statement at issue.

If a witness changes his/her views in connection with the above statement many times, then his/her testimony cannot serve as a suitable source for judging *p* in the sense of (5). Similarly, the testimony of a witness stating that the motorcyclist did not cross the double white lines does not allow us to assign a positive plausibility value to *p*, since it is against *p* and not for it. Nevertheless, it can be interpreted as a source supporting $\sim p$; that is, it allows for assigning a positive plausibility value to $\sim p$.

A further important feature of this interpretation of plausibility values is that the numerical values do not behave like 'normal' numbers. For example, one cannot state that a hypothesis to which a plausibility value 0.8 has been assigned on the basis of source *S* has a four times higher plausibility value than a statement with the plausibility value 0.2. The numerical values are only capable of a raw, rudimentary 'arithmetic'. They behave in some respects like *rough estimates* rather than like exact calculations. Their main function lies in the comparison of the plausibility of (rival) hypotheses as well as in the comparison of earlier and later plausibility values of the same hypothesis. Thereby, the guiding principle is simply 'a higher value indicates a higher degree of plausibility' (see also Rescher 1976: 11).

Motivation and background

Comparing (6) and (10), we see that no plausibility value can be assigned to *p* on the basis of *S* if *S* is not suitable for judging *p* in the sense of (5) or if it is against p. That is, if S judges p ambiguously, or makes p implausible or false with certainty, then one cannot say that S votes for p and supports it unequivocally to any extent. Quite the contrary holds true: it votes against it, inconsequently or unequivocally. In contrast, the plausibility value 0 indicates that the given source neither supports p nor refutes it to any extent. In such cases, one remains 'neutral': one does not take sides in the question of p's acceptance or rejection.

These stipulations make it evident that this interpretation of plausibility values substantially differs from objective/subjective probability. The value 0 does not indicate the falsity of the given statement, and values smaller than 0.5 do not mark improbability.

Nevertheless, the p-model does not exclude cases in which a source provides information on the basis of which the statement can only be judged ambiguously. As already mentioned, it lays down the methodological principle that unsuitable sources have to be divided into smaller, suitable ones. This means that one has to strive to identify the factors which might motivate the separation of the information for and against p, respectively.

It is important to note that there are no general, exhaustive criteria regarding the evaluation of the reliability of sources. Every theory or approach has its own traditions, which the researcher may consider as a starting point (but, when the need arises, they may be modified as well).[12] Thus, the (initial) plausibility value is often determined *conventionally* in the sense that within a given field of scientific research, adherents of a certain approach may reach a consensus about the ranking of the reliability of the sources. Such rankings may become standards that influence to a considerable extent, or even determine automatically, the plausibility of statements judged on the basis of these sources. These rankings, however, can – similarly to other methodological principles – be revised and re-evaluated (see Chapter 10).

Example 6

The source-dependence of plausibility and the consensual character of the judgement of the reliability of sources can be nicely illustrated by the history of experiments in science. Experiments were first applied in the seventeenth century when it became clear that pure reasoning, speculation, passive observation, reference to ancient authorities or to religious dogmas were not capable of providing enough information about nature. Previously, however, observation had been regarded as a totally unreliable source.[13] Of course, the usability of experimental devices and the acceptability of the results were fiercely debated at the outset. As a result, attempts were made to secure the reliability of experiments by diverse methods. First, scientists listed the names of prominent people who had been present at the experiment in the experimental report. In this way, the earlier strategy, according to which authorities were referred to, was applied to the new method. Thus, the reliability of an experiment and the plausibility of the hypotheses stemming from it as a direct source were directly proportional to *the authority of the experimenter and the witnesses*. As a next step, Boyle elaborated a new strategy insofar as he gave a *vivid and detailed account* of every phase of the experimental process in order to turn the reader, as Cantor (1989: 163) expresses it, into a *virtual witness*. This was a very important shift in the role of 'witnessing', since the reliability of the experiment was no longer based on authority but on the (real or merely imagined) *reproducibility* of the procedure. Thus, the reliability of an experiment and the plausibility of the hypotheses stemming from it as a direct source were directly proportional to *the grade of reproducibility of the experimental procedure*. A further far-reaching move was the use of an *impersonal style*, achieved by relying on the dominance of mathematical tools, schematisation and formalisation. These means were intended to create the impression that the authority of experimental results stems *directly from nature*. Thus, the reliability of an experiment and the plausibility of the hypotheses stemming from it as a direct source were directly proportional to *the alleged objectivity of the experimental report* and inversely proportional to the subjective steps included in it. Nevertheless, it was often the case that the arguments presented (calculations, formal/mathematical methods, the experimental design, the interpretation of the results) or the devices applied were criticised. Therefore, the argumentation for the acceptability and reliability of the results was *extended* to new elements such as possible systematic errors and their prevention, or statistical analyses enabling the elimination of effects of unavoidable sources of noise etc. These arguments have since grown in importance and come to be regarded as decisive factors in judging the acceptability of experimental results. At the same time, the description of the experimental procedure has become not only strongly schematic but also more theory-oriented and reduced. That is, the experimenter selects the relevant moves and events which are accounted for in the experimental report; she has the privilege of deciding what counts as an accidental, contingent mistake which may remain unmentioned and what, on the contrary, must be regarded as a systematic error that has to be reported together with its correction. Nevertheless, there are more or less explicitly formulated *norms* against which experimental reports are judged. These stem, however, not from general, a priori philosophical considerations. Rather, it is the *scientific community* which decides whether the experimental results are reliable and epistemologically useful, that is, whether they can be used for theory testing, explanation, or the elaboration of new theories etc. That is, the reliability of an experiment and the plausibility of the hypotheses stemming from it as a direct source are directly proportional to *the extent to which its elements conform to the norms set up by the given scientific community.*

Motivation and background

Following Rescher (1976), we use plausibility values for *comparative* purposes. Therefore, numerical values do not represent values with some exact meaning on a scale. Instead, they simply make it possible to compare the degree or strength of statements' plausibility. Rescher, however, does not speak of 'neutral plausibility' and he does not introduce the concept of 'implausibility'; nor does he differentiate between 'direct' and 'indirect' sources. A further difference between the two approaches to plausibility is that Rescher does not indicate the sources together with the plausibility values. That is, he does not use the term 'plausibility according to the source S' but he speaks simply of 'plausibility'. He also requires the assigning of a plausibility value to all statements, while the p-model permits the lack of plausibility values. A further dissimilarity is that the p-model does not postulate that the set of the statements with plausibility value 1 is consistent. The two approaches determine the relationship between the plausibility of the premises and the conclusion of inferences differently, too (see Section 9.5.5).

Nevertheless, we agree with the view that theories of inference which take into consideration plausibility values are also not formal systems; they are not logic. Rescher formulates this in connection with his approach as follows:

Plausibility theory takes us beyond logic and probability: it moves from the realm of *formal* into that of *'material'* considerations. (Rescher 1976: 2)

The theory of plausibility developed here departs in one very fundamental respect from all of its modern congeners. It is *nonprobabilistic*. Instead of deploying considerations from the theory of probability as the basis for plausibility it turns its back upon probabilistic considerations, and bases its approach on the traditional modal principle that the conclusion of a piece of reasoning takes its status from that of the 'weakest' premiss (pars deterior). Such appeal to a modal perspective makes for a conception of plausibility that is particularly undemanding in point of reliance on formal apparatus. Only deductive logic and ranking-comparisons enter in; there is no need for the more complex processes of probabilistic calculation. This plausibility theory is thus far more rudimentary than probability theory. On its approach, when working with plausibilities we need only make rank-comparisons and never engage in calculations that fuse various quantities together into a new result. Plausible reasoning is relatively basic: it reflects a relatively *primitive* – but for that no less *important* – mode of reasoning. (Rescher 1976: xi f.; emphasis as in the original)

This also means that plausibility values do not belong to the logical structure of statements, and the same is true of categorical plausibility as well. There are several reasons for this, which are not independent of each other. The interpretation of plausibility in (6)–(10) does not motivate the elaboration of a 'plausibility logic' – in fact, it does not even make it possible.

The p-model's concept of inference in (2) and the definition of indirect source in (7)(b) already signify that we will investigate in what cases the premises, their plausibility values and other relevant characteristics (logical, semantic structure) can be regarded as an indirect source on the basis of which it is reasonable and rational to deem the conclusion plausible because it is partially supported by this information. The reason for this is that the p-model aims at the interpretation and (in case of 'proper' use) legitimation of inferences that are often used and are considered to be reliable. As we will see in Section 9.5, however, the requirement that the conclusion's plausibility should (deductively) follow from the plausibility of the premises as well as from the logical structure of the inference would be such a strict criterion that it could not be met by most inferences applied in everyday situations or in scientific argumentation.

The point is not only that it would be unmotivated to elaborate a 'plausibility logic' but it is questionable for several reasons whether this task can be fulfilled:

(a) A logical functor/operator 'it is plausible that . . . ' cannot be defined in analogy to the modal functors/operators. The source-dependence and non-categorical character of plausibility (that is, the involvement of plausibility values) does not motivate this step because the two essential aspects of plausibility mentioned could not be accounted for. The interpretation of this functor/operator would be problematic as well: what semantic value should be assigned to the formula 'it is plausible that *A*'? One might attempt to treat sources as indices of possible worlds. Thus, 'it is plausible that *A*' would be true if and only if there is a possible world in which *A* is true. But how to interpret this '*A* is true'? It cannot mean 'absolute', 'objective' truth, since nothing excludes the possibility that one's source is a linguistic theory where *A* is also an uncertain, not totally reliable, that is, plausible statement. For similar reasons, '*A* is true' cannot mean '*A* is true with certainty.'

(b) A system of rules pertaining to the relationship between logical connectives and plausibility values (or even categorical plausibility) cannot be set either. On the basis of the plausibility values (or plausibilities) of the antecedent and the consequent, the plausibility (value) of a conditional statement cannot be determined, whichever logical connective has been applied (for example, conditional, strict implication). The same is true of negation as well: if we speak of plausibility without specifying its source, then from the fact that ~*A* is plausible, no conclusion can be drawn about the plausibility of *A*. It may happen that, for example, one source renders *A* plausible, while it is implausible in the light of another; on the other hand, a given source can make only one member of the pair {*A*; ~*A*} plausible. From this it follows that it is not possible to elaborate a logic in a broader sense which would apply to plausibility values instead of truth values or would comprise 'plausible' and 'implausible' besides truth values.

When one wants to determine the plausibility of a statement *p*, there may generally be more than one source which is relevant. If *p* can be judged plausible to different degrees on the basis of the members of a group of sources, then the decision may be based on the principle that states that *a number of sources all supporting the statement in question support this statement to a larger extent than any of the sources on their own*:

(11) (a) If $S = \{S_1, S_2, \ldots, S_n\}$, every member of *S* allows for assigning a plausibility value to *p*, and the plausibility value of *p* is positive on the basis of at least two elements of *S*, then **the plausibility value of statement *p* on the basis of the set of sources *S*** is $|p|_S \geq \max\{|p|_{S_1}, |p|_{S_2}, \ldots, |p|_{S_n}\}$.
(b) If every member of *S* allows for assigning a plausibility value to *p* but only $|p_{S_i}|$ is positive, then $|p|_S = |p_{S_i}|$.
(c) If the plausibility value of *p* is 0 on the basis of each member of *S*, then $|p|_S = 0$.
(d) If some member of *S* does not allow for assigning a plausibility value to *p*, neither does *S*.[14]

(11)(d) also involves the case that one judges *p* plausible on the basis of some member of *F* (that is, one assigns a plausibility value to it), another member, however, shows it to be implausible (and does not allow for assigning a plausibility value to *p*; see (10)).

It follows from (11)(a) that, contrary to probability, plausibility *cannot be defined as a calculus*. (11)(a) leaves the exact value of $|p|_S$ indefinite. The reason for this is that the value of the plausibility of *p* depends on the number of the elements in *S* and the information content originating from them. On the one hand, the more sources support *p*, the more plausible it will be. However, it may occur that, for instance, two sources with the plausibility value 0.9 cannot make *p* true with certainty; and it may also be possible that two sources complete each other in such a way that they can guarantee the truth of *p* together.

The treatment of plausible statements has several aspects that cannot be considered to be definite prescriptions. The point is that there are certain *limits* within which the criteria that might be clear instructions cannot be identified.

Examples 7(1)–(2)

(1) If utterances containing a construction can be found in several corpora, and native speakers judge such utterances unanimously correct, then the plausibility value of the hypothesis stating the grammaticalness of this construction on the basis of the totality of the sources mentioned is higher than its plausibility on the basis of any of the corpora alone or on the basis of acceptability judgements alone.

(2) If there is only one corpus from the early Middle Ages at one's disposal, and a given construction can be found in it, while further corpora stem from later periods, then only reference to the first corpus allows for assigning a positive plausibility value to the statement that this construction already existed in the early Middle Ages. The other corpora – since they capture later stages of the development of the given language – are not relevant in judging the plausibility value of this statement. Therefore, one has to assign the plausibility value 0 to it on the basis of these sources. From this, it follows that, on the basis of the set of sources consisting of all these corpora together, this statement's plausibility is identical to its value according to the corpus from the early Middle Ages.

Comparing (6), (10) and (11), we obtain the following extension of (6):

(12) (a) **Statement *p* is true with certainty on the basis of the set of sources *S*,** if *p*'s plausibility is at least neutral on the basis of each member of *S*, and there is at least one member of *S* that allows for judging *p* true with certainty; that is, if $|p|_S = 1$.

(b) **Statement *p* is plausible on the basis of the set of sources *S*,** if *p*'s plausibility is at least neutral on the basis of each member of *S*, no member of *S* allows for judging it true with certainty, and there is at least one member of *S* on the basis of which *p* is plausible; that is, if $0 < |p|_S < 1$.

(c) **Statement *p* is implausible on the basis of the set of sources *S*,** if on the basis of *S*, $\sim p$ is plausible; that is, if $0 < |\sim p|_S < 1$.

(d) **Statement *p* is false with certainty on the basis of the set of sources *S*,** if on the basis of *S*, $\sim p$ is true with certainty; that is, if $|\sim p|_S = 1$.

(e) **Statement *p* is of neutral plausibility on the basis of the set of sources *S*,** if *p* has neutral plausibility on the basis of each member of *S*; that is, if $|p|_S = 0$.

According to (12)(b), plausible statements are supported by certain considerations (that is, sources), but cannot be regarded to be true with certainty. Similarly, if one possesses information that is against a statement but does not refute it completely, then this statement is implausible on the basis of these sources. An important property of the above definition of plausibility is that it allows a statement to be plausible on the basis of some sources and implausible on the basis of others at the same time. In other words, the sources might differ from each other not only in the plausibility value they allow to be assigned to a given statement but also as to whether they deem it plausible or implausible.

Examples 8(1)–(2)

(1) It may be that one hits upon an utterance in a corpus that is judged unacceptable by one's linguistic intuition. In this case, one may deem the statement that the given utterance is grammatical plausible on the basis of one source (the corpus), while one may judge it implausible on the basis of another source (linguistic intuition). In this situation, the two sources form a set of sources which is not suitable in the sense of (5); thus, no plausibility value can be assigned to the statement at issue by relying on this set of sources taken together because it does not satisfy any of the criteria laid down in (12)(a)–(e). Therefore, the two sources and the plausibility values stemming from their application have to be treated separately.

(2) Indirect sources (inferences) may also lead to situations where there is a statement that is not judged unanimously as well. For example, the statement 'The dental affricate is biphonemic in German' is judged implausible by Wurzel (1981) on the basis of an inference whose third premise is based on a structural rule saying that 'If a vowel /V/ follows a formative-initial /$C_3C_2C_1$/ consonant cluster, then the consonant cluster /C_2C_1/ also occurs in the same position':[15]

(a) $0 <$ |If the dental affricate is biphonemic in German, that is, if its phonemic structure is /ts/, then the phonemic structure of *zwar* is /tsvɑ:r/.|$_W < 1$
|If the phonemic structure of *zwar* is /tsvɑ:r/, then a vowel follows the formative-initial /tsv/ consonant cluster.|$_W = 1$
$0 <$ |If the vowel /ɑ:/ follows the formative-initial /tsv/ consonant cluster, then the consonant cluster /sv/ occurs in the same position, too.|$_W < 1$
|The consonant cluster /sv/ does not occur formative-initially followed by a vowel.|$_W = 1$

$0 <$ |The dental affricate is not biphonemic in German.|$_{Ia} < 1$

The implausibility of the statement 'The dental affricate is biphonemic in German' (that is, the plausibility of its negation) is based on the plausibility of other statements, namely, that of the premises of the inference reconstructed in (a).

By relying on another structural rule stating that 'If the phoneme cluster /C_1C_2_/ occurs formative-initially, then there exists a formative in which the phoneme cluster /_C_2C_1/ occurs formative-finally', Wurzel considers the hypothesis mentioned plausible:

(b) $0 <$ |If the dental affricate is biphonemic in German, that is, if its phonemic structure is /ts/, then the phonemic structure of *zehn* is /tse:n/.$|_W < 1$
|If the phonemic structure of *zehn* is /tse:n/, then the phoneme cluster /ts_/ occurs formative-initially.$|_W = 1$
$0 <$ |If the phoneme cluster /ts_/ occurs formative-initially, then there exists a formative in which the phoneme cluster /_st/ occurs formative-finally.$|_W < 1$
$0 <$ |The consonant cluster /_st/ occurs formative-finally in *Nest* (/nεst/).$|_W < 1$

$0 <$ |The dental affricate is biphonemic in German.$|_{I_b} < 1$

In this case, Wurzel came to the opposite conclusion: the plausibility of the statement 'The dental affricate is biphonemic in German' has been obtained with the help of inference (b), that is, the plausibility of this hypothesis was supported by another indirect source. It has to be emphasised that this indirect source is not capable of proving the statement in the conclusion. That is, it provides only partial support for it; it makes it plausible but does not make it true with certainty. The reason for this is that this inference only captures the fact that the phoneme cluster /ts/ behaves as required by the structural rule above, and on the basis of this finding, the hypothesis according to which the dental affricate is biphonemic was supported to some extent.

Reconstruction and treatment of situations in which some of the sources support while others refute (weaken) the given statement is in most cases a very complicated task. We will return to this problem in Chapter 10 and Section 19.7.[16]

In what follows, we will examine how we can define and characterise inferences which *take the plausibility value of their premises as relevant factors into consideration.*

9.4 The concept of 'demonstrative inference'

An inference in the sense of (2) can be regarded as an indirect source on the strength of which the conclusion can be judged true with certainty if three criteria are fulfilled: there is a logical consequence relation between the premises and the conclusion; the semantic relation connecting the premises and the conclusion is reconstructible; and the premises are true with certainty according to some set of sources. Such inferences satisfy (9)(a) and are called *demonstrative inferences* (see Polya 1948: 223).

Examples 9(1)–(3)

(1) The following inference is an instance of demonstrative inference:

|If the sum of the digits of a number can be divided by 9, then this number can be divided by 9, too.$|_S = 1$
|The sum of the digits of 3276 can be divided by 9.$|_S = 1$

|3276 can be divided by 9.$|_I = 1$

The first premise is a theorem of mathematics that can easily be proven. Its truth is guaranteed by an indirect source: by the inferences that lead from the axioms of arithmetic (which are regarded to be true with certainty within arithmetic) to this theorem, constituting a proof. The truth of the second premise is secured by simple arithmetical regularities. These two sources together can be unified in the set of sources *S* because neither of them makes the premise obtaining a plausibility value from the other source implausible or false with certainty. If we reveal the logical structure of the premises and conclusion of this inference, we can show that there is a logical consequence relation between them. The semantic relation connecting the premises and the conclusion can also be reconstructed from the premises: the first premise is a conditional statement, according to which a certain property of numbers involves and guarantees the existence of another property; the second premise states that 3276 is a number possessing the property referred to by the antecedent of the conditional statement in the first premise; and the conclusion says that this number has the property mentioned in the consequent of this conditional statement. Thus, this inference *I* is an indirect source on the basis of which the conclusion can be considered true with certainty.

(2) The following inference is demonstrative as well:

|The defendant had attempted to commit a robbery.$|_S = 1$
|If somebody attempts to commit a robbery, then he/she must receive a prison sentence.$|_S = 1$

|The defendant must receive a prison sentence.$|_I = 1$

The judge accepts the first premise as true with certainty, since the eyewitnesses had unanimously told the court that the defendant tried to rob a bank. That is, the judge deems eyewitnesses' testimonies to be a perfectly reliable source. He/she holds the second premise to be certainly true on the basis of the relevant article of the criminal code as a direct source. From these two premises he/she draws the conclusion, which he/she can consider true with certainty as well, since there is a logical consequence relation between the premises and the conclusion, and the semantic connections can be easily reconstructed as well: the second premise specifies a consequence of the first premise, which appears in the conclusion, too.

(3) Negative results of tests of hypothetically assumed linguistic universals are often interpreted as instances of demonstrative inference as well. For example, the universal-candidate

(U) If the indefinite article is derived from the cardinal 'one', then non-numerable nouns cannot take indefinite article (Moravcsik 1969)[17]

can be refuted with the help of the following inference:

|If U, then if the indefinite article was derived from the cardinal 'one' in Coptic, then non-numerable nouns cannot take an indefinite article in Coptic.$|_S = 1$[18]

|In Coptic, the indefinite article was derived from the cardinal 'one', but non-numerable nouns can take an indefinite article.$|_S = 1$

$|{\sim}U|_I = 1$

The first premise can be judged true with certainty because the consequent is a special case of the antecedent. The second premise is supported by Frans Plank's finding that although the indefinite article was derived from the cardinal 'one' in Coptic, it can also be used with names of materials that are non-numerable. This source can be deemed perfectly reliable in that one trusts Frans Plank's expertise and the clear consensus among universal researchers on this question. Thus, if one acknowledges the conventional evaluation of the premises, then the premises are capable of securing the certainty of the conclusion, since there is a logical consequence relation between the premises and the conclusion, and there is a semantic relation between them, too. From (11) and (12)(d) it follows that every extension of the indirect source I by further sources which render U implausible or false with certainty will also assign ${\sim}U$ the plausibility value 1, too. If, however, other sources support U, that is, if they make it plausible, then U does not obtain a plausibility value on the basis of the set of sources containing all sources mentioned according to (11)(d).

The evaluation of the premises' plausibility in this case was conventional. One may, however, revise this decision and consider the second premise only plausible because it does not rely exclusively on linguistic data and its checking requires (historical) linguistic analysis as well, which might be contestable.

We can make this basic idea more precise with the help of the notions already introduced as follows:[19]

(13) By **demonstrative inference**, we mean an inference in the sense of (2)[20] such that:
- (a) the set of the premises is consistent;
- (b) on the basis of the logical structure of the premises and the conclusion it can be established that a logical consequence relation holds between them; that is, the conclusion is true, *provided* that the premises are also true;[21]
- (c) on the basis of the semantic structure of the premises and the conclusion, a semantic relation connecting them can be reconstructed;
- (d) the premises are true with certainty according to some set of sources *S*.

(13)(a), (b) and (c) pertain to the primary relevant characteristics of demonstrative inferences (logical vs semantic structure) in the sense of (3)(a), while (13)(d) deals with a secondary characteristic in the sense of (3)(b), namely, the 'factual' truth value of these statements (i.e. the truth value which is not hypothetical but has been assigned on the basis of some source). Since according to (13)(b) there is a logical consequence relation between the premises and the conclusion, and in addition, due to (13)(d), all premises are true with certainty on the basis of some set of sources *S*, the conclusion will necessarily be true with certainty as well.

(13)(c) concerns non-formalisable characteristics of the premises and the conclusion. It stipulates that one also has to take into consideration aspects of the meaning of statements that are not needed in order to reveal their logical structure. Demonstrative inferences are – unlike deductive ones – (also) motivated by *semantic relations* between statements. All premises have to be relevant to the conclusion; it is, indeed, well known that this criterion cannot be formulated with formal tools.

Example 10

Suppose that one does not know the books by A. A. Milne but reads in a publication by a renowned literary scholar that 'Winnie-the-Pooh likes honey' and 'If Winnie-the-Pooh likes honey then Piglet hates to have a bath.' Starting from this information, the following inference may be made:

(I) Winnie-the-Pooh likes honey.
If Winnie-the-Pooh likes honey then Piglet hates to have a bath.
―――――――――――――――――――――――――
Piglet hates to have a bath.

There is a logical consequence relation between the premises and the conclusion of (I). If one considers the paper mentioned as a perfectly reliable source, then both premises have to be judged true with certainty. If, however, the two clauses of the second premise are judged irrelevant to each other, then (I) cannot be regarded as a demonstrative inference, since (13)(c) has been violated. *A precondition of drawing demonstrative inferences is – besides logical analysis – the semantic interpretation of the statements.* In this case, for example, a semantic relation can be established between the two clauses (as well as the other premise and the conclusion) by supposing that each character of Milne possesses the typical features of the given animal.

A further important finding arises from the above considerations: employing statements as premises of inferences may lead to the re-evaluation of their plausibility value. It may happen that the semantic connections revealed during the interpretation turn out to be not strong enough. Then, of course, the reliability of the source at issue has to be revised, too.

As (13)(d) clearly indicates, demonstrative inferences are *source-dependent* insofar as one has to be in possession of a set of sources S that is capable of securing the truth of the premises. From the definition provided in (13), it also follows that demonstrative inferences *can be regarded as sources* securing the truth of a statement (conclusion). Hence, the truth value of the conclusion may be called the plausibility value of the conclusion stemming from the given inference as an indirect source. This plausibility value depends indirectly on the sources guaranteeing the certainty of the premises, as well as from the logical and semantic tools that allow for capturing the circumstance that there is a logical consequence relation and a semantic relation between the premises and the conclusion.

The primary relevant characteristics of the premises and conclusion as well as the premises' secondary characteristics determine whether a demonstrative inference I can be regarded as an indirect source which is capable of securing the certainty of the conclusion – that is, whether I is capable of extending the context[22] with a certainly true statement at a given stage of the argumentation process.[23] The plausibility value of the premises of demonstrative inferences originates from a set of sources S, while that of the conclusion comes from the given inference as an indirect source. This is a schematic reconstruction of a specific inference pattern:

(14) *Demonstrative modus ponens*

$$\frac{\begin{array}{l}|\text{if } A, \text{ then } B|_S = 1\\ |A|_S = 1\end{array}}{|B|_I = 1}$$

Nevertheless, (14) is incomplete, because some pieces of the primary characteristics are missing from it. Namely, (13)(c) requires that some semantic relation holds between the premises and the conclusion. Thus, in the case of premises of the type 'If *A*, then *B*', the plausibility of the conditional statement in question has to be based on some semantic relation between the content of *A* and *B* (e.g. causality etc.); it cannot originate solely from the circumstance that one knows that both *A* and *B* are true (see Example 10). The connection between the two clauses of conditional statements can be established by semantic relations such as *A* is a cause of *B*, or vice versa, *B* is a consequence of *A* (in this case, one infers the result from the cause or vice versa, one infers the cause from some 'state of affairs'); *B* is a sign of *A*; *B* is a necessary condition of *A*, or vice versa, *A* is a sufficient condition of *B*.

Motivation and background

Demonstrative inferences have two primary characteristics in the sense of (3)(a). The first is the logical structure of the premises and the conclusion, the second is of a semantic nature. Accordingly, the production and evaluation of demonstrative inferences relies – besides logical inference schemata and other logical tools – on semantic factors as well. The latter are also connected with the determination of the plausibility value of the premises: logically complex statements require that a semantic structure be attributed to them. As we have seen already in Example 10, this may lead to the revision of plausibility values originating from direct sources. With direct sources, the assignment of plausibility values is based in the sense of (7)(a) on some previous categorisation or convention that may require revision. That is, the use of demonstrative (and plausible) inferences enforces the interpretation of the statements and the re-evaluation of the reliability of the sources. In this way, in certain cases arguments of the type *argumentum ad verecundiam* (a faulty appeal to the testimony of an authority) can be avoided and the shortcomings of the sources (i.e. poor judgement of the plausibility of certain statements) can be identified.

This indicates a fundamental difference between on the one hand (purely formal) deductive inferences and on the other demonstrative and plausible inferences that take into consideration plausibility values and, via this, the content of the statements as well. While the former are impersonal and automatic, and aim at revealing the 'theoretical' possibilities, the latter are non-formal and involve content-related aspects; thus, they are non-automatic, and their use requires decisions. Nevertheless, it is important to emphasise that in scientific theorising, both kinds of inference are needed. Indeed, the clarification of their role is an urgent methodological task.

Demonstrative inferences can be considered the strongest possible tools for the extension of the set of information at issue, since they lead to a certainly true conclusion (relative to some fixed information state). They can be regarded as sources which *perfectly support* the statement employed as the conclusion (see (9)(a)).[24] On the other hand, however, they can be applied under very strict conditions: one can draw demonstrative inferences only if one possesses the total amount of information necessary for drawing a conclusion with a certain truth value.

To sum up, demonstrative inferences can be characterised as follows:

(15) (a) The first relevant characteristic of the premises and the conclusion is their logical structure. On these primary characteristics, the following criterion is based: a logical consequence relation has to hold between the premises and the conclusion.
(b) The second relevant characteristic of the premises and the conclusion is their semantic structure. On these primary characteristics the following criterion is based: the connection between the premises and the conclusion has to rely on semantic factors (causality, necessary condition etc.), and this relationship has to be reconstructible from the premises.
(c) The third relevant – secondary – characteristic of the premises and the conclusion is their truth value.[25] All premises have a truth value on the basis of some set of sources *S*; the truth of the conclusion is guaranteed by the premises and the relevant characteristics. That is, demonstrative inferences are sources which perfectly support the conclusion.

(15) indicates that the application of demonstrative inferences is significantly *limited*. These limitations are related to the peculiarities of the information at one's disposal. It is a truism that *in both everyday and scientific thinking one often does not possess the full amount of information needed for drawing demonstrative inferences*. Basically, this may have three reasons, which may co-occur. The first possible reason is that whereas the logical consequence relation holds between the premises and the conclusion, at least one of the premises is not true with certainty, but is only *plausible*. This means that there is at least one premise which does not possess the secondary characteristic mentioned in (15)(c). Second, it is also possible that while the premises at hand are true with certainty, there is no logical consequence relation between them and the conclusion (that is, the criterion mentioned in (15)(a) does not hold). Third, (15)(b) may be violated, that is, it may be the case that there is no semantic relation between the premises and the conclusion.

9.5 The notion of 'plausible inference'

9.5.1 Introductory remarks

At this point the question emerges how (2) can be specified in such a way that the resulting inference can serve as a source which cannot support the conclusion perfectly but is capable of giving it *partial support*, that is, which *makes it plausible*. Our task is, therefore, to determine the primary and secondary relevant characteristics that allow an inference to fulfil (9)(b). We try to answer this question by taking the criteria pertaining to demonstrative inferences as our starting point; then, we will gradually loosen them. We will investigate three cases. After summarising and generalising our findings, we will define the notion of plausible inference by spelling out the primary and secondary characteristics of the premises and the conclusion needed for considering the conclusion plausible.

9.5.2 *Case 1*

It may be the case that an inference-candidate fulfils (13)(a)–(c) but does not satisfy (13)(d), because instead of being true with certainty, at least one of its premises is only plausible according to the set of sources *S*. For instance, in (16), the premises of the inference in the first column are certainly true on the basis of *S*. Therefore, this inference is demonstrative. In the case of the inference given in the second column, however, one of the premises is only plausible; consequently, it is not a demonstrative inference:

(16)

Demonstrative modus ponens	*?*
|If Roger Federer won three sets in the final of the US Open, then he won the final.|$_S = 1$	|If Roger Federer won three sets in the final of the US Open, then he won the final.|$_S = 1$
|Roger Federer won three sets in the final of the US Open.|$_S = 1$	$0 <$ |Roger Federer won three sets in the final of the US Open.|$_S < 1$
|Roger Federer won the final.|$_I = 1$	|Roger Federer won the final.|$_I = ?$

The *demonstrative modus ponens* (see (14)) in the first column supports the conclusion perfectly: since one of the sufficient conditions of the conclusion is true, the conclusion will also be necessarily true. With the inference in the second column, the premises are not sufficient to support the conclusion perfectly, since the second premise is not true with certainty. It is clear, however, that if the plausibility of this premise increases (decreases), then the plausibility of the conclusion will also increase (decrease). If the plausibility value of the former is 0, then the conclusion is of neutral plausibility, too. If one, however, knew that Federer had won three sets in the final, then it would be considered as certain that he had won the final. From this it follows that if it is plausible that Federer won three sets, so then one is allowed to suppose that the plausibility that he won the final, too, lies between the two cases mentioned – that is, it is a plausible statement, because its plausibility value is between the minimal and the maximal plausibility values as it is stipulated in (10)(b). This means that the inference candidate in the second column can be regarded as an *indirect source* that partially supports the conclusion, that is, it makes the latter plausible. Therefore, this is an inference in the sense of (2), where the conclusion possesses the secondary characteristic in the sense of (3)(b) that it is a plausible statement on the basis of this inference as an indirect source. This finding can be generalised as follows:

(17) *Plausible modus ponens*

$|\text{if } A, \text{ then } B|_S = 1$

$0 < |A|_S < 1$

$0 < |B|_I < 1$

The pattern in (17) captures – similarly to the *demonstrative modus ponens* (14) – not only the logical structure of the premises and the conclusion, but also indicates the plausibility values of the premises on the basis of a set of sources. It does not, however, contain any hint as to the semantic characteristics of the premises and the conclusion. Therefore, it cannot count as an inference schema specifying the properties of an inference type exhaustively.

Example 11

Consider the following example which is an instance of *plausible modus tollens* (see Ross 1967: 15ff.):

$0 <$ |If the *wh*-transformation cannot apply twice to a given string, then the sentence *He told me about a book which I can't figure out where to obtain* is not correct.$|_S < 1$

|~(The sentence *He told me about a book which I can't figure out where to obtain* is not correct.)$|_S = 1$

$0 <$ |~(The *wh*-transformation cannot apply twice to a given string)$|_I < 1$[26]

The first premise is a conditional sentence. If one accepts the hypothesis that in the sentence *He told me about a book which I can't figure out where to obtain*, the *wh*-transformation was applied twice, then it is reasonable to assume a causal relation between the two clauses of this conditional. Thus, it is easy to see that there is a semantic relation between the premises and the conclusion which can be reconstructed from the premises. Although one cannot state that the first premise is true with certainty, it is legitimate to deem it plausible. The second premise ('The sentence *He told me about a book which I can't figure out where to obtain* is not correct') is regarded as false with certainty by the generativist tradition that treats judgements of linguistic intuition as evidence. On the strength of the logical structure of the premises and the conclusion, it can be established that there is logical consequence relation between them. Thus, this inference supports the implausibility of the statement 'The *wh*-transformation cannot apply twice to a given string' as an indirect source; it does not, however, guarantee its falsity. This, of course, does not rule out the possibility that other direct or indirect sources show this hypothesis to be plausible. Such a source is, for example, Chomsky's (1966 [1964]: 37ff.) argumentation, according to which while the sentences *who saw what?*, *you met the man who saw what?*, *you read the book that who saw?*, *you saw the book which was next to what?* are correct, the sentences *who what saw?*, *you saw the book which which was next to?* are not grammatical. Chomsky based the antecedent of the first premise of the above inference on these and some similar examples, because they support the first clause of the conditional sentence. This is a requisite for treating the prohibition of the twofold application of the *wh*-transformation not as a pure supposition, but as a serious, indeed possible cause of the statement in the second clause of the conditional sentence. The second premise of Ross' example, however, is a counterexample, that is, it renders this hypothesis implausible.

From this, we get the following characterisation of plausible inferences belonging to the first type:

(18) (a) The first relevant primary characteristic of the premises and the conclusion is their logical structure. Two criteria are based on these primary characteristics: a logical consequence relation holds between the premises and the conclusion, and the former make up a consistent set of statements.

(b) The second relevant primary characteristic of the premises and the conclusion is their semantic structure. On these characteristics the following criterion is based: the connection between the premises and the conclusion has to rely on semantic factors (causality, necessary condition etc.), and this relationship has to be reconstructible from the premises.

(c) The third relevant – secondary – characteristic of the premises and the conclusion is their plausibility value. All premises have a positive plausibility value (that is, they are either plausible or true with certainty) on the basis of some set of sources *S*, but at least one of them is not true with certainty. The conclusion is plausible on the basis of the premises and their relevant characteristics as a source.

9.5.3 Case 2

It may happen that the statements employed as premises are consistent, they are true with certainty according to a set of sources *S*, a semantic relation can be reconstructed that connects them with the conclusion, but that there is no logical consequence relation between them and the statement treated as the conclusion. That is, while (13)(a), (c) and (d) are met, (13)(b) does not hold.

Let us consider the former example with some modifications. Suppose that on the basis of the set of sources S, the statement *If Roger Federer wins three sets in the final of the US Open* (A), *then he wins the competition* (B) is true with certainty, and S also perfectly supports the information that he in fact has won the US Open, that is, on the basis of S, B is true with certainty. From these pieces of information one may attempt to obtain A. It is clear that this is not a demonstrative inference, since there is no logical consequence relation between the two premise-candidates and the conclusion-candidate. 'If A, then B' and 'B' in themselves are not sufficient to secure the truth of A. One cannot exclude the possibility, for example, that his opponent has not given up the match due to an injury (C_1), or that he has not been excluded from the tournament for doping (C_2), etc. Consequently, it cannot be stated that A is true with certainty. Thus, the question emerges whether one may state that it is plausible, and if so, under what conditions.

In order to answer this question, one has to start from the semantic connections between the premise-candidates and the conclusion-candidate, and one has to strive to find statements that, together with B, constitute a sufficient condition of A. For example, if C_3 means that *The opponent did not miss the match*, and C_4 means that *No objection has been raised against the opponent's eligibility to play*, then these two statements together with B, C_1 and C_2 constitute a sufficient condition of A. With the help of these statements, from the two premise-candidates ('if A, then B' and B) another inference can be obtained, namely, (19):

(19)	if A, then B	$\rightarrow$	if B & C_1 & C_2 & C_3 & C_4, then A
	B	$\rightarrow$	B & C_1 & C_2 & C_3 & C_4
	?A		A

There is a logical consequence relation between the statements resulting from the transformation of the premise-candidates in the left column and A. Therefore, if the former are plausible according to the set of sources S or on the basis of one of its extensions S', then the conclusion will also be plausible. The premises in the second column of (19) can be considered as *latent background assumptions* that have to be *at least of neutral plausibility* according to some extension of S so that A can be assigned a plausibility value, too.

These results can be generalised as follows. In the case of inference-candidates that do not meet (13)(b), *the premise-candidates within one's reach are not enough to secure the plausibility of the conclusion*. One also needs *latent background assumptions* which make it possible to transform the given inference-candidate into an inference in which there is a logical consequence relation between the premises and the conclusion. This transformation may consist of the extension of the set of the premise-candidates by further statements.

For example, with inductive inferences, the set of the premise-candidates has to be supplemented by the background assumption that the cases not examined also possess the characteristics that could be found in the investigated ones; the conclusion states the presence of these characteristics as a general rule. In other cases – such as in the case of the example above – this transformation is not confined to the addition of further statements, but some premise-candidates have to be deleted.

If S can be extended in such a way that one can assign a plausibility value to the premises of the inference resulting from the transformation (that is, they are true with certainty, plausible, or at least of neutral plausibility), and this extension does not alter the plausibility value of the premise-candidates, then from the statements and sources mentioned, an inference in the sense of (2) can be obtained that assigns a plausibility value to the conclusion as an indirect source. The inference partially reconstructed in (19) is called *strong reduction*.[27]

Whole–part inferences also belong to this type if their premises are true with certainty according to some set of sources. (20) shows a possible reconstruction. Latent background assumptions will be put between '[' and ']'.

(20) *Whole–part inference*

$|A \text{ is part of } B|_S = 1$

$|B \text{ has property } P|_S = 1$

$[0 \leq |\text{If } B \text{ has property } P\text{, then its parts possess } P \text{ as well}|_{S'} \leq 1]$

$0 \leq |A \text{ has property } P|_I \leq 1$

We cannot speak, of course, of an inference schema in the sense of logic in this case either. See also Examples 13(2) and 18.

Motivation and background

(20) clearly illustrates the difficulties emerging in connection with the evaluation of inferences belonging to the second type. These difficulties arise from the circumstance that in order to reconstruct these inferences and to judge the plausibility of the conclusion, one also has to take into consideration pieces of information not included in the premises.

The identification of the latent background assumptions is a challenging task for two reasons – and these difficulties point in certain respects in opposite directions. On the one hand, deductive inferences can be obtained in an infinite number of ways, starting from the premise-candidates. On the other hand, the majority of these extensions are only theoretically possible, since the latent background assumptions have to possess a plausibility value – that is, the set of sources S has to be extended by sources on the basis of which a plausibility value can be assigned to these statements, without making the premises implausible or false. Therefore, the evaluation of the plausible inferences belonging to the second type is a much more difficult task than that of the plausible inferences of the first type. The former includes, among others, the following factors:

- It is possible that two individuals evaluate an inference differently, although they agree on the plausibility value of the premises. For example, if one of them has no information about the plausibility value of the latent background assumptions, and the other knows that one of them is false, then the first person will deem the conclusion plausible, whereas the second will not.[28]
- The same situation may occur due to changes in information at one's disposal, which may lead to the revision of one's former judgement.
- A similarly contradictory result may be obtained if the premises are supplemented with latent background assumptions in different ways. It may occur that the conclusion and the inference are evaluated as plausible on the basis of one supplementation, whereas they are not considered as plausible on the basis of another.
- It may happen that the latent background assumptions cannot be identified.

Plausible inferences belonging to Type 2 (and 3, see Section 9.5.4) have – similarly to demonstrative inferences – two primary characteristics in the sense of (3)(a). One of them is the logical structure of the premises and the conclusion, the other is their semantic structure, on which relations between the content of the statements are based. In the production of plausible inferences, semantic factors are decisive, while it is both logical and semantic factors that are needed to evaluate them.

Nevertheless, it is no accident that there are typical inference patterns, such as reduction, induction, part–whole inferences or analogy (for more on this, see Rescher 1976: 90ff., the argumentation schemes of Kienpointner 1992 and Walton 1995, 1996, Walton & Reed 2005, Walton, Reed & Macagno 2008). The formation of these patterns and the way they work are influenced by semantic and cognitive factors which motivate the selection of certain frequent inference patterns.[29] For the reconstruction and the typology of inference patterns, see also Hample (1992 [1985]), Rigotti (2007a, b), as well as Section 9.5.6.

Example 12

Inferences belonging to the second type may serve in certain cases as the means of testing potential linguistic universals. For example:

(U) For every language, if there is a pronominal reflexive for the first person, then there is also one for the second person. If there is a pronominal reflexive for the second person, then there is also one for the third person. (Plank 2008: 165; Faltz 1985: 120; Comrie 1981: 19)

U can be tested as follows:

> |If *U*, then if there is a pronominal reflexive for the first person in German, then there is also one for the second and third person, respectively.$|_S = 1$
> |In German, there is a pronominal reflexive for the first and second person, respectively, and there is also one for the third person.$|_S = 1$
>
> ---
>
> $|U|_I = ?$

Although both premises can be considered to be true with certainty, they are not sufficient to support the certainty or the plausibility of the conclusion: there is a semantic relation but no logical consequence relation between the premises and the conclusion. Therefore, with the help of latent background assumptions, the premises have to be transformed into an inference of Type 1, for example, in the following way:

|If *U*, then if there is a pronominal reflexive for the first person in German, then there is also one for the second and for the third person, respectively.$\|_S = 1$	→	[|For every living language, every language that existed and every language that will exist in future, if there is a pronominal reflexive for the first and second person, respectively, and there is also one for the third person, then *U*.$\|_S = 1$]
|In German, there is a pronominal reflexive for the first and second person, respectively, and also one for the third person.$\|_S = 1$	→	|In German, there is a pronominal reflexive for the first and second person, respectively, and also one for the third person.$\|_S = 1$
		[|In English, there is a pronominal reflexive for the first and second person, respectively, and also one for the third person.$\|_S = 1$]
		[0 < |For every further living language, every language that existed and every language that will exist in future in which there is a pronominal reflexive for the first person, there is also one for the second and third person, respectively.$\|_S < 1$]
?		$0 < |U|_I < 1$

The first two latent background assumptions can be deemed true with certainty. The third one, however, is only plausible, since it cannot be checked exhaustively. Consequently, this statement cannot be treated as being true with certainty; one can only say that it possesses a high plausibility value. The same is true of the conclusion as well.

Generalising our results, we find that the inferences belonging to the second type can be characterised as follows:

(21) (a) The first primary characteristic of the premises and the conclusion is their logical structure. On these primary characteristics, two criteria are based: The premises make up a consistent set of statements, and there is no logical consequence relation between the premises and the conclusion.

(b) The second primary characteristic of the premises and the conclusion is their semantic structure. On these characteristics, the following criteria are based:

- the connection between the premises and the conclusion has to rely on semantic factors (causality, necessary condition etc.),
- this relationship has to be reconstructible from the premises, and
- it has to be extendable to latent background assumptions with the help of which the inference can be transformed (extended) into a deductively valid inference.

(c) The third relevant – secondary – characteristic of the premises and the conclusion is their plausibility value. All premises have to be true with certainty on the basis of some set of sources *S*. This alone, however, is not sufficient to secure the plausibility of the conclusion. To achieve the latter, the latent background assumptions mentioned in (b) have to be at least of neutral plausibility according to some extension of *S*.

From (21)(c) it is obvious that in the case of plausible inferences of the second group, the plausibility of the conclusion is strongly *source-dependent*. First, sources are needed according to which the premises can be deemed true with certainty. Second, one has to rely on sources which are capable of assigning a plausibility value to the latent background assumptions. This is one of the reasons why the p-model – unlike Rescher's approach – always uses plausibility by reference to the sources.

An important consequence of this context-dependence is that there is no guarantee that such inferences will be evaluated in a similar way and unequivocally in every context.[30] The plausibility of their conclusion depends on two factors. The first factor is the reliability of the sources on the basis of which the premises have been judged plausible and the comprehensiveness of this set of sources. The latter means whether this set contains all sources that assign a plausibility value to the premises in the given context, or only to some of them. From this it follows that the plausibility of the conclusion is only *relative*: it may happen that by considering a broader set of sources, the plausibility of the premises changes, or even gets completely lost. The second factor is whether the set of sources can be extended in such a way that the latent background assumptions are also plausible or at least of neutral plausibility.[31]

The above considerations underlie the formulation of the following methodological principle: *the plausibility of the premises and latent background assumptions has to be evaluated on the broadest range of sources possible.* This does not mean that if a set of sources deems a premise or latent background assumption plausible while another set makes it implausible, then one cannot draw a plausible inference on the basis of the former set. In certain situations (see Sections 10.5–6), this may be a legitimate or even a reasonable strategy. Nevertheless, one has to take into consideration that the conclusion is plausible only relative to a narrowed set of sources.

Motivation and background

At this point, we will briefly examine inference-candidates that – although there is no logical consequence relation between their premises and their conclusion – satisfy the following generalisation of the logical consequence relation:

(22) If the premises are true, then the conclusion is true as well.

(22) does not require that the truth of the conclusion is secured by the truth of the premises and the logical structure of the premises and the conclusion. For instance, (23) cannot be deemed a demonstrative inference but it satisfies (22):

(23) The sum of the digits of 3276 can be divided by 9.
―――――――――――――――――――――――――――
3276 can be divided by 9.

Cases similar to (23) are usually interpreted as enthymemes, that is, as deductive inferences in which one of the premises remains implicit. A precondition of this interpretation is that the missing premise can be clearly identified (cf. 'If the sum of the digits of a number can be divided by 9, then the number can also be divided by 9'). (23), however, is not a demonstrative inference in the sense of (13) because there is no logical consequence relation between the premise and the conclusion. It cannot be reconstructed as a plausible inference of the second type, either. The reason for this is that the missing premise cannot be regarded as a latent background assumption, since the first clause of (23) does not contain the semantic relation that connects it with the conclusion. Consequently, cases similar to (23) can be interpreted not as inferences in the sense of (2) but as direct sources. That is, the relationship between the 'premise' and the 'conclusion' can be considered to be direct: the divisibility of the sum of the digits may count as a perfectly reliable source on the basis of which the given number can also be 'automatically' deemed to be divisible by 9. Of course, this relationship can be converted into an indirect source (demonstrative inference). For this, one has to identify and make explicit the missing premise, and the source assigning a plausibility value to it has to be taken into consideration.

There are indeed enthymemes which are also represented in the p-model as inferences, that is, as indirect sources. These are extreme cases of the second type of plausible inferences, when the latent background assumptions extending the set of the premises are true with certainty according to some extension of S:

(24)
$$\begin{array}{l} |\text{if } A \,\&\, B, \text{ then } C|_S = 1 \\ |A|_S = 1 \\ [|B|_{S'} = 1] \\ \hline |C|_I = 1 \end{array}$$

(24) is not a demonstrative inference, since there is no logical consequence relation between the premises and the conclusion. Therefore, the premise 'if *A* & *B*, then *C*', the premise '*A*', and the source *S* jointly cannot guarantee the certainty of *C*. If, however, *S* can be extended in such a way that the missing latent background assumption becomes true with certainty, then the conclusion can be also regarded as certainly true. To sum up, inferences such as (24) can be transformed into a demonstrative inference by making the latent background assumptions explicit and by including the source guaranteeing the truth of the latter in the inference.

9.5.4 *Case 3*

Case 3 occurs when there is no logical consequence relation between the premises and the conclusion, further at least one of the premises is not true with certainty but only plausible – that is, if (13)(a) and (c) are satisfied, while (13)(b) and (d) are not. For instance, in the example analysed in Section 9.5.3, it may happen that *B*, that is, the statement *Federer has won the US Open* is not true with certainty but only plausible according to the sources at one's disposal:

(25)
$$\begin{array}{lcl} & & \textit{Weak reduction} \\ |\text{if } A, \text{ then } B|_S = 1 & \rightarrow & [0 < |\text{if } B \,\&\, C_1 \,\&\, C_2 \,\&\, C_3 \,\&\, C_4, \text{ then } A|_{S'} \leq 1] \\ 0 < |B|_S < 1 & \rightarrow & 0 < |B|_{S'} < 1 \\ & & [0 \leq |C_1 \,\&\, C_2 \,\&\, C_3 \,\&\, C_4\,|_{S'} \leq 1] \\ \hline ? & & 0 \leq |A|_I < 1 \end{array}$$

It is easy to see that inferences belonging to Type 3 are the *most uncertain*. At the same time, however, this type is the *most frequent*, since it covers (among others) analogical inferences, part–whole inferences, induction etc. which have at least one plausible premise.

The only difference between the characterisation of the inferences in the third type and the features summarised in (21) is that the former have at least one premise that is only plausible but not true with certainty. Therefore, the inferences belonging to the third group can be characterised by repeating (21) with this modification:

(26) (a) The first primary characteristic of the premises and the conclusion is their logical structure. On these primary characteristics, two criteria are based: the premises make up a consistent set of statements, and there is no logical consequence relation between the premises and the conclusion.

(b) The second primary characteristic of the premises and the conclusion is their semantic structure. On these characteristics, the following criteria are based:

- the connection between the premises and the conclusion has to rely on semantic factors (causality, necessary condition etc.),
- this relationship has to be reconstructible from the premises, and
- it has to be extendable to latent background assumptions with the help of which the inference can be transformed (extended) into a deductively valid inference.

(c) The third relevant – secondary – characteristic of the premises and the conclusion is their plausibility value. All premises have to be plausible on the basis of some set of sources *S*. This alone, however, is not sufficient to secure the plausibility of the conclusion. To achieve the latter, the latent background assumptions mentioned in (b) have to be at least of neutral plausibility according to some extension of *S*.

Examples 13(1)–(4)

(1) The following inference is an instance of weak reduction[32] (see (25), Example 12; see also Example 11):

$0 <$ |If the *wh*-transformation cannot apply twice to a given string, then the sentence *He told me about a book which I can't figure out when I should read* is not correct.$|_S < 1$ (see Ross 1967: 15ff.).

|The sentence *He told me about a book which I can't figure out when I should read* is not correct.$|_S = 1$

|The *wh*-transformation cannot apply twice to a given string.$|_I = ?$

The first premise is plausible provided one accepts the hypothesis that in the sentence *He told me about a book which I can't figure out when I should read* the *wh*-transformation was applied twice – that is, if the incorrectness of the sentence in question is ascribed to the circumstance described in the first clause. The second premise is regarded as true with certainty by the generativist tradition that accepts grammaticality judgements as evidence. There is no logical consequence relation between the premises and the conclusion. In such cases, one has to try to transform the set of premises with the help of latent background assumptions in such a way that a logical consequence relation is created between this set and the conclusion. This goal can be achieved, for example, in the following way:

$0 <$ |If the *wh*-transformation cannot apply twice to a given string, then the sentence *He told me about a book which I can't figure out when I should read* is not correct. $|_S < 1$	→	[|If no sentence is correct that has been gained from an English sentence by a twofold application of the *wh*-transformation, then the *wh*-transformation cannot apply twice to a given string. $|_{S'} = 1$]
|The sentence *He told me about a book which I can't figure out when I should read* is not correct. $|_S = 1$	→	|The sentence *He told me about a book which I can't figure out when I should read* is not correct. $|_{S'} = 1$
		[$0 <$ |In the sentence *He told me about a book which I can't figure out when I should read*, the *wh*-transformation was applied twice. $|_{S'} < 1$]
		[$0 <$ |Every further sentence is incorrect that has been gained from an English sentence by a twofold application of the *wh*-transformation. $|_{F'} < 1$]
?		$0 <$ |The *wh*-transformation cannot apply twice to a given string. $|_I < 1$

The third latent background assumption is only plausible for two reasons. First, there are an infinite number of sentences in a language, from which an infinite number of transformed sentences can be derived. Second, it is only supposed that the sentences taken into consideration have been produced this way. Therefore, the inference only supports (but does not prove) the hypothesis of Chomsky's generative grammar that the *wh*-transformation cannot apply twice to a given string.

(2) Sometimes, one infers from a characteristic of the part to the corresponding characteristic of the whole (see e.g. Bierwisch & Lang 1989a, Kertész 2004b, Lang 1989):

$0 <$ |Knowledge of language is part of human cognitive behaviour. $|_S < 1$
$0 <$ |Knowledge of language is organised in a modular way. $|_S < 1$

|Human cognitive behaviour is organised in a modular way. $|_I = ?$

The premises cannot be regarded as true with certainty because one has no access to an unquestionably reliable source that could perfectly support the statements that knowledge of language is an autonomous part of cognition and that it is organised in a modular way. Moreover, it is easy to see that these premises would not guarantee the truth of the conclusion even if they were true with certainty. Therefore, in order to support the plausibility of the conclusion latent background assumptions are also needed. One can, for example, look for a source that assigns at least neutral plausibility to the statement that the characteristic of the part mentioned involves the corresponding characteristic of the whole:

$0 <$ |Knowledge of language is part of human cognitive behaviour.|$_{S'} < 1$
$0 <$ |Knowledge of language is organised in a modular way.|$_{S'} < 1$
[$0 \leq$ |If a part of human cognitive behaviour is organised in a modular way, then human cognitive behaviour is organised in a modular way, too.|$_{S'} > 1$]

$0 \leq$ |Human cognitive behaviour is organised in a modular way.|$_{I} < 1$

(3) The following analogical (inductive) inference originating in Lakoff & Johnson (1980) belongs to the third group of plausible inferences, too, since the premises do not contain any information about the further abstract concepts:

$0 <$ |The concepts of ARGUMENT, TIME and QUALITY are part of the conceptual system.|$_{S} < 1$
$0 <$ |The concepts of ARGUMENT, TIME and QUALITY are metaphorically structured.|$_{S} < 1$
[|Other concepts within the conceptual system are metaphorically structured, too.|$_{S} = 0$]

$0 \leq$ |Most of our conceptual system is metaphorically structured.|$_{I} < 1$

(4) A move in Levinson's (2000: 56) argumentation can be reconstructed as an inductive inference:

$0 <$ |The sentence *John has two children, if not more* contains the clause 'John has two children', and the first clause implicates that 'he has no more'.|$_{S} < 1$
$0 <$ |The sentence *John has two children and perhaps more* contains the clause 'John has two children', and the first clause implicates that 'he has no more'.|$_{S} < 1$
$0 <$ |The sentence *John has two children and in fact, now I come to think of it, maybe more* contains the clause 'John has two children', and the first clause implicates that 'he has no more'.|$_{S} < 1$
$0 <$ |The sentence *John has two children; he had two more by his first wife but they are grown up now* contains the clause 'John has two children', and the first clause implicates that 'he has no more'.|$_{S} < 1$
$0 <$ |The sentence *John has two children. Actually Sue says he has three, but I've never seen the third so I doubt he or she exists* contains the clause 'John has two children', and the first clause implicates that 'he has no more'.|$_{S} < 1$

$0 \leq$ |The clause 'John has two children' always implicates that 'he has no more'.|$_{I} < 1$

In this case, the latent background assumption can be assumed that every sentence that has not been examined in the premises but contains the clause 'John has two children' shares the characteristic formulated in the conclusion. At the same time, however, as Levinson emphasises, in the light of the literature on pragmatics, the premises cannot be regarded as true with certainty.

9.5.5 *The connection between the plausibility of the premises and the conclusion*

To sum up the insights gained from the investigation of the three types of plausible inferences, one can also draw inferences in the sense of (2) in cases in which the information at one's disposal (statements, sources, characteristics) does not allow for making demonstrative inferences – provided that certain conditions are fulfilled. Such inferences are capable of supporting the plausibility of the conclusion as an indirect source. By generalising from (18), (21) and (26), the concept of plausible inference can be defined as follows:

(27) By **plausible inference**, we mean an inference in the sense of (2) such that
- (a) the set of the premises is consistent;
- (b) on the basis of the semantic structure of the premises and the conclusion, a semantic relation connecting them can be reconstructed;
- (c) the premises are plausible or true with certainty according to some set of sources *S*;
- (d) if there is no logical consequence relation between the premises and the conclusion, then the set of the premises can be extended by further statements (*latent background assumptions*) for which it holds that
  - the semantic relation in (b) can be extended to them;
  - they are at least of neutral plausibility according to some extension of *S* that does not modify the plausibility of the premises, and
  - a logical consequence relation holds between the extended set of statements and the conclusion;
- (e) at least one premise or latent background assumption is not true with certainty.

From the definition of the plausibility value in (10) as well as the definition of demonstrative inferences (see (13)) and the latter's properties as summarised in (15) it follows that if the plausibility value of the premises and latent background assumptions approaches 1, then the same is true of the conclusion, too. This also means that *demonstrative inferences are limiting cases of plausible inferences*.[33] In a similar way, it follows that if the plausibility value of a premise or latent background assumption approaches 0, then that of the conclusion does as well. From these two considerations it follows that *the conclusion of plausible inferences is a plausible statement*:[34] the premises of plausible inferences support the conclusion only partially, since they do not lead to a certainly true statement but they do influence the plausibility of the conclusion. Therefore, plausible inferences can be considered to be indirect sources that make the statement in the conclusion plausible. To put it another way: plausible inferences are inferences in the sense of (2); the secondary characteristic of the premises and the conclusion in the sense of (3)(b) is their plausibility value. If the conclusion already has a plausibility value, then it will increase according to (11).

Nevertheless, (27) does not determine the plausibility value of the conclusion. An essential characteristic of plausible inferences is that the relationship between the plausibility values of the premises and the conclusion cannot be calculated exactly, because several factors should be taken into consideration about which one does not possess enough information. Therefore, one has to confine oneself to imposing the *limits* within which the conclusion of a plausible inference should lie.

In the literature on argumentation theory, the connection between the plausibility values of the premises and the conclusion is often supposed to follow *the weakest link principle*. Rescher and Pollock, for example, formulate it as follows:

> When a certain group of (mutually consistent) propositions in S entails some other proposition in S, then this resulting proposition cannot be less plausible than the least plausible among them. (Rescher 1976: 15)

> The argument strength of a defeasible argument is the minimum of the strengths of the defeasible reasons employed in it and the degrees of justification of its premises. (Pollock 2001: 244)

We will accept this principle, too. In order to apply it, however, the plausibility value of the latent background assumptions has to be taken into consideration as well, since with plausible inferences belonging to the second and third group, there is no logical consequence relation between the premises and the conclusion. Thus, the principle has to be modified in such a way that it applies to the least plausible premise *or* latent background assumption.[35]

Nevertheless, the weakest link principle is in some cases *counterintuitive*, as is illustrated by the following example:

(28)

$\lvert\text{if } A, \text{ then } B\rvert_S = 1$	$\lvert\text{if } A, \text{ then } B\rvert_S = 0.5$
$\lvert A\rvert_S = 0.3$	$\lvert A\rvert_S = 0.3$
$\lvert B\rvert_I \geq = 0.3$	$\lvert B\rvert_I \geq = 0.3$

According to Pollock's interpretation of the weakest link principle, the plausibility of the conclusions of the two inferences in (28) is identical – it is the plausibility value of the second premise. Our intuition, however, says that the conclusion of the second inference is somewhat weaker, since one of its premises is weaker as well. Since Rescher does not determine the exact value of the plausibility value of the conclusion but imposes only a lower limit for it, his proposal is not in conflict with this example. Nevertheless, the difference between the two conclusions cannot be captured by his model. The following principle, however, should be applied not only in (logical) semantics:

> The ultimate test of a semantics is that validates the intuitively right reasoning. It is human intuitions about correct reasoning that we want to capture. (Pollock 2001: 238)

Intuitively, an upper limit should also be set which could be the value of the most plausible premise. Thus, we get the following hypothesis:

(29) If I is a plausible inference in the sense of (27) such that
- its premises are $p_1, p_2, \ldots, p_n$,
- its conclusion is c,
- its latent background assumptions are $l_1, l_2, \ldots, l_m$ ($m \geq 0$), further
- there is a logical consequence relation between $p_1, \ldots, p_k$ ($k \leq n$), $l_1, l_2, \ldots, l_m$ and c,

then I can be regarded as an indirect source on the basis of which the plausibility value of the conclusion lies between the plausibility values of the premise or the latent background assumption with the lowest and highest plausibility value, respectively:

$$\min\{|p_1|_S, \ldots, |p_k|_S, |l_1|_S, \ldots, |l_m|_S\} \leq |c|_I \leq$$
$$\leq \max\{|p_1|_S, \ldots, |p_k|_S, |l_1|_S, \ldots, |l_m|_S\}$$

With the exception of a few special cases, (29) does not determine the plausibility value of the conclusion exactly, but only imposes limits on it. These limits must not be exceeded by any valuation, and they can be tightened. For example, one may try to achieve some refinement of this estimation. To this end, two starting points present themselves. First, in the case of inferences with many premises, (29) is sensitive only to the values of the two 'extreme' premises/latent background assumptions. Second, the plausibility value of the conclusion might lie near a mean of the values of the premises and latent background assumptions.

From these considerations it follows that a possible estimation is that *in the case of plausible inferences belonging to the first type*, we choose the geometric mean of the plausibility values of the premises (that is, the nth root of their product) as the lower limit, and their 'average' (arithmetical mean) as the upper limit:

(30) If I is a plausible inference in the sense of (27) with the premises $p_1, p_2, \ldots, p_n$ and the conclusion c, and there is a logical consequence relation between $p_1, p_2, \ldots, p_n$ and c, then I can be regarded as an indirect source on the basis of which the plausibility value of the conclusion lies between the geometric and the arithmetic mean of the plausibility values of the premises:

$$\sqrt[n]{|p_1|_S \cdot \ldots \cdot |p_n|_S} \leq |c|_I \leq \frac{|p_1|_S + \ldots + |p_n|_S}{n}$$

Motivation and background

(30) does not result from the calculation of the plausibility value of the conclusion with the help of some algorithm. It has been motivated by the following considerations:

- Both means are sensitive to changes in the plausibility value of the premises: they move in the same direction as the plausibility value of the premises.
- By starting from the definition of the arithmetic and the geometric mean, it is easy to show that their value lies between the values of the premises with the lowest and the highest plausibility values, respectively. Since $|c|_I$ is between the two means, it lies in this interval, too. This finding is much more informative than the weakest link principle stating only that the plausibility of the conclusion is at least as high as that of the premise with the lowest plausibility value.
- If all premises are true with certainty, then from (30) we obtain that the conclusion is also true with certainty. Thus, (30) is capable of accounting for the finding that demonstrative inferences are limiting cases of plausible inferences.
- (30) predicts correctly that if all premises have the same plausibility value, then the conclusion will have this value as well.

Example 14

Suppose that in Example 11, the premises have the following plausibility values:

|If the *wh*-transformation cannot apply twice to a given string, then the sentence *He told me about a book which I can't figure out where to obtain* is not correct.$|_S = 0.6$

|~(The sentence *He told me about a book which I can't figure out where to obtain* is incorrect.)$|_S = 1$

By applying (30), the plausibility value of the conclusion can be estimated as follows:

$$\sqrt{0.6 \cdot 1} \leq |c|_I \leq \frac{0.6 + 1}{2}$$

That is,

$0.77 \leq$ |~(The *wh*-transformation cannot apply twice to a given string)$|_I \leq 0.8$

This means that the plausibility of the conclusion lies somewhere 'halfway' between the plausibility values of the premises.

If the plausibility of the first premise is higher, for instance 0.8, then one obtains higher limits for the plausibility of the conclusion, too:

$0.894 \leq |\sim$(The *wh*-transformation cannot apply twice to a given string)$|_I \leq 0.9$

In cases in which the first premise possesses a low plausibility value (0.1), the conclusion will have a rather low plausibility:

$0.316 \leq |\sim$(The *wh*-transformation cannot apply twice to a given string)$|_I \leq 0.55$

It is easy to see that the gap between the lower and upper limit decreases whenever there is little difference in the plausibility values of the premises.

If their latent background assumptions can be identified, the treatment of *plausible inferences belonging to the second and third type* (that is, of deductively invalid plausible inferences) can be traced back to the above case. Namely, with these inferences, there is a logical consequence relation between the conclusion, a part of the premises (or in certain cases, all of them) and the latent background assumptions. Therefore, the plausibility value of the conclusion can be estimated with the help of the geometric and arithmetic mean of the plausibility values of the relevant premises in the above sense and the latent background assumptions:

(31) If I is a plausible inference in the sense of (27) with the premises p_1, $p_2, \ldots, p_n$, the latent background assumptions $l_1, l_2, \ldots, l_m$ and the conclusion c, further there is no logical consequence relation between p_1, $p_2, \ldots, p_n$ and c, but a logical consequence relation holds between $p_1, \ldots, p_k$ $(k \leq n)$, the latent background assumptions and the conclusion, then I can be regarded as an indirect source on the basis of which the plausibility value of the conclusion lies between the geometric and arithmetic mean of the plausibility values of the premises and latent background assumptions:

$$\sqrt[k+m]{|p_1|_{S'} \cdot \ldots \cdot |p_k|_{S'} \cdot |l|_{S'} \cdot \ldots \cdot |l_m|_{S'}} \leq |c|_I \leq$$
$$\leq \frac{|p_1|_{S'} + \ldots + |p_k|_{S'} + |l_1|_{S'} + \ldots + |l_m|_{S'}}{k+m}$$

Similarly to (30), (31) also remains within the boundaries set by (29). See Figure 1.[36]

The notation in Figure 1 is as follows:

A = the plausibility value of the 'weakest' premise/latent background assumption

B = the plausibility value of the 'strongest' premise/latent background assumption

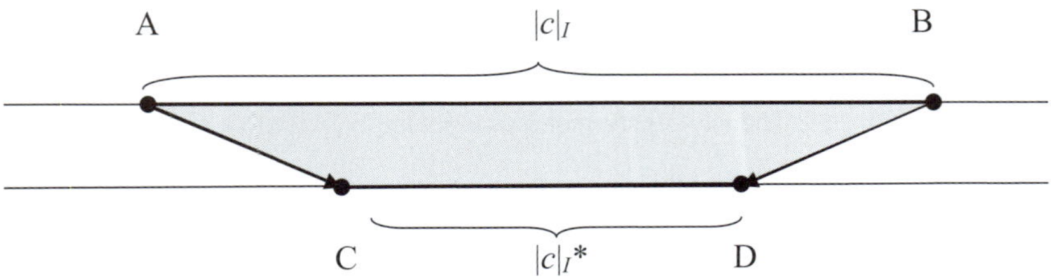

Figure 1. Domain of the possible values of the conclusion's plausibility on the basis of (29)–(31)

C = geometrical mean of the plausibility values of the premises and latent background assumptions
D = arithmetical mean of the plausibility values of the premises and latent background assumptions
$|c|_I$ = possible values of the conclusion's plausibility on the basis of (29)
$|c|_I$* = possible values of the conclusion's plausibility on the basis of (30)/(31)

Examples 15(1)–(2)

(1) (31) requires the transformation of the plausible inferences belonging to the second or third type into a deductively valid inference (that is, into a plausible inference of Type 1). This was done with the inference in Example 12 in the right-hand column. Therefore, let's suppose that the premises and latent background assumptions possess the following plausibility values:

- Premises:

  |In German, there are pronominal reflexives for the first/second person, and also one for the third person.$|_{S'} = 1$

- Latent background assumptions:

  |For every living language, every language that existed and every language that will exist in future, if there are pronominal reflexives for the first/second person, and there is also one for the third person, then $U.|_{S'} = 1$

  |In English, there are pronominal reflexives for the first/second person, and also one for the third person.$|_{S'} = 1$

  |For every further living language, every language that existed and every language that will exist in future in which there are pronominal reflexives for the first/second person, there is also one for the third person.$|_{S'} = 0.2$

With the help of (31), the plausibility of the conclusion can be estimated as follows:

$$\sqrt[1+3]{1 \cdot 1 \cdot 1 \cdot 0.2} \leq |c|_I \leq \frac{1+1+1+0.2}{1+3}$$

That is, the linguistic universal at issue has relatively high plausibility:

$0.67 \leq$ |For every language, if there is a pronominal reflexive for the first person, then there is also one for the second person. If there is a pronominal reflexive for the second person, then there is also one for the third person.| ≤ 0.8

See also Examples 16(1) and 17(1).

(2) (31) can be applied to the inference in Example 13(4) as well:

- Premises:

|The sentence *John has two children, if not more* contains the clause 'John has two children', and the first clause implicates that 'he has no more'.$|_S = 0.5$

|The sentence *John has two children and perhaps more* contains the clause 'John has two children', and the first clause implicates that 'he has no more'.$|_S = 0.5$

|The sentence *John has two children and in fact, now I come to think of it, maybe more* contains the clause 'John has two children', and the first clause implicates that 'he has no more'.$|_S = 0.5$

|The sentence *John has two children; he had two more by his first wife but they are grown up now* contains the clause 'John has two children', and the first clause implicates that 'he has no more'.$|_S = 0.5$

|The sentence *John has two children. Actually Sue says he has three, but I've never seen the third so I doubt he or she exists* contains the clause 'John has two children', and the first clause implicates that 'he has no more'.$|_S = 0.5$

- Latent background assumption:

|Every sentence that has not been examined in the premises but contains the clause 'John has two children' implicates that 'he has no more'.$|_S = 0.2$

With the help of (31), the plausibility of the conclusion can be estimated as follows:

$$\sqrt[5+1]{0.5 \cdot 0.5 \cdot 0.5 \cdot 0.5 \cdot 0.5 \cdot 0.2} \leq |c|_I \leq$$
$$\leq \frac{0.5+0.5+0.5+0.5+0.5+0.2}{5+1}$$

That is, the conclusion has a rather low plausibility:

$0.43 \leq$ |The clause 'John has two children' always implicates that 'he has no more'.$|_I \leq 0.45$

See also Example 16(2).

From (31) it follows that with plausible inferences belonging to the second and third type, the plausibility value of the conclusion does not necessarily lie between the plausibility value of the premises with the lowest and the highest plausibility value. The reason for this is that the latent background assumptions have to be taken into consideration as well. Moreover, if one of the latent background assumptions has the plausibility value 0, then the conclusion can (but must not) be judged to be of neutral plausibility, too.

Nevertheless, it often happens that the missing latent background assumptions cannot be identified. In such cases, one may try to assign the plausibility value 0 to the hypothesised missing latent assumption(s) in (31), which yields the following estimation:[37]

(32) $$0 \leq |c|_I \leq \frac{|p_1|_S + \ldots + |p_n|_S}{n+1}$$

(32) enables several strategies of plausibility assignment. If the unidentified latent background assumptions seem to pose too high a risk and lead to considerable uncertainty in the evaluation of the conclusion's plausibility, then one should proceed with caution and judge the conclusion to be of neutral plausibility. In contrast, if the plausibility of the premises is high and they seem to yield a secure basis for the conclusion, then the value on the right side of (32) may be chosen. The latter is indeed lower than the average of the plausibility values of the premises, since it takes into account at least one latent background assumption with the plausibility value 0.

Examples 16(1)–(2)

(1) If the inference in Example 12 cannot be transformed into another one which is of Type 1, then (32) should be applied to the premises in the left column:

$$0 \leq |c|_I \leq \frac{1+1}{2+1}$$

That is, this estimation results in considerably wider limits as was the case with the use of (31) in Example 15(1):

$0 \leq$ |For every language, if there is a pronominal reflexive for the first person, then there is also one for the second person. If there is a pronominal reflexive for the second person, then there is also one for the third person.| ≤ 0.67

Since the transformation of plausible inferences of Types 2 and 3 introduces new pieces of information into the estimation of the plausibility value of the conclusion, it may lead to narrower limits and a higher plausibility value.

(2) The application of (32) to the inference in Example 13(4) yields the following estimation:

$$0 \leq |c|_I \leq \frac{5 \cdot 0.5}{5 + 1}$$

Similarly to the outcome of Examples 15(1) and 16(1), we obtained wider limits and lower minimum/maximum values than was the case with Example 15(2):

$0 \leq$ |The clause 'John has two children' always implicates that 'he has no more'.$|_I \leq 0.417$

Of course, other estimations are also possible that narrow down the limits given in (29) in different ways. One may apply, for example, weighted means if it seems to be reasonable to take into consideration the plausibility values of the premises to different extents, or one may turn back to the *weakest link principle*.

Motivation and background

(29)–(32) clearly indicate that there are fundamental differences between the p-model's concept of inference and those of the formal models. The former sets certain limits without providing a method which would make it possible to calculate the plausibility value of the conclusion exactly. The major reason for this is that the plausibility of the conclusion is influenced, beyond the plausibility value of the premises, by a series of factors that cannot be formalised. Therefore, there is no method which could be applied mechanically and would always lead to results in accord with one's intuitions. If, for example, one follows Rescher, then one finds that if *Q* is a logical consequence of *P*, then *Q* has at least as high a plausibility as *P*. According to (29) and (30), however, these two values are identical, which seems to be more appropriate – and the list could be continued.

Nevertheless, estimations based on (30)–(32) remain within the boundaries set up in Walton (1992) and referred to in Walton (2001):

> In a linked argument, both (or all) premises are functionally related to support the conclusion. In a convergent argument, each premise is an independent line of evidence to support the conclusion. In a linked argument, Theophrastus' Rule applies. The plausibility value of the conclusion must be at least as great as that of the least plausible premise. In a convergent argument, the value of the conclusion must be at least as great as that of the most plausible premise. (Walton 2001: 149)

In the terminology of the p-model this means two things. First, the plausibility value of the conclusion of a plausible inference is always at least as high as that of the least plausible premise/latent background assumption. This follows from the circumstance that, as we have seen, (30)–(32) are refinements of the weakest link principle captured by (29). Second, according to (11), if a statement is supported by several sources, then the resulting plausibility value will be higher than any of the plausibility values provided by any of the sources on their own. At this point, there is a difference to Rescher's standpoint, which equates the resulting plausibility value with the highest single value (see Rescher 1976: 12, 19).

Examples 17(1)–(2)

(1) As we have seen in Example 15(1), the application of (31) yields relatively high lower and upper limits for the plausibility of the conclusion with the inference in Example 12. This may be evaluated to be counterintuitive. Therefore, in this case it seems to be reasonable to try to work with weighted means. In such a way, one can take into account the (low) plausibility value of the latent background assumption to a larger extent.

(2) Walton (1992: 37) analyses the following inference:

P_1: Jones is less than five feet tall.
P_2: Jones is an All-Star forward of the NBA Los Angeles Lakers.

C: Jones is a less than five-foot tall All-American forward of the NBA Los Angeles Lakers.

In his view, although both P_1 and P_2 might be made highly plausible by their sources, their conjunction in C is implausible, and this contradicts the rules of plausibility indexing set by Rescher which stipulate that C is at least as plausible as the weakest premise of the above inference. There is, however, an alternative analysis possible which is based on the source-dependence of plausibility. Namely, C obtains a plausibility value from an indirect source; this value can be estimated with the help of (30) as follows:

$|\text{Jones is less than five feet tall.}|_{S_1} = 0.8$
$|\text{Jones is an All-Star forward of the NBA Los Angeles Lakers.}|_{S_2} = 0.8$

$$\sqrt{0.8 \cdot 0.8} \leq |\text{Jones is a less than five-foot tall All-American forward of the NBA Los Angeles Lakers.}|_I \leq \frac{0.8 + 0.8}{2},$$

which yields that

$|\text{Jones is a less than five-foot tall All-American forward of the NBA Los Angeles Lakers.}|_I = 0.8$

S_1 may be personal information from some acquaintance of Jones, while S_2 may be a newspaper article. If there is a source S which keeps the evaluations of S_1 and S_2, respectively, then C has the plausibility value 0.8 according to this inference. There is, however, a direct source S_3 as well which judges C to be implausible: it is a platitude that forwards of NBA teams are very tall people. Therefore, the plausibility value 1 can be assigned to $\sim C$ on the basis of S_3. From this it follows that on the basis of both sources together one cannot assign a plausibility value to C. There are four possible solutions of this inconsistency:

(a) The reliability of S_1 in judging the current height of Jones is questioned and P_1 is rejected. It may be the case, for example, that one finds out that P_1 does not refer to Jones' current height but to his height at the age of 10. Thus, the indirect source I is no longer capable of supporting C, because one of its premises does not have a plausibility value. From this it follows that C is implausible on the basis of the information at issue (S_3).

(b) The reliability of S_2 is questioned because one realises that this newspaper contains many typos and names are often misspelled; indeed, in the next passage one finds 'Johns', and reject P_2. Thus, the indirect source I is no longer capable of supporting C, because one of its premises does not have a plausibility value. From this it follows that C is implausible on the basis of the information at hand (S_3).

(c) One cannot find a source S keeping the evaluations of S_1 and S_2, respectively. That is, the personal source S_1 disagrees with P_2 stating that Jones is a jockey, or the newspaper article (S_2) mentions another height. This may be the case, for example, when there are two Jones who are only namesakes.

(d) Theoretically there is a fourth possibility, questioning the reliability of S_3. Thus, the direct source S_3 would no longer be capable of supporting $\sim C$. From this it could follow that C is plausible on the basis of the indirect source I – but in this case, this possibility can be excluded.

9.5.6 *Summary*

To sum up, plausible inferences can be characterised as follows:

(33) (a) The first primary characteristic of the premises and the conclusion is their logical structure. Two criteria are based on these primary characteristics. First, the premises have to make up a consistent set of statements Second,

either there is a logical consequence relation between the premises and the conclusion, or the set of the premises can be transformed into a set of statements with the help of latent background assumptions of at least neutral plausibility in such a way that there is a logical consequence relation between the resulting set of statements and the conclusion.

(b) The second primary characteristic of the premises and the conclusion is their semantic structure. It is the criterion that the connection between the premises and the conclusion has to rely on semantic factors (causality, necessary condition etc.) that is based on these characteristics. This relationship has to be reconstructible from the premises and has to be extendable to the latent background assumptions as well.

(c) The third relevant – secondary – characteristic of the premises and the conclusion is their plausibility value.[38] All premises have a positive plausibility value on the basis of some set of sources *S*, the latent background assumptions are of at least neutral plausibility according to an appropriate extension of *S*, and the conclusion is plausible on the basis of the premises and their relevant characteristics. That is, plausible inferences are indirect sources partially supporting the conclusion.

There are, of course, also enthymematic plausible inferences. Such cases can be treated in a similar way as demonstrative inferences from which a premise is missing (see Section 9.5.3). Thus, if (33)(b) is not violated, then one is dealing with a plausible inference belonging to the second or third group. It may happen, however, that the missing premise would be needed to meet (33)(b). Under such circumstances, the inference-candidate has to be interpreted not as an indirect but as a direct source; that is, it cannot be regarded as a plausible inference. In such cases, however, there is a smaller amount of explicit information at one's disposal for judging the plausibility of the conclusion, since at least one of the premises required by (33) remains hidden. Therefore, the assignment of the plausibility value of the conclusion is less well established and less controllable.

Motivation and background

Comparing (15)(a) and (33)(a), a further important difference can be detected between demonstrative and plausible inferences. While with the former, the logical structure of the premises and the conclusion is a primary characteristic in the sense of (3)(a) on which a purely logical criterion is based, in the case of the latter, the logical structure provides a criterion in certain cases (that is, in the case of plausible inferences belonging to the second and third types) only together with other relevant characteristics. This finding reinforces our claim that with plausible inferences, great significance has to be attached to criteria related to non-formal characteristics such as semantic properties or plausibility value and purely formal criteria are insufficient.

At this point, it is worth comparing the p-model's concept of plausible inference with Rescher's proposal. Rescher interprets plausible inferences belonging to the first type as deductive inferences whose premises have been assigned plausibility values. He deems inferences of the second and third type to be inductive inferences and reconstructs them as enthymematic deductive inferences:

> inductive reasoning is not a matter of using a characteristic sort of 'inductive logic', but is a matter of leaping to conclusions by gapfilling, by supplementing the resources of ordinary (deductive) logic with *substantive* materials. Such a substantively committal process can never be validated *a priori* by reasoning from general principles alone . . . Induction represents a cognitively serious effort at closing an information-gap in such a way that – everything considered – we can regard it as epistemically well-advised to accept the indicated results . . . The present approach . . . sees induction not as a characteristic mode of drawing conclusions, but as an estimation technique, a methodology for obtaining answers to our factual questions through optimal exploitation of the information at our disposal. (Rescher 1980: 17ff.; emphasis as in the original)

Rescher's stance is at several points close to the p-model; there are, however, differences as well. We are in agreement on the finding that plausible inferences belonging to the second and third type cannot be interpreted as the weakening of (1). We also share the view that both logic and plausibility theory complementing the formal apparatus of logic with content-related elements are needed for the reconstruction of induction, analogy, part–whole inferences, reduction etc. A further common idea is that the drawing and reconstruction of plausible inferences is not mechanical and cannot be formalised. Instead, it is a heuristic task which often does not have a unique, objectively controllable solution.

We disagree with Rescher in that such inferences are always produced with the tools of logic. We think that the 'gap' between the premises and the conclusion is not filled with the help of deductive inferences created *ad hoc* but by the application of semantically motivated, *typical inference patterns*. These characteristic inference patterns can be regarded as heuristics that narrow down considerably the range of possibilities insofar as they – at least during the first attempts – lead the search for the latent background assumptions in certain directions.

We also think that it is very worthwhile to reveal possible links between the concept of 'plausible inference' as it is interpreted and characterised by the p-model and Douglas Walton's *argumentation schemes*. Walton, Reed & Macagno (2008) introduces the concept of 'argumentation scheme' in connection with that of plausible (defeasible, presumptive, abductive) inferences:

> Argumentation schemes are forms of argument (structures of inference) that represent structures of common types of arguments used in everyday discourse, as well as in special contexts like those of legal argumentation and scientific argumentation. They include the deductive and inductive forms of argument that we are already so familiar with in logic. However, they also represent forms of argument that are neither deductive nor inductive, but that fall into a third category, sometimes called defeasible, presumptive, or abductive . . . Such an argument can rightly carry weight, or be a plausible basis for acceptance, on a balance of considerations in an investigation or discussion that is moving forward, as new evidence is being collected. The investigation can then move ahead, even under conditions of uncertainty and lack of knowledge, using the conclusion tentatively accepted. (Walton, Reed & Macagno 2008: 1f.)

By characterising the schemes belonging to the third group, in his writings Walton does not start from a unique (formal) definition but from a long list of schemes. That is, he does not derive argumentation schemes from a single, abstract concept of 'correct inference' or 'presumptive/plausible/defeasible/abductive etc. inference' but he proceeds from a rich variety of schemes towards possible generalisations. This method has historical grounds, because research into plausible inferences has its origins partly in the study of *fallacies*. It was one of the most important insights at the beginnings of argumentation theory that there are inferences which are acceptable, non-fallacious forms of inference in spite of being deductively invalid.[39] Therefore, for several decades the study of deductively invalid but acceptable inferences consisted in the analysis of a series of different inference/argument types which were traditionally judged to be fallacious but which in the view of modern argumentation theorists seemed to cover non-fallacious, acceptable uses as well. The unease about the *unsystematicity* of fallacies as well as their correct counterparts was formulated by Walton as follows:

> The basic problem for informal logic as a scientific discipline is that forms of argument corresponding to the types of arguments used to commit the fallacies have never been identified as well-defined structural units, in the way that forms of argument have been identified and defined in formal logic. (Walton 1995: 3)

Walton (1995, 1996) and Walton, Reed & Macagno (2008) developed a hierarchical system of argumentation schemes and revealed several possible generalisations. They came to the conclusion that most schemes have a defeasible *modus ponens* form (Walton, Reed & Macagno 2008: 364ff.). Nevertheless, they raised two problematic points. First, defeasible *modus ponens* seems to be only a rough description of the structure of these inferences because they usually contain 'many special premises and variables that are also parts of the form of the argument', too (Walton, Reed & Macagno 2008: 367). Second, argumentation schemes involve not only a structural description of an argument form but also a set of so-called *critical questions* which allow for the evaluation of 'a given argument in a particular case, in relation to a context of dialogue in which the argument occurred' (Walton, Reed & Macagno 2008: 11f.). The formalisation of these questions needs further research as well (see Walton, Reed & Macagno 2008: 379, 382). For example, the scheme *Argument from Correlation to Cause* is supposed to have the following structure and linked critical questions:[40]

Structure:

> *Premise*: There is a positive correlation between *A* and *B*.
> *Conclusion*: Therefore, *A* causes *B*.

Critical questions:

> CQ1: Is there really a correlation between *A* and *B*?
> CQ2: Is there any reason to think that the correlation is any more than a coincidence?
> CQ3: Could there be some third factor, *C*, that is causing both *A* and *B*?

If we compare this analysis with a possible reconstruction obtained by the p-model, it is easy to see that CQ1 can be interpreted as referring to the plausibility (reliability, acceptability) of the premise, CQ2 to the plausibility of the second latent background assumption, and CQ3 to the third latent background assumption:

$0 <$ |There is a positive correlation between *A* and *B*.$|_S < 1$
[$0 <$ |If there is a positive correlation between *A* and *B*, then there is more than a coincidence between them.$|_S < 1$]
[$0 <$ |*B* is not a cause of *A*.$|_S < 1$]
[$0 <$ |There is no third factor *C*, that is causing both *A* and *B*.$|_S < 1$]
[$0 <$ |If there is more than a coincidence between *A* and *B*, *B* is not the cause of *A* and there is no third factor *C*, that is causing both *A* and *B*, then *A* causes *B*.$|_S < 1$]

$0 <$ |*A* causes *B*.$|_S < 1$

From this, the following hypothesis presents itself:

(34) The inferences captured by Walton's argumentation schemes are plausible inferences in the sense of (27) in Section 9.5.5. The schemes themselves indicate the syntactic and semantic structure of the inferences, while the critical questions refer to the evaluation of the plausibility of the premises and latent background assumptions.

By accepting (34) it seems to be possible to provide a systematic theoretical background which allows for analysing plausible (defeasible, presumptive, or abductive, etc.) inferences in such a way that we start from a unique, well-defined concept of 'plausible inference' and proceed systematically towards more and more specific types and instances by relying on the comprehensive and detailed analyses provided by Walton's model of argumentation schemes. Thus, while the p-model could contribute to the identification of the structure and the latent background assumptions of inferences primarily by revealing how the set of premises can be completed to a deductively valid inference, Walton's model, on the other hand, invites us to undertake a semantically and pragmatically motivated search for them helped by raising critical questions. At this point, there seems to be a chance of a fruitful dialogue between the two approaches.

Nevertheless, there are also some differences between our view and Walton's which can be best illustrated by two schemes related to scientific argumentation. The argumentation scheme *Argument from Evidence to a Hypothesis* has the following two versions:[41]
Structure:

Argument from Verification
Major premise: If A (a hypothesis) is true, then B (a proposition reporting an event) will be observed to be true.
Minor premise: B has been observed to be true, in a given instance.
Conclusion: Therefore, A is true.

Argument from Falsification
Major premise: If A (a hypothesis) is true, then B (a proposition reporting an event) will be observed to be true.
Minor premise: B has been observed to be false, in a given instance.
Conclusion: Therefore, A is false.

Critical questions:

CQ1: Is it the case that if A is true, then B is true?
CQ2: Has B been observed to be true (false)?
CQ3: Could there be some reason why B is true, other than its being because of A being true?

If we analyse these argumentation schemes using the tools provided by the p-model, then we can reach the following conclusions:

- CQ1 is related to the plausibility (reliability, tenability) of the major premise, CQ2 to the plausibility of the second premise, while CQ3 refers to a latent background assumption in the case of an *Argument from Verification*.
- Neither of the schemes has a *modus ponens* structure: *Argument from Verification* is a *reduction* (see (19), (25)), while the logical structure of the *Argument from Falsification* is an instance of *modus tollens*. In scientific contexts, certain types of plausible inferences belonging to the first and third group (such as plausible *modus tollens*, as well as weak reduction (see (25) in Section 9.5.4), analogy, part–whole inference etc.) seem to be more common than (plausible) *modus ponens*.
- Although inferences fitting the scheme *Argument from Verification* are deductively invalid, the conclusion is formulated as if the truth of A

could be secured by the premises 'If *A*, then *B*' and '*B*'. Moreover, in scientific contexts in most cases hypotheses as well as statements capturing the result of sense perception or measurement are only plausible rather than being true or false with certainty. Thus, there is a tension between the terminology used in the formulation of the schemes ('true', 'false', 'observation') and the alleged plausible (defeasible, presumptive, abductive) character of these inferences.

9.6 The fallibility of plausible inferences

An important characteristic of plausible inferences is their *fallibility*. Since they have at least one premise or latent background assumption that is not true with certainty but only plausible (or is of neutral plausibility), their conclusion is not certainly true but only plausible to some extent. Moreover, taking into consideration a wider scope of sources, one may come into possession of information that makes the premises, the latent background assumptions or the conclusion implausible or false. Therefore, it is always the case that the conclusion is plausible only relative to the premises, the latent background assumptions and the sources supporting them. With inferences belonging to the second or third type, it may be the case that they are no longer capable of supporting the conclusion even though the premises are true or plausible. For example, information may emerge that refutes (makes implausible or false) a latent background assumption that has been accepted so far in the absence of pieces of information pointing in the opposite direction. In the latter case, the conclusion may lose its plausibility even when the plausibility value of the premises remains intact.[42]

From the above considerations it follows that the *reconstruction* of plausible inferences belonging to the second and third group is a process full of uncertainties. The circumstance that the latent background assumptions cannot be identified definitely poses a serious problem. This stance has two important consequences. First, by the evaluation of a given inference one can only choose that extension which seems to be the most satisfactory in the given context. In connection with this, there are also translation problems contributing to the uncertainty of plausible inferences. Such problems are well known in the logical literature, and they cannot be eliminated by the further elaboration of the analytic (logical or argumentation-theoretical) tools entirely (see Rescher 1977a). The second consequence is that inferences are often created in such a way that identification and control of the latent background assumptions is carried out only *partially*. This means that one checks the plausibility of the premises, and supposes – on the basis of more or less systematic considerations – that the context does not contain components that could make the latent background assumptions which are partially or wholly known, implausible or false. From this it follows that the identification of the latent background assumptions is not a prerequisite for drawing plausible inferences. It is required, however, for their evaluation. The amount of information used has to be maximally extended; that is, it has to contain all sources, semantic and logical characteristics as well as applicable methods that are accessible in the given context.

These findings explain why plausible inferences belonging to the second and third group do not have a formal counterpart, as is the case with demonstrative inferences, whose formal counterparts are the deductive inferences. For the plausibility of the conclusion, it is not sufficient to suppose that the premises are true or plausible; rather, starting from the semantic relations reconstructed from the premises, the set of the premises has to be complemented by latent background assumptions which are assigned a plausibility value on the basis of a given set of sources.

Nevertheless, one can speak of *plausible inference patterns*. These, however, differ considerably from the inference schemata of logic. They do not indicate content reduction (that is, the omission of elements that are irrelevant to the logical structure) but they capture semantic relations (for example, part–whole, causal, or analogical relations). See also Sections 9.2 and 9.5 on this.

Example 18

In the next two examples, some property of the part is inferred from the corresponding property of the whole. If we take our everyday knowledge as a set of sources, then only (b) can be regarded as a plausible inference:

(a) $|$Peter's car is blue.$|_S = 1$
$|$The wheels of Peter's car are parts of Peter's car.$|_S = 1$

? The wheels of Peter's car are blue.

(b) $|$Peter's car is in the garage.$|_F = 1$
$|$The wheels of Peter's car are parts of Peter's car.$|_S = 1$

$0 < |$The wheels of Peter's car are in the garage.$|_I < 1$

This difference is due to the circumstance that while in the case of (a), the missing latent background assumption has to be judged false with certainty, if we take our everyday knowledge as a source, while in the case of (b), it is plausible:

(a′) $|$Peter's car is blue.$|_S = 1$
$|$The wheels of Peter's car are parts of Peter's car.$|_S = 1$
[$\sim$(If a car is blue, then all parts of it are blue.)$|_S = 1$]

$|$The wheels of Peter's car are blue.)$|_I = ?$

(b′) $|$Peter's car is in the garage.$|_S = 1$
$|$The wheels of Peter's car are parts of Peter's car.$|_S = 1$
[$0 <$ $|$If a car is in the garage, then all parts of it are in the garage.)$|_S < 1$]

$0 <$ The wheels of Peter's car are in the garage.)$|_I < 1$

Nevertheless, (b) can be faulty as well, since it is possible that Peter has taken away the wheels of his car and taken them to the mechanic in order to get the tyres changed.

9.7 The dynamism of plausible inferences

In general, the plausibility values assigned to the premises and background assumptions cannot be considered to be fixed, since they may change if new sources are taken into consideration or if the reliability of their source changes. The modification of the plausibility values of the premises and background assumptions brings about the change in the plausibility value of the conclusion: it will be more or less plausible, too. This dynamism is also manifested in the finding that demonstrative inferences can be interpreted as limiting cases of plausible inferences:

> our pattern of plausible inference has a 'limiting form', which is a pattern of demonstrative inference. As the premises of the plausible inference 'tend' to the corresponding premises of the limiting form, the plausible conclusion 'approaches' its extreme limiting strength. Still shorter: there is a continuous transition from the heuristic pattern to a demonstrative pattern. (Polya 1954: 42)

Therefore, due to the dynamism of plausible inferences, their model naturally involves demonstrative inferences as limiting cases.

The dynamism of plausible inferences is manifested not only in their relationship with demonstrative inferences as limiting cases. If we compare the plausibility value of the conclusion at a given moment to its plausibility value in an earlier state, we can see that if the plausibility of any premise decreases or increases, the plausibility of the conclusion will also change along with that of the premises. Nevertheless, the plausibility of the conclusion does not only depend on the 'strength' or 'weight' of the premises, but is also influenced by new pieces of information related to the latent background assumptions.[43]

Plausible inferences can be interpreted not only statically, but also dynamically. See, for instance:

(35)

$$\frac{|\text{if } A, \text{ then } B|_{S_1} = 1 \qquad 0 < |B|_{S_1} < 1}{0 < |A|_{I_1} < 1} \quad \rightarrow \quad \frac{|\text{if } A, \text{ then } B|_{S_2} = 1 \qquad |B|_{S_2} = 1}{0 < |A|_{I_2} < 1,\ |A|_{I_1} < |A|_{I_2}}$$

Comparing the two columns of (35), we can see that the plausibility of *A* increased after *B* had become certain. This also means that plausible inferences can be interpreted as indirect sources that are sensitive to changes in the plausibility of the premises and latent background assumptions.

The dynamism of plausible inferences is especially important because the plausibility of a statement is often examined in comparison with its alternatives (for instance, its negation or one of its former values, or any other alternative assumption).

Example 19

Cole and Sung proposed the following universal-candidate:

(U) Monomorphemic reflexives can take long-distance antecedents whereas polymorphemic reflexives cannot (Cole & Sung 1994: 365).[44]

As we have seen in Example 12, linguistic universals cannot be tested exhaustively because one cannot examine whether they hold in all languages that existed, exist and will exist in future but the investigations are reduced to living languages and a few dead ones. With the help of (32), the initial plausibility of *U* can be estimated as follows:

(a) |If *U*, then monomorphemic reflexives can take long-distance antecedents whereas polymorphemic reflexives cannot in living languages.$|_C = 1$
|Monomorphemic reflexives can take long-distance antecedents whereas polymorphemic reflexives cannot in living languages.$|_C = 0.2$

$0 \leq |U|_{I_a} \leq 0.4$

Cole & Sung (1994) tested the second premise, among others, on Chinese. They found that this hypothesis holds in this language. From this we obtain the following plausible inference, where the plausibility of the conclusion can be estimated with the help of (32) again:

(b) |If monomorphemic reflexives can take long-distance antecedents whereas polymorphemic reflexives cannot in living languages, then the same holds true in Chinese, too.$|_C = 1$
|Monomorphemic reflexives can take long-distance antecedents whereas polymorphemic reflexives cannot in Chinese.$|_C = 0.8$

$0 \leq$ |Monomorphemic reflexives can take long-distance antecedents whereas polymorphemic reflexives cannot in living languages.$|_{I_b} \leq 0.6$

As regards the initial plausibility of the second premise of (a) and its plausibility value stemming from inference (b), on the basis of (11)(a) we obtain that the plausibility value of this statement has increased. If we choose its highest possible value, than we arrive at the following:

$|$Monomorphemic reflexives can take long-distance antecedents whereas polymorphemic reflexives cannot in living languages.$|_{I_b} = 0.6$

This finding can be applied to the premises of inference (a) as follows:

(c) $|$If U, then monomorphemic reflexives can take long-distance antecedents whereas polymorphemic reflexives cannot in living languages.$|_C = 1$
$|$Monomorphemic reflexives can take long-distance antecedents whereas polymorphemic reflexives cannot in living languages.$|_{I_b} = 0.6$

$0 \leq |U|_{I_c} \leq 0.53$

As we see, the upper limit of U's plausibility has become higher.

Cole and Sung obtained similar results in the case of Korean, English, Italian and Icelandic as well:

(d) $|$If monomorphemic reflexives can take long-distance antecedents whereas polymorphemic reflexives cannot in living languages, then the same holds true in Chinese, Korean, English, Italian, and Icelandic.$|_C = 1$
$|$Monomorphemic reflexives can take long-distance antecedents whereas polymorphemic reflexives cannot in Chinese.$|_C = 0.8$
$|$Monomorphemic reflexives can take long-distance antecedents whereas polymorphemic reflexives cannot in Korean.$|_C = 0.8$
$|$Monomorphemic reflexives can take long-distance antecedents whereas polymorphemic reflexives cannot in English.$|_C = 0.8$
$|$Monomorphemic reflexives can take long-distance antecedents whereas polymorphemic reflexives cannot in Italian.$|_C = 0.8$
$|$Monomorphemic reflexives can take long-distance antecedents whereas polymorphemic reflexives cannot in Icelandic.$|_C = 0.8$

$0 \leq |$Monomorphemic reflexives can take long-distance antecedents whereas polymorphemic reflexives cannot in living languages.$|_{I_d} \leq 0.71$

It is easy to show that the more languages are investigated and tested positively, the more plausible is the second premise of the inference (a), and, consequently, its conclusion:

(e) $|$If U, then monomorphemic reflexives can take long-distance antecedents whereas polymorphemic reflexives cannot in living languages.$|_{C'} = 1$
$|$Monomorphemic reflexives can take long-distance antecedents whereas polymorphemic reflexives cannot in living languages.$|_{C'} = 0.71$

$0 \leq |U|_{I_e} \leq 0.57$

It may happen, however, that a universal-candidate is implausible according to an inference as indirect source. In this case, for example, Subbarao (1998:

19) is such a source. Its application leads to the following inferences, which belong to Type 1 of plausible inferences, therefore the plausibility of their conclusion can be established with the help of (30):

(f) |If monomorphemic reflexives can take long-distance antecedents whereas polymorphemic reflexives cannot in living languages, then the same holds true in Marathi as well.$|_S = 1$
|Both monomorphemic and polymorphemic reflexives can take long-distance antecedents in Marathi.$|_S = 0.8$[45]

$0.89 \leq |\sim$ (Monomorphemic reflexives can take long-distance antecedents whereas polymorphemic reflexives cannot in living languages.)$|_{I_f} \leq 0.9$

Since the conclusion of (f) has a very high plausibility, both premises of inference (g) are of high plausibility, too:

(g) |If U, then monomorphemic reflexives can take long-distance antecedents whereas polymorphemic reflexives cannot in living languages.$|_S = 1$
$|\sim$ (Monomorphemic reflexives can take long-distance antecedents whereas polymorphemic reflexives cannot in living languages.)$|_{I_f} = 0.9$

$0.949 \leq |\sim U|_{I_g} \leq 0.95$

Therefore, U has become highly implausible on the basis of the indirect sources (f) and (g). Subbarao achieved similar results for Oriya (see Subbarao 1998: 19). Therefore, the implausibility of the universal-candidate has increased.

If the plausibility of the second premise above is judged on the basis of all languages mentioned, then this set of sources does not make it possible to assign a plausibility value to this hypothesis according to (11)(d) in Section 9.3. Thus, one cannot build an indirect source on this set of sources which would enable one to judge the plausibility of the universal examined.

Nevertheless, one may take into consideration the latent background assumption of inferences (b) and (d) saying that monomorphemic reflexives can take long-distance antecedents whereas polymorphemic reflexives cannot in every living language besides Chinese, Korean, English, Italian and Icelandic. By estimating the plausibility value of the conclusion of these inferences, we supposed that this statement is of neutral plausibility in the sense of (6)(e). As inference (f) has shown, this is not the case. Consequently, the inferences (b)–(e) are no more capable of making their conclusion plausible. Thus, U should be given up and $\sim U$ should be kept. This decision would lead, however, to information loss since, as we have seen, there are languages in which U seems to hold true. In such situations, there seems to be a better strategy: we should clarify the criteria which make it possible to decide which languages belong to the group where U is valid and which to the other where $\sim U$ holds. That is, one may attempt to divide the set of sources into smaller sets of sources and to refine the original hypothesis.

9.8 The p-context-dependence of plausible inferences

As we have seen in Section 9.2, deductive inferences are purely formal in the sense that the fulfilment of the logical consequence relation is not influenced by any new information that is related to the plausibility of the premises of the given inference. Nevertheless, revealing the logical structure of the premises and the conclusion, and via this, the decision as to whether there is a logical consequence relation between the latter depends on the logical system applied and the translation of the sentences from natural language.

In contrast, demonstrative inferences are not formal in the above sense, since they require that one is in possession of sources that secure the truth of the premises. If the reliability of these sources decreases or vanishes, or one intends to determine the plausibility value of the premises on the basis of a wider set of sources that does not judge them unanimously, then the conclusion can no longer be deemed to be true with certainty.

The same holds for plausible inferences as well. As we have seen in the previous section, plausibility values cannot be considered to be fixed, since new pieces of information may strengthen or weaken the plausibility of the premises. Therefore, the plausibility of the conclusion may change dynamically as well. With inferences belonging to the second or third group, the plausibility of the premises, as we have seen, is not capable of securing the plausibility of the conclusion, but latent background assumptions are also needed.

Moreover, the applicability of different types of inferences may be influenced by the situation in which one intends to use them. If, for instance, one needs a conclusion that is true with certainty, then one cannot be satisfied with the application of plausible inferences. This means that the applicability of inferences depends, albeit to a considerably different extent, on a number of factors that have to be considered to be a relevant part of their evaluation. So far, we have used the term 'context' without explication. These considerations underlie the following definition of the notion of *p-context*:

(36) The **p-context** covers
(a) the accepted methodological norms, for instance, the criteria of the acceptability of the statements, the permissible type(s) of inferences, methodological rules pertaining to the relevant characteristics of the accepted inference types (the useable logical, semantic etc. systems, the methods of the translation of the sentences from natural language to some logical and semantic system), the methods of the treatment of contradictions, the criteria for the judgement of the reliability of sources etc.;
(b) the direct and indirect sources (inferences) judged as reliable on the basis of the criteria in (a);
(c) statements and their relevant characteristics at one's disposal according to (a) and (b),[46] or some subset of this set.

From (36)(c) it follows that, on the one hand, only statements possessing relevant characteristics belong to the p-context; on the other hand, the p-context may contain manifold instances of a given statement whose plausibility value originates from different sources or whose logical structure has been revealed with the help of diverse logical systems.

Motivation and background

In the sense of (36), all types of plausible inferences presented are p-context-dependent but to a different extent:

- Although deductive inferences are the least p-context-dependent, they are p-context-dependent from three important points of view. First, they can be used in situations in which one need not 'actually' know the truth value of the conclusion, but it is enough to know it hypothetically, only by supposing the truth of the premises. They do not depend on the 'actual' truth or plausibility value of the statements. Second, one can only draw those deductive inferences whose premises are included in the p-context. Third, the logical tools employed to reveal the logical structure of the premises and the conclusion and to check the presence of the logical consequence relation may vary from p-context to p-context.
- Demonstrative inferences are p-context-dependent to a greater extent, since besides the second and the third p-context-dependent characteristic of deductive inferences, they possess two further ones. First, demonstrative inferences can be created only from premises that are true with certainty according to some set of sources in the given p-context. Second, the certainty of the conclusion is not absolute and final, but only relative for several reasons. It indirectly depends on the certainty of the premises; therefore, if the reliability of the sources guaranteeing the truth of the premises decreases or vanishes, the plausibility value of the conclusion reduces or vanishes as well. The extension of the set of sources

guaranteeing the certainty of the premises by sources which judge the premises to be implausible or false with certainty leads to a situation where – in the sense of (11)(d) – on the basis of this wider set of sources, no plausibility value can be assigned to the premises at issue. From this it follows that this inference is no longer capable of providing support to its conclusion. Furthermore, the p-context may contain direct or indirect sources that also assign a plausibility value to the conclusion of the given inference; it may happen, for example, that another source deems the conclusion false with certainty. In this case, the given inference is only one of the sources on the basis of which the plausibility of the conclusion can be judged in the given p-context.

- Plausible inferences are strongly p-context-dependent. With plausible inferences of the first type, this is partly due to the same factors as in the case of demonstrative inferences. In the case of plausible inferences, however, the premises do not have to be true with certainty, and one may draw such inferences if the conclusion is not required to be certain but may be only plausible. Therefore, the extension of the set of sources supporting the plausibility of the premises may change (increase) the plausibility value of the premises. In such cases, the conclusion becomes more plausible, too. Plausible inferences belonging to the second and third group are also p-context-dependent in a 'negative way' as well: since the latent background assumptions have to be at least of neutral plausibility, one can often only demand that they either cannot be identified or they must not be implausible or false. The fulfilment of these criteria is, of course, heavily influenced by the range of the sources that have been taken into consideration.

Examples 20(1)–(3)

(1) The first premise of the demonstrative inference in Example 9(2) (*The defendant had attempted to commit a robbery*) was deemed to be true with certainty by the judge because he regarded eyewitness testimonies as perfectly reliable sources. If, however, the defendant's lawyer destroys the credibility of some of the witnesses in his speech (for example, he proves that one of them has committed perjury and finds out that another is a chronic alcoholic), then he modifies the p-context insofar as he decreases the reliability of the set of sources determining the plausibility value of the first premise, and via this, the plausibility of this premise as well. Thus, in this modified p-context, the plausibility of the conclusion will decrease, too:

$0 < |$The defendant had attempted to commit a robbery.$|_{S'} < 1$
$|$If somebody attempts to commit a robbery, then he has to receive a prison sentence.$|_{S'} = 1$

$0 < |$The defendant has to receive a prison sentence.$|_{I} < 1$

If the lawyer manages to find a new witness who provides a different description of the bank robber, and this testimony is added to the set of sources consisting of the testimonies, then this set of sources becomes unsuitable, since it does not judge the first premise unanimously (see (5) in Section 9.3). Therefore, in this p-context, no indirect source (plausible inference) can be established with reference to the testimonies as a set of sources. Nevertheless, the latter may be divided into two sets of sources: the testimonies of the prosecution and those of the defence. According to the first group, the first premise is plausible, while the second group deems it implausible. The conclusions point in opposite directions, too: in the opinion of the prosecution, the prison sentence seems to be well founded, while according to the defence, it does not. It is left to the judge to resolve the inconsistency.

(2) As we have already mentioned, a given inference is usually only one of the relevant sources when judging the plausibility of the conclusion. This characteristic of plausible inferences can be nicely illustrated with the help of implicational universals. We will see that the usability (motivatedness) of plausible inferences in a given p-context also depends on what further (direct and indirect) sources are present in the p-context which assign a plausibility value to the conclusion of the inference.

Let's revert to the linguistic universals mentioned in Example 12:

(U) For every language, if there is a pronominal reflexive for the first person, then there is also one for the second person. If there is a pronominal reflexive for the second person, then there is also one for the third person. (Plank 2008: 165; Faltz 1985: 120; Comrie 1981: 19)

The two components of conditionals (if *A*, then *B*) in implicational universals are related in such a way that the presence of *A* involves the presence of *B*. *A* and *B* are both statements that can be checked easily in a language – in this case, *A* is the hypothesis that there is a pronominal reflexive for the first person in a language, while *B* is the statement that there is also one for the second and the third person, respectively. They are supposed to bear no causal relationship to each other, but they are regarded as inductive generalisations based on the investigation of a few languages. That is, one states only that in the presence of *A*, *B* is always present, too.

The following inference pertains to the first type of plausible inferences:

(a) $|$If U, and there is a pronominal reflexive for the first person in language X, then there is also one for the second and third person, respectively.$|_S = 1$
$0 < |U|_S < 1$
$|$In language X, there is a pronominal reflexive for the first person.$|_S = 1$

$0 < |$In language X, there is a pronominal reflexive for the second and the third person, respectively.$|_I < 1$

Although (a) satisfies all criteria for plausible inferences as summarised in (27), it cannot be used as an indirect source allowing the determination of the plausibility value of the statement in the conclusion. Since we are in possession of a perfectly reliable source supporting the conclusion, (a) would be pointless and unmotivated. It is not B (that is, the second clause of the implicational universal) that has to be tested but the universal-candidate U. This can be done with the help of (b) or (c) – depending on which statements (and plausibility values) are contained in the p-context at our disposal. If we know that in the language X, there is a pronominal reflexive for the third person, then we can set up the following indirect source, and the p-context can be extended with the conclusion of this inference:

(b) $|$If U, and there is a pronominal reflexive for the first person in language X, then there is also one for the second and the third person, respectively.$|_S = 1$
$|$In language X, there are pronominal reflexives for the first, the second and the third person as well.$|_S = 1$

$0 < |U|_I < 1$

We know from another source that the second premise is true with certainty; the first premise is true with certainty, too, since the second clause is a special case of the first one. Nevertheless, inference (b) contains latent background assumptions as well, which cannot be regarded as true with certainty, as we have shown in Example 12 in Section 9.5.3.

This inference extends the p-context, since by supporting U's plausibility, it increases the plausibility value of U along the lines of (11)(a).

If, however, the p-context includes the information that there is no pronominal reflexive for the third person in language X, then (c) presents itself:

(c) $|$If U, and there is a pronominal reflexive for the first person in language X, then there is also one for the second and the third person, respectively.$|_S = 1$
$|$In language X, there is a pronominal reflexive for the first and second person, respectively, but there is no pronominal reflexive for the third person.)$|_S = 1$

$|{\sim}U|_I = 1$

Since we know that the second premise is true with certainty (this is the case if we treat statements capturing the characteristic of language X at issue as perfectly reliable sources), U has to be judged to be false with certainty.

There is an asymmetry between (b) and (c): while (b) makes U only plausible, (c) makes it false with certainty.

(3) In most cases, inferences in favour and against a hypothesis behave symmetrically in the sense that one of them makes it plausible and the other one implausible. That is, they neither prove nor falsify it but support or oppose it to some extent. One reason for this is that in most cases the antecedent of linguistic hypotheses formulated as conditional statements does not capture the necessary conditions of the consequent exhaustively; thus, it is not sufficient to guarantee the truth of the latter. For instance:

(a) $0 <$ $|$We systematically talk about arguments in terms of war.$|_S < 1$
$0 <$ $|$If we systematically talk about arguments in terms of war, then there is a tightly structured mapping from the conceptual domain WAR to the conceptual domain ARGUMENT when we talk about arguments.$|_S < 1$

$0 <$ $|$There is a tightly structured mapping from the conceptual domain WAR to the conceptual domain ARGUMENT when we talk about arguments.$|_I < 1$

The consequent of the second premise formulates only one possible cause of the statement in the first premise. Thus, we cannot state that the truth of the antecedent is not compatible with the falsity of the consequent.

A further recurrent manifestation of the uncertainty of 'linguistic facts' is that theories do not confront their hypotheses with certainly true 'linguistic facts' or 'raw data' but with representations of linguistic utterances, that is, with statements that describe a certain aspect of the language investigated with the help of some theoretical apparatus, therefore, with plausible hypotheses again. Thus, phonological theories apply phonological representations, syntactic theories interpret sentences with the help of the notions of GB theory or of some version of LFG etc.

The uncertainty of introspective data (for example, in generative grammar) is partly due to the circumstance that people's linguistic intuition is not uniform and its reliability is strongly influenced by several factors (see Sternefeld 2007).

9.9 The heuristic function of plausible inferences

It is no accident that plausible inferences are very often used in both scientific inquiry and everyday thinking. The latent background assumptions that influence the plausibility of the conclusion are not only responsible for the uncertainty and fallibility of the conclusion, but they also make it possible for the conclusion to state *more* than the information content of the premises (see, for instance, Polya 1948: 221; Rescher 1976: 60ff., 97ff.). As a result, plausible inferences are *heuristic tools* of problem solving that can provide us with new pieces of information.[47] Their function is to find solutions to current problems which are, due to their fallibility, not final, only provisional, but still the most acceptable in a given information state in comparison with other alternatives.

Example 21

Induction (analogy) is one of the most frequently used plausible inferences. Starting from individual cases, inductive inferences bring us to general hypotheses, as in the following case (see Kiefer 2007: 349f.):

$0 <$ |The sentence *Peter forgot that the key was in his pocket* contains a factive predicate, and the sentence has a presupposition.$|_S < 1$
$0 <$ |The sentence *Ann was angry that Peter arrived late* contains a factive predicate, and the sentence has a presupposition.$|_S < 1$
$0 <$ |The sentence *Ann is happy because Steve arrived* contains a factive predicate, and the sentence has a presupposition.$|_S < 1$

$0 <$|If a sentence contains a factive predicate, then the sentence has a presupposition.$|_I < 1$

The structure of the above inference can be reconstructed as follows:

$0 < |a_1$ possesses properties S and $T.|_S < 1$
$0 < |a_2$ possesses properties S and $T.|_S < 1$
$0 < |a_3$ possesses properties S and $T.|_S < 1$
[$0 <$ |Every x distinct from a_1, a_2, a_3 possessing characteristic S exhibits characteristic T as well.$|_S < 1$]

$0 <$ |Every x possessing characteristic S exhibits characteristic T as well.$|_I < 1$

The information content of the conclusion clearly exceeds that of the premises, since it involves the content of the latent background assumption as well.

9.10 Conclusions

In the present chapter we laid the foundations of the p-model by outlining a novel approach to plausible inference. After having clarified the basic notions of 'plausible statement', 'inference', 'deductive inference', 'demonstrative inference' and 'plausible inference', we discussed the properties of the latter. To sum up our considerations:

(37) Plausible inferences are
 (a) fallible,
 (b) dynamic,
 (c) p-context dependent, and
 (d) perform heuristic functions.

Among the insights of the present chapter, it is of special importance to highlight the nature of plausibility values. One of the most important characteristics of plausibility values is that they are capable of indicating the *changes* in the reliability of hypotheses as a consequence of changes in the p-context. The introduction of the notion of 'plausible inference' and the methods presented to 'calculate' the plausibility of the conclusion on the basis of the plausibility values of the premises and other characteristics of the given inference make it possible to determine which elements of the p-context influence the plausibility of a given statement and to what extent. Besides, it is important to remark that these 'rules' (see (11), (29)–(31)) leave ample room to choose the degree of the refinement of the estimation of the plausibility values. Thus, one may set looser or stricter limits and provide only rough or even more refined estimates. The aim is not to make linguists do calculations in every case but to make them reflect on the fact that they use hypotheses and other statements of different strengths and of different grades of uncertainty.

Nevertheless, the elaboration of the 'numerical' details of the model is also motivated by the need to legitimise the p-model by showing that it is feasible and theoretically well founded. Moreover, there are research situations where more exact 'calculations' might be useful tools.

Relying on these findings, now we are in a position to take the next step which will lead from plausible inferences to plausible argumentation.

10 Plausible argumentation

10.1 Overview

Chapter 10 expands the framework introduced in Chapter 9 by the notion of *plausible argumentation*. Plausible argumentation is a process aiming at the gradual transformation of a problematic (incomplete and/or inconsistent) informational state into one that is no longer (or at least less) problematic. It is a complex process which makes use of plausible inferences during the successive re-evaluation of the information at hand. Its aim is to detect the available solutions to a given problem or problems and to decide which of them is to be accepted.

The argumentation process is basically *not linear*, because in order to find all available solutions, one has to turn back to the initial problem and try another route. Moreover, the re-evaluation of the information one has access to usually does not lead immediately to the solution of the initial problem(s) but it gets stuck. In such situations one has to revise one's latest decisions and return to some earlier stage of the argumentation process in order to choose another route. Therefore, throughout the argumentation process one returns to the problems at issue again and again, and re-evaluates the earlier decisions about the acceptance or rejection of statements, the reliability of the sources, the plausibility values of the statements, the workability of methodological norms, the conclusions previously reached by inferences etc. In sum: one *retrospectively re-evaluates* the information at issue.

Retrospective re-evaluation is *cyclic* in nature. However, it is not only cyclic but also *prismatic*. This means that the cycles continuously change the perspective from which the pieces of information constituting the p-context are evaluated.

The cyclic and prismatic retrospective re-evaluation is realised by the application of a series of *problem-solving strategies*. Besides being *effective* in that it yields the solution of problems, the effectiveness of the process of plausible argumentation may in certain cases turn into ineffectiveness and lead to *fallacies*.

10.2 Informational under- and overdetermination, problems and their solution

In Section 9.3, we said that one can assign a plausibility value to statements in two ways: either directly, that is, on the basis of the reliability of their source, or in an indirect way, starting from statements whose plausibility values are known, with the help of plausible or demonstrative inferences. As already mentioned, in certain cases one has to deal with *informational overdetermination*: the sources in the p-context include too much information in the sense that the statements originating from them cannot be true at the same time (see Rescher 1976: 2; Rescher & Brandom 1980: 3ff.).[1] For instance, the p-context contains a statement *p* that is plausible on the basis of some sources, and implausible on the basis of others. In such cases, the p-context becomes p-inconsistent, since both *p* and ~*p* are plausible statements:

(38) The p-**context** ***C*** is called **p-inconsistent** if there is a statement *p* such that both *p* and ~*p* have a positive plausibility value according to any source[2] in *C*.[3]

Nevertheless, it is also possible that the p-context is incomplete, since the sources provide too little information in the sense that there are statements that are neither true or false with certainty, nor plausible or implausible in the given p-context. In this case, one is dealing with *informational underdetermination* (see Rescher & Brandom 1980: 3ff.). In this sense, all p-contexts are underdetermined, since they do not assign a plausibility value to every possible statement. Still, manifestations of underdetermination are unequal in weight. One tries to eliminate them only if the statement at issue is considered relevant. In such cases, one attempts to find sources with the help of which it can be decided whether this statement can be regarded as plausible, implausible, or even true or false with certainty. It is possible that – at least at the outset – one fails to find reliable, relevant and suitable sources (see (6)(e), (10)(c)). Therefore, we will deal with a special case of informational underdetermination when the p-context contains a statement *p* such that *p* is of neutral plausibility on the basis of the totality of sources which make it possible to assign a plausibility value to it, and the same is true of its negation, ~*p* as well:

(39) The **p-context *C* is p-incomplete** if it contains a statement *p* such that $|p|_{S_1} = 0$ and $|{\sim}p|_{S_2} = 0$, where S_1 is the set of the sources on the basis of which a plausibility value can be assigned to *p* and S_2 is the set of sources on the basis of which a plausibility value can be assigned to ~*p*.

It is important to remark that p-incompleteness may be eliminated in certain cases with the help of information obtained from direct or indirect sources of the p-context that have not yet been taken into consideration. A p-context can be informationally under- and overdetermined at the same time; it can be p-inconsistent in relation to certain statements as well as p-incomplete in connection with other ones.

Instances of p-inconsistency and p-incompleteness are called *p-problems*. A *p-context* is *p-problematic* if it is p-inconsistent and/or p-incomplete.

Motivation and background

The concept of 'problem' is itself problematic, since its definition is fraught with difficulties. Therefore, the above description cannot be regarded as a definition.

There are, of course, several other types of problems. For example, the concept of 'informational underdetermination' can be easily and naturally extended to cases where a statement is plausible according to the sources in the p-context but for its acceptance, a higher plausibility value is required. Such situations occur typically in mathematics, where one cannot be content with conjectures but hypotheses have to be proved, that is, made true with certainty. A third and more basic type of problem – preceding cases of informational over/underdetermination mentioned so far in the problem-solving process – is when one cannot decide whether a set of criteria can be satisfied at the same time, and if so, then how. Polya calls them, in contrast to 'problems to prove', 'problems to find'. For instance, one has to find those values of the variables x and y which are the solutions of the system of equations $x^2 + y^2 = 25; x - y = 1$; or the task is to find the line that is at an equal distance from a circle and a line etc. A fourth problem type which is also closely related to p-problematicness consists of cases when one wants to find those p-contexts in which a given hypothesis is plausible. To put it otherwise, it is to find out how the scope of an overgenerating hypothesis can be narrowed down. Undergenerating hypotheses raise a similar problem as well: namely, how they can be complemented by further hypotheses/conditions in such a way that they no longer undergenerate. Of course, there are several other types of problems as well.

The concept of 'p-problem' and 'p-problematicness' can be generalised: p-contexts characterised by informational over- and/or underdetermination can be regarded as problematic. P-problematicness is a special case of problematicness that covers instances of problems that are *explicit* (identified) and *related to plausibility values*. A set of statements can be, of course, implicitly inconsistent; this means that it does not contain a contradictory pair of statements. Indeed, such cases do not belong to the scope of (38). Similarly, it may happen that one has not yet tried to assign a plausibility value to a statement important for some reason; thus neither it nor its negation possesses a plausibility value.

One's aim is to eliminate or at least reduce the informational over- and/or underdetermination by starting from the information involved in the p-context, that is, to find the solutions (see (40)) and the resolution of the p-problems (see (41)):

(40) The **solution to a p-problem** is a p-context in which

(a) the statement generating the given instance of p-inconsistency or p-incompleteness is either plausible or implausible (in the extreme case: true/false with certainty),

or

(b) the statements generating p-inconsistency can be represented in such a way that they become separated systematically and this separation is well motivated.[4]

(40)(a) means that the sources are unanimously for or against the statement generating p-inconsistency or p-incompleteness.

Examples 22(1)–(2)

(1) The linguistic universal in Example 4(1) is plausible according to Head's (1978) investigations into more than 100 languages. Simon (1997), however, deems *U* implausible because he shows that German data from the eighteenth–nineteenth centuries do not support this hypothesis. These two sources make the context p-inconsistent. A possible solution to this p-problem in the sense of (40)(a) may be to keep only Head (1978) and question the reliability of Simon (1997) – this can only be done, however, in possession of strong enough arguments. That is, it should be shown that Simon's (1997) analyses are faulty. Another solution to this p-problem in the sense of (40)(a) is the reverse of the former proposal: to doubt Head's (1978) reliability because it does not cover the examination of older language states and, therefore, it does not rely on an appropriately wide range of data. Namely, as we have seen in Examples 4(1), 12, 19 and 20(2), tests of universal-candidates with a positive outcome rely on plausible inferences belonging to Type 2 or 3. Therefore, they make use of latent background assumptions stating that the test would be positive in the case of languages which have not been examined yet, and assign them the plausibility value 0. Simon (1997), however, shows that this assumption is not of neutral plausibility but is implausible. Not even in this case must *U* be given up; one might try to find criteria with the help of which its scope can be narrowed down to cases where it is satisfied. This could lead to a solution in the sense of (40)(b). See also Examples 19 and 23(1).

(2) A heavily discussed p-problem of metaphor research is, for example, whether or not there is only one mechanism of cognitive metaphor processing for all metaphors. Therefore, the p-context of cognitive metaphor research is p-inconsistent because it contains sources on the basis of which the statement *There is only one mechanism of metaphor processing for all metaphors* is plausible, as well as sources which deem the negation of this statement plausible. The conceptual metaphor theory of Lakoff and Johnson or Gluckberg's property attribution theory, for instance, presuppose this hypothesis and seem to regard it to be true with certainty. As opposed to this standpoint, Gentner's structure mapping theory argues that there are different processing mechanisms in the case of conventional and novel metaphors. This approach presents several indirect sources in support of the negation of the above-mentioned hypothesis and argues for its rejection. This means that the two groups of theories propose rival solutions for the treatment of this p-problem.

In order to work out a solution to a p-problem, one has to transform the p-context: new information has to be gained from the sources in the p-context, the reliability of the sources has to be revised, some of them even have to be declared unreliable etc. In this way, statements that have been considered plausible so far may turn out to be implausible or vice versa. Hence, if one tries to solve a problem, *new problems may emerge*, and the p-context may become problematic again. Attempts to solve these new problems may lead to further problems, and so on. Therefore, one arrives at different solutions to the given p-problem which may contain more or less new p-problems. This necessitates the introduction of a further concept:

(41) The **resolution of a p-problem** is one of the solutions to the given p-problem in the sense of (40) so that according to the accepted criteria it is better than the other solutions which can be put forward on the basis of the information at hand.

Motivation and background

(41) relies on two, closely related preconditions. On the one hand, its application requires a system of criteria allowing for the comparison and ranking of rival solutions. On the other hand, problems are usually not of equal weight: some of them have to be resolved, while others can be – at least temporarily – tolerated.[5]

Examples 23(1)–(2)

(1) In Example 22(1), the alternative deeming U implausible seems to be the resolution of the given p-problem on the basis of the literature presented so far. As we have seen, the reliability of the indirect sources supporting U has to be re-evaluated, because they rely on latent background assumptions which turned out to be implausible instead of being of neutral plausibility. Thus, only $\sim U$ remains plausible. Nevertheless, further argumentation cycles should be carried out in order to examine whether there is a solution in the sense of (40)(b). This could be a better solution because it provides an account of cases where U holds.

(2) The resolution of the p-problem presented in Example 22(2) is a more complicated task, since all rival solutions refer to a series of direct and indirect sources (such as results of psycholinguistic experiments) in order to support their standpoint and weaken that of the others. The state of the art can be characterised in such a way that there are several alternative solutions but none of them can be regarded as the resolution of the p-problem at issue (see Gentner & Bowdle 2008; Bowdle & Gentner 2005; Glucksberg 2003; Glucksberg & McGlone 2001; Dodge & Lakoff 2005; Gibbs 2006; Gibbs & Perlman 2006; Rohrer 2006).

To find the solutions and the resolution of a p-problem, a *heuristic tool* is needed which provides clear guidelines and criteria for the accomplishment and control of the transformation and evaluation of the p-context.

10.3 The notion of 'plausible argumentation'

As a first approximation, plausible argumentation is the gradual transformation of a p-problematic p-context into one that is no longer (or at least less) p-problematic. The p-context which contains the initial p-problems will be called the *starting p-context*; the p-context at which the transformation process comes to an end is the *final p-context*. That is, we introduce the notion of plausible argumentation as follows:

(42) By **plausible argumentation**, we mean a process which develops *rival solutions* in the sense of (40) to the p-problems included in the starting p-context and terminates when their *resolution* in the sense of (41) has been achieved.

From (42) it follows that the process of plausible argumentation seeks as many solutions to the p-problems in the starting p-context as possible within the given informational state, and tries to find out which one is the most acceptable of them according to a certain set of criteria. This means in most cases that the decision among the available solutions is not final, only provisional, but is the most acceptable compared to other alternatives.

If the p-context is *p-incomplete* in the sense of (39), then first new direct/indirect sources have to be found that make it possible to assign a positive plausibility value to the given statement or to its negation. If these sources make only one of the rival statements plausible, then the resolution of the p-problem in question has been obtained. Nevertheless, it is often the case that both a given statement and its negation are made plausible by some sources or sets of sources, and the informational underdetermination leads to informational overdetermination.

If the starting p-context is *p-inconsistent* in the sense of (38), then one has to strive to find sources which make one or another component of the contradiction plausible. In a second step, the acceptability of these sources (in the case of direct sources, their reliability, and in the case of indirect sources the plausibility of the premises and the latent background assumptions in the given p-context) has to be revised. A choice between the two members of the contradiction is possible if the reliability of the sources for one of them can be questioned, and these sources as well as the statements supported by them can be eliminated from the p-context. In such cases, one arrives at a possible solution of the p-problem. It cannot be ruled out, however, that new information originating from further sources undermines the acceptability of the sources which this solution is based on. They may also call the arguments into question which led us to deem certain sources unreliable or invited us to consider statements applied as premises implausible, etc. In this way, new rival solutions may emerge.

Accordingly, conducting the process of plausible argumentation may be a highly complex task. First, a p-context may contain numerous p-problems. Second, as we have already seen in Section 10.2, the search for the solution to a p-problem may give rise to the emergence of further p-problems. Third, initiation of new sources or changes in the reliability of the sources may alter the plausibility of certain statements. As a consequence of the dynamism and the p-context-dependence of plausible inferences presented in Sections 9.7 and 9.8, this may lead to changes in the plausibility value of further statements as well.

Therefore, in order to reach a well-founded decision among the solutions developed, one weighs up simultaneously a series of points of view in order to find that solution which seems to be the best on the basis of the *totality* of these viewpoints. One takes into consideration, among other things, how problematic the solutions are, how comprehensive they are in the sense of how many statements and sources they involve, how serious their p-problems are, or which of them contains a relatively high number of statements with high plausibility and a relatively smaller set of statements of low plausibility value etc. The argumentation process terminates – at least provisionally – when all achievable solutions in the given informational state have been found, elaborated and compared, and one is either able to decide which of them can be regarded as a resolution of the starting p-problems, or one shows that there is no such solution. Nevertheless, new information might necessitate the continuation of the argumentation process.

Due to the complexity of the process sketched, in the following subsections we will discuss the constitutive properties of plausible argumentation separately: its subdivision into argumentation cycles, its prismatic nature, the problem-solving strategies it makes use of and its heuristic effectiveness. Let us turn to its cyclic structure first.

10.4 The cyclic nature of plausible argumentation

The above characterisation of plausible argumentation indicates that the argumentation process is basically *not linear*, but rather, it is a series of *argumentation cycles*. First, as we have seen in Section 10.3, one cannot be content with the development of a single solution but one has to try to reveal *all available solutions*. Since these solutions are different *re-evaluated versions* of the starting p-context, the argumentation process may turn back to the p-problems included in the starting p-context in order to search for a new solution. Second, the re-evaluation of the p-context usually does not lead immediately to the solution of the initial p-problem(s), either. It may happen that the argumentation process seems to reach a dead end and one has to revise the latest decisions and return to some earlier stage of the re-evaluation of the p-context in order to choose another route. Third, a given solution to the starting p-problem(s) is not necessarily a non-problematic p-context, since – as we have already shown in Section 10.2 – the argumentation process may raise further p-problems. In such cases, it has to be examined whether these newer p-problems are resolvable. Thus, at this point the argumentation process will branch into different paths towards possible solutions to these newer p-problems.

All three cases require the revision of previous decisions, the consideration of new perspectives, the assessment of other alternatives etc., that is, the *repeated re-evaluation of the p-context*. Consequently, argumentation is a *cyclic* process that returns to the given problems again and again, and revises former decisions (see Rescher 1987, 1977a, 1979: 73). In the course of the *cyclic returns*, one's aim is to gradually eliminate hypotheses that are unacceptable for some reason and to get rid of, or at least to reduce, the p-problematicness of the p-context on the basis of different – sometimes even contradictory – considerations.[6]

As illustrated in Figure 2, argumentation cycles consist of three main stages.

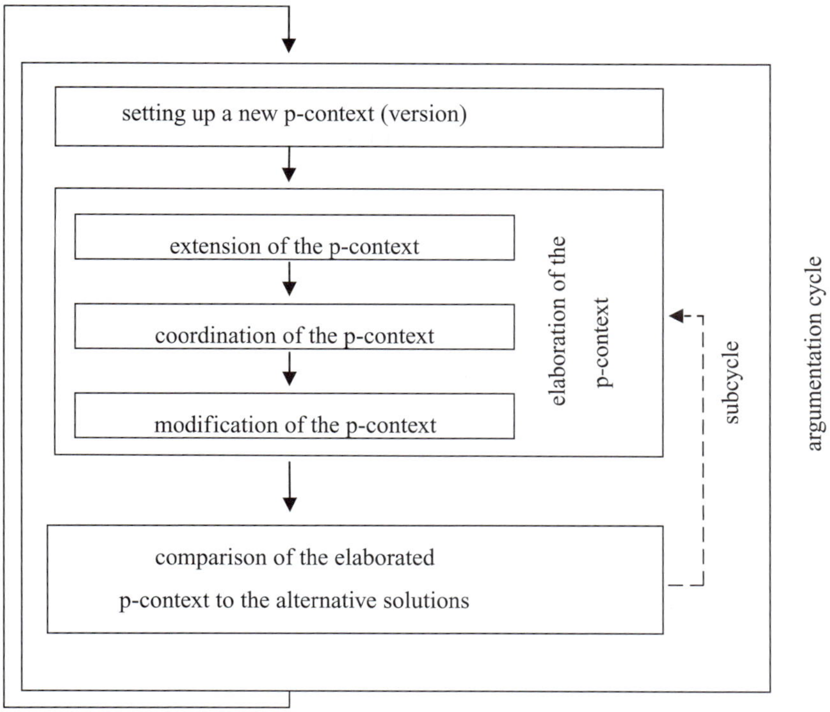

Figure 2. The structure of the argumentation cycle

First, a new p-context version has to be *set up*. This is in most cases a twofold task. On the one hand, hypotheses, sources and methodological norms are presented which one accepts and which are regarded as the starting points of the next stage (cycle) of the argumentation process. On the other hand, one revises some elements of the earlier cycle(s) and reduces the p-context by their elimination. The new p-context version may contain the starting p-problem (that is, it may cover both members of a p-inconsistency or remain p-incomplete), it may be developed around one of the rival hypotheses by omitting the other one, it may be the continuation of an earlier p-context variant (that is, the argumentation process may turn back to an earlier stage), or it may combine and develop two alternative p-context versions in parallel but systematically separated.

Second, the new p-context version has to be *elaborated*. With this aim in view, one has to search for pieces of information from the direct and indirect sources in the p-context that seem to be relevant to the solution of the starting p-problem(s). That is, the p-context has to be *extended* in such a way that relevant characteristics (plausibility values) are assigned to further statements with the help of direct sources not used so far and by drawing new inferences, or methods not yet used are applied, or new criteria are made use of, etc. The extended p-context has to be *coordinated*: the plausibility values of statements stemming from the old and the new sources, their relevant characteristics, as well as old and new pieces of information related to the reliability of the sources have to be compared. Then, the coordinated context has to be *modified*; one has to work out the p-context that will be regarded as the revised, re-evaluated version of the starting p-context, as a *solution* to the starting p-problem. For example, one has to determine the plausibility value of the statements on the basis of the sources available; a decision has to be taken as to which sources should be considered unreliable, and the information originating from them has to be omitted; certain methodological norms have to be abandoned or modified or new ones have to be accepted; on the basis of these new norms, further sources can be deemed reliable and may be used etc.

Third, the elaborated p-context version has to be *compared* to its rivals: is it a better solution of the starting p-problem, is it a resolution (that is, the best solution available) or not? If it is no better than the solutions obtained in the earlier cycles, then a new cycle has to be started; if it is not yet a solution, then one has to turn back to this cycle and further elaborate it by starting a new subcycle. In sum:

(43) **An argumentation cycle**

(a) is a phase of the plausible argumentation process which develops *a new solution* in the sense of (40) to the p-problems contained by the starting p-context and *examines* whether with this solution their resolution in the sense of (41) has been achieved;

(b) consists of the three main stages illustrated in Figure 2, and

(c) may have **subcycles** revising certain decisions made within the given argumentation cycle, and continuing the argumentation process by turning back to an earlier stage of the argumentation cycle.

Example 24

Schütze (2009: 154f.) presents an argumentation which consists of two cycles. *Cycle 1* starts with setting up the first p-context version by raising the problem addressed in Manning (2003) of whether an occurrence of the sequence *as least as* in a novel is part of English or is only a typo. Thus, the starting p-context is *p-inconsistent*, since both the statement

(P) The sequence *as least as* is not a typo but part of English.

and its negation are plausible on the basis of some source: *P* is supported by its presence in the novel, $\sim P$ by Manning's linguistic intuition as a source. Schütze cites Manning's argumentation aimed at resolving the p-inconsistency. Manning begins the *elaboration* of the first p-context version by *extending* the p-context by corpus data such as

(D_1) The sequence *as least as* cannot be found in 1994 *New York Times* newswire.
(D_2) There are 4 examples with the sequence *as least as* in 1995 *New York Times* newswire.
(D_3) There are 2 examples with the sequence *as least as* in 1996 *New York Times* newswire.
(D_4) There are hundreds of examples with the sequence *as least as* on the Web.
(D_5) The sequence *as least as* is about 175 times less common than *at least as* in the corpus investigated.
(D_6) There are several examples with the sequence *as least as* that can be found with *at least as* in a neighbouring sentence.
(D_7) Many of the examples with the sequence *as least as* on the Web appear in conjunction with an *as Adj as* construction.

Manning interprets the data D_2–D_4 as pieces of evidence for P. Although the passage cited by Schütze contains only hints rather than full-fledged arguments, it can be reconstructed as the following set of inferences:

The first inference makes use of D_2 and D_3 as premises; it also contains a latent background assumption:

(a) 0 < |If the sequence *as least as* is just a typo, then it should occur relatively rarely in the *New York Times* newswire.$|_M$ < 1[8]
|There are 4 occurrences of the sequence *as least as* in 1995 *New York Times* newswire.$|_M = 1$
|There are 2 occurrences of the sequence *as least as* in 1996 *New York Times* newswire.$|_M = 1$
[0 < |6 occurrences of the sequence *as least as* in 1995–96 *New York Times* newswire count as relatively many instances.$|_M$ < 1][9]

---

0 < |The sequence *as least as* is not a typo.$|_{I(a)}$ < 1

where M indicates Manning's text, its implications or presuppositions as a direct source. (a) is not deductively valid and two of its premises are only plausible; therefore, this inference belongs to Type 3 of plausible inferences (see Section 9.5.4). Thus, P becomes plausible.

Inference (b) comes to a similar conclusion on the basis of D_4, and increases P's plausibility:

(b) 0 < |If the sequence *as least as* is just a typo, then it occurs relatively rarely on the Web.$|_M$ < 1
|There are hundreds of examples with the sequence *as least as* on the Web.$|_M = 1$
[0 < |Hundreds of occurrences of the sequence *as least as* on the Web count as relatively many instances.$|_M$ < 1][10]

---

0 < |The sequence *as least as* is not a typo.$|_{I(b)}$ < 1

In relation to D_6, the following inference presents itself as a possible reconstruction of the inferences behind Manning's text:

(c) |The sequence *as least as* often occurs together with *at least as* in a neighbouring sentence.$|_M = 1$
$0 <$ |The sequence *as least as* is part of English and it has the same meaning as the sequence *at least as*.$|_M < 1$
[$0 <$ |If a linguistic construction occurs together with a similar form with the same meaning in a neighbouring sentence, then these forms show intraspeaker variation.$|_M < 1$]

$0 <$ |The sequences *as least as* and *at least as* show intraspeaker variation.$|_{I(c)} < 1$

In contrast to (a) and (b), (c) already presupposes *P* instead of concluding it from pieces of information given in the p-context. Manning's argumentation related to D_7 is similarly sketchy; a possible reconstruction is presented in (d):

(d) |The sequence *as least as* often appears in conjunction with the construction *as Adj as*.$|_M = 1$
$0 <$ |The sequence *as least as* is a new construction.$|_M < 1$[11]
[|If the sequence *as least as* is a new construction and it often appears in conjunction with the construction *as Adj as*, then it may have developed from the conjunction of *at least as* and *as Adj as*.$|_M = 0$]

$0 <$ |The sequence *as least as* may have developed from the conjunction of *at least as* and *as Adj as*.$|_{I(d)} < 1$

As the second premise shows, (d) presupposes *P* as well. Nevertheless, this inference provides further support for this hypothesis because its application has led to a plausible explanation of the historical development of the hypothesised new form *as least as*.

Manning's argumentation contains only one argument in favour of $\sim P$:

(e) $0 <$ |If the sequence *as least as* is just a typo, then it should occur relatively rarely in the *New York Times* newswire.$|_M < 1$[12]
|The sequence *as least as* cannot be found in 1994 *New York Times* newswire.$|_M = 1$

$0 <$ |The sequence *as least as* is a typo.$|_{I(e)} < 1$

The *coordination of the p-context* is simple: the initial plausibility of *P* as a conjecture was increased by two indirect sources, by inferences (a) and (b). Further, (c) and (d) show that this hypothesis can be easily connected to other hypotheses. Therefore, a coherent hypothesis system can be established. In contrast, $\sim P$ is supported by only one indirect source (by inference (e)).

Thus, by comparing the plausibility of P and $\sim P$, Manning rejects the latter and votes for the former hypothesis. This is the *modified (and final) p-context* elaborated by Manning.

Schütze, however, does not find this argumentation persuasive. His main concern is that Manning not only narrowed down his investigations to an exclusive application of the tools of corpus linguistics but he did this superficially insofar as instead of comparing the relative frequency of occurrences of *as least as* to some carefully chosen base rate, he interpreted the terms 'relative frequently/rarely' subjectively. Therefore, Schütze starts a new argumentation cycle by *revising* Manning's decisions at several points.

Schütze *sets up* a new p-context version in *Cycle 2* by pointing out that the p-context is *informationally underdetermined* in the sense that sources which could provide data relevant in judging the plausibility of $\sim P$ are missing from the p-context. Specifically, collecting intuitive judgements of native speakers about the acceptability of *as least as* could increase $\sim P$'s plausibility value to a large extent. Therefore, Schütze revises Manning's decision about the rejection of $\sim P$ and reintroduces it in the p-context. Then, he *extends the p-context* with new data whose initial plausibility originates from an intellectual source, namely, from his conjectures; of course, Schütze argues that this initial plausibility value has to be re-evaluated by experiments. As a second step, Schütze extends the p-context with a further datum, namely, with a hypothesis presenting an alternative explanation of the development of the sequence *as least as*. He points out that this explanation is in harmony with $\sim P$ instead of with P as it was the case with inference (d):

(f) $0 <$ |If the sequence *as least as* is a typo, then its development may be explained as a case of anticipatory substitution.|$_S < 1$
$0 <$ |The development of the sequence *as least as* may be explained as a case of anticipatory substitution insofar as a slip from *at least as* to *as least as* is an anticipation of the *s* triggered by the fact that at least two other *a–s* sequences need to be typed imminently in the same phrase, including one with the identical context (#_#), and sometimes three, in the frequent situation where the sequence *Adj as* follows *as least as*.|$_S < 1$

$0 <$ |*As least as* is a typo.|$_{I(f)} < 1$,

where S is Schütze's intuition as a direct source.

According to Schütze, both premises of (f) have to be assigned a high plausibility value. Therefore, he deems the conclusion very plausible, too.[13]

As a third step of Cycle 2, Schütze *re-evaluates* the plausibility of Manning's conclusions by revising the reliability of the indirect sources that support them. Namely, as we have seen, inferences (a) and (b) make use of latent background assumptions stating that the occurrences of the sequence *as least as* found in 1995–96 *New York Times* newswire and on the Web count as relatively many instances. Although Manning seems to assign a positive plausibility value to these statements, Schütze raises the problem that their acceptability heavily depends on the question of what 'relatively many' means in connection with the occurrences of *as least as*. It is clear that without further clarification, the number of occurrences alone cannot be interpreted properly and it remains only a subjective label. Thus, in order to reach a well-founded decision, Schütze proposes to conduct an experiment to reveal the relative frequency of typing *as least as* instead of *at least as* in the kinds of typing situations where they have been found on the Web. Experiment E is a direct source which might provide data allowing for the *re-evaluation* of the two latent background assumptions mentioned by making them more plausible or by showing them to be implausible and supporting the rival hypothesis:

(g) $0 <$ |If the relative frequency of the occurrence of *as least as* against *at least as* in typing situations is lower than its relative frequency in the corpus investigated by Manning, then *as least as* is part of English.|$_E < 1$
|The relative frequency of the occurrence of *as least as* against *at least as* in typing situations is lower than its relative frequency in the corpus investigated by Manning.|$_E = ?$

|*As least as* is part of English.|$_{I(g)} = ?$

(h) $0 <$ |If the relative frequency of the occurrence of *as least as* against *at least as* in typing situations is higher than its relative frequency in the corpus investigated by Manning, then *as least as* is a typo.|$_E < 1$
|The relative frequency of the occurrence of *as least as* against *at least as* in typing situations is higher than its relative frequency in the corpus investigated by Manning.|$_E = ?$

|*As least as* is a typo.|$_{I(h)} = ?$

Schütze reveals a further instance of *informational underdetermination* in the p-context after conducting Cycle 1. He reproaches Manning for an overhasty interpretation of the close occurrences of *at least as* and *as least as* as instances of intraspeaker variation (see the first latent background assumption of (c)) without clearing the relative frequency of neighbouring occurrences of two *as*-variants. He thinks that from D_5 and D_6 one can conclude that this frequency is rather low. From this he obtains the following system of inferences:

(i) $0 <$ |If the sequence *as least as* is about 175 times less common than *at least as* in the corpus investigated and there are several examples with the sequence *as least as* that can be found with *at least as* in a neighbouring sentence, then it is relatively rare to find the *as* variant used consistently within a passage.|$_S < 1$

|The sequence *as least as* is about 175 times less common than *at least as* in the corpus investigated.$|_S = 1$
|There are several examples with the sequence *as least as* that can be found with *at least as* in a neighbouring sentence.$|_S = 1$

---

0 < |It is relatively rare to find the *as* variant used consistently within a passage.$|_{I(i)} < 1$

(j) 0 < |If it is relatively rare to find the *as* variant used consistently within a passage, then *as least as* is a typo.$|_S < 1$
0 < |It is relatively rare to find the *as* variant used consistently within a passage.$|_{I(i)} < 1$

---

0 < |*As least as* is a typo.$|_{I(j)} < 1$

The *coordination* of the p-context yields the result that the plausibility of $\sim P$ is very high, while the plausibility of P is low. This seems to be a reasonable motivation to modify the p-context in such a way that one gives up P. After having *elaborated* the new p-context version in Cycle 2, Schütze *compares* the two p-context versions elaborated in Cycles 1 and 2, respectively. As a result, he comes to the opposite conclusion to Manning and judges the p-context version around $\sim P$ to be the better founded alternative. Therefore, he proposes to resolve the p-inconsistency of the starting p-context by giving up P and accepting the p-context version elaborated in Cycle 2.

During the argumentation process, the argumentation may divide into rival p-context versions, but it may return to a former p-context variant as well, elaborating new versions of it.[14] However, this *globally cyclic* process may, of course, have *local* stages which are related to each other *linearly*.

10.5 The prismatic nature of plausible argumentation

As we have seen in Section 10.4, the argumentation process examines and compares a series of p-context variants and solutions. Therefore, it is not only cyclic, but also *prismatic*, since, in the course of the cycles that constantly re-evaluate the information, one is trying to view the given problem from different, partly incompatible *perspectives* (Rescher 1987: 306f., 313; Polya 1981, vol. II: 68).[15]

The 'prism' through which, during the argumentation cycles, one re-evaluates the information at issue and/or views new pieces of information to be considered, has different sides which do not follow prefabricated patterns. However, the stages of the argumentation cycles discussed in the previous section are closely related to the following *basic types of perspectives*:

- diagnostic
- contrastive

- exclusive
- combinative
- evaluative.

There is no one single correct sequence of the application of the five perspectives. Within a relatively complicated argumentation process usually every perspective is taken many times. It may also happen that an argumentation process does not make use of all perspectives, and there may be considerable differences in terms of the length and depth of their usage.

In what follows we will elucidate the prismatic nature of plausible argumentation by characterising these kinds of perspectives.

By setting up the starting p-context, the p-context remains p-inconsistent because a decision based on the comparison of the plausibility of the conflicting statements (the rejection of the less plausible member of the p-inconsistency) would be premature and would not be well founded.[16] Instead, one attempts to reveal the nature and scope of the conflict; that is, one takes a *diagnostic perspective*. In order to find out which statements, sources, methodological principles etc. are involved in the conflict, one extends the problematic p-context by further elements. For example, the starting p-problem may arise from hypothesis testing: it may be the case that a hypothesis leads to a prediction which is evaluated to be false with certainty or implausible by some other source(s). In this case, one investigates further predictions of the hypothesis at issue, examines the source from which the hypothesis at issue and the contradictory datum originates, respectively, raises hypotheses which seem to be capable of providing an explanation of the 'disobedient' data and tries to reveal the relationship between the hypothesis and other hypotheses of the theory etc. It may also happen that the p-inconsistency of the p-context is triggered by hypotheses obtained from generalisations about different data sets.

With the continuous extension of the p-context by new, relevant elements and through revealing the relationship between the new and the old elements, the systems of statements and sources connected to the conflicting statements become more and more elaborated and differentiated. Thus, at a certain point of the coordination of the p-context, the direct and indirect sources, the methodological principles used and the statements and other elements which support the one and the other conflicting statements, respectively, may become connected to such an extent that they become integrated into unified, coherent, but only partially elaborated systems, into *germs of p-context versions*. A key stage of this process is that both these p-context version germs become organised around *rival hypotheses*, that is, around incompatible (contradictory or contrary) hypotheses from which the one and the other of the conflicting statements can be inferred, respectively.[17] These rival hypotheses are also involved in several indirect sources allowing for the judgement of the plausibility of further statements. Of course, it may also be the case that the two members of the p-inconsistency belong to *rival theories*; thus, they belong to two different systems of hypotheses, methodological principles etc. from the outset. In such cases, the diagnostic perspective is reduced to the presentation of the (from the point of view of the given p-inconsistency) relevant parts of the two theories.

Working within a diagnostic perspective usually does not lead to a solution of the starting p-problem. The conflicting statements, the sources supporting them, the methodological principles leading to incompatible hypotheses etc. fall within the same p-context and their separation is in most cases *not motivated* yet. Despite this, the *ad hoc* separation of the two p-context version germs organised around rival hypotheses fulfils three important tasks. First, it ensures that one does not draw conclusions from inconsistent sets of premises. Second, it is the first step towards a more comprehensive view of the p-problem at issue insofar as it becomes clearer and clearer that one has to compare p-context versions (that is, system of statements, sources, methodological norms, tools, etc.) instead of simply comparing two conflicting statements. Third, it paves the way for the adoption of further perspectives which may lead to possible solutions of the starting p-problem.

Example 25

The starting p-context in **Zubizarreta** (1982) is *p-incomplete* because neither the statement *H* nor its negation has a plausibility value assigned to it on the basis of the sources in the p-context:

(H) Modals behave in Spanish and Italian like main verbs (and unlike auxiliaries).
(~H) Modals behave in Spanish and Italian like non-main verbs.

Zubizarreta applies several tests which can provide useful information for the solution of this p-problem.

She takes a *diagnostic perspective* and tries to collect all sources that support *H* and its negation, respectively. Therefore, she *extends* the p-context by a series of indirect sources.

I. *H* is supported by the following indirect sources (systems of plausible inferences):

(a) $0 <$ |If modals allow for null-complement anaphora in Spanish, then the sentences *Juan podría/debería visitar a María y Pedro también podría/debería* are grammatically correct.|$_Z < 1$

$0 <$ |The sentences *Juan podría/debería visitar a María y Pedro también podría/debería* are grammatically correct.|$_Z < 1$

$0 <$ |Modals allow for null-complement anaphora in Spanish.|$_{I_a} < 1$[18]

(b) $0 < |$If auxiliaries allow for null-complement anaphora in Spanish, then the sentence *Juan ha visitado a María y Pedro también ha* is grammatically correct.$|_Z < 1$
$0 < |$The sentence *Juan ha visitado a María y Pedro también ha* is not grammatically correct.$|_Z < 1$

$0 < |$Auxiliaries do not allow for null-complement anaphora in Spanish.$|_{I_b} < 1$

(a) and (b) are plausible inferences: (a) belongs to Type 3 (see Section 9.5.4), because there is no logical consequence relation between its premises and the conclusion, and the premises are only plausible, while (b) is of Type 1, because it is deductively valid but its premises are not true with certainty. Therefore, they lead to a plausible conclusion.

Relying on the conclusions of (a) and (b), Zubizarreta draws the following inference:

(c) $0 < |$Main verbs allow for null-complement anaphora in Spanish.$|_Z < 1$
$0 < |$Modals allow for null-complement anaphora in Spanish.$|_{I_a} < 1$
$0 < |$Auxiliaries do not allow for null-complement anaphora in Spanish.$|_{I_b} < 1$
[$0 < |$If main verbs and modals allow for null-complement anaphora in Spanish while auxiliaries do not, then modals behave in Spanish like main verbs (and unlike auxiliaries).$|_Z < 1$]

$0 < |$Modals behave in Spanish like main verbs (and unlike auxiliaries).$|_{I_c} < 1$

On the basis of the indirect source (c), *H* has become plausible. The second system of inferences makes use of premises about the placement of negation:

(d) $0 < |$If the negation word is placed between the modal and the verb in Spanish, then the sentences *Pedro podría/debería no contestar la carta* are grammatically correct.$|_Z < 1$
$0 < |$The sentences *Pedro podría/debería no contestar la carta* are grammatically correct.$|_Z < 1$

$0 < |$The negation word is placed between the modal and the verb in Spanish.$|_{I_d} < 1$

(e) $0 < |$If the negation word is placed between the auxiliary and the verb in Spanish, then the sentence *Pedro ha no contestado la carta* is grammatically correct.$|_Z < 1$
$0 < |$The sentence *Pedro ha no contestado la carta* is not grammatically correct.$|_Z < 1$

$0 < |$The negation word cannot be placed between the auxiliary and the verb in Spanish.$|_{I_e} < 1$

From the conclusions of (d) and (e) Zubizarreta draws the following conclusion:

(f) 0 < |The negation word is placed between the main verb and its verbal argument in Spanish.$|_Z$ < 1
0 < |The negation word is placed between the modal and the verb in Spanish.$|_{I_d}$ < 1
0 < |The negation word cannot be placed between the auxiliary and the verb in Spanish.$|_{I_e}$ < 1
[0 < |If the negation word is placed between the main verb and its verbal argument in Spanish, and the same holds true for modals, while it cannot be placed between the auxiliary and the verb, then modals behave in Spanish like main verbs (and unlike auxiliaries).$|_Z$ < 1]

---

0 < |Modals behave in Spanish like main verbs (and unlike auxiliaries).$|_{I_f}$ < 1

Comparing the conclusions of (c) and (f), we see that the plausibility of *H* increased, since there are two indirect sources which enable a positive plausibility value to be assigned to it, and *H*'s plausibility value on the basis of both sources is according to (11)(a) higher than $|H|_{I_c}$.

The third test is related to cliticisation:

(g) 0 < |If clitics can be attached to the verbal argument of modals in Spanish, then the sentences *Pedro puede/debe contestarla* are grammatically correct.$|_Z$ < 1
0 < |The sentences *Pedro puede/debe contestarla* are grammatically correct.$|_Z$ < 1

---

0 < |Clitics can be attached to the verbal argument of modals in Spanish.$|_{I_g}$ < 1

(h) 0 < |If clitics can be attached to the verbal argument of auxiliaries in Spanish, then the sentence *Pedro ha contestadola* is grammatically correct.$|_Z$ < 1
0 < |The sentence *Pedro ha contestadola* is not grammatically correct.$|_Z$ < 1

---

0 < |Clitics cannot be attached to the verbal argument of auxiliaries in Spanish.$|_{I_h}$ < 1

On the basis of (g) and (h), we obtain:

(i) 0 < |Clitics can be attached to the argument of main verbs in Spanish.$|_Z$ < 1
0 < |Clitics can be attached to the verbal argument of modals in Spanish.$|_{I_g}$ < 1
0 < |Clitics cannot be attached to the verbal argument of auxiliaries in Spanish.$|_{I_h}$ < 1

[0 < |If clitics can be attached to the argument of main verbs and to the verbal argument of modals in Spanish, while this is not the case with auxiliaries, then modals behave in Spanish like main verbs (and unlike auxiliaries).$|_Z$ < 1]

---

0 < |Modals behave in Spanish like main verbs (and unlike auxiliaries).$|_{I_i}$ < 1

Zubizarreta quotes Rizzi (1978), who states that modals in Italian behave in several respects like main verbs, too. Thus, the plausibility of *H* has increased again.

II. ~*H* is supported by the following indirect sources (systems of plausible inferences):

(j) 0 < |If clitics can be attached to modals in Spanish and Italian, then the sentences *Pedro le pudo/debió hablar personalmente* and *Gianni gli ha dovuto/potuto parlare personalmente* are grammatically correct.$|_Z$ < 1
0 < |The sentences *Pedro le pudo/debió hablar personalmente* and *Gianni gli ha dovuto/potuto parlare personalmente* are grammatically correct.$|_Z$ < 1

---

0 < |Clitics can be attached to modals in Spanish and Italian.$|_{I_j}$ < 1

(k) 0 < |If clitics can be attached to main verbs in Spanish and Italian, then the sentences *Pedro le prometió hablar personalmente* and *Gianni gli ha promesso di parlare personalmente* are grammatically correct.$|_Z$ < 1
0 < |The sentences *Pedro le prometió hablar personalmente* and *Gianni gli ha promesso di parlare personalmente* are not grammatically correct.$|_Z$ < 1

---

0 < |Clitics cannot be attached to main verbs in Spanish and Italian.$|_{I_k}$ < 1

On the basis of (j) and (k), Zubizarreta finds that ~*H* is plausible:

(l) 0 < |Clitics can be attached to modals in Spanish and Italian.$|_{I_j}$ < 1
0 < |Clitics cannot be attached to main verbs in Spanish and Italian.$|_{I_k}$ < 1
[0 < |If clitics can be attached to modals, while this is not the case with main verbs, then modals behave in Spanish and Italian like non-main verbs.$|_Z$ < 1]

---

0 < |Modals behave in Spanish and Italian like non-main verbs.$|_{I_l}$ < 1

The next system of inferences increases this plausibility value:

(m) 0 < |If modals allow for impersonal *se*-passive in Spanish and *si*-passive in Italian, then the sentences *Estos libros se deberían/podrían comprar ya* and *Questi libri si dovrebbero/potrebbero comprare gia* are grammatically correct.$|_Z$ < 1

0 < |The sentences *Estos libros se deberían/podrían comprar ya* and *Questi libri si dovrebbero/potrebbero comprare gia* are grammatically correct.$|_Z$ < 1

---

0 < |Modals allow for impersonal *se*-passive in Spanish and *si*-passive in Italian.$|_{I_m}$ < 1

(n) 0 < |If main verbs allow for impersonal *se*-passive in Spanish and *si*-passive in Italian, then the sentences *Estos libros se prometieron comprar* and *Questi libri si promissero di comprare* are grammatically correct.$|_Z$ < 1
0 < |The sentences *Estos libros se prometieron comprar* and *Questi libri si promissero di comprare* are not grammatically correct.$|_Z$ < 1

---

0 < |Main verbs do not allow for impersonal *se*-passive in Spanish and *si*-passive in Italian.$|_{I_n}$ < 1

From (m) and (n), we obtain the following indirect source which raises ~*H*'s plausibility value:

(o) 0 < |Modals allow for impersonal *se*-passive in Spanish and *si*-passive in Italian.$|_{I_m}$ < 1
0 < |Main verbs do not allow for impersonal *se*-passive in Spanish and *si*-passive in Italian.$|_{I_n}$ < 1
[0 < |If modals allow for impersonal *se*-passive in Spanish and *si*-passive in Italian, while main verbs do not, then modals behave in Spanish and Italian like non-main verbs.$|_Z$ < 1]

---

0 < |Modals behave in Spanish and Italian like non-main verbs.$|_{I_o}$ < 1

As a result of the extension of the starting p-context, it has become *p-inconsistent*, because on the basis of certain tests, she judges hypothesis *H* to be plausible while on the basis of other tests its negation.

The *coordination* of the p-context is a simple task: it is easy to see that both *H* and ~*H* possess a relatively high plausibility value.

One may take the *contrastive* perspective after the (*ad hoc*) separation of the germs of p-context versions within a diagnostic perspective by considering and contrasting their tenability during the elaboration of the p-context. In such cases, the separation of the two rival p-context versions remains *ad hoc*, and aims at their better elaboration in order to arrive at a situation where a *decision* can be made between them. Therefore, the p-context is extended by new pieces of information which seem to be useful in weighing up different components of the two rival p-context versions. If a situation is arrived at where a decision seems to be possible, an *exclusive perspective* may be taken by trying to give up one of the rivals and keep only the other one and investigate whether it leads to a *solution* of the starting p-problem.

Example 26

In Example 24, in the first cycle Manning first adopts a *diagnostic perspective* by realising that his linguistic intuition and the presence of the sequence *as least as* in a novel are both reliable sources to some extent, so that both are capable of securing a low (but positive) plausibility value to P and $\sim P$, respectively. Then, he takes a *contrastive perspective*. Namely, he deems the two p-context version germs (the one which makes use of his linguistic intuition as a direct source and the other one which relies on a corpus datum) to be rivals and confronts them continuously. He extends the starting p-context by the data D_1–D_7 as well as by the indirect sources (a)–(e) in order to find out which sources and statements support the two members of the p-inconsistency and to what extent. He weighs the two p-context versions against each other and comes to the conclusion that the p-context version around P is the more differentiated, more comprehensive one, and it assigns to P a higher plausibility value than the rival p-context version does to $\sim P$. Therefore, in the spirit of an *exclusive perspective*, he modifies the p-context by giving up $\sim P$ and eliminating the sources supporting it from the p-context.

Schütze makes use of the same perspectives but he applies them more thoroughly insofar as he not only takes into consideration significantly more sources and data in favour of both members of the contradiction, but he also checks their reliability more carefully. As a result, he comes to the opposite conclusion and gives up P within an *exclusive perspective*.

The *combinative perspective* may be taken during the elaboration of the p-context if one believes that both members of the contradiction illuminate *under different circumstances* a certain aspect of the examined phenomena correctly and neither of them can be given up – that is, both the maintenance and the separation of the two inconsistent statements is motivated. Then one retains and separates the rival hypotheses and the two p-context versions containing them *within the same p-context* in a *well-motivated way*. In such cases, the two p-context versions exist side by side, at the same time and illuminate the phenomena under investigation from different viewpoints. The task of the next stages of the argumentation cycle is to elaborate the partial context-variants and the p-context arising from the combination (superposition) of the latter. This means that although *the contradiction in question is tolerated*, a logical chaos is avoided.[19]

Example 27

If we continue the analyses presented in Example 25, then we will see that Zubizarreta (1982: 138) reveals that the application of *H* and ~*H* can be *separated* in a non-*ad hoc* way:

(S) When modals behave as non-main verbs with respect to the phenomena mentioned in (j)–(o), they also behave as non-main verbs with respect to Cleft-formation, Right-node raising, Heavy-NP shift, Wh-movement, null-complement anaphora or placement of negation.

She supports *S* by two plausible inferences:

(p) |If *S*, then modal verbs do not allow for null-complement anaphora whenever a clitic is attached to them in Spanish.$|_Z = 1$
$0 <$ |If modal verbs do not allow for null-complement anaphora whenever a clitic is attached to them in Spanish, then the sentences *Juan podría/debería visitar a María y Pedro también la podría/debería* are not grammatically correct.$|_Z < 1$
$0 <$ |The sentences *Juan podría/debería visitar a María y Pedro también la podría/debería* are not grammatically correct.$|_Z < 1$

$0 < |S|_{I_p} < 1$

(q) |If *S*, then the negation word cannot be placed between the modal and the verb in Spanish whenever a clitic is attached to the modal in Spanish.$|_Z = 1$
$0 <$ |If the negation word cannot be placed between the modal and the verb in Spanish whenever a clitic is attached to the modal, then the sentences *Juan la podría/debería no contestar* are not grammatically correct.$|_Z < 1$
$0 <$ |The sentences *Juan la podría/debería no contestar* are not grammatically correct.$|_Z < 1$

$0 < |S|_{I_q} < 1$

Thus, the first argumentation cycle presented by Zubizarreta ends with a *modified* p-context version which contains both members of the p-inconsistency in such a way that they are *systematically separated* into two p-context versions along the lines of *S*: if there is a clitic attached to the modal or if the modal is in *se*-passive, then it behaves as a non-main verb; in all other cases, it behaves as a main verb. This paves the way for a *combinative perspective* where both conflicting statements are kept simultaneously within the same p-context but in different p-context versions. After further elaboration of the p-context, the argumentation process presented by Zubizarreta ends with a proposal for a representation with two parallel structures as in Figure 3.

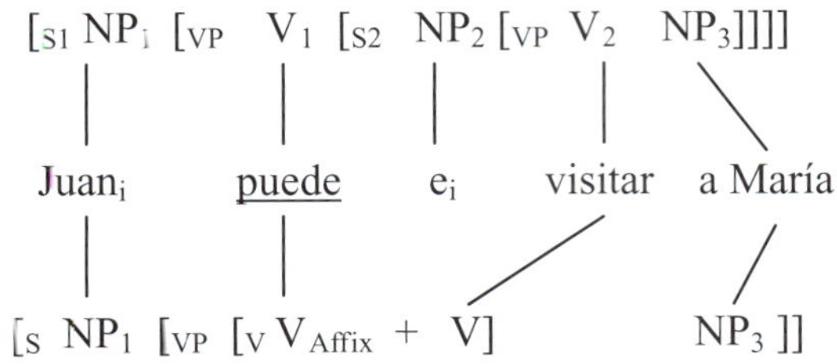

Figure 3. Parallel structures analysis

That is, the conflict between *H* and ~*H* is resolved in the following way:

(R) Modals are argument-taking predicates *and* verbal affixes modifying the verb, that is, adjunct-predicates. If there is a clitic attached to the modal or if the modal is in *se*-passive/*si*-passive, then it behaves as a non-main verb; in all other cases, it behaves as a main verb.

At the end of an argumentation cycle, one adopts an *evaluative perspective*. This involves a twofold task. First, as a final step in the elaboration of the p-context, one modifies it in order to arrive at a solution to the initial p-problem. Therefore, one has to check whether in fact a *solution* in the sense of (40)(a) has been elaborated if one was working within a contrastive perspective or in the sense of (40)(b) if one was working within a combinative perspective. Second, the currently obtained solution has to be *compared* to the solutions gained in the previous cycles. Thus, one has to investigate whether a well-founded decision can be made between the alternative solutions at one's disposal – that is, in every cycle one asks the question of whether the *resolution* of the starting p-problem has been arrived at. Of course, the p-context may turn out to be p-inconsistent and/or p-incomplete as well; attempts at the solution of a p-problem may lead to new p-problems. Therefore, one examines the current state of the p-context carefully, and tries to find weak points in the evaluation of the reliability of the direct and indirect sources applied, in the assignment of plausibility values, in the comprehensiveness of the analyses etc. in order to find out whether this is the best solution so far or whether there are further improvements possible and thus it seems to be reasonable to start a new argumentation cycle.

In this way, one modifies the p-context again and again and – if no resolution of the starting p-problem is achieved – sets up new, re-evaluated versions of it. Thus, the newer and newer argumentation cycles gradually elaborate diverse constellations of statements, plausibility values, sources, methodological principles etc., that is, *rival solutions*. Of course, cyclic returns are also possible within an argumentation cycle, as we have seen in Figure 2. If one is not satisfied with the fulfilment of some step during the current cycle in the face of the information obtained in a later stage, then one may start a new *subcycle*.

Example 28

The cyclic and prismatic nature of retrospective re-evaluation can be well illustrated by the development of generative grammar, the stages of which are built – as is well known – on the re-evaluation of previous stages on the basis of new points of view. Consequently, the history of generative grammar is a complicated network of cycles working at different levels. The lowest level consists of argumentation cycles within a paper. Higher-level cycles result from the continuous modification and revision of the hypotheses at lower levels and lead to the elaboration of different versions of generative grammar – such as the Standard Theory, the Revised Standard Theory, the Extended Revised Standard Theory, the Government and Binding Theory, the Minimalist Program, and their different variants.

Motivation and background

Pullum interprets the process of linguistic theorising as a cyclic process, too, during which hypotheses and methodological principles are checked with the help of manifold data types, modified in the light of counter-examples and gradually refined until one finds the best-supported, most plausible theory-variant. Pullum thinks that this methodology may cast new light on the analysis of the structure and function of linguistic data:

> The linguist tentatively formulates some proposals about the rules and checks their consequences against *intuition* (the linguist's own, or those of other speakers, or other grammarians). Those are cross-checked against the evidence of what *corpora* contain. The latter may quite often change the linguist's mind about the former. Sometimes it will be clear that the current proposal about the rules should be *revised*. Other times a cluster of rules may start to look stable enough that it seems preferable to *rethink* the issue of grammaticality for certain sequences. That might mean *another* corpus check to re-stimulate intuitions or provide a corrective. And sometimes things may be rather more subtle: the linguist finds that a distinction was missed, and while the rule is right about *one* class of cases, it is wrong about *the others*, for which a different generalisation holds. (Pullum 2007: 40; emphasis added)

10.6 Problem-solving strategies

A constitutive characteristic of plausible argumentation is that usually the re-evaluation of the p-context cannot be complete. There are often practical *limits* that do not allow us, for example, to take every source of the starting p-context into consideration, to produce all information potentially inherited by them, or to perform a complete test of inconsistency during the coordination of the p-context etc. During the cyclic returns, one cannot elaborate and compare every possible solution. Therefore, one has to rely on *problem-solving strategies* that are capable of ensuring that the argumentation process takes a relatively comprehensive range of information into consideration. On the basis of the partial accomplishment of the steps in (42) and (43), such *heuristics* make it possible to arrive at a fair number of solutions to the p-problems investigated, and as a result, they may lead to a reliable resolution of the p-problems within the given practical limits. During the three main stages within an argumentation cycle mentioned in (43) and represented in Figure 2, the following strategies are typically applied:[20]

(a) Problem-solving strategies applied while setting up a new p-context version. While setting up a new p-context version, one has to consider which pieces of information seem to be relevant to the solution of the starting p-problem. This means that the scope of one's investigations has to be narrowed down to an amount of information which seems to be manageable. A further important question is which hypotheses, methodological norms, tools etc. have to be made explicit and which ones may remain in the background (for example, because they seem to be generally accepted and secure). One can neither take into consideration nor present all the results, conjectures, methods etc. available which could serve as potential starting points. Therefore, provisional, more or less *ad hoc* choices have to be made which, however, may be modified in later cycles of the argumentation process.

(b) Problem-solving strategies applied during the elaboration of the p-context. During the elaboration of the p-context, one first *extends* the p-context with new information that might be useful for the solution of the starting p-problem with the help of direct and indirect sources (that is, plausible/demonstrative inferences) not taken into consideration so far. Above all, one tries to construct *systems of inferences* in which the inferences are linked together in such a way that they lead in many steps from the information given in the p-context to plausible statements that may make it possible to get rid of the p-inconsistency or p-incompleteness of the p-context.

Examples 29(1)–(2)

(1) Such systems of inferences are (a)–(c), (d)–(f), (g)–(i), (j)–(l) and (m)–(o) in Example 25.

(2) In mathematics, one aims at providing proofs (systems of demonstrative inferences) of conjectures. With this end in view, one has to find the

axioms and already proven theorems (that is, statements which are considered to be true with certainty within the given mathematical theory) and a series of demonstrative inferences which lead from these secure statements to the statement at issue. This means that one has to think and infer in a 'reverse direction': one proceeds from the conjecture(s), and, with the help of plausible inferences, tries to find the (already proven) theorems which a proof can be based on. Thus, the synthesis is preceded by the analysis. (See Polya 1948: 129ff.)

Then, one *coordinates* the p-context. Thereby, one summarises, among other things, the plausibility values of the statements originating from the old and new sources, respectively. A tool for this is (11), with the help of which one can determine how plausible the statements are according to the totality of the sources supporting them. However, (11) can be applied only to sources that judge unanimously whether a statement is plausible. This means that, with the help of (11), one can *separately summarise* the strength of the sources supporting the plausibility of the given statement and those supporting its implausibility. At this point, however, one cannot decide on how to handle p-inconsistency. Since a decision has to take into consideration a number of other factors, it cannot be restricted to the mechanical comparison of the plausibility values of a hypothesis and that of its rival. One never compares isolated statements. Instead, statements have to be evaluated along with the entire p-context.

Motivation and background

The coordination of the plausibility values of the statements involves the checking of the p-context's consistency, too. One examines whether the statements obtained by the extension of the p-context are p-consistent with the other elements of the p-context, that is, with the data at one's disposal. For example, whether they provide good predictions or they are supported by the data if the theory is extended to new areas. In addition, one also examines if they are p-consistent with the conjectures, or with important, central hypotheses of the theory etc.

In the course of the *modification* of the p-context, the coordinated p-context is *revised* and *transformed* in the following ways, among others:

- One may try to eliminate the statements that had been evaluated as plausible in the initial stage of the argumentation cycle, while in the extended p-context one ended up possessing information that supported their implausibility. So, one can reduce the set of statements belonging to the p-context, thereby making it less p-problematic. However, one has to reckon with the possibility that information has also been lost, since the statement in question has not been clearly refuted (as it turned out to be only implausible, not false with certainty). Thus, it has to be considered whether the maintenance of the rejected statement and the rejection of the preferred one lead to a globally better solution – that is, whether it is not reasonable to elaborate a new, rival p-context version.

- Initial plausibility values express only rankings of the reliability of the sources within a given state of the p-context. These values (and even the rankings) may change dynamically whenever the p-context changes.
- Statements may be eliminated only if the acceptability of the sources which made them plausible has been revised.[21]
- As the p-context variants produced in previous cycles are the rivals of the p-context variants in the current cycle as well, one may return to them and include again formerly excluded sources or statements by revising previous decisions.
- If one does not manage to produce a p-context that solves the initial p-problems, then the modification of the applied methodological norms may also be attempted.

Motivation and background

If the coordinated p-context is p-inconsistent or p-incomplete, then it has to be modified. The violation of the consistency suggests that the p-consistency of the p-context should be restored by abandoning one of its statements. This usually requires one to start new argumentation cycles, and to compare several alternatives. This is a complex decision-making process during which one has to consider, among other things, what consequences the abandonment of a given statement will have with respect to the entire p-context: whether it can restore the consistency of the p-context, or whether it leads to the loss of hypotheses with a high plausibility value, etc.[22]

Ignoring the confrontation with the data, failing to check the p-consistency, or systematically and arbitrarily narrowing it down, poses the danger that the theory may become unproductively circular. This is unacceptable for three reasons. First, circular theories – since they refuse to revise their hypotheses – cannot provide an explanation for the behaviour of those data that do not fit the accepted schemes, rules, generalisations, or hypotheses. Second, they do not develop but legitimatise their theses by repeating them in an unaltered form again and again (for more on this, see Kertész & Rákosi 2009b). Third, they may misguide the process for the decision among rival solutions; thus, the preference for the given theory or theory-variant may become unfounded.

Accordingly, in scientific theories (similarly to other forms of knowledge and communication), the p-context is constantly changing. One gains new information in the course of the argumentation cycles when extending the p-context; in the course of the re-evaluation of the p-context, one may abandon statements which have been accepted in previous cycles, or, under certain circumstances, one may modify the methods or one may even change the methods of the control of p-consistency. Nevertheless, the checking of p-consistency may relate to only one momentary state, since the p-context may, any time, become p-inconsistent again.

(c) Problem-solving strategies applied during the comparison of rival solutions. The comparison of the p-context obtained in the last cycle to the rival solutions gained in the previous cycles cannot be carried out completely, either. This is partly due to the insight that the solutions to be compared are partial, since their set-up and elaboration are based on heuristics, too, instead of being fully completed. Moreover, one should compare the solutions achieved from several different points of view such as the plausibility of the statements, the comprehensiveness, the p-problematicness of the p-context etc. That is, it is not only the plausibility values of the rival hypotheses that have to be compared. One must also examine, for example, which solution is, *as a whole*, the less p-problematic p-context. As we have already mentioned in Sections 10.2 and 10.4, the solution of the starting problem may generate further problems. It may happen that a statement is more plausible than its rival, but the p-context variant containing it is more p-problematic than that involving its rival.

This means that a definite and final decision among the rival solutions can be reached only when a fair amount of relevant information obtained from the starting p-context has been taken into consideration. If one of the rival solutions contains a consistent and coherent set of statements with relatively high plausibility values, while the others involve a set of statements with considerably lower plausibility values and/or a p-problematic set of statements, then the former solution should be preferred. In most cases, however, things are not so simple. First, there may become sources available that have not yet been taken into account but from which information may be obtained which fundamentally changes the current situation (and even leads to the opposite decision). Second, solutions may turn out to be p-problematic in several ways. On the one hand, the plausible inferences applied may generate further contradictions. On the other hand, with p-incomplete p-contexts it may happen that the informational underdetermination cannot be eliminated, since one does not find sources on the basis of which a plausibility value could be assigned to the statement at issue or to its negation. In most cases, however, as we have already seen, after the extension of the p-context both statements are made plausible by a source or set of sources. Thus, the informational underdetermination usually leads to informational overdetermination.

(d) Problem-solving strategies related to the choice of the prismatic perspective. The choice of the *perspective* from which one examines the current state of the elaboration of the p-context (see Section 10.5) requires the use of heuristic considerations as well, because there are no exact criteria which would determine conclusively which perspective has to be taken in a given situation. This is partly a consequence of the cyclic and heuristic character of the argumentation process, where it is always possible and often necessary to turn back to an earlier stage and to make it more thorough. Furthermore, while the diagnostic perspective is bound to the setting up of the initial p-context, and the evaluative perspective to the later phase of the modification of the p-context as well as to the comparison of its result to the existing solutions, the contrastive, the combinative and the exclusive perspectives are alternatives which can be chosen during the elaboration of the p-context. This means that one can basically choose between three strategies based on a contrastive, an exclusive or a combinative perspective, respectively:

- **The Contrastive Strategy**. The essence of this strategy is that it develops the p-context version germs obtained within the diagnostic perspective in such a way that it treats the p-context versions containing the contradictory statements as *rival alternatives*. That is, by applying a *contrastive perspective*, one aims at reaching a decision between them on the basis of the information available.
- **The Exclusive Strategy**. This strategy is applied after the Contrastive Strategy when a decision has been reached between the two rival p-context versions elaborated. It is based on an exclusive perspective and aims at checking as comprehensively as possible whether the p-context version chosen can be extended in such a way that it is capable of explaining phenomena that could be accounted for within the rejected p-context version. This, of course, may lead to the emergence of new p-problems.
- **The Combinative Strategy**. This strategy consists in treating the two rival p-context versions in the spirit of a combinative perspective not as rivals but as two parts of a whole which have to be maintained simultaneously. The two coexisting p-context versions making up the whole p-context have to be gradually elaborated. In such cases, one has to try to elaborate two unproblematic p-context versions. If one succeeds, then the starting p-problem is solved by the simultaneous but systematically separated maintenance of the two rival p-context versions.[23] Nevertheless, it has to be checked whether the separation of the two p-context versions is *well-motivated* within the whole p-context.

Motivation and background

The heuristic, cyclic and prismatic nature of plausible argumentation in linguistics is nicely illustrated in the following passage by Pullum:

> The goal is an *optimal fit* between a general linguistic theory (which is never complete), the proposed rules or constraints (which are [not] quite as conformant with the general theory as we would like), the best grammaticality judgments obtainable (which are not guaranteed to be veridical), and facts from corpora (which may always contain errors). *All are revisable, at every point*... There are no one-answer-fits-all solutions to the problems of knowledge acquisition in our subject. (Pullum 2007: 40; emphasis added)

10.7 The effectiveness of plausible argumentation

Plausible argumentation is a heuristic tool in the sense of (42). Its task consists in finding the best solution (resolution) of the p-problems in the starting p-context. Consequently, plausible argumentation is *effective*. If, however, an argumentation process is not capable of contributing to the solution of the given p-problems, it is called *ineffective*. Similarly, we call a *component* of the argumentation process (see (42), (43)) *effective* if it contributes to the resolution of the given problem(s); otherwise it is *ineffective*. To sum up:

(44) **Fallacies** are ineffective components of the argumentation process, preventing a given stage or the whole of the argumentation process from fulfilling its heuristic function.

Fallacies may appear at any stage in the re-evaluation of the given p-context and may be triggered by any element of the argumentation process. It is often the case that they do not appear in isolation but are linked with other mistakes and tendentiously misguide the whole argumentation process. For example, the overestimation of the plausibility of the conclusion, the faulty judgement of the reliability of a source, the preference for a less plausible statement over a more plausible one, the disregarding of relevant sources or statements, the insufficiency of the control of consistency, involving irrelevant information etc. are fallacies in the sense of (44).

Consequently, on the basis of what has been said above, plausible argumentation and fallacious argumentation cannot be distinguished primarily on the basis of formal, structural criteria, but only *heuristically*. While plausible argumentation, when properly applied, is a means of *gaining new and reliable information*, fallacies may result in *unfounded decisions* and *the defective solution of problems*.

One of the most frequently committed fallacies is *circular argumentation*. The argumentation process is circular if it does not re-evaluate the p-context or a part of it but leaves it unaltered. With *cyclic and prismatic argumentation*, however, 'one indeed returns to "the same point" but does so at a different cognitive level' (Rescher 1976: 119), since a modified, prismatically re-evaluated, qualitatively new information state is created. Accordingly, cyclic argumentation is effective. Therefore, cyclic argumentation does not mean circularity because the argumentation process does not return to the starting p-context but to a re-evaluated variant of it with altered information content.[24]

10.8 Conclusions

To sum up, what we have discussed in the present chapter boils down to the following findings:

(45) **Plausible argumentation**

(a) consists basically of a system of plausible inferences, while it may rely on deductive and demonstrative inferences as well;
(b) is globally cyclic, but may locally contain linear stages as well;
(c) pursues heuristic goals and applies a series of problem-solving strategies;
(d) is, in contrast to fallacious argumentation, effective;
(e) prismatically re-evaluates the p-context;
(f) elaborates solutions and the resolution of the p-problems in the starting p-context or shows that the latter cannot be achieved on the basis of the information at hand.

Figure 4 illustrates how those aspects of plausible argumentation which we have discussed in the previous sections are related.

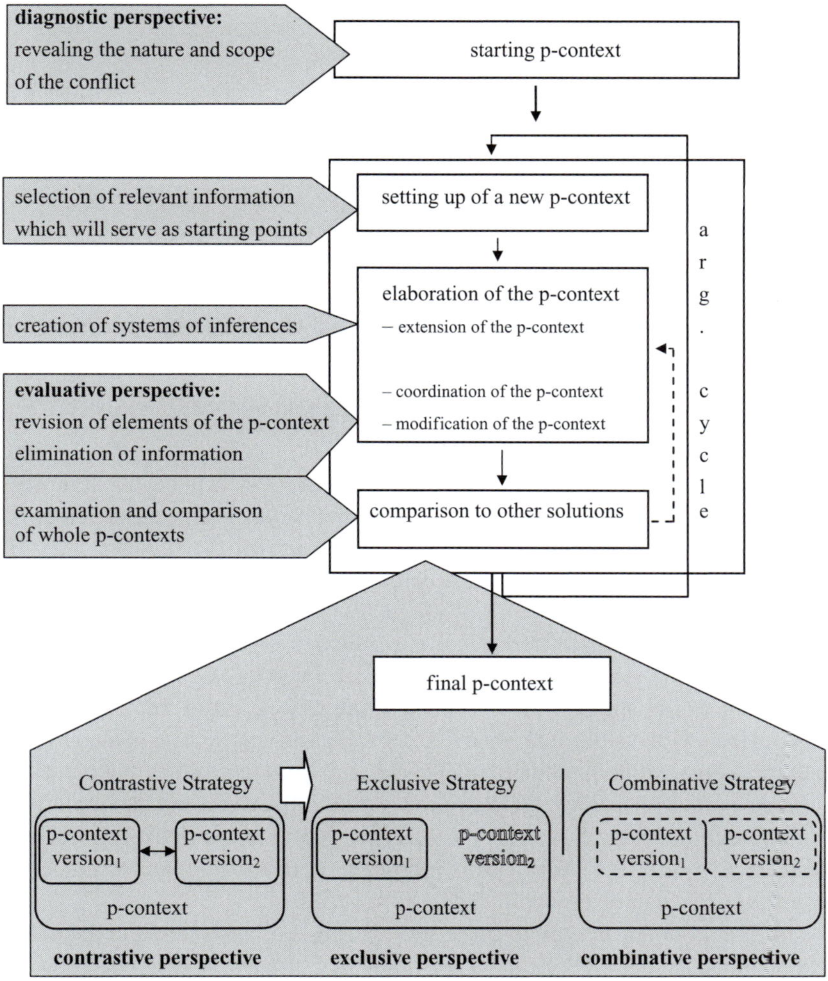

Figure 4. The process of plausible argumentation

11 The solution to $(P)_{II}$

On the basis of what was said in Chapters 9–10, we put forward the following hypothesis as the solution to $(P)_{II}$:

$(SP)_{II}$ The p-model is a metatheoretical model that allows for defining the concepts of 'data' and 'evidence' in linguistics.

The p-model interprets linguistic theorising as a process of plausible argumentation in the sense of (42). It enables us to involve such aspects of scientific theorising in the scope of metascientific reflection that the standard view of the analytical philosophy of science could not handle, but raised as unsolved problems:[1]

(a) An important characteristic of the p-model is that unlike the standard view of the analytical philosophy of science, it does not reduce scientific rationality to the application of deductive inferences. From the fact that the conclusion of plausible inferences is not true with certainty – but they are only plausible, fallible, p-context-dependent – it does not follow that plausible inferences and plausible argumentation built on them are not rational. This attitude significantly differs from the standard view of the analytical philosophy of science, which restricts scientific rationality to deductivity and to inductive inferences that can be probabilistically reconstructed.

(b) The p-model interprets linguistic theories not as systems of hypotheses obtained as the final results of the theorising process. Rather, we consider linguistic theorising to be the application of heuristics, which our model reconstructs, continues, and evaluates at a metalevel in the course of new argumentation cycles, also with the help of the tools of heuristics (that is, with the help of a plausible argumentation process). This means that we get a different picture of the structure of linguistic theories as well. We do not consider linguistic theories to be closed systems of hypotheses, in which one has to put the hypotheses in a hierarchical order with the help of deductive logic. Rather, the p-model considers the process of linguistic theorising – as we have seen in Chapter 10 – to be plausible argumentation, while the latter is explicated as a system of transformations elaborating and comparing a series of p-context versions.

(c) Although one of the most important driving forces of linguistic argumentation – and scientific theorising, in general – is the striving to get rid of contradictions, consistency cannot be considered to be the main criterion in the evaluation of scientific theories.[2] The consistency of theories cannot be examined in isolation, but has to be judged with other criteria – such as, simplicity, coherence, elegance, etc.[3] One cannot treat consistency as an absolute criterion, which needs to be fulfilled at all stages of the theorising process. Rather, in certain cases, the toleration of inconsistency may be perfectly legitimate. This, however, does not mean that contradictions can be tolerated under any circumstances and without further ado. There are very strict criteria for the application of paraconsistent solutions, that is, the maintenance of both members of a contradictory pair of statements.[4]

Part III

Data and evidence

12 The problem $(P)_{III}$

In Part II, we argued for the hypothesis $(SP)_{II}$ which says that the p-model enables us to define the concepts of 'data' and 'evidence'. Part III will be devoted to the realisation of $(SP)_{II}$ in that we will show *how* the two notions which the book centres on – namely, 'data' and 'evidence' – can be defined with the help of the p-model.

Therefore, this part of the book has to solve the following problem:

$(P)_{III}$ *How* does the p-model define the concepts of 'data' and 'evidence'?

In Chapter 13, we show how constitutive features of linguistic data and evidence can be identified. In Chapter 14, we will summarise the solution to $(P)_{III}$.

In discussing what notion of 'data' and 'evidence' follows from the tenets of the p-model, our starting point will be that the standard view of linguistic data and evidence (SVLD) interprets data as statements capturing experiences directly, whose reliability is secured by general methodological rules. According to this view, from the set of data one can select a special subset called 'evidence', whose certainty is guaranteed by experience and intersubjective testability. Evidence is supposed to provide a firm base for the testing of theories. However, this view is untenable for several reasons:

(46) (a) It has become generally acknowledged in the philosophy of science that experience by itself cannot guarantee the truth of a statement, and it only leads to fallible judgements affected by subjective factors.

(b) Although intersubjective testability reduces subjectivity immanent in individual experience as a source of knowledge, it does not eliminate it completely. If n persons evaluate a phenomenon in the same way, it does not follow that the $n+1$th person will also agree. This means that the criterion of intersubjectivity is built on induction (that is, on a type of plausible inference), since it infers from a finite number of cases to an infinite number of cases.

(c) Phenomena require interpretation. The object of one's experience has to be described with the help of a category system, that is, a theoretical apparatus. Consequently, it is not directly the experience to which one compares the hypotheses of the theory, but statements gained by processing the observed phenomena with the help of the conceptual apparatus of the theory. The thesis of the theory-ladenness of observation refers to this finding.[1]

13 The concept of 'datum' and 'evidence'

13.1 Overview

As already mentioned in the previous chapter, the task of the present chapter is to provide definitions of the central notions 'datum' and 'evidence' with the help of the p-model. By 'datum', we will mean a statement with a positive plausibility value originating from some direct source. Following this, three different kinds of 'evidence' will be obtained from the p-model: weak, strong and relative evidence.

13.2 The concept of 'datum'

In accordance with the p-model, *data cannot be restricted* to their information content, but we have to assign them a structure consisting of two components. They consist of a statement capturing an information content and a plausibility value (see Rescher 1979: 69):

(47) A **datum** is a statement with a positive plausibility value originating from some direct source.

In the sense of (47), one cannot state that data are in all cases true with certainty. Usually, they can be considered to be only more or less reliable '*truth-candidates*', which are supported by their source to a certain extent, without being made by them true with certainty (Rescher 1976: 8, 1977a: 213, 1987: 307).

It is important to remark that in the sense of (47), the source on the basis of which the plausibility value is assigned to a datum is not necessarily identical to the entity usually referred to as 'data source', because the former is often more complex. This complexity is due to the circumstance that in linguistic theories, data usually contain more information than can be gained from the corpus, intuitive judgements, responses of participants in experiments etc., because they involve the results of a certain amount of linguistic analysis as well. If a datum is an 'example' which says only that a sentence or string of words etc. belongs to a given language or that it can be found in a corpus, then the p-context has to be extended by another datum which captures the linguistic structure of this sentence. Without this, the ‘example’ cannot be involved in the process of linguistic theorising.

Motivation and background

Nevertheless, it is very important to emphasise that this otherwise rather open characterisation of the notion of datum is by no means unconstrained. Thus, we do not consider any piece of information to be a datum. The plausibility of data is initially determined by the reliability of their source. The more reliable the source is on the basis of which a plausibility value is assigned to a datum, the higher initial plausibility value one can associate it with. A datum must possess a certain degree of plausibility when it comes into contact with other hypotheses of the theory. On this, we agree with Rescher completely:

> We do not intend the conception of datahood to ‘open the floodgates’ in an indiscriminate way. Not *everything* is a datum: the concept is to have *some* logico-epistemological bite . . . Data are . . . not created as equal. All of them have *some* degree of positive plausibility in the epistemic circumstances at issue, but need certainly not be *the same* degree. (Rescher 1976: 10; emphasis as in the original)

In the sense of (47), hypotheses obtained not by inference but originating from some linguistic paper count as data as well. The source of such data is the reference to the linguistic paper at issue. At the same time, if one gives a detailed account of a psycholinguistic experiment instead of only summarising its outcome, then one is not endowed with data (receiving their plausibility value from some direct source). Instead, statements summarising the results of the experiment obtain their plausibility value from indirect sources, namely, by plausible inferences presented in the experimental report. In such cases, those statements count as data in the sense of (47) which serve as the starting points of the presented argumentation (systems of inductive generalisations, analogical inferences) such as authenticated and interpreted perceptual data etc. For more on this, see Chapter 16 and Section 19.6.

Examples 30(1)–(4)

(1) Statements capturing introspective judgements based on the linguistic intuition of native speakers are data. What counts as a datum in the sense of (47) is not the *linguistic expression or utterance* whose grammaticality is judged, but the *statement* expressing the judgement about

the grammaticality of this expression or utterance. Accordingly, the statement

(a) The sentence *Wer*$_i$ *meint Lydia, liebt t*$_i$ *Jakob?* is correct.

or the statement

(b) The sentence *Wer*$_i$ *meint Lydia, liebt t*$_i$ *Jakob*? is more correct than the sentence *Wer*$_i$ *meint Lydia, dass t*$_i$ *Jakob liebt?*.

are data if the judgements are based on the linguistic intuition (introspection) of the linguist *X* or on an experiment carried out on a totality of 100 informants. Nevertheless, neither the sentence

(c) *Wer*$_i$ *meint Lydia, liebt t*$_i$ *Jakob?*

can be considered to be a datum, nor do (a) or (b), if the latter's plausibility stems from an indirect source, that is, if they are inferred from hypotheses of the theory.[1]

We interpret judgements as plausible statements. This means that we do not deem them true with certainty. This decision is motivated by the problems raised in Schütze (1996) which centres around the complexity and the resulting uncertainty of judgements. The reason for this is, among other things, that non-linguist native speakers do not judge grammaticality directly, but rather they provide acceptability judgements. Acceptability judgements, however, are products of linguistic performance (see Schütze 1996: 24). Therefore, even if one evaluates the statement "Sentence *X* is unacceptable" to be true with certainty on the basis of the judgement of person *Y*, it cannot be stated that the statement "Sentence *X* is grammatically not correct" is also true with certainty, because the unacceptability may result not only from the contribution of linguistic competence but may be traced back to some other factor.

Linguists often evaluate the grammaticality of sentences in a direct way when providing 'introspective data' for their theory. The term '(un)grammatical', however, refers not only to their intuitive judgement about the correctness of the given sentence but inevitably presupposes some theory of grammar, too, which serves as a reference point against which violations of syntactic rules can be evaluated (and other kinds of violations of the rules of the language can be excluded). Thus, such statements are data, too, but the source on the basis of which they receive their plausibility value is more complex and cannot be reduced to the linguist's linguistic intuition alone.

(2) An example from Featherston (2007: 275ff.) illustrates impressively the uncertainty of grammaticality judgements and the problems which

arise from ignoring this uncertainty. Several syntacticians agreed on the grammaticality judgement according to which the sentences (a)–(c) are not better than (d):

(a) Wen$_i$ meint Lydia, liebt Jakob t$_i$?
whom thinks Lydia loves Jakob t$_i$
'Who does Lydia think Jakob loves?'
(b) Wer$_i$ meint Lydia, liebt t$_i$ Jakob?
who thinks Lydia loves t$_i$ Jakob
'Who does Lydia think loves Jakob?'
(c) Wen$_i$ meint Lydia, dass Jakob t$_i$ liebt?
whom thinks Lydia that Jakob t$_i$ loves
'Who does Lydia think that Jakob loves?'
(d) Wer$_i$ meint Lydia, dass t$_i$ Jakob liebt?
who thinks Lydia that t$_i$ Jakob loves
'Who does Lydia think that loves Jakob?'

As Featherston remarks, Haider, Grewendorf, Stechow & Sternefeld, Bayer and Lutz presuppose that native speakers judge (a)–(d) similarly. Therefore, on the basis of their linguistic intuition, they regarded the statement

(A) The sentences (a)–(d) are equally grammatical.

as a certainly true datum. From this they concluded that *A* clearly and perfectly refutes the following hypothesis:

(T) In standard German, there is a *that*-trace effect. That is, subjects and objects behave differently in complement clauses with a complementiser insofar as only the latter can be extracted.

Featherston refers to a paper by Grewendorf (see Grewendorf 1995) where he writes some years later that in standard German, *A* is a datum that is true with certainty, while this is not the case in North German dialects. Conversely, Fanselow (1987) holds that *A* cannot be treated as a datum in South German.

Featherston's experiments (see Featherston 2007: 276f.), however, yielded the result that *A* is not true with certainty – what is more, it is not even a plausible statement. Therefore, it cannot be treated as a datum. The participants of the experiments judged (a) and (b) to be better than (c) or (d). Consequently, on the basis of this experiment as a source one has to judge *A* to be implausible. Therefore, *A* cannot support the non-existence of the *that*-trace effect as part of an indirect source. Quite the contrary seems to be the case: Featherston's experiments serve with data in favour of T, since they can be interpreted as sources making A' plausible:

(A′) Sentences (a)–(b) are better than (c)–(d).

(3) Corpus data are statements capturing characteristics of utterances in some corpus; thus, they do not necessarily have the same structure. They may, for example, have the form 'The utterance *U* containing the linguistic phenomenon *P* can be found in corpus *C*.', or 'The structure *S* can be identified in corpus *C* and it had the characteristics *X*', etc. They often have the form 'The sentence in Example *x* is contained in Corpus *C*' and occur together with further data such as 'The sentence in Example *x* contains the occurrence of the construction *S*'. They have to be interpreted as data in the above sense, that is, as plausible statements originating from a direct source. This source, however, is not the corpus alone. Rather, it is a compound of (sub-)sources such as the historical document itself, the linguist's linguistic intuition and his/her skills in the application of some linguistic theory, etc. The reliability of each of these sub-sources influences the plausibility of the datum. Therefore, corpus data usually cannot be considered to be certainly true statements. It is not only the case that factors deciding over the genuineness of the historical document are relevant; difficulties or uncertainties in the identification and interpretation of the given linguistic phenomenon must be taken into account as well. There are several reasons for this:

(a) Both the occurrence of the investigated structure in the corpus ('positive evidence') and the lack of its occurrence ('negative evidence')[2] raise serious problems, which are unsolvable or at least difficult to handle with the methodologies at the researchers' disposal:

- It is often difficult to decide how to differentiate relevant occurrences from insignificant, isolated, unreliable, dubious information.
- Linguists inevitably have to fall back on their own linguistic intuition when processing corpora. The interpretation of the utterances in the corpus, the identification of utterances containing the given linguistic phenomenon (syntactic structure, semantic or pragmatic phenomenon etc.) and the selection of the reliable examples require the active involvement of linguistic intuition; therefore, these operations contain subjective elements as well. For example, if a cognitive linguist searches for metaphors in a corpus, then he/she cannot rely on observable, 'objective' criteria. Therefore, he/she has to decide which expressions he/she is

willing to consider – at least partly – metaphorical on the basis of his/her own linguistic intuition.

- The absence of a certain form or construction does not necessarily mean that this form/construction is faulty. It may happen that the phenomenon at issue appears rarely, and it can be found in a larger corpus or in a corpus covering another linguistic register.

(b) 'Quantitative data' indicate that a given phenomenon's occurrence is statistically significant. Of course, the identification of the occurrences raises the problems mentioned in (a), too. The reliability of such examples also depends on the range of data which their relative frequency is compared to, as well as on the statistical method applied. Thus, for example, the representativeness of the corpus is a factor that has to be checked in order to obtain reliable results.

(c) In connection with questionnaires, manifestations of the 'observer's paradox' (see Section 4.2) lead to uncertainty as well.

Meurers (2007) enumerates several factors evincing that the use of corpus data presupposes the involvement of the linguist's linguistic intuition. Therefore, such data cannot be deemed certainly true statements:

- The linguist has to decide which sentences of the corpus are relevant to a particular research problem. He/she has to select and reconstruct data. This requires the analysis of the sentences in the corpus with the help of the given theory and the identification of the syntactical, pragmatic etc. parameters.
- One needs to decide whether a piece of information from the corpus is part of the language one is studying. This means that the normal, grammatical sentences have to be identified.
- Corpora are finite representations of language use. Therefore, it is possible that they do not contain information relevant to the actual research problem.

(4) Adherents of the standard view of linguistic data and evidence (SVLD) (see Section 3.3) – followers of both the introspective and the corpus-based tradition – do not use statements related to ungrammatical (deviant) sentences produced during spontaneous language use as data. They simply presuppose that such sentences can be easily identified and do not contain any relevant information; therefore, they are useless and have to be dismissed from linguistic research. In contrast, Foster (2007) regards them as valuable and reliable (although not certainly true) data. She argues that

> naturalistic ungrammatical sentences are of interest to linguists studying language production, language loss and language learning. (Foster 2007: 73)

She points out that in order to create computer parsers that are capable of parsing 'real' sentences stemming from language production (and can eventually create these and similar sentences), one has to make a distinction not only between grammatical and ungrammatical sentences but between sentences which contain frequently and routinely committed, 'realistic' errors and which can be easily understood on the one hand, and sentences which contain invented, unrealistic mistakes on the other hand. Foster is of the opinion that this dual task can be accomplished only by relying on one's linguistic intuition. From this it follows that one has to deal with data which are not true with certainty but are inevitably affected by subjective factors, that is, with uncertain data:

> Of course the decision over whether a sentence contains an error is a subjective one because it depends on a person's opinion about what constitutes an error but I would argue that some level of subjectivity is unavoidable in any linguistic task whether that be applying a grammaticality judgement or building a treebank. (Foster 2007: 80)

We may conclude from Foster's argumentation that the standard view of linguistic data and evidence (SVLD) is built on a *paradox*: corpora can be regarded as perfectly reliable, objectively controllable sources only after their unreliable, faulty elements have been eliminated – and this can be done only by relying on our subjective opinion.

To summarise these considerations, the following characteristics of data can be highlighted:

(48) (a) In linguistic theories, data are, according to (47), statements that are supported by some direct source at one's disposal but which are often not true with certainty. Rather, they are only plausible, that is, truth-candidates.

(b) The initial plausibility of data is based on the weighing of the reliability of their source at the beginning of the argumentation process or cycle. This may, however, dynamically change at later stages of the cyclic and prismatic argumentation process.

(c) Data are theory-dependent (p-context dependent). First, from different manifestations of linguistic behaviour one can obtain statements capturing characteristics of these manifestations with the help of the conceptual apparatus of a theory. Second, different theories (plausible argumentation processes) may judge the plausibility of statements differently.

(d) Data are 'given' in the sense that – since they receive a plausibility value from direct sources – their initial plausibility is judged not with the help of inferences constructed within the given argumentation process but directly on the basis of the reliability of their source.

(e) If the reliability of a data source is called into question, then the usability of this source as well as the plausibility of the statements originating from it have to be re-evaluated. This means that information concerning the reliability of the source and the relationship between the source and the statements stemming from it have to be integrated into the argumentation process. In this way the data stemming from this source will lose their data status (but not necessarily their plausibility).

(f) Data supply the theory with plausibility values. These values can be used to determine the plausibility of other statements with the help of plausible inferences.

Examples 31(1)–(2)

(1) The p-context-dependence (theory-dependence) of data and the well-motivatedness of interpreting data as plausible statements rather than as instances or products of linguistic behaviour can be nicely illustrated with the help of the analysis of different interpretations of the annotations and degrees of 'badness' as summarised by Schütze (1996: 44ff.):

(a) In the generative literature, ungrammatical sentences are usually marked by asterisks. This, however, leaves open several possibilities of interpretation. According to Householder (1973: 370ff.), for example, '**X*' may be interpreted as

- 'I would never say *X*';
- 'I have never seen or heard a sentence of the type of *X* and hereby wager you can't find an example';
- 'This is quite comprehensible, and I have heard people say it, but they were all *K*'s [foreigners, Southerners, etc.]; in my dialect we would say *Y* instead.'

(b) The use of the question mark is ambiguous, too, since '?*X*' may indicate that

- *X* shows interspeaker variation, i.e. *X* is good for some people but bad for others;
- most speakers rate *X* marginal;
- *X* has a very literary ring, but it is not unacceptable.

Schütze cites Andrews (1990: 203) who developed a system of symbols in order to make the meaning of the markings used explicit. This system involves a six-point scale:

√: completely acceptable and natural;
?: acceptable, but perhaps somewhat unnatural;
??: doubtful, but perhaps acceptable;
?*: worse, but not totally unacceptable;
*: thoroughly unacceptable;
**: horrible.

The application of this system means that it is not the linguistic examples themselves that one treats as data but rather *statements* about their acceptability such as 'Sentence *X* is doubtful, but perhaps acceptable' on the basis of the linguistic intuition of speaker *Y* as a direct source. Since the linguistic intuition of (single) native speakers cannot be regarded as a completely reliable source, one obtains *plausible* statements which may serve as data in the theory at issue. These data are *theory-dependent*, because they involve elements of the above system, which is, of course, only one of the possible scales which have been elaborated and can be applied in collecting and evaluating judgements from informants. In this way, acceptability judgements become integrated into the process of linguistic theorising, and they may function as starting points for the estimation of the plausibility value of hypotheses about the grammaticalness of the given sentence or structure. Namely, the degree of acceptability of a sentence cannot be equated with the degree of its grammaticalness, because the former is also determined by semantic, pragmatic, and general cognitive factors. Consequently, the plausibility of '*X* is ungrammatical' is lower than the plausibility of '*X* is unacceptable' on the basis of the linguistic intuition of a native speaker, and the plausibility of the statement 'Structure *Y* is ungrammatical/bad' is even lower. In such cases, the source on the basis of which the statements '*X* is ungrammatical' and 'Structure *Y* is ungrammatical/bad' are evaluated is not direct, because these statements are inferred from acceptance judgement data and other information about other possible reasons of badness; therefore, in such p-contexts they are not data.

(2) Another aspect of the *theory-dependence (p-context dependence) of data* is that it may happen that a datum is evaluated to be true with certainty in one theory (p-context) but it may be deemed to be implausible (and, of course, not regarded as a datum) in another. Schütze (1996: 38f.) mentions several such cases in order to illustrate the unreliability of unsystematically collected judgement data.

One of his examples is the case of the alleged *that*-trace effect of adjunct *wh*-words. Lasnik & Saito (1984) deemed sentences like *Why do you think that he left*? ambiguous because in their opinion, *why* may relate to the reason for the thinking or to the reason for the leaving. In the terminology of the p-model this means that in this p-context (theory), the statement 'The sentence *Why do you think that he left*? is ambiguous' is a datum which is true with certainty on the basis of the two linguists' linguistic intuition as a direct source. In the p-context (theory) of Aoun *et al.* (1987), however, similar statements are held to be implausible and not treated as data on the basis of two indirect sources.

The first indirect source (system of inferences) refers to the uncertainty and inaccuracy of the judgement of informants who claim that they have two readings of such sentences. The second indirect source (system of inferences) bases the refusal to accept the existence of a second reading on the argument that if such sentences were grammatical, then certain similar sentences such as *Who remembers what we bought why*? should be acceptable, too, which is, however, not the case.

Since the sources used by the two theories do not judge the plausibility/implausibility of the statements at issue unequivocally, they cannot be regarded as a set of sources on the basis of which a plausibility value could be assigned to the statements at issue. Schütze (1996: 39) tries to re-evaluate the reliability of the sources mentioned. He comes to the conclusion that all sources used by the authors are unreliable. Since the judgements provided by the speakers he has surveyed are strongly divided, he concludes that without carefully conducted experiments it is not possible to make a decision. Therefore, the statement 'The sentence *Why do you think that he left*? is ambiguous' loses its data status because it has lost its plausibility value.

13.3 The concept of 'evidence'

The p-model makes the introduction of several concepts of 'evidence' possible. Thus, it provides us with tools that enable us to grasp the relationship between data and other hypotheses of the theory in a subtle way. As a first approximation, evidence is a datum whose function is to *contribute to the judgement and comparison of the plausibility of rival hypotheses*, that is, incompatible (contradictory or contrary) hypotheses (see Section 10.5). We distinguish between three types of evidence.

Weak evidence for a hypothesis h simply means that one can build inference(s) on the given datum that make(s) *h* plausible (in the extreme case true with certainty). *Weak evidence against a hypothesis h* can be defined in a similar way. It means a datum on which one can build inference(s) that make(s) *h* implausible (in the extreme case false with certainty):

(49) (a) A datum *e* is **weak evidence for hypothesis *h***, if the p-context contains statements that extend *e* into an indirect source on the basis of which a positive plausibility value can be assigned to *h*.

(b) A datum *e* is **weak evidence against hypothesis *h***, if the p-context contains statements that extend *e* into an indirect source on the basis of which a positive plausibility value can be assigned to $\sim h$.

Weak evidence for *h* is a datum that is suitable to assign a positive plausibility value to *h* as part of an indirect source, thereby partially supporting its truth. At the same time, however, (49) allows that e serves as weak evidence for a rival of h as well. Therefore, its use may lead to informational overdetermination.

Examples 32(1)–(2)

(1) Wurzel (1981) aims to decide between the following rival hypotheses concerning the structure of German affricates:

(h_1) The labial affricate is biphonemic, that is, its phoneme structure is /pf/.
(h_2) The labial affricate is monophonemic, that is, its phoneme structure is /p^f/.

The datum e_1 is weak evidence for hypothesis h_1:

(e_1) *Pfropfen* is an existing German word,

since with the help of e_1 as well as the following two plausible statements an indirect source can be created that makes h_1 plausible:

(p_1) If a vowel /V/ follows a formative-initial /$C_3C_2C_1$/ consonant cluster, then the consonant cluster /C_2C_1/ and /C_1/ also occur in the same position.
(p_2) There exist German formatives with the structure /frɔ_ / and /rɔ_ /.

With the help of the statements mentioned, we gain the following plausible inferences:

$$\frac{0 < |\text{If } h_1 \ \& \ e_1 \ \& \ p_1, \text{ then } p_2.|_S < 1 \qquad |p_2|_S = 1}{0 < |h_1 \ \& \ e_1 \ \& \ p_1|_I < 1}$$

$$\frac{0 < |h_1 \ \& \ e_1 \ \& \ p_1|_I < 1}{0 < |h_1|_{I'} < 1}$$

It is easy to see that, on similar grounds, e_1 is weak evidence for h_1's rival h_2, too.

(2) As we have already seen in Example 30(4), adherents of the standard view of linguistic data and evidence (SVLD) do not consider statements about ungrammatical sentences which have been obtained from spontaneous language use as relevant data. The main reason for this lies in their conviction that sentences of this kind result from the linguistic performance of the native speaker; therefore, it is not possible to infer properties of linguistic competence from them. As opposed to this, Arppe & Järvikivi (2007) – similarly to Foster (2007) – argue that data of this type, too, are relevant insofar as they may serve as (weak) evidence for the grammaticality of linguistic constructions:

> Slips of the Tongue, i.e., output *errors* that are produced by normal native speakers unintentionally and spontaneously (and sometimes unconsciously) are another well-documented case in point. These *errors* are not random, but instead follow the way the language system is organised . . . On many occasions, the speaker in fact corrects the error – therefore even the corrections can tell us quite a lot about how our linguistic system is organised . . . (Arppe & Järvikivi 2007: 101f.; emphasis as in the original)

Relative evidence stipulates stricter requirements:

(50)

(a) A datum e is **relative evidence for hypothesis *h***, if

(i) e is weak evidence for hypothesis h;

(ii) the inference(s) connecting the premises and h allow(s) us to assign a higher plausibility value to h than the plausibility value of h's rivals assigned by inferences also using e as a premise.

(b) A datum e is **relative evidence against hypothesis *h***, if

(i) e is weak evidence against hypothesis h;

(ii) the plausible inference(s) connecting the premises and $\sim h$ allow(s) us to assign a higher plausibility value to $\sim h$ than the plausibility value of h assigned by the inferences also using e as a premise.

(50)(a) allows e to be weak evidence for rivals of h, too. In the latter case, however, e cannot be regarded as relative evidence for h's rival, since according to (50)(a)(ii), the plausibility of h is higher than that of its rivals. To put it another way: whereas a datum may be relative evidence only for one of the rivals, it may function as weak evidence for rivals of h as well.

Example 33

In Example 32(1), e_1 is relative evidence for hypothesis h_2, since with the help of hypothesis p_3 a further indirect source can be obtained which makes h_2 plausible, while in the case of h_1, this is not the case:

(p_3) If the phoneme cluster /C_1C_2_/ occurs formative-initially, then there exists a formative in which the phoneme cluster /_C_2C_1/ occurs formative-finally.

(p_4) There exist German formatives with the structure /_rpf/.

With the help of these statements, the following plausible inferences can be formulated:

$$\frac{\begin{array}{l} 0 < |\text{If } h_2 \,\&\, e_1 \,\&\, p_3, \text{ then } p_4.|_S < 1 \\ |p_4|_S = 1 \end{array}}{0 < |h_2 \,\&\, e_1 \,\&\, p_3|_I < 1}$$

$$\frac{0 < |h_2 \,\&\, e_1 \,\&\, p_3|_I < 1}{0 < |h_2|_{I'} < 1}$$

Here there is only one indirect source supporting h_1, while there are two for h_2. Moreover, the latter provide h_2 with a higher plausibility value than the first source in Example 32(1) does with h_1.

The third type is *strong evidence:*

(51)

(a) A datum *e* is **strong evidence for hypothesis *h***, if
  (i) *e* is weak evidence for hypothesis *h*; and
  (ii) *e* is not weak evidence for any of *h*'s rivals.

(b) A datum *e* is **strong evidence against hypothesis *h***, if
  (i) *e* is weak evidence against hypothesis *h*; and
  (ii) *e* is not weak evidence against any of *h*'s rivals.

(51)(a) requires that *e* exclusively makes only *h* plausible, that is, while *e* makes *h* plausible, it either makes its rivals implausible or it may not be extended into an indirect source on the basis of which a positive plausibility value can be assigned to the rivals of *h* in the given p-context. In a similar way, (51)(b) requires that *e* exclusively makes only *h* implausible. Consequently, relative as well as strong evidence may contribute to the decision among rival hypotheses and to the treatment of p-inconsistency.[3]

Examples 34(1)–(2)

(1) Bowdle & Gentner (1999) mention the following rival hypotheses in cognitive metaphor research:

(h_1) Metaphors are based on the comparison of two conceptual domains and on the matching of their related properties.
(h_2) Metaphors are stable, unidirectional mappings between two conceptual domains.
(h_3) Metaphors are special cases of categorisation.
(h_4) Conventional metaphors are special cases of categorisation, while novel metaphors are special cases of analogy.

According to the authors, results of psycholinguistic experiments comparing the interpretation and processing of conventional and novel metaphors make h_1–h_3 equally implausible because the latter describe all metaphors with the same processing model. They support only h_4 and work therefore as strong evidence for h_4 in the above sense.

(2) Hoffmann (2007) presents a case study illustrating that it may happen that a problem cannot be solved solely by relying on corpus data since they serve as weak evidence for both the given hypothesis and its rival; experimental data, however, may function as strong evidence. He characterises the problematic nature of the starting p-context as follows:

> the corpus results allow for two competing hypotheses: on the one hand it is possible that sequences such as *the way* ***which*** *the satire is achieved* ***in***... is just an accidental gap in the data that speakers would use just as they might *the world* ***which*** *I was working* ***in***... On the other hand, it might be a construction that is not provided by the grammar, i.e., a systematic gap on par with pied piping with *that/ø*-relativisers..., which is generally considered ungrammatical... (Hoffmann 2007: 94; emphasis as in the original)

That is, the statement

(e_1) The corpus contains neither manner adjunct PPs with the structure *which* + P or P + *that/ø*, nor locative PPs with this structure.

is interpreted by Hoffmann as weak evidence for hypotheses h_1 and h_2 alike:

(h_1) Manner adjunct PPs and locative adjunct PPs of the structure *which* + P, P + *that/ø* are grammatical but rare.
(h_2) Manner adjunct PPs and locative adjunct PPs of the structure *which* + P, P + *that/ø* are ungrammatical.

The reason for this decision is that both hypotheses can be supported by plausible inferences which make use of e_1 as a premise:

(a) 0 < |If the corpus contains neither manner adjunct PPs with the structure *which* + P or P + *that/ø*, nor locative PPs with this structure, then there is an accidental gap in the data that speakers would use.|$_H$ < 1
0 < |If there is an accidental gap in the data that speakers would use, then manner adjunct PPs and locative adjunct PPs of the structure *which* + P, P + *that/ø* are grammatical but rare.|$_H$ < 1
0 < |The corpus contains neither manner adjunct PPs with the structure *which* + P or P + *that/ø*, nor locative PPs with this structure.|$_H$ < 1

---

0 < |Manner adjunct PPs and locative adjunct PPs of the structure *which* + P, P + *that/ø* are grammatical but rare.|$_{I_a}$ < 1

(b) 0 < |If the corpus contains neither manner adjunct PPs with the structure *which* + P or P + *that/ø*, nor locative PPs with this structure, then there is a systematic gap in the data.|$_H$ < 1
0 < |If there is a systematic gap in the data, then manner adjunct PPs and locative adjunct PPs of the structure *which* + P, P + *that/ø* are ungrammatical.|$_H$ < 1

0 < |The corpus contains neither manner adjunct PPs with the structure *which* + P or P + *that/ø*, nor locative PPs with this structure.$|_H < 1$

---

0 < |Manner adjunct PPs and locative adjunct PPs of the structure *which* + P, P + *that/ø* are ungrammatical.$|_{I_b} < 1$

In order to take a well-founded decision between h_1 and h_2, Hoffmann extends the p-context with new data:

(e_2) Participants of an introspection experiment judged the structures in the following order acceptable:
V + P > which + P (locative adjunct) > which + P (manner adjunct) >> >> P + that/ø = word order violations = agreement errors etc.

Referring to Sorace & Keller (2005), Hoffmann makes use of e_2 as follows:

(c) 0 < |If e_2, and clines of acceptability usually indicate the violation of a soft grammatical constraint, then the grammatical structure of a stranded preposition is provided by the grammar, but the decreasing acceptability scores mirror increasing problems in semantically interpreting the resulting structure.$|_H < 1$[4]
0 < |If the grammatical structure of a stranded preposition is provided by the grammar, but the decreasing acceptability scores mirror increasing problems in semantically interpreting the resulting structure, then manner adjunct PPs and locative adjunct PPs of the structure *which* + P, P + *that/ø* are grammatical but rare.$|_H < 1$
$0 < |e_2|_H < 1$
0 < |Clines of acceptability usually indicate the violation of a soft grammatical constraint.$|_H < 1$

---

0 < |Manner adjunct PPs and locative adjunct PPs of the structure *which* + P, P + *that/ø* are grammatical but rare.$|_{I_c} < 1$

(d) 0 < |If manner adjunct PPs and locative adjunct PPs of the structure *which* + P, P + *that/ø* are ungrammatical, then they violate a hard grammatical constraint.$|_H < 1$
0 < |If they violate a hard grammatical constraint, then they are judged as bad as the ungrammatical fillers.$|_H < 1$
0 < |If they are judged as bad as the ungrammatical fillers, then $\sim e_2.|_H < 1$
$0 < |e_2|_H < 1$

---

0 < |~ Manner adjunct PPs and locative adjunct PPs of the structure *which* + P, P + *that/ø* are ungrammatical.$|_{I_d} < 1$

To sum up, e_2 is strong evidence for hypothesis h_1 and against h_2 in the sense of (51), since inferences were set up that made h_1 plausible and h_2 implausible.

Motivation and background

It is easy to see that none of the notions of 'evidence' gained by the p-model satisfies the criteria laid down by the standard view of the analytical philosophy of science (SVAPS). The former do not provide criteria whose fulfilment could ensure that the datum in question perfectly supports or refutes the given hypothesis. First, since the connection between the datum and the hypothesis is in most cases established by plausible inferences relying on plausible premises, they cannot guarantee the truth or falsity of the hypothesis. Second, nothing excludes the possibility of gaining evidence against the given hypothesis on the basis of other data.

(49)–(51) are related to situations in which the datum does not guarantee but only supports or questions the given hypothesis to a certain extent. However, as a limiting case (51)(a) also covers situations in which it is guaranteed that the hypothesis is true with certainty. This is the case if the evidence e is certainly true and the p-context contains statements with the help of which e can be extended into a demonstrative inference the conclusion of which is the hypothesis h. These requirements are, of course, extremely strict stipulations.

To sum up what we have said in connection with (49)–(51), we can highlight the following properties of evidence:

(52) (a) Data may be tools for eliminating informational overdetermination insofar as they may contribute to the evaluation and comparison of the plausibility of hypotheses which are the sources of p-inconsistency.

(b) Data are not evidence in general but they count as evidence with respect to some hypothesis. That is, they may be weak/relative/strong evidence for or against a given hypothesis h.

(c) During the argumentation process, a statement may lose its evidence status. First, statements playing the role of evidence are data, that is, plausible or certainly true statements which get their plausibility value from a direct source. Therefore, when their source loses its reliability, their data status will vanish as well. Second, further sources may evaluate them as implausible. In such cases, they do not have a plausibility value on the basis of all sources which assign a plausibility value to them because the latter do not judge them unequivocally as required in Section 9.3. Thus, they are evidence for this hypothesis on the basis of a part of this set of sources but they cannot function as evidence for it on the basis of the set of all sources. Third, a premise of the inference connecting the evidence and the hypothesis supported/questioned by it may lose its plausibility as a result of changes in the p-context.

(d) Evidence is theory-dependent. On the one hand, it is a theory-dependent datum. On the other hand, it depends on the methodology of the given theory whether the evidence and the (type of) inference connecting it with the given hypothesis is considered to be legitimate.

13.4 Conclusions

(47)–(51) introduce concepts at a highly abstract level. The reason for this is – as is also emphasised in the current literature on linguistic data and evidence – the enormous diversity of linguistic data (see Kertész & Rákosi 2009c). It is well known that the source of this diversity is that linguistics is far from being a homogeneous discipline. Rather, it is a network of theories which involve various combinations of several, in certain cases radically different, methods relying on ontological and methodological background assumptions originating from the 'empirical' natural sciences, from hermeneutics, or philosophy. In some cases, these theories behave complementarily, while in other cases they overlap or are in conflict with each other (see Penke & Rosenbach 2004a; Kepser & Reis 2005a; Lehmann 2004: 189f.). From this it follows that a number of data types can be found in linguistics that are characteristic of other disciplines. Consequently, the notions of 'linguistic datum' and 'linguistic evidence' *do not have differentia specifica* which would definitively distinguish them from the *genus proximum* of 'scientific datum/scientific evidence'. Therefore, the highly general definitions given in (47)–(51) are not specifiable to 'linguistics', but must be narrowed down to specific – that is, documented – argumentation processes implemented by the methods of specific theories.

14 The solution to $(P)_{III}$

The definitions provided in (47)–(51) lead to a *radical reinterpretation* of the concept of 'evidence' in several respects:

(a) The concept of 'datum' in (47) serves as a basis for the introduction of the three types of evidence (i.e. weak, strong and relative), allowing us to make subtle differentiations in the relationship between a datum and two or more rival hypotheses. It may be the case that indirect sources can be built upon a datum which make at least one of the rival hypotheses plausible (weak evidence). It may happen that by comparing the strengths of the indirect sources which can be built on this datum one finds that one of the rival hypotheses is made more plausible than its rival (that is, this datum seems to vote for one of the rivals as relative evidence). Finally, it is also possible that the datum is one of the premises of inferences which make one of the rivals plausible and the other one implausible (strong evidence); this may, of course, legitimise a stronger preference for the given hypothesis. Consequently, as we have put it, data may be tools for eliminating informational overdetermination insofar as they may contribute to the evaluation and comparison of the plausibility of hypotheses which are the sources of p-inconsistency. Moreover, with weak evidence, data may be the sources of p-inconsistency as well.

To sum up, with the help of the concept 'evidence' it can be clarified which data can be used as elements of indirect sources, either for a given hypothesis or against it. The identification of data which are strong evidence for/against a hypothesis is especially important because this is a first step towards the (re)solution of the p-problematicness of the p-context.

(b) It is crucial that 'evidence' as a concept does not classify data in the traditional sense. As we emphasised in Section 13.3, data are not evidence in general but they count as evidence relative to some hypothesis. Moreover, evidence is strongly *p-context-* and *theory-dependent*. It is not 'objective' in the sense of the standard view of the analytical philosophy of science (SVAPS), it is not 'given' at the outset of inquiry, it is not 'primary' to the theory etc.

Consequently, in the present part of the book we have obtained the following solution to $(P)_{III}$:

$(SP)_{III}$ The p-model defines the concepts of 'data' and 'evidence' as introduced in Chapter 13.

Part IV

Application of the p-model: a case study

15 The problem $(P)_{IV}$

The p-model interprets linguistic theorising as *problem solving*, that is, as a heuristic process. As we have mentioned in Section 8.3, we suppose that the structure of linguistic theories/approaches/models cannot be separated from the problem-solving activities applied during linguistic theorising. Namely, the p-model assumes that linguistic theorising is based on the techniques of plausible argumentation, and it interprets the presentation of the results of the research as a certain stage in the process of theory formation. Consequently, linguistic papers are regarded as pieces of plausible argumentation, too, from which the process of problem solving can in most cases be partially – not completely, of course, but to a considerable extent – *reconstructed*. We suppose that papers presenting the results of linguistic research contain several *traces* of the heuristic process from which these results originate.

Part IV will be devoted to the presentation of a detailed case study which illustrates how the p-model can be applied to the *reconstruction* of the process of linguistic theorising. Therefore, we raise the following problem:

$(P)_{IV}$ How can the p-model be applied to the practice of linguistic inquiry?

16 A case study: a reconstruction of Gentner & Wolff (1997)

16.1 Overview

The case study in the present chapter elucidates that the p-model is indeed capable of bridging the gap between linguistic research practice and metatheoretical reflection on this practice. We exemplify how the concepts and the argumentation strategies that have been introduced in the previous parts of the book can be used to analyse the emergence and the resolution of inconsistency, the integration of data sources and the role which evidence plays in the choice between alternative hypotheses etc.

The case study focuses on the comparison and evaluation of models of metaphor processing by Dedre Gentner and Phillip Wolff with the help of *data* obtained from psycholinguistic experiments. Gentner & Wolff (1997) presents three model types in such a way that they are organised around three *rival hypotheses*. According to pure matching models, metaphor processing involves the search for common properties; according to abstraction-first processing, properties are projected from the base to the target; finally, alignment-first processing models state that after an initial search for common properties, in a second stage further properties are projected from the base. After a short introduction of the main hypotheses of the theories belonging to the three model types, different kinds of *evidence* for and against them are put forward and evaluated. On the basis of the explanatory power of their hypotheses in comparison to the other models as well as the evidence for/against them, pure matching models are rejected, but no decision is made between abstraction-first and alignment-first models; both of them are made *plausible* by several sources. Thus, the p-context is *p-inconsistent*: besides their incompatible hypotheses, the two models also make contradictory predictions. Therefore, Gentner and Wolff tried to resolve this inconsistency by testing these predictions. They conducted three experiments which, however, led to contradictory results: while the first two experiments provided *(strong) evidence against* abstraction-first models, the third experiment offers *(strong) evidence for* them. This means that the p-context remained p-inconsistent; the application of the *Contrastive Strategy* (that is, the treatment of the rival p-context-variants as rivals, see Sections 10.5 and 10.6) failed. At this point, the *Combinative Strategy* (see

Section 10.6) is proposed by Gentner and Wolff: the two p-context-versions (that is, the two models) are not rivals but they have to be maintained *simultaneously* by separating their scope of application. Abstraction-first models seem to give good descriptions of the processing of metaphors whose bases are highly conventional while their bases and targets are low in metaphorical similarity; alignment-first models, however, seem to be appropriate for novel metaphors. Thus, a new *argumentation cycle* is started where with the career of metaphor hypothesis, a *revised* version of both rival hypotheses, is tested with the help of Experiment 4, and, on the basis of the results, further modified and compared to a newer, *re-evaluated* version of abstraction-first models proposed in Glucksberg, McGlone & Manfredi (1997).

16.2 Argumentation cycle 1: three model types of metaphor processing

16.2.1 Setting up the starting p-context

The case study focuses on a paper by Dedre Gentner and Phillip Wolff about the comparison of diverse model types of the metaphor comprehension process. We will follow their argumentation and try to reconstruct the steps they make with the help of the notions of the p-model. In order to secure maximal closeness to the paper analysed as well as to maintain textual flow, we will make extensive use of quotations and only slightly rephrased passages by referring in endnotes precisely to their occurrence in Gentner and Wolff's study. We emphasise that our aim is not to investigate metaphor comprehension and thereby to *apply* Gentner and Wolff's findings. Rather, we will *reconstruct at a metalevel* Gentner and Wolff's object-scientific argumentation. We intend to reveal the peculiarities of the *argumentation process* in the course of which their findings have been put forward.

In Section 10.3, we characterised plausible argumentation as a process aiming at the gradual transformation of a p-problematic p-context into one that is no longer (or at least less) p-problematic. The *p-context* (see (36) in Section 9.8) includes, first, a set of *sources* in terms of which the plausibility value of statements can be judged. Second, it covers a set of *statements* together with their *relevant characteristics* (in particular, their plausibility values with respect to the sources in the p-context, their logical and semantic structure). Third, the *accepted methodological norms* related to the components of the p-context (for instance, the permissible type(s) of inferences, the criteria of the acceptability of the statements, the methods of the treatment of inconsistencies, the criteria for judging the reliability of the sources etc.) also belong to the p-context. *P-problems* were introduced in Section 10.2 as special cases of informational under- or overdetermination related to statements of the p-context. From these definitions it follows that these concepts can be applied not only to publications, theories or approaches, but to larger units such as research frameworks, research fields etc., as well.

The first paragraph of Gentner & Wolff (1997) *sets up* the starting p-context (see Section 10.4) by specifying it as the comprehensive p-context of research into the psycholinguistics of metaphor interpretation. The paper presents three model types of metaphor processing by adopting a *diagnostic perspective* in the sense of Section 10.5. That is, with the separate introduction and analysis of the three model types, Gentner and Wolff differentiate between three *p-context versions* in the sense of Section 10.5 within the comprehensive p-context of research into the psycholinguistics of metaphor interpretation. In this way, it becomes possible to reveal which hypotheses are accepted by the different models (or by two of them) and where there is conflict among the three views.

The three model types constituting the three p-context versions cover several models sharing some basic assumptions:[1]

(53) (a) According to *pure matching models*, metaphor processing involves the search for common properties.
(b) According to *abstraction-first models*, properties are projected from the base to the target.
(c) *Alignment-first processing models* state that after an initial search for common properties, in a later stage further properties are projected from the base.

These p-context versions are organised around three central hypotheses which are plausible on the basis of some source in the sense of (8)(b) in Section 9.3:

(h_1) Metaphors are interpreted by searching for common properties and by matching identical elements in the target and base.[2]

(h_2) The interpretation of metaphors takes place in three steps: '(1) finding or deriving an abstraction associated with the base; (2) projecting this abstraction from the base to the target; (3) verifying the information in the target typically, by matching the selected abstraction with the target representation.'[3]

(h_3) The process of interpretation begins with an alignment of representations between the base and target, continues with matching the elements as well as the relations between them, and results in a match of connected structures allowing further inferences.[4]

h_1–h_3 are related to the models mentioned in (53) as follows:

(54) (a) On the basis of source S_1 (works by Aristotle, Demetrius, Tversky, Malgady and Johnson, Ortony, etc.),[5] the statement h_1 is plausible.
(b) On the basis of source S_2 (papers by Carbonell, Kennedy, Shen, Way, Glucksberg and Keysar, etc.)[6] the statement h_2 can be regarded as plausible.
(c) Source S_3 (publications by Gentner, Clement, Falkenhainer, Skorstad, Wolff, Isenberg, Verbrugge and McCarrell, etc.)[7] supports the statement h_3.

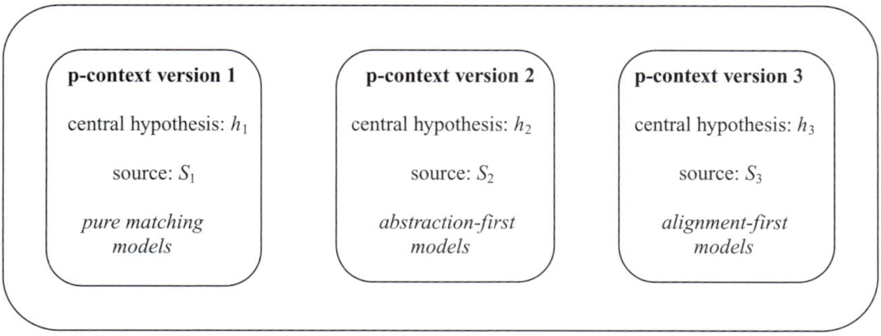

Figure 5. Starting p-context: comprehensive p-context of research into the psycholinguistics of metaphor interpretation

The starting p-context involves, of course, not only these central hypotheses but several other claims as well which are accepted by all or by eminent researchers working within some version of the given model type. All the sources S_1–S_3 are direct sources in the sense of (7)(a) in Section 9.3, which means that the initial plausibilities of these hypotheses stem from the reliability of their sources: that is, they are based on the authority of the linguists who proposed them as well as on the acceptance of the theories in which they occur. These values can, of course, change dynamically during later stages of the argumentation process.

Figure 5 illustrates the starting p-context.

The three p-context versions contain partly different statements, assign different plausibility values to several hypotheses, apply different methodological norms etc.; that is, researchers working within their framework adopt different perspectives from which they investigate the processing of metaphors.

16.2.2 The elaboration of the starting p-context

The starting p-context is *p-inconsistent* (see (38), Section 10.2), since it contains incompatible hypotheses which are, however, supported by some source. In order to weigh up their tenability, Gentner and Wolff take a *contrastive perspective* in the sense of Section 10.5. With the aim of coming to a well-founded decision as to which of them should be accepted, they elaborate the three p-context-variants by *extending* them by new data, by *coordinating* them in that they judge the plausibility/implausibility of their hypotheses in the light of the new data, and producing a *modified* version of them.

The authors mention only one common point of the three model types: all of them agree upon the claim that metaphor interpretation arises from the interaction between its base and target concepts.[8] Then, they characterise the three model types in such a way that they present some of their central tenets as well as arguments (results of psycholinguistic experiments, considerations weighing up their explanatory power, etc.) for and against them.

First, Gentner and Wolff evaluate the tenability of h_1. To do so, they enumerate several *experimental data* which can be used to increase its initial plausibility value:[9]

(55) (a) 'Metaphors judged high in similarity were also judged to be of high goodness.'
(b) 'Metaphors rated high in similarity have been found to have a greater number of shared features.'
(c) 'Metaphors with many shared features have been judged to be of higher goodness than those with few.'
(d) 'Participants who rated metaphors high in semantic relatedness also tended to rate them as easier to interpret.'
(e) 'Similarity can aid in the selection of an interpretation.'
(f) 'The matching features tended to be of higher salience in the base than in the target.'[10]

The statements (55)(a)–(d) originate from *direct sources* (see Section 9.3), since their initial (positive) plausibility value is determined by the reliability of the sources which are the papers cited in Gentner & Wolff (1997: 332ff.). Thus, (55)(a)–(f) are *data* in the sense of (47). They can be regarded as *weak evidence for* h_1 in the sense of (49)(a), because it is possible to create plausible inferences supporting h_1 whose set of premises contains these statements.

For example, one can deem the following statement plausible, because it captures that (55)(a) is a prediction of the model based on h_1:

If h_1, then metaphors high in similarity are also judged to be of high goodness.

According to the literature cited in Gentner & Wolff (1997) (that is, to source S_4), this prediction is correct. From this we obtain the following plausible inference:

$0 <$ |If h_1, then metaphors high in similarity are also of high goodness.|$_{S_4} < 1$
$0 <$ |Metaphors judged high in similarity were also judged to be of high goodness.|$_{S_4} < 1$

$0 < |h_1|_{I_1} < 1$

This inference belongs to *Type 3 of plausible inferences*, because it fulfils all criteria laid down in Section 9.5.4. More exactly, it is weak reduction (see (25) in Section 9.5.4, Example 13(1) in Section 9.5.4).

Similar plausible inferences can be created with (55)(b)–(f) as well. These inferences are *indirect sources for* h_1 in the sense of (7)(b) in Section 9.3. Since all of them make h_1 plausible, they function as a *set of sources* supporting this hypothesis. According to (11)(a) in Section 9.3, the plausibility value of h_1 on the basis of this set of sources is higher than its plausibility value assigned by the sources at issue separately. Consequently, these indirect sources increase the initial plausibility value of h_1 and provide a stronger support for it.

Gentner & Wolff (1997) does not examine the relationship between the statements in (55) and h_2/h_3. Thus, since the authors do not elucidate the question whether (55)(a)–(f) also provide weak evidence for or against h_2 or h_3, they leave open the question whether these data could also function as *relative* or *strong evidence for* h_1 in the sense of (50)(a) and (51)(a) in Section 13.3.

For example, (55)(a) would function as *relative evidence for* h_1 if it were also weak evidence for h_2 and h_3 but the plausibility of h_1 were the highest on the basis of the inferences connecting (55)(a) and these hypotheses (see (50)(a)(ii) in Section 13.3). This would be the case if pure matching models offered a better explanation for this datum than abstraction-first or alignment-first models did. (55)(a) could be interpreted as *strong evidence for* h_1 if it were also weak evidence against h_2 and h_3 or if it could be applied to create plausible inferences supporting neither h_2 nor h_3 (see (51)(a)(ii) in Section 13.3). This would be the case if h_2 and h_3 predicted its negation or if h_2 and h_3 were inapplicable to (55)(a) in the given p-context; that is, if only pure matching models were capable of explaining it.[11]

Gentner and Wolff criticise only (55)(f) by referring to two direct sources which show this statement to be implausible. Thus, according to (11)(d) and (12), on the basis of the set of every relevant source, no plausibility value can be assigned to (55)(f). From this it follows, that it loses its data status (see (47)) and cannot be used as weak evidence for h_1.

The two authors also put forward evidence which makes the central hypotheses of the first model type *implausible*:[12]

(56) (a) 'Not every shared feature is included in an interpretation', although according to h_1, 'those features that enter into an interpretation should be those that are shared by both of the terms.'
(b) 'It is not clear how non-identical but similar properties are matched.'
(c) Models around h_1 'cannot explain why metaphors are more asymmetric than are literal comparisons'.
(d) Models around h_1 'fail to predict *feature importation* (or projection of *candidate inferences*): the fact that features apparently present in only one of the terms can enter into an interpretation'.[13]

These data presented in the literature can be interpreted as *weak evidence against* h_1.

Motivation and background

It is important to see that the data listed in (56) do not decrease the plausibility of h_1 but make it implausible – that is, they make its negation plausible. For example:

$0 < |$If h_1, then those features that enter into an interpretation should be those that are shared by both of the terms.$|_{S_5} < 1$
$0 < |$Not every shared feature is included in an interpretation.$|_{S_5} < 1$

$$0 < |{\sim}h_1|_{I_2} < 1$$

This inference belongs to the *first type of plausible inferences* (see Section 9.5.2); namely, it is a *plausible modus tollens*. This inference is deductively valid while its premises are not true with certainty but only plausible according to the publications mentioned by Gentner and Wolff (S_5 indicates this set of sources).

From (55) and (56) one can conclude that the acceptance and testing of h_1 leads to *p-inconsistency*, because both h_1 and its negation are plausible on the basis of some sets of source (S_4 and S_5, respectively). Moreover, Gentner and Wolff remark that both abstraction-first and alignment-first models are capable of offering solutions to the problems in (56); therefore, in their view, the data in (56) provide *strong evidence against* h_1 in the sense of (51)(b) and *weak evidence for* h_2 and h_3 along the lines of (49)(a) in Section 13.3.[14] This leads to p-inconsistency, too.

In a second step, evidence for and against h_2 is listed, as it is summarised in (57) and (58), respectively. The following data (hypotheses about the explanatory power of h_2 and 'linguistic data') have to be regarded as *weak evidence for* h_2 in the opinion of Gentner and Wolff:[15]

(57) (a) h_2 provides a possible explanation for the partiality of feature selection: 'only those properties that are part of the category referred to by the base are incorporated into the interpretation'.
(b) h_2 predicts that metaphor processing is asymmetrical, 'since reversing the terms should result in an entirely different categorisation'.
(c) h_2 can 'explain how metaphors might convey new knowledge about the target' insofar as 'feature-importation from base to target is possible by inheritance of properties from the abstraction associated with the base'.
(d) 'Metaphors have the syntactic form of class-inclusion statements' which 'leads to a suggestive grammatical difference between literal and figurative comparison statements. For literal sentences, a comparison cannot be converted into a category assertion . . . ; in contrast, for figurative statements, comparisons (similes) . . . can often be converted into category form . . .

This suggests that simile, like metaphor, should be viewed as a kind of class-inclusion statement.'

(e) 'Individual terms can come to be associated with abstract categories'; 'languages sometimes use prototypical members to refer to the category itself.'[16]

It is easy to see that the data in (57)(a)–(e) are also *strong evidence against* h_1, since the phenomena touched upon by them (feature selection, asymmetry, feature importation, difference between literal and metaphorical comparisons, polysemy of base terms) cannot be explained with the help of h_1, as we have seen in (56).

At this point, Gentner and Wolff level criticism at the explanatory power of h_2 in comparison to that of h_1 and h_3. They judge the following datum to be *strong evidence against* h_2, since it refers to a problem which does not arise in the case of pure matching models and alignment-first models:

(58) Since h_2 rejects matching as the underlying process, it 'loses the intuition that metaphors reveal deep commonalities'.[17]

(58) is, of course, also *weak evidence for* h_1 and h_3 in Gentner and Wolff's judgement. That is, due to (58), the acceptance of h_2 leads to *p-inconsistency* as well.

In a third step, the authors provide arguments in favour of h_3. The following hypotheses about the explanatory power of h_3 are highlighted as *weak evidence for* h_3:[18]

(59) (a) Models around h_3 are 'sensitive to the structural bindings in the base and target representations'.

(b) Models around h_3 describe the initial stages of metaphor comprehension as a process operating 'in a rather blind and local manner, allowing the maximal structure to emerge without having to be anticipated'.

(c) In accordance with h_3, the first stage – where 'all identical predicates in the target and the base are matched in parallel without regard for structural consistency' and 'nonidentical entities and operators . . . are placed into correspondence if they fill identical argument positions in the corresponding relational structures' – is followed by a second stage, where 'structurally consistent connected clusters' emerge. These 'are merged into one or more maximal structurally consistent interpretations' in the third stage, 'for which *candidate inferences* may be carried over from the base to the target' which extend the target's representation by new predicates. The candidate inferences are then 'inserted into the target structure, subject to verification of their correctness'. 'The choice between interpretations is guided partly by context' (this explains the context-sensitivity of metaphor interpretation) 'but more generally by the *systematicity* principle, which states that, all else being equal, people prefer the interpretation that preserves the *largest* and *deepest* connected representational structure'.

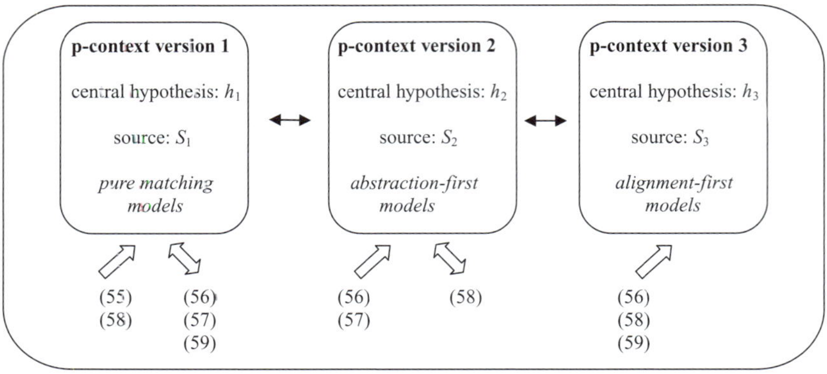

Figure 6. Cycle 1: extension of the starting p-context by the data listed in (55)–(59)

(d) The systematicity principle is capable of explaining feature selection: 'only information that is part of the maximal common connected structure gets included in the interpretation'.
(e) 'The problem of feature importation is addressed by the projection of candidate inferences.'
(f) 'The problem of matching similar but non-identical features is addressed by the fact that nonidentical functions and objects can be placed in correspondence by virtue of common roles in a like relational structure.'
(g) h_3 offers an explanation for the asymmetry of metaphors: 'Because candidate inferences are directional (from base to target), reversing the order will change the interpretation.'[19]

At the same time, (59)(c)–(g) are *strong evidence* against h_1. On the basis of the above considerations, we can review the current state of the p-context as in Figure 6.[20]

After the extension and the coordination of the p-context, Gentner and Wolff *modify* it, that is, they revise the plausibility and through this, the tenability of the three rivals. At this point, they change their perspective because they take the *evaluative perspective* in the sense of Section 10.5 insofar as they ponder whether the modified p-context provides a *solution* of the p-inconsistency rooted in h_1–h_3 in the sense of (40) in Section 10.2. The answer is a partial yes. On the basis of the p-inconsistency generated by the statements in (55) and (56) (that is, by the weak evidence for and against h_1), as well as by judging the explanatory power of h_1 in comparison to the other models on the basis of (57)–(59) (that is, the strong evidence against h_1 and in favour of h_2 and/or h_3), pure matching models are rejected. No decision is made, however, between abstraction-first and alignment-first models. Thus, the p-context remains p-inconsistent in the sense of (38) in Section 10.2:

(60) The *central p-problem* of Gentner and Wolff's paper can be reconstructed as follows:

(a) The statement
There is 'an initial process of projection from the base followed by a later verification process'
is plausible, while the hypothesis
There is 'an initial process of alignment between the base and target representations followed by projection of inferences'
is implausible according to the source S_2 as well as the indirect sources built upon (57).

(b) The statement
There is 'an initial process of projection from the base followed by a later verification process'
is implausible, while the hypothesis
There is 'an initial process of alignment between the base and target representations followed by projection of inferences'
is plausible according to the source S_3 as well as the indirect sources built upon (58) and (59).[21]

This p-inconsistency is rooted in the incompatibility between the two central hypotheses h_2 and h_3.

Although the hypotheses of both models are made *plausible* by several sources, and p-inconsistency has been made explicit only in the case of h_2, no attempt is made to compare these plausibility values and the whole of the p-context versions and to take a decision on this basis. The indirect sources (plausible inferences) which can be built upon (58) are not strong enough to serve as a base for a well-founded decision. Instead, Gentner and Wolff initiate a new argumentation cycle by *extending the p-context* with new *sources*: they try to *resolve the p-inconsistency* captured in (60) by testing the predictions of the two model types with the help of a series of experiments.

16.3 Argumentation cycle 2: application of the Contrastive Strategy

16.3.1 Setting up the new p-context

In order to resolve the p-inconsistency (60), Gentner and Wolff *start a new argumentation cycle* by *extending the p-context by new data sources*, namely, by psycholinguistic experiments. Within this cycle, they apply the Contrastive Strategy (see Section 10.6): they treat h_2 and h_3 as incompatible hypotheses belonging to *rival p-context versions*, and they try to come to a *decision* between them. Therefore, if the data obtained from the new sources provide evidence for h_2, then the p-context version labelled 'abstraction-first models' will be kept as the solution of the starting p-inconsistency and the context-variant based on h_3 discarded; if the new data support h_3, then the p-context version 'alignment-first models' will be retained and its rival rejected. This means that the authors make an attempt to elaborate a *consistent solution* in the sense of (40)(a) (see Section 10.2) to the p-problem (60).

16.3.2 Subcycle 1: Experiment 1

In order to further elaborate the p-context covering the two rival p-context versions, Gentner and Wolff intended to contrast the predictions of the two models. With this end in view, they tried to find out whether the speed of metaphor processing can be influenced by priming it by the target or the base term. The *experimental design*[22] was relatively simple: participants had to interpret thirty-two metaphors preceded by one of four primes: the target, the base, neither of them (blank lines) or both of them (the entire metaphor). The stimulus material was produced carefully insofar as the metaphors were chosen either from the literature or constructed by the authors, and the preferred direction of metaphors, that is, the ordering of base and target, was controlled with the help of another experiment. In order to compare the interpretation times of metaphors preceded by the different prime types, the time taken by subjects to begin typing an interpretation of the metaphor was measured. Gentner and Wolff formulated a series of conjectures about the possible outcomes of the experiment and their relationship to the rival hypotheses:[23]

(61) (a) If h_2 holds, then subjects should be faster to interpret a metaphor when it is primed by the base than when it is primed by the target, because the first step of the interpretation process is the derivation of an abstract category from the base term.

(b) According to h_3, there should be no difference in these processing times, since both terms are required to start the alignment between them.

(c) From h_3 it follows that priming with both terms should reduce the comprehension time of metaphors in comparison to priming with only one term.

(d) No priming should lead to the longest processing time in the case of both models.

Motivation and background

The *experimental design* is a comprehensive preliminary description of all facets of the process of experimentation. It is always necessarily only partial in the sense that the researcher cannot identify and rule out in advance all potential sources of error that may bias the outcome of the experiment.

This experimental design relies on a series of *theoretical constructs*: concepts, hypotheses and models. It is supposed, for example, explicitly or implicitly, that

(62) (a) metaphors consist of an interaction between two concepts, the base and the target;
(b) metaphor processing can be influenced by presenting people with the base and/or target term;
(c) all people use the same (or very similar) processing methods;
(d) the time which elapses from reading the metaphor to begin typing an interpretation of it is proportional to the processing time of the metaphor; therefore,
(e) differences in the times between reading the metaphors and starting to write can be interpreted as indices of the differences of processing times.

Motivation and background

One has to have at least a rough idea of what one intends to investigate. The problem which the experimenter raises is usually related to one or more imperceptible, rather low-level theoretical construct(s), *phenomena* that may be relevant in judging hypotheses about high-level theoretical constructs or require theoretical explanation relying on high-level theoretical constructs. In our case, for example, low-level theoretical constructs such as 'base term', 'target term', or 'response time for interpreting sentences containing metaphorical expressions primed by both terms/the target term/the base term/none' etc. are applied to obtain information which is used to produce and evaluate hypotheses about high-level theoretical constructs such as 'alignment of base concept and target concept', or 'projection of an abstraction from the base to the target representation', etc.

The theoretical model of the phenomena expected to be detected is, similarly to higher-level hypothesis systems, fallible, and the same is true of the researcher's hypotheses concerning the relationship between the constructs at the higher and lower levels. Moreover, there may be an overlap between the theoretical model of the phenomena and the theory which is tested by the experiment.

As for the *experimental procedure*,[24] sixty undergraduates took part in the experiment for a course credit. The thirty-two metaphors appeared on a computer screen in a random order for each participant. Four levels of prime type were run in a within-subjects design, and four between-subjects groups were used in order to counterbalance the assignment of metaphors to priming types.

There were three practice trials, where the participants received instructions on the computer screen. They were informed that their task will consist of interpreting metaphors by making use of the primes preceding them. They were also told that they could write interpretations of up to two lines in length and that they should begin typing the interpretation as soon as they were ready with their formulation. The backspace key was disabled in order to prevent editing after a too early start. The primes were presented in sentence frames; null terms were indicated by blank lines. Subsequently, four more practice trials followed with the same conditions as in the experimental trials. A line of asterisks was followed after 500 ms by the prime, which was shown for 1500 ms. Then a blank screen was presented for 100 ms, before the entire metaphor was displayed; at the same time, below the metaphor a cursor appeared with a prompt for the interpretation. When participants pressed the enter button to indicate they had finished typing, a 1500 ms break followed before the next item. Not only was the time between the appearance of the metaphor and the first keystroke of the interpretation measured to millisecond accuracy but also the time required to type in an interpretation. In this way, *perceptual data* were obtained by capturing the results of the measurements in the form of statements such as

(63) The time between the appearance of the metaphor No. x and the first keystroke by person No. y in item set B was z ms.

Motivation and background

The *experimental procedure* is a material procedure where an experimental apparatus is set up and its working is monitored and recorded under controlled circumstances, in an experimental setting. Nevertheless, the experimental apparatus as well as the devices monitoring it and recording the results may malfunction. Moreover, experimentation is also practice-dependent in the sense that the experimental apparatus applied allows solely for a limited detection of the properties of the investigated phenomenon, and the abilities and skill of the researchers performing experiments may also differ.

After collecting the perceptual data, their *authentication* took place. Namely, responses in which it took longer than 20 s to type in an interpretation were excluded from the statistical analysis because the authors supposed that in such cases, participants had not yet had a fully elaborated interpretation. Cases in which the time between the appearance of the metaphor and the first key stroke was more than 15,000 ms were also discarded.

Motivation and background

The experimenter has to evaluate the outcome of the experimental procedure. He/she has to decide whether the experimental apparatus was working properly so that *perceptual data* (statements containing information gained by sense perception such as records of measurements, photographs etc.) are stable and reliable; he/she has to check whether sources of noise were excluded, or at least whether their effect can be eliminated with the help of statistical methods. This is the *authentication of perceptual data.*

The authentication of perceptual data is not capable of securing totally reliable data. Although the researcher may be totally sure, for example, that he/she has seen the digit *X* on the reader of the experimental apparatus, perceptual data are always underdetermined by the act of observation insofar as the statement capturing the circumstances and result of the experimenter's observation contains elements that cannot be controlled by sense perception. In (63), for instance, it is merely supposed that person No. *x* has in fact seen the metaphor mentioned on the screen, that it was in fact a metaphor (and not only according to Gentner and Wolff's linguistic intuition), that he/she has identified it as a metaphor and understood it properly, or that the computer measured and recorded the presentation and interpretation times properly. Although with the exclusion of too long interpretation times and too long response times an attempt was made to eliminate such factors, one cannot say that 'normal' interpretation and response times always indicate the perfect performance of the task and that Gentner and Wolff are in possession of completely reliable data.

In accordance with current practice in psycholinguistics, perceptual data are not presented in Gentner & Wolff (1997). Instead, the remaining authenticated perceptual data were *interpreted*: they were sorted into prime types (base, target, both, none), averaged out and evaluated with the help of statistical tools such as one-way repeated-measures analysis of variance and the Neuman-Keuls procedure. Thus, the following *experimental data* were obtained and made public:[25]

(64) (a) Mean response time (and standard deviation) with priming type 'both' in Experiment 1 was 3730 ms (1418 ms).

(b) Mean response time (and standard deviation) with priming type 'base' in Experiment 1 was 4315 ms (1713 ms).

(c) Mean response time (and standard deviation) with priming type 'target' in Experiment 1 was 4233 ms (1483 ms).

(d) Mean response time (and standard deviation) with priming type 'blank' in Experiment 1 was 4753 ms (1160 ms).

(e) 'Both targets . . . and bases . . . resulted in [significantly] faster interpretations than blanks' in Experiment 1.

(f) 'Metaphors preceded by both primes . . . were [significantly] faster than metaphors preceded by either targets . . . or bases . . . ' in Experiment 1.
(g) 'Base primes resulted in non-significantly slower interpretation than target primes' in Experiment 1.

Motivation and background

The experimenter has to establish a *connection* between the perceptual data gained and the phenomena investigated. It has to be decided whether the former are relevant, real and reliable in relation to the latter, and it has to be spelled out what conclusions can be drawn from the former: the perceptual data indicate the presence of the given phenomenon, they indicate its absence, or they require the modification of its supposed properties etc. To this end, perceptual data have to be *interpreted*: a relationship to a phenomenon has to be established. Phenomena, however, are (low or high level) theoretical constructs; thus, the interpretation of perceptual data is *theory-dependent*.

The researcher, of course, intends to give an explanation not for the outcome of the individual measurements but for the link between results of a *series of measurements* and the expected phenomenon. Consequently, although observation is a necessary component of scientific experiments, its role is rather modest: what is perceived is only readings of the experimental apparatus, the smell of a liquid, a photograph taken with the help of a microscope etc. but not the phenomena themselves that the researcher is interested in. Theoretical considerations from different disciplines are active in the creation of the link between perceptual data and hypotheses about the phenomena investigated such as statistical tools, models of the background phenomena, investigation of other possible interpretations, calculation of the effects of known distorting factors etc. These considerations may, to varying extents, overlap with the given theory which aims at the explanation of the phenomenon investigated.

From this it follows that experimental data are always *theory-laden*, too. This theory-ladenness may concern high-level (that is, very abstract) and specific hypotheses of the given theory, but it may be related to rather low-level and non-specific hypotheses as well. This means that researchers with different background knowledge or of a different theoretical persuasion may look for different phenomena and, as a result, for different perceptual data. It may also happen that they judge different aspects of phenomena relevant, or interpret the perceptual data differently insofar as they may find they indicate different phenomena.

Gentner and Wolff *coordinated* the p-context insofar as they evaluated the relationship between the experimental data gained and the rival hypotheses under investigation as follows:[26]

(65) (a) (64)(e) indicates that 'the primes were effective' (see (61)(d)).
(b) (64)(f) was correctly predicted by alignment-first models (see (61)(c)).
(c) (64)(g) contradicts the prediction of abstraction-first models but it is in accord with alignment-first models (see (61)(a), (b)).

Differences in response times (processing times and the time required for the elaboration of an interpretation) were taken as indicating differences in processing times.

The relationship between statements in (64) and h_2/h_3 can be reconstructed as follows:

(a) $0 < |$If h_2, then no prime leads to the longest processing time.$|_{E_1} < 1$ (see (61)(d))
$0 < |$No prime led to the longest processing time.$|_{E_1} < 1$ (see (64)(e))

$0 < |h_2|_{I_a} < 1$

This inference is not deductively valid. There is, however, a semantic relationship between the premises, since the second clause of the first premise contains a consequence of the first clause: it formulates a prediction of the model based on h_2. The second premise states that this prediction is supported by the results of Experiment 1. The conclusion declares that on the basis of these pieces of information, one may conclude that hypothesis h_2 holds. Both premises are plausible according to Experiment 1 as a source, and this inference can be transformed into a deductively valid inference with the help of latent background assumptions which are at least of neutral plausibility as required in (27)(d).[27] Therefore, this inference belongs to the Type 3 of plausible inferences (see (26) in Section 9.5.4). It is capable of making the conclusion plausible but cannot guarantee its certainty. Thus, it functions as an indirect source making h_2 plausible. This means that the statement in the second premise is *weak evidence for* h_2 in the sense of (49)(a) in Section 13.3.

(b) $0 < |$If h_3, then no prime leads to the longest processing time.$|_{E_1} < 1$ (see (61)(d))
$0 < |$No prime led to the longest processing time.$|_{E1} < 1$ (see (64)(e))

$0 < |h_3|_{I_b} < 1$

This inference has the same primary and secondary characteristics as the inference in (a); the only difference is that in this case, h_3 plays the role of h_2. Consequently, the statement in the second premise is *weak evidence for both* h_2 *and* h_3.

With priming type 'both', a prediction was made only in relation to h_3:

(c) $0 < |$If h_3, then priming with both terms reduces the comprehension time of metaphors in comparison to priming with only one term.$|_{E_1} < 1$ (see (61)(c))
$0 < |$Priming with both terms reduced the comprehension time of metaphors in comparison to priming with only one term.$|_{E_1} < 1$ (see (64)(f))

$0 < |h_3|_{I_c} < 1$

This inference belongs to Type 3 of plausible inferences, too; it makes h_3 plausible as an indirect source. Moreover, since the statement in the second premise cannot be extended to an indirect source on the basis of which a positive plausibility value can be assigned to h_2 as required in (51)(b)(ii) in Section 13.3, the second premise is also *strong evidence for h_3*. That is, the datum (64)(f) makes only this hypothesis plausible.

The second premise of the next two inferences provides *strong evidence for h_3* and, at the same time, *strong evidence against h_2* in the sense of (51)(b), too, since it is a premise of Inference (d) making h_2 implausible as well as one of the premises of Inference (e) which renders h_3 plausible:

(d) $0 < |$If h_2, then subjects are faster to interpret a metaphor primed by the base than primed by the target.$|_{E_1} < 1$ (see (61)(a))
$0 < |$Base primes resulted in non-significantly slower interpretation than target primes.$|_{E_1} < 1$ (see (64)(g))

$0 < |{\sim}h_2|_{I_c} < 1$

(e) $0 < |$If h_3, then there should be no difference in the processing times of metaphors primed by the base and primed by the target, respectively.$|_{E_1} < 1$ (see (61)(b))
$0 < |$Base primes resulted in non-significantly slower interpretation than target primes.$|_{E_1} < 1$ (see (64)(g))

$0 < |h_3|_{I_e} < 1$

To sum up, according to Gentner and Wolff, (64)(g) can be regarded as *strong evidence against h_2 and for h_3* in the sense of (51) in Section 13.3, while (64)(f) is *strong evidence for h_3*. (64)(e) is *weak evidence for both rivals* in the sense of (49)(a).

As for the *modification* of the p-context, in the view of the authors these inferences neither prove nor falsify the rival hypotheses but make them more plausible and implausible, respectively. Thus, instead of giving up h_2, they summarise the outcome of Experiment 1 with great care:

> In summary, the results provide no evidence for abstraction-driven processing and are consistent with the predictions of the alignment-first model. (Gentner & Wolff 1997: 338)

One reason for this caution is that they judge Experiment 1 as data source fallible, because there are some circumstances which might indicate possible *systematic errors* that question the reliability of Experiment 1 and, consequently, the plausibility of the experimental data gained.

Motivation and background

While random errors are unpredictable but with statistical methods controllable, *systematic errors* systematically distort the results. It is very difficult to reveal their presence because they bias every single measurement in the same way, in the same direction and to the same extent. Therefore, they cannot usually be detected by a repetition of the measurement procedure and their effect cannot be eliminated by statistical means. They can be identified only with the help of another apparatus, by an experiment of a different type, or by comparison with calculations based on theoretical considerations.

Gentner and Wolff mention two findings of the subsequent analysis of Experiment 1 which may be indices of systematic errors:[28]

(66) (a) The ISI between the moment the prime disappeared and the moment the metaphor appeared was rather brief (only 100 ms). It may be the case that 'participants would have required more time to process the primes'.

(b) The variability of the response time was somewhat high. This may be due to the fact that the dependent measure was the time taken to begin typing an interpretation instead of the indication that participants had an interpretation.

Thus, Gentner and Wolff do not take an *exclusive perspective* in the sense of Section 10.6 and they do not give up the p-context version around h_2, because they think that this would not lead to a satisfactory solution of the initial p-problem. Instead, they start a new subcycle and conduct a revised version of Experiment 1 in order to control for the impact of these potential sources of error.

Motivation and background

Although Experiment 1 clearly meets the general requirements for psycholinguistic experiments, one cannot say that it confronts hypotheses of theories directly with empirical evidence in the sense as defined by the standard view of the analytical philosophy of science summarised in (E) in Section 3.2. Following the standard practice in this field, we do not see the 'raw data' (that is, the whole stimulus material and the numerical values belonging to the stimuli; as we have already mentioned, the perceptual data are missing from Gentner and Wolff's paper) and a deductively valid system of inferences leading to the result of the experiment which is then confronted with the hypotheses/theories tested but a highly complex *argumentation*. This argumentation is not strictly deductive and contains a strongly reduced set of 'raw data' in the above sense, the upshot of statistical analyses as well as the presentation of considerations concerning the interpretation and the reliability of the results, their impact on the theories at hand, and the explanatory power and other strengths of the theories investigated as well as their weak points, etc.

This does not mean, of course, that this practice could be deemed to be purely rhetorical and would per se prevent a thorough evaluation of the experimental results by the scientific community. Since experiments are not private but public affairs aimed at supplying data for scientific theorising, it is not only the results of the experiment which are put forward but every element of the experimental procedure which is judged *relevant* to the evaluation and acknowledgement of the results. Therefore, the experimenters have to present an argumentation that contains all information that may have any significance for the scientific community when they decide whether the experimental results are reliable and epistemologically useful, that is, whether they can be used for theory testing, explanation, the elaboration of new theories etc. To this end, relevant pieces of information have to be selected and arranged into a well-built system of arguments leading from the previous problems raised through the description of the experimental design and the experimental procedure to the evaluation (authentication and interpretation) of perceptual data. This, however, also unavoidably results in a *reduction* of the amount of information at the reader's disposal.

In our case, for example, Gentner and Wolff do not make public the perceptual data obtained; instead, the latter remain the private affair of the experimenters. From this it follows, however, that these statements cannot assume the role of data in the argumentation presented in the paper summarising the results of the experiment. That is, they are data for Gentner and Wolff but not for the reader – or, to use the terminology presented in Figure 7 in the next section, they are data in the argumentation process connecting the stages of the experimentation process but they do not appear in the argumentation put forward in the experimental report. Conversely, the statements in (64) do not assume the role of data in the experimental process for Gentner and Wolff, because they have calculated their plausibility value on the basis of the perceptual data, the applied statistical methods, the reliability of the grouping of the perceptual data etc. That is, the plausibility value of these statements does not originate from a direct source for the experimenters but from indirect ones. Nevertheless, (64)(a)–(g) are data for the reader, since Gentner and Wolff's paper does not contain the premises from which they could be obtained. The plausibility value of these statements is based on the reliability of the argumentation presented in Gentner & Wolff (1997) as well as on the authority of these researchers.

From this it follows that the source from which the plausibility value of experimental data in (64) originates is remarkably *complex* – and the same is true of experiments as data sources in general as well. They are not monolithic but comprise several sub-sources (or, they are sets of sources). This also means that the decision about which statement counts as a datum is strongly *p-context dependent.*

16.3.3 Subcycle 2: Experiment 2

In Experiment 2, the same stimulus material was applied as in Experiment 1. There were only two changes in comparison to Experiment 1 in the experimental design:[29] the ISI between the prime and the metaphor was increased to 2500 ms (see (66)(a)), and participants were required to press the space bar after having thought out an interpretation; in contrast to Experiment 1, the time from the offset of the metaphor until the space bar was hit was measured (see (66)(b)). This time, there were forty undergraduates who took part in the experiment. The perceptual data were authenticated along similar lines to the previous case: response times over 15,000 ms as well as cases in which the interpretation was missing were omitted. This means that it was not the time of typing an interpretation that was used to control for the correct accomplishment of the task but the presence of an interpretation. The following *experimental data* were obtained:[30]

(67) (a) Mean response time (and standard deviation) with priming type 'both' in Experiment 2 was 1577 ms (1150 ms).
(b) Mean response time (and standard deviation) with priming type 'base' in Experiment 2 was 2779 ms (1245 ms).
(c) Mean response time (and standard deviation) with priming type 'target' in Experiment 2 was 2756 ms (1197 ms).
(d) Mean response time (and standard deviation) with priming type 'blank' in Experiment 2 was 3143 ms (1185 ms).
(e) 'Seeing the target or the base alone did not result in significantly faster processing than seeing neither' in Experiment 2.
(f) 'Seeing both terms . . . led to [significantly] faster interpretation times than seeing either targets or bases' in Experiment 2.
(g) 'Metaphors were interpreted no faster when primed by bases than when primed by targets' in Experiment 2.

The relationship between these data and the two models was captured as follows:[31]

(68) (a) (67)(e) contradicts the predictions of both models (see (61)(d)).
(b) (67)(f) was correctly predicted by alignment-first models (see (61)(c)).
(c) (67)(g) contradicts the prediction of abstraction-first models but it is in accord with the prediction of alignment-first models (see (61)(a), (b)).

Gentner and Wolff regard (67)(g) as *strong evidence against* h_2. As for the *coordination of the p-context*, they point out that h_2 has become implausible again:

the results failed to bear out the predictions of abstraction-first models. (Gentner & Wolff 1997: 339)

16.3.4 *The modification of the p-context and comparison of the solutions obtained in Cycles 1 and 2*

Within an *evaluative perspective*, the authors argue that the similarity among the experimental designs of Experiment 1, Experiment 2 and two only slightly different earlier experiments (see Wolff & Gentner 1992), as well as the harmony among their results, make the results of Experiments 1 and 2 highly reliable. Therefore, they form a *set of sources* which provide data that make h_2 highly implausible:

The results from Experiments 1 and 2 offer little encouragement for abstraction-first models. These results . . . argue against abstraction-first models as a general account of metaphor processing. (Gentner & Wolff 1997: 339)

This means that it is possible to give up h_2 and to deem the modified p-context version as a *consistent solution* of the p-problem (60) in the sense of (40)(a) in Section 10.2. This is, however, not seen as a *resolution* of (60) in the sense of (41) by Gentner and Wolff, because there are, as we will see in Section 16.5, further pieces of information which have not been taken into consideration but might yet lead to a better solution. Therefore, a new cycle was started.

16.4 Intermezzo: on the cyclic nature of psycholinguistic experiments

The relationship between Experiments 1 and 2 reveals a characteristic of psycholinguistic experiments of the utmost importance, that is, their *cyclic nature*. The experimental process should be viewed as a search for the best fit achievable between the experimental design, the theory of the experimental apparatus, the process of experimentation, the perceptual data gained, the authentication and interpretation of the latter, the theory of the phenomenon investigated, etc. To find this fit, one has in most cases to turn back to earlier stages of the experimentation process and *modify* some component. Every component can

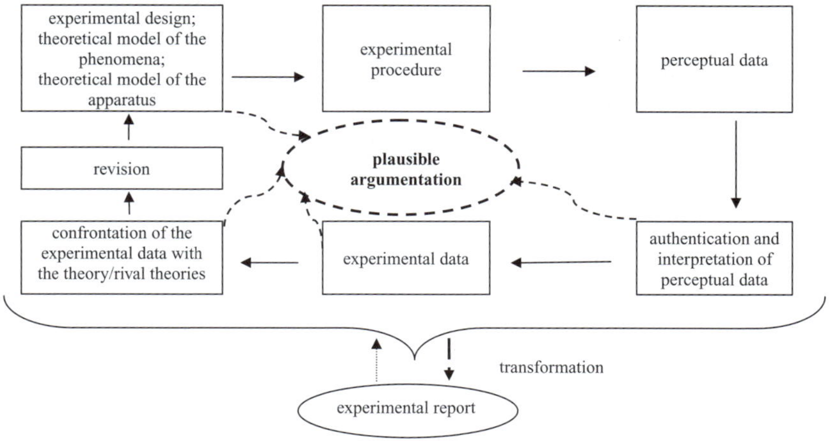

Figure 7. The structure of the experimental process

be *revised* and the revisions have to be repeated again and again till there is mutual support among the constituents.

Thus, we will raise the hypothesis that this cyclic process is organised and conducted by an *argumentation process* which tries to clarify the relationship among hypotheses of the experimental design, the theoretical model of phenomena, the theoretical model of the experimental apparatus, the theory under test and its rivals as well as statements describing the events of the experimental procedure, capturing the results of the interpretation and authentication of perceptual data etc. See Figure 7.

One of the most substantial characteristics of this argumentation process is that it operates with and manages *uncertain, fallible and often conflicting pieces of information.*

Hypotheses used in the experimental design, the theoretical model of the phenomena and of the apparatus make up the starting point of the experimental process. They are not true with certainty but they are supported to some extent by theoretical considerations, by earlier experiments, or are simply (reasonable) conjectures. They allow for a rough estimation of the outcome of the experiment – the experimenter has in most cases some ideas about the results to be expected. After the experimental procedure, in possession of the perceptual and experimental data, this preliminary guess may be strengthened. Nevertheless, it may happen that the perceptual data cannot be interpreted properly, or they seem to be in conflict with the predictions. In such cases, the reliability of the previously accepted hypotheses has to be revised. The interpretation and authentication of the perceptual data may also indicate shortcomings in the experimental procedure, in the experimental design, or in the theoretical model of the phenomena or of the apparatus. Therefore, all facets of the experiment conducted have to be *re-examined*, and, if it seems to be necessary, control experiments have to be carried out, or the experimental design has to be modified and the experiment repeated. Moreover, even the interpretation or the authentication of the perceptual data itself may be faulty and be in need of modification. The tenability of the hypotheses raised can undergo changes, either directly or indirectly. For example, mistakes revealed by the use of statistical methods undermine not only the reliability of the authentication of the perceptual data but require the re-evaluation of the experimental results as well. From this it follows that it is of crucial importance that one reveals the connections between the statements which capture different aspects of the experimental procedure, and makes the checks and cross-checks as comprehensive as possible. Consequently, the effectiveness and comprehensiveness of the plausible argumentation process organising the conduct and control of the experiment largely determines the reliability of the experimental results.

This argumentation process does not consist of purely formal, logical inferences because it takes into consideration the uncertainty of the statements as well. It is not acted out in public; rather, it is to a considerable extent a *private affair* of the experimenters. This does not mean, however, that there are no rules which govern it. Since experimental results have to be acknowledged by the scientific community, the experimenters have to strive to fulfil the norms against which experiments are judged. That is, they have to convince themselves of the reliability and acceptability of the outcome of the experiment and after this, they have to persuade the scientific community as well. Therefore, the researchers have to transform the argumentation process into an experimental report summarising and making public the results of the experiment.

The *presentation of the results* of the experiment, however, not only leads to a concise and coherent report on the experiment but also conceals several details of the experimentation process. Therefore, it *replaces* the original, real event as well as the argumentation process governing it with an edited, selective, informationally reduced and/or modified picture. Thus, there is a danger that the researcher eliminates relevant information from the published report so that important decisions remain outside public control, and he/she overestimates the plausibility of the results. From this it follows that the acceptability of the experimental report depends not only on the reliability of the experiment itself but it is also influenced by the specific process of the *transformation* of the non-public argumentation process into its public version. If the transformation results in a distorted picture of the experimental process insofar as the plausibility of the results and that of other hypotheses is systematically overestimated, weak points are suppressed, or if relevant facets of the experimental procedure cannot be reconstructed and evaluated, then the experimental report has to be deemed unreliable.

The *evaluation* of experimental results, however, has to start from the experimental report which is nothing other than an edited, transformed version of the non-public argumentation process. While the latter is part of an ontologically complex process of scientific experiment, the former is purely argumentative. It is a mixture: it contains elements or traces of the original argumentation process as well as argumentative tools needed to make this reduced set of information coherent, comprehensible and persuasive for the reader. Clearly, this transformation can be regarded as acceptable when it does not change the plausibility value of the hypotheses of the original argumentation. This can be achieved if it contains all information which is relevant for the evaluation of the steps of the experimental process. This means that the reader should be in a position to reconstruct and continue the non-public argumentation process. In this way, the reader could become a *virtual participant of the creation, analysis and evaluation of the perceptual and experimental data*. This means that he/she has to be equipped to reconstruct not only the experimental procedure but also the interpretation and authentication of the perceptual data and the significant steps of the argumentation process which organises the elaboration of the experimental results.

16.5 Argumentation cycle 3: change from a Contrastive to a Combinative Strategy

16.5.1 Setting up a new p-context

Gentner and Wolff argue that although the experiments conducted so far provide strong evidence against h_2, a closer examination of abstraction-first models reveals that they comprise two subcases which apply to different types of metaphors and make use of different hypotheses:

(69) (a) There is 'a preexisting metaphorical abstraction or category associated with the base term' which 'allows processing to proceed via access to a conventionalised meaning'.

(b) 'There is no preexisting category association: the abstraction must be derived on the spot', that is, 'an ad hoc category must be derived from the base term in order to process the metaphor'.[32]

Gentner and Wolff raise the conjecture that (69)(b) is incorrect and this might have been the reason why h_2 fails; thus, if one narrows down the scope of application of h_2 to conventional metaphors and rejects (69)(b), then abstraction-first models may gain experimental support. They mention some approaches which propose similar hypotheses such as the lexical representation hypothesis (see Swinney & Cutler 1979), or findings by Blank (1988), Blasko & Connine (1993) etc. These results increase the plausibility of (69)(a). To test this, Experiment 3 was performed.

16.5.2 *Subcycle 1: Experiment 3*

There was a substantial change in the experimental design in comparison to Experiments 1 and 2.[33] The stimulus material was produced in such a way that twenty metaphors with high base conventionality and low metaphorical similarity were selected. The aim of this choice was to create circumstances where the use of the processing mode predicted by abstraction-first models is the most likely and the processing mode suggested by alignment-first models seems to be the least likely. The dependent measure was the time taken to press the first key of an interpretation as in Experiment 1; further, the ISI between the prime and the metaphor was 2500 ms as in Experiment 2. Four levels of prime type were run within subjects, and four between-subjects groups were used to counterbalance the assignment of metaphors to conditions. Participants were forty undergraduates for course credit.

The low similarity of base and target as well as the conventionality of the base term were secured with the help of two prior control experiments.[34] With the help of the control experiments, two relevant factors of the stimulus material were controlled for not with the help of the experimenters' linguistic intuition but on the basis of the linguistic intuitions of twenty-four and thirty-two undergraduates, respectively. This step, of course, contributes to the reliability of Experiment 3 as a data source. Nevertheless, one cannot state with certainty that every metaphor used was low in metaphorical similarity and high in conventionality. First, people's intuition cannot be regarded as a completely reliable source. Second, it was Gentner and Wolff who interpreted and evaluated the similarity/conventionality ratings gained; therefore, the procedure cannot be judged to be completely objective and without any subjective decisions.

For the authentication of the perceptual data, Gentner and Wolff kept the principles applied in Experiments 1 and 2: cases with response times over 15,000 ms, without interpretation or with interpretation times over 20 s were discarded. The following *experimental data* were obtained:[35]

(70) (a) Mean response time (and standard deviation) with priming type 'both' in Experiment 3 was 2894 ms (1360 ms).
(b) Mean response time (and standard deviation) with priming type 'base' in Experiment 3 was 3706 ms (1487 ms).
(c) Mean response time (and standard deviation) with priming type 'target' in Experiment 3 was 4389 ms (1729 ms).
(d) Mean response time (and standard deviation) with priming type 'blank' in Experiment 3 was 4601 ms (1515 ms).
(e) 'Base primes led to [significantly] faster interpretation times than did blanks, while targets did not' in Experiment 3.
(f) 'Participants were [significantly] faster to interpret a metaphor when it was preceded by both terms . . . than when it was preceded by either the target . . . or the base . . . ' in Experiment 3.
(g) 'Metaphors preceded by bases were interpreted [significantly] faster than metaphors preceded by targets' in Experiment 3.

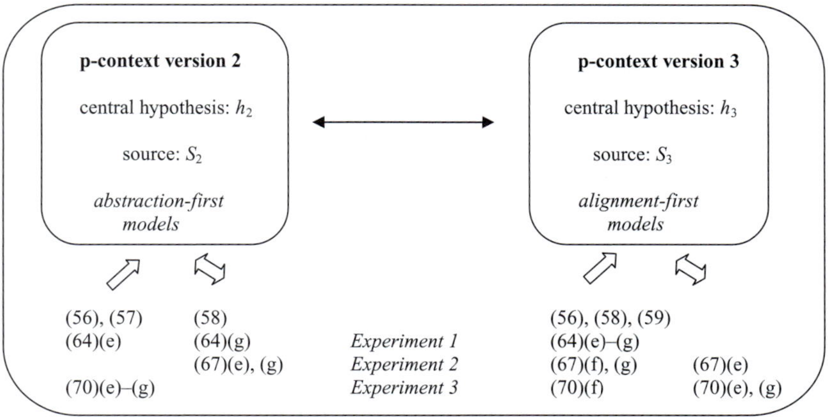

Figure 8. Cycle 3: the p-context after conducting Subcycle 1

These data were confronted with the predictions obtained from the application of abstraction-first models and (69)(a) as follows:[36]

(71) (a) (70)(e) is consistent with the hypothesis of abstraction-first models that 'seeing the base first allows processing to begin early, while seeing the target does not' (see (61)(d)).

(b) (70)(f) is consistent with both models and with the results of Experiment 1 (see (61)(c)).

(c) (70)(g) is in accord with the prediction of abstraction-first models (see (61)(a)).

On the basis of (71), Gentner and Wolff regard (70)(g) as *strong evidence for* h_2:

For the first time, clear support was obtained for abstraction-first models . . . The results of Experiment 3 suggest that abstraction-first processing may obtain when base conventionality is high and metaphorical similarity is low. (Gentner & Wolff 1997: 341)

The results of Experiment 3 as summarised in (71) and the results of Experiments 1 and 2 as summarised in (65) and (68) indicate that the p-context remained *p-inconsistent* even after its extension by the sources Experiments 1–3 and the coordination of the extended p-context. Namely, h_3 can be applied to novel metaphors and to many conventional metaphors but it fails in the case of high-conventionality and low-similarity metaphors; conversely, h_2 succeeded only in the latter case. Since data gained from the sources Experiments 1 and 2 support h_3 while data gained from Experiment 3 support h_2, the plausible inferences built on them do not form a set of sources which would assign a plausibility value to h_2 or h_3.

Figure 8 illustrates the coordinated p-context.

16.5.3 Modification of the p-context: strategy change

By taking an *evaluative perspective* in the sense of Section 10.5, Gentner and Wolff seem to have come to the conclusion that the application of the *Contrastive Strategy* (that is, the treatment of the different p-context variants as rivals, see Section 10.6) failed, because it did not lead to a *solution* of the starting p-problem in the sense of (40) in Section 10.2. Neither the statement *There is an initial process of projection from the base followed by a later verification process and it is not the case that there is an initial process of alignment between the base and target representations followed by projection of inferences* (see (60)(a)) nor its negation (see (60)(b)) is plausible or implausible on the basis of *all sources* available in the current state of the p-context:

> it appears that abstraction-driven processing may occur for conventional metaphors, whose bases have prestored stock meanings . . . Although the abstraction-driven model can be applied to novel metaphors as well, by postulating that an ad hoc abstract category is derived from the base and then applied to the target . . . , the results of the first two studies are not encouraging for this possibility. (Gentner & Wolff 1997: 341f.)

Abstraction-first models seem to provide a good description of the processing of metaphors whose bases are highly conventional; alignment-first models, however, seem to be appropriate for novel metaphors. Therefore, giving any of them up would be unmotivated because it would lead to information loss. Instead, Gentner and Wolff *modify the p-context* at another point: they give up a common latent background assumption of the two rival models according to which the processing of metaphors takes place in a single, uniform way in the case of all metaphors. As a second step in the modification of the p-context, a *revised version* of both rival hypotheses is put forward in order to find an explanation for the results of Experiments 1–3:

(72) *The career of metaphor hypothesis (h_4)*:
- (a) 'For a novel metaphor, the comprehension process is one of structural alignment and projection' between the literal base and target representations along the lines of h_3.
- (b) 'If the base term is used repeatedly to yield this interpretation, then the metaphoric abstraction will gradually come to be stored as an alternative sense of the base term.'
- (c) 'When the conventionalised sense becomes sufficiently accessible, it can be accessed as part of the process of metaphor comprehension.' Thus, an abstraction-guided process may apply to stock metaphors in accord with h_2.[37]

(72) can be reconstructed as the application of the *Combinative Strategy* (see Sections 10.5–6): the two models are seen not as rivals but p-context versions which have to be maintained *simultaneously* by *separating* their scope. With the strict separation of the field of application of h_2 and h_3, the conflict between the

contradictory statements in (60)(a) and (60)(b) does not emerge, since neither p-context-version includes them together.

In this way, Gentner and Wolff maintain *both* statements h_2 and h_3, since they believe that both of them capture certain aspects of metaphor processing correctly and neither of them can be given up. Thus, they treat the two p-context-versions around h_2 and h_3 not as rivals but as *coexisting* p-context versions.

16.5.4 Subcycle 2: Experiment 4

A new *argumentation cycle* is started to test this new, more complex hypothesis. This requires the extension of the p-context by a new source, by Experiment 4. The *experimental design* is motivated by two considerations (see Gentner & Wolff 1997: 342). First, (72) covers hypotheses which have been tested separately, in the course of different experiments, or have been proposed only on the basis of a subsequent analysis of the experimental results. Therefore, testing of these statements with the help of a single experiment seems to be reasonable and could increase their plausibility considerably. Second, further investigation of Experiment 3 revealed a weak point which might decrease its reliability and, via this, the plausibility of the data it provides. Namely, there were two different factors (high base conventionality and low metaphorical similarity of base and target) but their impact has not been tested separately. Consequently, it cannot be decided on this basis which one of these two factors is a sufficient determinant of abstraction-driven processing. That is, (72) leaves open two possibilities because it does not decide whether conventionality alone is a relevant factor, or whether, besides high conventionality, low metaphorical similarity is also required for abstraction-guided processing. Therefore, the p-context is not only informationally overdetermined but it is *informationally underdetermined* as well in the sense of (39) in Section 10.2: both the statement *Metaphorical similarity is a decisive factor in metaphor processing* and its negation are of neutral plausibility on the basis of the sources in the given state of the p-context.[38] Thus, h_4 covers two versions of (72)(c), but on the basis of the information at hand, no choice can be made between them:

(73) An abstraction-guided process may apply to conventional metaphors in accord with h_2.

(74) An abstraction-guided process may apply to high-conventional and low-similarity metaphors in accord with h_2.[39]

Figure 9 captures the p-context version around h_4 before conducting Experiment 4.[40]

In order to gain data from Experiment 4 which might enable a decision to be taken between (73) and (74), the *stimulus material* was constructed by crossing

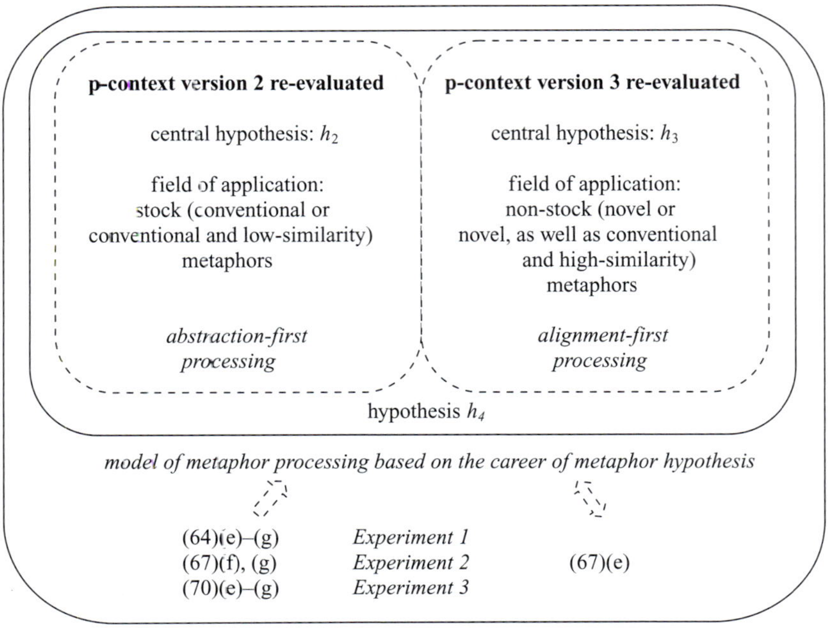

Figure 9. Cycle 3: setting up the p-context at the start of Subcycle 2

high/low base conventionality and high/low metaphorical similarity, resulting in four conditions. Gentner & Wolff (1997: 342) summarise the possible outcomes of the experiment and their relationship to h_2 and h_4 as follows:

(75) (a) If h_2 is correct and the abstraction-first model holds for every metaphor, then 'we will see a base advantage in all four cells'.
(b) If no base advantage can be found anywhere, then h_2 is completely wrong and h_4 fails as well (see (72)(c)).
(c) 'If abstraction-first processing applies only when conventionalised base abstractions exist' (that is, if h_2 is bound to base conventionality, see (73)), that is, if h_4 & (73) holds, 'then a base advantage will obtain in the two cells that have high conventional metaphorical meanings'.
(d) If 'abstraction-driven processing occurs only when base conventionality is high and relational similarity is low as in Experiment 3' (that is, if h_2 is restricted to the combination of these two factors as in (74), thus h_4 & (74) holds), then 'a base advantage occurs in only one cell'.
(e) h_4 predicts 'no base advantage for novel metaphors'.
(f) If h_4 is correct, then 'metaphors high in relational similarity should be faster to comprehend than low-similarity metaphors' (cf. (72)(a)).

Two sets of sixteen bases were chosen to test these possibilities; one set consisted of terms high in conventionality, the other set involved terms of

Table 1 *Means and standard deviations in Experiment 4*

	Prime type				
	Both	Base	Target	Blank	Overall
High conventionality					
High similarity	2487 (2161)	3143 (1749)	3358 (3358)	3750 (2062)	3181 (2200)
Low similarity	2947 (2630)	3403 (2052)	3897 (2667)	4130 (2208)	3598 (2439)
Low conventionality					
High similarity	3158 (2397)	3636 (2882)	3516 (2665)	4353 (2750)	3668 (2536)
Low similarity	3613 (2875)	4538 (2882)	4049 (2849)	4860 (2875)	4276 (2739)
Overall means	3048 (2552)	3677 (2303)	3718 (2535)	4274 (2514)	

low conventionality. Every base was paired with target pairs: one target had high relational similarity with the base, the other low, but the members of the target pairs had similar meanings.[41] The grades of conventionality and similarity were controlled with the help of two prior experiments consisting of rating tasks performed by undergraduates.[42] Thus, the experimental design was based on the interpretation of thirty-two metaphor pairs which were carefully counterbalanced among the factors investigated. A 2x2x4 design was used, and all three factors (conventionality, similarity, prime type) were within-subjects. Four assignments of subjects to groups were used to achieve counterbalancing over the first two factors. Each participant received one member of each of the thirty-two metaphor sets. The ISI between the prime and metaphor was 0 ms. Response times were measured as in Experiment 2. A total of 112 undergraduates took part in the experimental procedure; this is a considerable number. The perceptual data were *authenticated* in a similar way to those in the earlier experiments: response times over 16,000 ms as well as cases where the interpretation was not supplied or where a time longer than 20 s was taken to enter the response were excluded.[43] The following *experimental data* were obtained with the help of analyses of variance and the Bonferroni method of error protection:

(76) (a) Table 1 shows the means and standard deviations in Experiment 4.
(b) 'Overall, metaphors primed by their bases were comprehended no faster than metaphors primed by their targets' in Experiment 4.
(c) 'Metaphors with high relational similarity . . . were comprehended [significantly] faster than metaphors with low relational similarity . . . ' in Experiment 4.
(d) 'High-conventionality metaphors . . . were comprehended [significantly] faster than low-conventionality metaphors . . . ' in Experiment 4; nevertheless, the result was only 'marginally significant across items'.

(e) Interpretation was significantly faster after priming by the base than by priming with the target in the cell of high base conventionality and low relational similarity in Experiment 4.
(f) There was no base advantage in the other three cells in Experiment 4. There was either no difference or, with the low-conventionality, high-similarity condition, a reverse result was found.[44]

Motivation and background

It can be questioned whether (76)(b) is a datum in the sense of our definition provided in (47) in Section 13.2, because it can be inferred from (76)(a) and does not require the use of statistical methods and further data not provided in the experimental report. Thus, it may be reconstructed in such a way that it originates from an indirect source, since it can be inferred from the values in the second and third cell in the last row of Table 1. This finding raises the question whether the concept of 'evidence' should be built upon that of the 'datum'. The possibility of allowing for all statements with a positive plausibility value to play the role of the evidence should be considered, provided they fulfil the criteria laid down in points (i)–(ii) in the definitions (49)–(51)(a) and (b), respectively.

Gentner and Wolff compare the predictions of the two models and the experimental data as follows:[45]

(77) (a) From (76)(b) it follows that h_2 is not supported (see (75)(a)).
(b) Alignment-driven models predicted (76)(c) correctly (see (75)(f)).
(c) (76)(d) is consistent with h_4 (see (75)(b), (c), (d)).
(d) (76)(e) provides evidence for abstraction-based processing when base conventionality is high and metaphorical similarity is low, that is, for h_4 & (74) (see (75)(c)).
(e) (76)(f) shows that the possibility that abstraction-driven processing holds whenever base conventionality is high (that is, h_2's restriction to high base conventionality as required by h_4 & (73)) was not supported (see (75)(c)).

Within an *evaluative perspective* the authors judge that (76)(b)–(c) is *strong evidence* for h_4 and *against* h_2. Moreover, Experiment 4 provided data (see (76)(e)–(f)) which enable a decision to be taken between (73) and (74) as well:

the results again fail to bear out a general abstraction-driven model. What about the abstraction-driven model restricted to high-conventional metaphors? This version also fails... These results are consistent with the career of metaphor hypothesis, which holds that novel metaphors are processed in alignment-first manner and that conventional metaphors may (but need not) be processed in abstraction-first manner... One *plausible account* is that alignment-driven and abstraction-driven processes can occur simultaneously... Then the existence of a prestored metaphorical abstraction for the

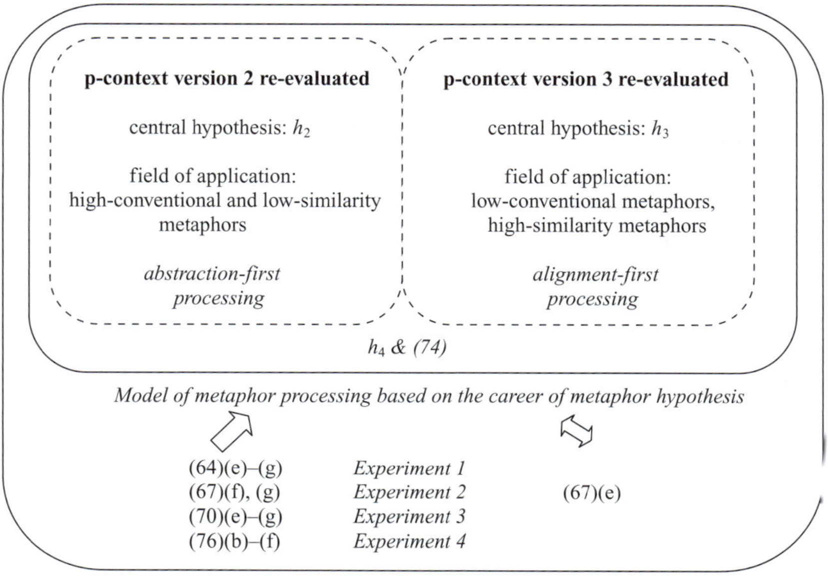

Figure 10. Cycle 3: the p-context after conducting Subcycle 2

> base term permits abstraction-driven processing; accessing that base category can occur early in the metaphor comprehension process. On the other hand, the more similar the two terms, the greater the likelihood that alignment-driven processing will finish first. (Gentner & Wolff 1997: 345; emphasis added)

A possible interpretation of this quotation is that the p-context built around h_4 & (74) provides a *solution to the starting p-problem* in the sense of (40)(b) which is shown in Figure 10.

Although the solution-candidate presented in Figure 10 is in almost full accord with the experimental data obtained so far, Gentner and Wolff do not find it satisfactory because they judge *this separation of the field of application of the two models unmotivated.* Namely, it is not clear why exactly these combinations of the two relevant factors result in alignment-driven and abstraction-driven processing, respectively; that is, there is *no explanation* for the finding that conventionality seems to be capable of guaranteeing abstraction-driven processing only in the presence of low relational similarity between the base and target terms.

Therefore, the authors' evaluation of the situation can be interpreted in such a way that in their view, the p-context around h_4 & (74) *cannot be regarded as a solution* to the starting p-problem in the sense of (40)(b) and the separation of the two p-context versions has to be grounded on some other principle.

16.5.5 Subcycle 3: the race model of metaphor processing

As we have already mentioned, (72)(c) was formulated very carefully, because it left open two possibilities: a base advantage should be present either for all high-conventional metaphors or only for those whose terms are of low similarity. In order to find a better motivation for the separation of the two coexisting p-context versions, Gentner and Wolff first propose two rival hypotheses as possible alternative elaborations of (72)(c) instead of (73) and (74):

(78) 'Processing shifts entirely to abstraction-driven processing with conventionalisation.'

(79) 'Alignment-driven and abstraction-driven processes occur simultaneously in processing conventional metaphors, as in the race models proposed for the processing of idioms.'[46]

From the experimental data captured in (76), Gentner and Wolff conclude that the existence of metaphorical abstraction associated with the base is not enough to guarantee abstraction-driven processing. Thus, (76)(f) provides *strong evidence for* (79) and *against* (78).

Adding (79) to h_4 and rejecting (78) and (74) also means that there is a *change in the application of the Combinative Strategy*: the two p-context versions (models) are not separated with the help of their restriction to different fields of application, that is, to different types of metaphors. Instead, the simultaneous operation of the two processing modes is enabled but only one of them is regarded as *the* processing mode of the given metaphor: the one which provides a faster interpretation. In this way, the parallelism of h_2 and h_3 is reduced to stages of the process but not to the reaching of the final stage, that is, to the entire process. This also means that the question whether an alignment-driven or an abstraction-driven procedure has produced the interpretation of a particular metaphor cannot be predicted in every case on the basis of some characteristic of the given metaphor. Instead, the plausibility of the latent background assumption of a strict division of metaphors into ones with purely abstraction-driven processing on the one hand and with purely alignment-driven processing on the other (see (60)) is questioned. Gentner and Wolff argue for the hypothesis that there is a continuum where in most cases both processing modes are present and run in parallel with each other for different lengths of time depending on the grade of conventionality of the base term and the degree of relational similarity.

16.5.6 Comparison of the solutions obtained in Cycles 1, 2 and 3

The p-context in Figure 11 is a possible *solution* to the starting p-problem in the sense of (40)(b).

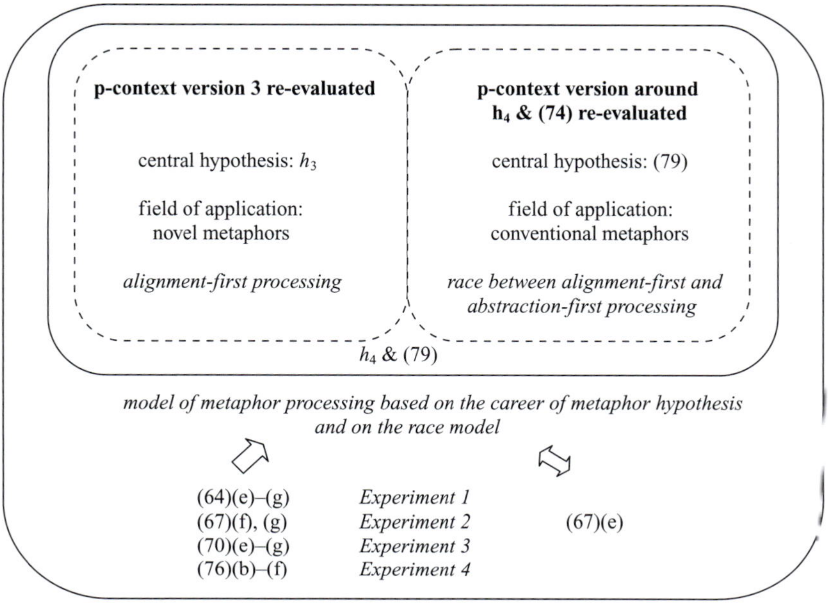

Figure 11. Cycle 3: the p-context after conducting Subcycle 3

The 'General discussion' in Gentner and Wolff's paper summarises the results of the four experiments conducted. At this point, Gentner and Wolff could have settled the argumentation process by declaring h_4 & (79) to be the *resolution* of the initial p-problem in the sense of (41), that is, to the best solution achievable on the basis of the information collected so far. Instead, they start a new *argumentation cycle* and *extend the p-context* with further data. The aim of this step might be twofold. First, the authors increase the plausibility of the career of metaphor hypothesis by showing its potential for development and further elaboration. Second, they compare it against the newest version of the rival abstraction-first model type.

16.6 Argumentation cycle 4: return to the Contrastive Strategy

16.6.1 Setting up the p-context

Gentner and Wolff raise a *rival hypothesis* of (79):

(80) 'The process continues to be alignment-driven, even for conventional metaphors.'[47]

The acceptance of (80) leads to a new turn in the argumentation strategy aimed at reaching a decision between h_2 and h_3: it is nothing else but a return to the application of the *Contrastive Strategy*.[48] Since the p-context version around h_2 (and via this, (60)(a) as well) is completely rejected by (80), the Contrastive Strategy results in the *Exclusive Strategy* in connection with the rival hypotheses h_2 and h_3.

16.6.2 The elaboration of the p-context

After the elimination of h_2 from the p-context, the following hypothesis is put forward as a new rival of h_4 & (79):

(81) *Re-evaluated version of the career of metaphor hypothesis (h_5):*[49]

(a) 'For a novel metaphor, the comprehension process is one of structural alignment and projection' between the literal base and target representations along the lines of h_3. (= (72)(a))

(b) 'If the base term is used repeatedly to yield this interpretation, then the metaphoric abstraction will gradually come to be stored as an alternative sense of the base term.' (= (72)(b))

(c) 'When the conventionalised sense becomes sufficiently accessible, it can be accessed as part of the process of metaphor comprehension' and may facilitate processing. Nevertheless, the process remains alignment-driven in accord with h_3 even for conventional metaphors.

Within an *evaluative perspective* one may conclude that (81) is a *solution* to the starting p-problem because it meets the criteria laid down in (40)(a). Thus, the two rival p-context versions (solutions) built around h_4 & (79) and h_5, respectively, confront the two strategies, the Contrastive and the Combinative Strategy, too.

Motivation and background

The continuation of the argumentation process and the starting of a new argumentation cycle again bears witness that Gentner and Wolff do not consider experimental data to be true with certainty or decisive among rival theories. Instead, they treat them as pieces of evidence making (central) hypotheses of theories/theory-variants plausible if they reinforce their predictions or implausible in cases when they are in conflict with the predictions of the given model. Therefore, they are treated as arguments among other types of data such as hypotheses of a theory, 'linguistic data' etc. They are neither decisive in the sense that one could preclude the possibility of the emergence of a new theory/theory-version with which they are also compatible.

Experimental data do not lead to ultimate results but they always underdetermine the range of their possible explanations. From this two conclusions present themselves. First, the role of data in linguistic theories cannot be reduced to testing hypotheses/theories because data contribute to the *development (re-evaluation)* of theories by motivating the elaboration of further, more sophisticated explanations which can be tested and compared against the prevalent rivals of the theory in new experimental settings. Second, as we have mentioned in Section 10.2, the continuous emergence of p-inconsistencies is inevitable.

Gentner and Wolff offer several arguments in favour of the re-evaluated version of the career of metaphor hypothesis:[50]

(82) (a) On the basis of h_5 predictions can be made which are entirely consistent with the results of Experiments 1–4.
(b) h_5 is capable of explaining a further experimental result by Gentner & Wolff according to which the alignment of high-conventional high-similarity metaphors is especially rapid.
(c) The plausibility of h_5 is also increased by findings of Gibbs suggesting that 'even idioms can retain some semantic productivity'.

While (82)(a) is *weak evidence for* h_5 in the sense of (49)(a) in Section 13.3, (82)(b)–(c) can be regarded as *strong evidence for* this hypothesis in the sense of (51)(a).

16.6.3 *Comparison of the solutions obtained in Cycles 1–4*

The two authors do not compare the plausibility value of h_4 & (79) and h_5, nor weigh up the tenability of the two p-context versions around these hypotheses. Consequently, the p-context is still *p-inconsistent*, but this p-inconsistency is caused by two versions of the career of metaphor hypothesis.

It is important to remark that, as this case study witnesses, the application of the Contrastive Strategy and the Combinative Strategy does not obey strict rules: one can neither establish their order nor base their preference on some simple general criteria. The authors present some further arguments in favour of both versions of the career of metaphor hypothesis (see Gentner & Wolff 1997: 346f.):

(83) (a) h_4 & (79)/h_5 is 'consistent with recent work on the effects of conventionality on the processing of metaphors . . . , suggesting that conventionalisation results in a shift in the dominant processing mode from on-line active interpretation to retrieval of stored meanings'.
(b) h_4 & (79)/h_5 provides an explanation for the creation of metaphorical categories. Thus, structural alignment can be regarded as 'a source of metaphorical polysemy in word meaning'.
(c) h_4 & (79)/h_5 'offers a way in which metaphorical and literal comparisons can be captured within a single mechanism'.

Gentner and Wolff interpret three further arguments not simply as *weak evidence for* the career of metaphor hypothesis but also as *strong evidence for* this view and *against* abstraction-first models (h_2):[51]

(84) (a) Onishi & Murphy (1993)'s experimental results according to which the processing time of metaphors depends on the distance between the two terms of the metaphor can be easily accounted for by the alignment view but cannot be explained by an abstraction-driven model.

(b) 'It is not clear . . . how an abstraction-first process would easily yield different interpretations for metaphors having the same base but different targets . . . '. The model relying on the career of metaphor hypothesis, in contrast, is capable of creating and coordinating several metaphorical interpretations and choosing the best of them with the help of the candidate inference mechanism.

(c) As Murphy (1996) has pointed out, targets must constrain the information from the base, because not all of it can be applied to the target concept. If, however, 'the role of targets occurs late in processing, many inferences may need to be created and rejected before an acceptable inference is found'; that is, the abstraction-first approach 'could prove computationally expensive'.

(d) Linguistic data and experimental results 'suggesting large-scale conventionalised mappings between different domains' . . . 'can readily be accounted for by a model based on h_4 & (79)/h_5', 'which is geared toward the alignment of relational systems'. It is unclear, however, how a model around h_2 'could handle large-scale parallel structures, because of its emphasis on a single, specific class-inclusion relationship, rather than a system of relationships'.

In connection with (84)(c), Gentner and Wolff refer to a *re-evaluated* version of abstraction-first models proposed by Glucksberg, McGlone & Manfredi (1997) which is capable of solving this problem:

(85) Re-evaluated version of the h_2 hypothesis (h_6):[52]

(a) 'Base and target are both active from the outset of metaphor comprehension.'

(b) 'Base and target each independently provide separate aspects of the information required for an interpretation.'

(c) 'In the first stages of metaphor processing, the base provides the metaphoric category abstraction, and, simultaneously, the target provides its preferred dimensions of attribution.'

Moreover, h_6 can explain the results of Experiments 1 and 2, too: since both the target and the base are active from the beginning, both the base and target terms should be effective early primes. Therefore, no base advantage follows from this hypothesis.

With the inclusion of the p-context version around h_6 in the (comprehensive) p-context, Gentner and Wolff increase the *p-problematicness* of the latter again without making an attempt at its resolution. They do not clarify the relationship

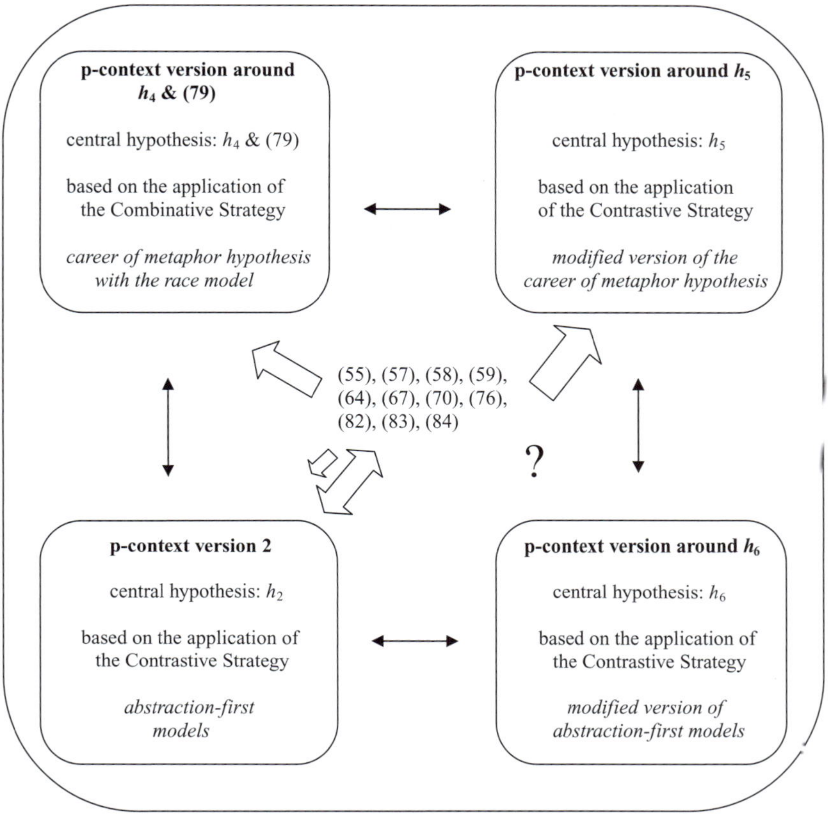

Figure 12. The final p-context

of this hypothesis to the results of Experiments 3 and 4 nor to the data presented in (55)–(59), (70), (76) and (82)–(84).[53] Consequently, the plausibility of h_5 on the basis of the inferences built on these data cannot be compared to that of its rivals. In the case of h_2, h_4 & (79) and h_5, however, it is possible to make such a comparison. As we have seen in Section 9.3, (11) makes it possible to estimate the plausibility value of a statement on the basis of a set of sources. Therefore, the higher the number of the indirect sources relying on the data (55)–(59), (64), (67), (70), (76) and (82)–(84) which make a given hypothesis plausible, the higher is its plausibility on the basis of this set of sources.[54] Similarly, the higher the number of the indirect sources relying on the data (55)–(59), (64), (67), (70), (76) and (82)–(84) which make a given hypothesis implausible, the higher is its implausibility on the basis of this set of data.[55] Thus, Gentner and Wolff's argumentation in this paper ends with the p-context illustrated in Figure 12.

16.7 Conclusions

If we compare the results of our reconstruction with the characterisation of *plausible argumentation* provided in (45) in Section 10.8, we can come to the following conclusion:

(86) (a) The argumentation presented in Gentner & Wolff (1997) involves a system of plausible inferences, since it relies mostly on plausible inferences belonging to Type 3 (weak reduction) and Type 1 (plausible *modus tollens*).
(b) The argumentation process is globally cyclic, but locally it contains linear stages as well, since the authors elaborate and re-evaluate several theory-versions (p-contexts). During the cyclic returns, they extend the information presented in the literature and summarised in the opening sections of their paper with new sources and data, they coordinate the old and new pieces of information, and they continuously modify the hypotheses raised. In this way, they return to the starting p-problem again and again and examine it in the light of the information available after the previous cycles.
(c) The authors' argumentation pursues heuristic goals, since it intends to solve the problem of modelling the process of metaphor comprehension (see (60)(a)–(b)).
(d) It prismatically re-evaluates the p-context, since it compares many different theories and theory-versions (see h_1–h_6) and with this, it investigates the problems related to the cognitive processes of metaphor comprehension from different points of view.
(e) Gentner and Wolff elaborate several solutions to the p-problems in the starting p-context (p-context versions built around h_2, h_3, h_4, h_5 and h_6) and show that none of them can be regarded as the resolution of the p-problems which emerged on the basis of the information at hand. Nevertheless, they narrow down the range of possible resolutions considerably (namely, to the application of h_4 & (79) and h_5, respectively).

Of course, this conclusion is only *plausible* in the light of our argumentation presented in Sections 16.2–7 but not true with certainty. A comparison between the concepts of data and evidence provided by the p-model as summarised in (48) and (52) in Sections 13.2–3 and our reconstruction in the present chapter leads to the following (plausible) conclusions:

(87) (a) Experimental data in Gentner & Wolff (1997) are plausible statements that are supported by Experiments 1–4 as direct sources only partially, since the authentication and interpretation of perceptual data do not result in certainly true pieces of information.
(b) They obtain their initial plausibility on the basis of the reliability of their sources Experiments 1–4. These values, however, dynamically changed at later stages of the cyclic and prismatic argumentation process. For example, on the basis of Experiment 1 as a direct source, Gentner and Wolff assigned

a positive plausibility value to the data in (64). This value decreased when the p-context was extended by the considerations about possible systematic errors in the experimental design in Experiment 1 as summarised in (66). But after conducting Experiment 2 which was a slightly modified version of Experiment 1, the similarity of the results indicated that the concern over the reliability of Experiment 1 as a data source in (66) was unfounded. Thus, the plausibility of the statements in (64) increased.

(c) These data are theory-dependent. First, they capture characteristics of phenomena which are (rather low-level) theoretical construct(s). Second, they result from the authentication and interpretation of perceptual data. These operations clearly require the use of several theoretical tools such as the conceptual system of a theory, statistical tools, models of the background phenomena etc.

(d) The data are 'given' in the sense that their initial plausibility is judged not with the help of inferences constructed and presented within the given argumentation process but directly on the basis of the reliability of the experiment from which they originate. The reason for this is that the experimental report does not contain every piece of information that could allow these statements to be obtained on the basis of other statements: perceptual data and several minor details of the experimental process are not made public but remain the private affairs of the experimenters.

(e) The experimental data may be subject to a re-evaluation of their plausibility and data status if the reliability of the experiment from which they originate is called into question, for example, by revealing systematic errors in the experimental procedure.

(f) One of their functions is that they supply the theory with plausibility values. These values were used to determine the plausibility of the hypotheses h_2–h_6 with the help of plausible inferences belonging to Types 1 and 3.

(g) Their other function consists in being tools to eliminate informational overdetermination, because the authors apply them to evaluate and compare the plausibility of the hypotheses h_2–h_6 in order to resolve the p-inconsistency between the statements in (60)(a) and (b). That is, they serve as weak/strong evidence for or against the hypotheses h_1–h_6.

(h) Nevertheless, these data are also sources of informational overdetermination in the sense that they allow for and motivate the elaboration of incompatible hypotheses which provide alternative explanations for them, as was the case with the data in (76) and the rival hypotheses h_4 & (79) and h_5.

(i) However, not every datum can be used to judge the plausibility or implausibility of a given hypothesis from this set.

(j) Experimental data do not provide support for the hypotheses at a fixed strength. First, their plausibility/implausibility changes dynamically when the p-context changes as we have shown in (b). Second, although the plausibility of (70)(e) did not change after the extension of the p-context with data originating from Experiment 4, this datum has lost its evidence status for hypothesis (73).[56]

(k) Experimental data function as theory-dependent pieces of evidence. On the one hand, they are theory-dependent data (see (c) above). On the other hand, adherents of rival theories may judge their usability for the evaluation of the hypotheses h_2–h_6 differently and question, for example, the plausibility of the hypotheses stating that a given datum may count as a prediction of the model at issue as stated by Gentner and Wolff.

The considerations we presented in (86)–(87) made the hypothesis that the p-model can be successfully applied to the *reconstruction* of the process of linguistic theorising plausible. From this finding alone, of course, it does not follow that it is also a reasonable and useful undertaking. We think that the metascientific reconstruction of the process of linguistic theorising with the help of the p-model is not only possible but it is also *fruitful*, since it allows us to reveal *starting points for the evaluation and development* of scientific theories:

(88) (a) The interpretation of the concept 'datum' as a plausible statement originating from a direct source requires the identification of the source from which the given datum originates. Thus, the initial plausibility of the datum can be checked and re-evaluated by revealing the factors which may influence the reliability of the source. In the case study presented, the plausibility of the experimental data (64), (67), (70) and (76) can be judged by a systematic analysis of the experimental design, the experimental procedure and the authentication and interpretation of the perceptual data on the basis of general considerations related to experiments as data sources. For example, a more thorough analysis of Gentner and Wolff's argumentation shows that they did not pay attention to some possible systematic errors in some cases. First, although the experimental data gained from Experiment 1 and from a similar earlier experiment referred to in Gentner & Wolff (1997: 339)[57] are almost identical, there is a great difference between the results in the both-prime cell (3730 ms vs 3048 ms). Second, it is not clear why the response time of the blank-prime type decreased in Experiment 2 in comparison to its value in Experiment 1. Moreover, in contrast to Experiment 1, with Experiment 2, there is no significant difference between blanks and priming with base or target alone (see (64)(e) and (67)(e)), and in Experiment 3, there is a significant difference only between blanks and base but not between blanks and target (see (70)(e)). Third, in Experiment 4, there seems to be a significant difference between low-conventionality and low-similarity metaphors when primed by the base term and the target term, respectively; that is, there is a target advantage. Fourth, the mean and the standard deviation of high-conventional and high-similarity metaphors by prime type target are identical. Moreover, the overall mean of the standard deviation in the column 'Target' is lower than any of the standard deviation in the cells in this column.

(b) The analysis of the argumentation presented in the experimental report makes it possible to identify and evaluate the inferences using experimental data as premises. In this way, the evidential support provided by the data for the hypotheses of the theory/rival theories can be more exactly estimated. For example, the finding that the datum (67)(e) contradicts the predictions of both models around h_2 and h_3, respectively, provides weak evidence against both rival hypotheses. As mentioned in Section 16.3, the clarification as to whether earlier experimental data summarised in (55) can be explained by abstraction-first and alignment-first models has an impact on the plausibility of their central hypotheses as well as on the decision among the three rival model types.

(c) Not only does the revision of the experimenters' argumentation gain a firmer basis but one may also more effectively exploit resources for further development of the experiments and/or theoretical model. That is, the incompleteness of the extension of the p-context by further relevant data/data sources, the imperfection of the coordination of the information gained from the old and the new sources or shortcomings during the re-evaluation of the resulting p-context all motivate the continuation of the argumentation process. As a result, one can obtain more reliable and sophisticated theories. For example, Gentner and Wolff refer to a paper by Glucksberg, McGlone and Manfredi without presenting and analysing their experiments. The involvement of the data presented in Glucksberg, McGlone & Manfredi (1997) could contribute to the decision between different versions of the career of metaphor hypothesis, or may even provide strong evidence against them and for the model based on h_6. That is, these experimental data require a new argumentation cycle to be started which might lead to a re-evaluation of the results of Gentner & Wolff (1997). The inclusion of the perceptual data and other missing details in the experimental report could be a further important step towards more reliable experimental data and towards the improvement of theories. It might contribute to a deeper analysis and evaluation of the experimental data because it would become possible to check the interpretation and the authentication of perceptual data (for example, the adequacy of the statistical methods applied by the authors), and perceptual data might suggest further refinement of the hypotheses.

17 The solution to $(P)_{IV}$

On the basis of the case study presented in Chapter 16, the following solution to the problem $(P)_{IV}$ presents itself:

$(SP)_{IV}$ The p-model is applicable to the reconstruction of the process of linguistic theorising.

The analysis of an argumentation process is, of course, only the first step of the application of the p-model. There are several other possible fields of application. Rákosi (in preparation) shows, for example, how the p-model can be applied to the evaluation of the *rhetorical tools* applied in papers on cognitive metaphor research. It is a task for the future to apply the p-model during linguistic theorising, that is, to use the p-model as a *guide* to linguistic problem solving.

Nevertheless, if the p-model can be successfully applied to the reconstruction of argumentations which were put forward by an unreflected application of the techniques of plausible argumentation, then this finding increases the plausibility of the claim that the *reflected*, conscious application of the tools of the p-model makes linguistic problem solving more effective.

Part V

The answers to the open questions

18 The problem $(P)_V$

In Part I, we revealed a series of questions which the current literature on linguistic data and evidence does not offer any answer to, or which are answered merely by controversial and incompatible proposals. Now, after having introduced the p-model in Part II, derived the notions of 'data' and 'evidence' from it in Part III and exemplified its workability in Part IV, we have to show how it answers the questions which current approaches to linguistic data and evidence could not. Thus, Part V will focus on the following subproblem:

$(P)_V$ How does the p-model answer (OQ1)–(OQ7)?

19 The answers to (OQ1)–(OQ7)

19.1 Overview

In Part I the following questions were left open and summarised in Chapter 6:

(OQ1) Under what conditions is the diversity of data legitimate and how can data belonging to different data types be combined?
(OQ2) What role do data sources play in the judgement of the reliability of data?
(OQ3) How can the complexity of data be accounted for?
(OQ4) How can the uncertainty of data be treated?
(OQ5) What is the relationship between data and theories?
(OQ6) On the basis of what criteria can it be decided whether a contradiction may be tolerated, and what strategies should we adopt for inconsistency resolution?
(OQ7) What data can serve as evidence in linguistic theories, if, on the one hand, evidence has to be capable of supporting or weakening hypotheses, and, on the other hand, data cannot be regarded as true with certainty?

In this chapter we systematically discuss the answers compatible with the p-model.

19.2 Ad (OQ1): the diversity and the combinability of data

The concept of 'data' provided in (47) allows for the acknowledgement of the diversity of data. It enables us to consider not only one but many kinds of data to be legitimate insofar as they can be regarded as plausible on the basis of some source in the given p-context. It does not require data to be certainly true facts. Therefore, it also permits data types that are judged not to be perfectly reliable. It stipulates, however, that data have to be deemed unanimously reliable by their source. If this is not the case, then the statement in question cannot be treated as a datum. Instead, the reliability of its source has to be revised. That is, we agree with the view mentioned in Section 5.2 according to which every statement capturing some manifestation of linguistic behaviour is a *potential* datum. Nevertheless, it is always the given argumentation process that decides whether, from some direct source, a positive plausibility value can be assigned to this datum-candidate or not – that is, whether this statement can be regarded *actually* as a datum in the given theory.

The p-model also allows for the combination of data of different types. Moreover, it shows why it is advisable and favourable to apply several data types. Namely, if different data types function as evidence in the sense of (49)–(51) for a hypothesis *h*, then according to (11) they allow us to assign a higher plausibility value to *h* than any of them does individually. Similarly, if different direct sources allow us to assign a positive plausibility value to a hypothesis, then the plausibility value of these statements increases. Therefore, one has to strive to *support the hypotheses of the theory at issue by as many types of data and sources as possible*, since in this way, their plausibility can be increased and the uncertainty resulting from the application of a single data type/source can be reduced. If, however, one of the data is evidence against *h* or is judged implausible on the basis of some direct source, then one has to face p-inconsistency. One strives to resolve this inconsistency by re-evaluating the p-context, that is, by applying the tools of plausible argumentation.

Nevertheless, as we have seen, theories may disagree on whether a given statement should be regarded as a datum. Therefore, the combinability of data types has its limits. Data are not data in general, but relative to some theory, or more exactly, to a given argumentation process. Consequently, it is not possible to work out a theory-independent typology of data, since aspects of linguistic behaviour are represented and evaluated by different theories in different ways. Nevertheless, the methodological norms which govern the evaluation of the reliability of different data types are revisable, too. Thus, the cyclic and prismatic argumentation process may re-evaluate the acceptability of data types and may make it possible to combine data types which have previously been seen as incompatible or unreliable.

For the *theoretical background* motivating these conclusions see Section 9.3 (plausible statements, plausibility value of a statement on the basis of a set of sources), Section 13.2 (concept of 'data'), Section 13.3 (concept of 'evidence'), Section 10.2 (p-inconsistency, solution of p-problems), Sections 10.3–6 (plausible argumentation process).

Relevant examples

Example 2 in Section 9.3 illuminates the fundamental importance of the suitability of sources by referring to psycholinguistic experiments in which there is no statistically significant difference between the opposing acceptability judgements of the participants. It also mentions the most frequent strategy used in such situations: the plausibility of such data can be revised (restored) if one is capable of identifying factors which facilitate the separation of the opposing judgements and arrive at two different sources supporting statements about the acceptability and the unacceptability of the sentences at issue, respectively.

Example 30(4) in Section 13.2 emphasises the theory-dependence (p-context dependence) of the evaluation of the plausibility/implausibility of statements: while statements related to deviant sentences produced during spontaneous language use were regarded as irrelevant by followers of generative linguistics and by corpus linguists for several decades, Foster (2007) proposes we treat them as reliable and valuable data.

Example 7(1) in Section 9.3 exemplifies the principle according to which the combination of different sources makes it possible to assign a higher plausibility value to our hypotheses. Nevertheless, Example 7(2) suggests caution about the assignment of plausibility values on the basis of a set of sources, because it may happen that a source (for example, a corpus) is not relevant for judging the plausibility of a statement.

We have seen in Section 16.3.4 that the plausibility of a hypothesis can be considerably increased if it is supported by many experiments as direct sources.

In Section 16.5.4, the reliability of the sources supporting a hypothesis decreased considerably. Therefore, a new data source (an experiment with a more sophisticated experimental design) was introduced in order to ensure its plausibility.

19.3 Ad (OQ2): the role of the sources in the reliability of data

The definitions (6)–(12) introduced in Section 9.3 are built on the connection between the plausibility of statements and the reliability of the sources of plausibility. (47) characterises data as statements with a positive plausibility value stemming from some direct source; they are true with certainty or plausible according to a direct source. Therefore, the categories introduced make it possible to examine, first, how and to what extent a source has contributed to the plausibility of a datum or set of data in a particular linguistic investigation. Second, in a particular linguistic investigation the sources satisfying the above definitions can be typologised and their contribution to different data types can be revealed, too.

At the outset, the plausibility of data is determined by the reliability of the source on the basis of which their plausibility value is assigned. During the argumentation process, however, this value may change, since further direct and indirect sources may assign a plausibility value to the data, and the reliability of the source of the data may increase or decrease as well. Consequently, the source of data from which its initial plausibility value stems is only one of the factors that determine the plausibility of data. (11) extends the concept of the assignment of plausibility values to sets of sources. In the sense of (11), if a datum is supported by many sources, then the plausibility of this datum increases. Thus, if the linguist judges at a certain point of his/her research that a sole data source is not capable of making a datum or data type plausible enough, then he/she has to seek further (direct or indirect) sources that can be used to determine the plausibility of these data. If these sources deem the data at issue to be plausible, then the plausibility of the data increases; if, however, any of the sources shows the data to be implausible, then the p-context becomes p-problematic. In such cases, one has to strive to resolve this p-problem by further argumentation cycles, by re-evaluating the reliability of the data and their sources as well as by collecting new data.

It is important to remark that sources of plausibility value are not necessarily identical to sources of information that are treated as data sources in the linguistic literature. For example, if one borrows a datum from a linguistic paper, then its plausibility value depends on the extent to which the given paper can be regarded as reliable in judging it. Nevertheless, from the paper one may find out that the datum at issue is an introspective datum based on the linguistic intuition of the author, or that it originates from a corpus. This information can be applied to determine the type and the plausibility of the data as well. Namely, one can revise the source and plausibility value of this datum in such a way that it is not the paper but the classification that is regarded as the source of the plausibility value. This means that one interprets this datum as an introspective datum or as a corpus datum and determines its plausibility value along these lines.

The *theoretical background* against which our answer to (OP2) can be interpreted covers Section 9.3 (sources, plausible statements, plausibility value of a statement on the basis of a set of sources) and Section 13.2 (concept of 'data').

Relevant examples

Example 4(2) in Section 9.3 enumerates several arguments for the standpoint that neither linguistic intuition nor corpora can be regarded as totally reliable sources and reinforces the view that both judgement data and corpus data are not entirely but only partially reliable. This supports our suggestion that these data types should be interpreted as plausible statements – and, as a consequence of this finding, as data in the sense of (47).

Example 4(1) in Section 9.3 outlines a situation in which, on the one hand, a statement is deemed plausible on the basis of a direct source (namely, a hypothesis is accepted as a linguistic universal by reference to a linguistic paper reporting Head's investigations on more than one hundred languages). On the other hand, however, this hypothesis is implausible on the basis of another direct source (Simon's paper summarising his investigations into German around the year 1800). Thus, while the linguistic universal can be regarded as a datum in the sense of (47) by taking into consideration the first direct source, it does not count as a datum when applying the second direct source mentioned above.

Example 31(2) in Section 13.2 is similar insofar as it refers to the conflicting evaluation of the ambiguity of sentences like *Why do you think that he left*?

The plausibility rankings presented in Example 5(1) in Section 9.3 also exemplify the connection between the reliability of the source and the initial plausibility of data. For instance, the application of a well-known, generally accepted experimental procedure allows us to assign a higher plausibility value to a statement than guesswork on the basis of some uncertain estimate.

Example 6 in Section 9.3 illustrates the source-dependence of plausibility and the consensual character of the judgement of the reliability of sources by the history of experiments in science.

In Section 13.2, Examples 30(1) and (2) deal with the factors which may diminish the reliability of judgement data, while Example 30(3) summarises the weak points of corpus data which necessitate interpreting them as not totally reliable but only plausible statements.

Section 16.2.1 illustrates the point that different sources (theories) may judge the initial plausibility of data differently, while Section 16.2.2 shows how these initial plausibility values may change (increase or vanish) during the argumentation process.

19.4 Ad (OQ3): the complexity of linguistic data

In the sense of (47), one component of the structure of data is a statement capturing some information related to properties of linguistic phenomena. This information content is described with the help of the *conceptual apparatus of the given theory*, that is, it is interpreted by means of a category system. The conceptual apparatus of the theory – which is closely related to the methodological principles and methods involved in the p-context at issue – determines the level of abstraction at which the investigated phenomena are captured. Thus, it is possible that in the case of one theory, statements which cover information at a relatively high level of abstraction are regarded as the starting points of the argumentation process, while in another theory, statements at a lower level of abstraction play the role of data.

The conceptual apparatus used also determines the range of aspects of the linguistic phenomena that can be grasped and the way these aspects can be described. Some aspects may remain undetected by the application of one theory but may be revealed by relying on another. This provides a further argument for the reliance upon many data types during linguistic theorising, because more data types make it possible to reveal more properties of the linguistic phenomenon under investigation and to develop more complex models of them by revealing the connections among these properties, too. This requires, of course, the integration of information stemming from many theories into the plausible argumentation process instead of restricting it to a single theory.

To sum up, complex models of linguistic phenomena can result from argumentation processes making use of complex data and/or a complex of many theories.

The *theoretical background* against which (OQ3) can be treated was discussed in Section 9.3 (plausible statements), Section 9.8 (p-context), Section 13.2 (concept of 'data').

Relevant examples

Example 30(1) in Section 13.2 analyses the structure of judgement data along the lines of the considerations in Schütze (1996), and shows how the complexity of judgement data resulting from the indirectness of grammaticality can be represented with the help of the p-model's concept of 'data'.

Example 30(3) in Section 13.2 examines the structure of corpus data and reveals not only their complex nature but their diversity, too. It points out the presence of the linguist's linguistic intuition in their interpretation.

Example 31(1) in Section 13.2 provides further arguments for the interpretation of judgement data as plausible statements with the help of the analysis of different interpretations of the annotations and degrees of badness as summarised in Schütze (1996). It shows that (47) allows us to represent judgement data as complex entities involving not only the sentence judged but the grade of its acceptability and the plausibility (reliability) of the latter, too.

19.5 Ad (OQ4): the treatment of the uncertainty of data

Since data are statements with a positive plausibility value (that is, they are plausible or true with certainty) in the p-model's view, the degree of their acceptability can be characterised with the help of their plausibility value. This value depends primarily on the reliability of the source on the basis of which a plausibility value is assigned to them, as well as on other factors within the p-context (such as the methodological background assumptions of the theory, the direct and indirect sources in the p-context), and can change dynamically during the argumentation process.

The p-model makes it possible to assign different plausibility values to different data and data types. Thus, differences between their reliability can be accounted for, and this can give us an insight into the reasons why a given data type has been preferred to another. Moreover, while the plausibility value of statements represents the degree of the reliability of their source, the notion of 'implausibility' (see (8)–(9)(c) in Section 9.3) allows us to grasp situations where a source provides information against a statement.

The p-model also illuminates how inferences from uncertain premises (data) can be drawn. It does not require the truth of the pieces of evidence used to test the hypotheses of the theory; rather, it makes it possible to estimate the plausibility of the conclusion on the basis of the plausibility value of the premises and latent background assumptions.

Section 9.3 (direct/indirect sources, plausible/implausible statements, plausibility value of a statement), Section 9.5 (plausible inferences) and Section 9.7 (dynamism of plausible inferences) constitute the *theoretical background* to our answer to (OQ4).

Relevant examples

The *relevant examples* relate to the application of the concepts 'plausible statement', 'plausibility value' and 'plausible inference'.

Examples 2–4 in Section 9.3 illustrate the concepts of 'suitable source', 'plausible statement on the basis of a source', 'implausible statement on the basis of a source', and 'neutral plausibility on the basis of a source'.

Examples 5(1)–(2) concern the assignment of plausibility values to statements.

Examples 11–13 in Section 9.5.2–4 present different types of plausible inference and show under what circumstances and how one can draw inferences from uncertain premises.

Examples 14–16 in Section 9.5.5 illustrate how the plausibility of the conclusion can be estimated on the basis of the plausibility value of the premises and latent background assumptions, as well as the structure of the inference at issue.

Example 19 in Section 9.7 shows how changes in the plausibility value of the premises influence the plausibility of the conclusion. Example 18 in Section 9.6 does the same in connection with the latent background assumptions of plausible inferences belonging to Types 2 and 3.

Examples 20(1)–(2) in Section 9.8 illustrate the impact of changes of the p-context on plausible inferences.

In Section 16.2.2 we can see how Gentner and Wolff manage to create inferences from not certainly true but only plausible statements in order to test the consequences of different theoretical assumptions made by rival theories of metaphor processing.

19.6 Ad (OQ5): the relationship between data and theory

In Chapter 10, we interpreted linguistic theorising as a cyclic and prismatic argumentation process based on the retrospective re-evaluation of information. This definition provides an answer to the question raised.

An important characteristic of the p-model's concept of 'datum' provided in (47) is that it does not indicate an absolute notion but determines what counts as data with respect to the given argumentation process. In order to evaluate the initial plausibility of data, that is, the reliability of the source supporting the datum, one has to examine every factor that may influence their reliability: for instance, the strictness of their testing, the complexity of the situation from which they originate etc. This means that one has to make use of inferences – above all, analogical inferences and induction – also in the case of data (which stem from a direct source) to check whether the source at issue satisfies certain methodological criteria. These inferences, however, usually remain outside the argumentation process presented, and it is only their final result – that is, the statement and the plausibility value assigned to it – that enters the cyclic process of re-evaluation. Thus, from the point of view of the public argumentation process, the assignment of a plausibility value is often *conventional* in the case of direct sources. For instance, the correctness of the principle on which the functioning of a well-known and acknowledged experimental apparatus is based is usually not supported with arguments. It is enough to provide the description of the experiment and the data obtained (that is, the statements recording the results of the experiment and the plausibility value assigned to them). However, this may change if problems occur during the argumentation process that question the reliability of the given source. In such cases, by the re-evaluation of the p-context, one has to revise the reliability of the source. This can be achieved by including those pieces of information in the argumentation process that concern the reliability of the source as well as the relationship between the source and the statements originating from the source. As a result, pieces of information stemming from this source no longer count as data, since their source becomes indirect. At the same time, the p-context is extended by new data: plausible statements constituting the starting point for the argumentation concerning the reliability of the source.

Another open question in connection with the relationship between data and theories pertains to the inferences connecting the data and the hypotheses of the theory. The p-model represents the relationship between data and further hypotheses of the theory with the help of plausible (in the limiting case, demonstrative) inferences and systems of inferences. Therefore, the relationship between the data and the reliability of the hypotheses can be accounted for.

Section 9.3 (direct/indirect sources, plausible/implausible statements, plausibility value of a statement), Section 9.5 (plausible inferences), Section 9.8 (p-context), Sections 13.2–4 (data, evidence), Chapter 10 (plausible argumentation) and Sections 19.7–8 serve as the *theoretical background* to our answer to (OP5).

Relevant examples

Example 6 in Section 9.3 points out the conventionality of the judgement of the reliability of data sources in a historical context, by referring to the stages of the treatment and evaluation of scientific experiments.

Examples 7(1) and (2) in Section 9.3 exemplify the increase in the initial plausibility value of data as a result of the involvement of further sources in the p-context.

Examples 20(1)–(3) in Section 9.8 illuminate the way in which adding not certainly true but plausible data to the p-context may influence the range and plausibility of the conclusions (hypotheses) which can be reached with the help of plausible inferences.

Example 21 in Section 9.9 shows that plausible inferences which are not deductive but rely on latent background assumptions as well – such as analogy or induction – are capable of supporting hypotheses the information content of which goes beyond that of their premises. Thus, the theory becomes more instructive than the set of data it includes.

Example 31(1) in Section 13.2 reveals how acceptability judgements become integrated into the process of linguistic theorising, and may function as starting points for the estimation of the plausibility value of hypotheses about the grammaticalness of a given sentence or structure.

Example 31(2) focuses on another aspect of the theory-dependence (p-context dependence) of data: namely, it presents a case showing that it may happen that a datum is evaluated to be true with certainty in one theory (p-context) but it may be deemed to be implausible (and, of course, not regarded as a datum) in another.

Examples 32–34 in Section 13.3 show how data may serve as part of plausible inferences as weak/relative/strong evidence for or against hypotheses of a theory and, as such, contribute to the decision between them and their rivals.

Sections 16.2.2, 16.3.2, 16.3.3, 16.5.2, 16.5.4 and 16.6.2 include several examples of plausible inferences connecting data and hypotheses, and elucidate how different kinds of data are constructed with the help of the theoretical tools of the given theory during the experimentation process.

Sections 16.4 and 16.7 reveal and analyse the cyclic argumentation process which establishes the relationship among the elements of the experimental design, the experimental procedure, the experimental data obtained and the experimental report.

19.7 Ad (OQ6): data and the treatment of inconsistencies

In Chapter 10, we analysed the connection between the characteristics of plausible argumentation and the emergence and (re)solution of inconsistencies. This relationship is of vital significance to data. Namely, if a statement is judged to be plausible, then it is treated as a datum and can be related to the other data and hypotheses with the help of different inferences and systems of inferences. In this way, it becomes part of a complex system of relations: it may contradict other data, support or weaken hypotheses etc. It contributes, however, not only actively to this system of relations but has to undergo changes as well: its plausibility may increase, decrease or even be lost depending on the extent to which it and the other hypotheses of the theory fit together. This means that the plausibility of the data is not fixed once and for all; the data source only determines the initial plausibility value of the given statement. Without further ado, it may occur that a datum that one has initially evaluated as reliable will gradually lose its plausibility, or vice versa: a datum with a relatively low plausibility value at the outset may become more plausible at later stages of the argumentation process.

The set of data may be p-inconsistent, since nothing excludes the possibility that different sources support data which conflict with each other (see Section 9.3; Rescher 1976: 40). This means that the p-context may contain data that are evaluated as plausible by different sources, but are incompatible (see Section 10.2; Rescher 1976: 15). It may also happen that one of the sources turns out to be unsuitable insofar as it evaluates both a statement and another statement that contradicts it as plausible. In this case, one has to revise the reliability of this source and, for instance, divide it into smaller sources while assigning them to different perspectives (for more on this, see Kertész & Rákosi 2006, 2009a).

Data may also be sources of p-inconsistency in such a way that one set of data makes a hypothesis plausible (that is, provides weak evidence for it) but another data set makes this hypothesis implausible (provides weak evidence against it by supporting its negation).

Recently, problems closely related to the emergence and the treatment of inconsistencies have been addressed more and more sharply in different syntactic theories. Although these problems do not pertain directly to the current debate on data and evidence, they are related to the debate's metatheoretical background assumptions. In order to illustrate their relevance, let us mention briefly the following examples:

(i) The emergence and systematic (re)solution of contradictions play a crucial role in most current syntactic theories. This problem manifests itself in optimality theory in an especially instructive manner (see e.g. Prince & Smolensky 2004). In optimality theory, the systematic generation and resolution of contradictions is a basic tool for judging the grammaticality of the forms investigated. Starting from the lexical form, generator GEN generates all possible forms (candidates). The evaluation mechanism EVAL compares the forms obtained as the output and chooses the surface form. During the evaluation, forms are confronted with constraints. These constraints are ranked in the given language and can be violated by the candidate forms. As a result, it becomes clear which forms violate which constraints. The form which violates the more dominant constraints to a lesser extent counts as the optimal one.

(ii) One of the most important recent contributions to the clarification of the methodological problems in theoretical linguistics is Moravcsik (2006, 2010). She investigates the question why there are different syntactic theories. She puts forward the following answer to this question:

> (1) Many of the various conceptual tools employed by syntacticians are designed to resolve conflicts in the data.
>
> (2) Given that there is a limited range of the logically available ways of conflict resolution, the range of syntactic theory types is limited as well and *their diversity can be systematically characterised in terms of the conflict-resolving constructs they employ*. (Moravcsik 2006: x; emphasis added)

Consequently, the process of the emergence (and the resolution) of inconsistencies is a *constitutive* characteristic of linguistic theorising. One of the most substantial results of the p-model is that it provides a systematic solution to this problem.

The p-model allows us to describe the different strategies of the treatment of contradictions related to data sets, considering the latter to be an integral part of linguistic theorising, that is, of a cyclic and prismatic argumentation process. These strategies allow us to deem inconsistency *not as a fatal failure*. They do not compel us to treat all contradictions in a unique way but license several possible methods for their handling:

- with the help of cyclic argumentation based on plausible inferences, one may try to resolve them;
- in the absence of an acceptable solution, the inconsistencies may be temporarily tolerated;
- one may tolerate them with the help of their paraconsistent representation; moreover, they may be regarded not as temporary phenomena but as constitutive elements of the given theory.

For the *theoretical background*, above all Chapter 10 (plausible argumentation) should be consulted. Further relevant passages can be found in Section 9.3 (the source-dependence of the plausibility/implausibility of statements), and Section 13.3 (data and the treatment of p-inconsistency).

Relevant examples

Example 8(1) in Section 9.3 presents a typical manifestation of p-inconsistency, namely, the conflict between corpus data and judgement data based on the linguist's linguistic intuition as a source.

Example 8(2) shows that indirect sources (inferences) which start from data as premises and try to support hypotheses may lead to p-inconsistency, too.

Examples 22–23 in Section 10.2 exemplify the concepts of the 'solution' and 'resolution' of a p-inconsistency.

In Example 24 in Section 10.4, the cyclic nature of plausible argumentation, the emergence and resolution of inconsistencies during the cyclic returns is explained with the help of the reconstruction of Schütze's (2009) argumentation related to Manning's considerations in favour of the hypothesis 'The sequence *as least as* is not a typo but part of English.'

Examples 25–28 in Section 10.5 serve to illuminate the prismatic nature of plausible argumentation. Chapter 16 reconstructs and provides a detailed analysis of techniques of inconsistency resolution in Gentner & Wolff (1997).

19.8 Ad (OQ7): linguistic evidence

(49)–(52) attempt to resolve the contradictions in the tendencies outlined in Part I and summarised in $(SP)_I$. Above all, they accept – albeit with several changes – the intention motivating $(SP)_I$(a), according to which 'scientific hypotheses' (in some sense) must be (in some sense) 'supported' by or 'confronted' with 'facts' (in some sense). However, they interpret this intention in a peculiar manner. First, according to (49)–(51), evidence is not necessarily true with certainty, but – in the sense of (8)(b) and (10)(b) – it is a statement with a positive plausibility value. Second, the hypothesis *h* and the evidence *e* are in most cases connected by a plausible inference. This means that the p-model breaks with $(SP)_I$ (a).

We have seen that in the current linguistic literature, the elements listed in $(SP)_I$(a) and $(SP)_I$(b), respectively, are not compatible with each other. Whereas $(SP)_I$(a) considers evidence to be a secure basis of scientific knowledge, $(SP)_I$(b) emphasises the uncertainty and relativism of evidence. (49)–(52) make the resolution of this conflict possible without abandoning the intention behind $(SP)_I$(a). The reason for this is that according to (49)–(51), the question of what counts as evidence is context-, theory- and problem-dependent.

Consequently, evidence cannot be considered to be an objective and neutral arbiter in situations when a decision has to be made between rival theories. This does not preclude the possibility that there are cases where it tilts the balance in favour of one of two rival alternatives. However, it may not serve as an exclusive basis for a decision, but can only be one of the factors to be weighed.

Evidence is not primary to the theory; its selection is not a step preceding the process of scientific theorising, serving as its starting point, but an integral part of this process.

Plausible inferences are by definition heuristic tools. Since we consider evidence to be part of a plausible argumentation process aiming to solve a problem by supporting hypotheses, we define evidence, too, as a heuristic tool aimed at the solution of the given problem. It is, consequently, obviously problem-dependent. The p-model can, therefore, grasp the characteristics of linguistic evidence in that it basically fulfils two functions in the theorising process: it plays an important role not only in the evaluation of the acceptability of the already existing hypotheses, but also in the discovery of hypotheses. Just like the evaluation process, the discovery is also the result of a series of revisable decisions. The stages of discovery and justification cannot be separated, but continuously follow each other and become inextricably intertwined. The ‘discovery’, that is the formulation of hypotheses, does not result from data-collection carried out in a haphazard way or from pure guesswork, but involves right from the outset preliminary ideas, conjectures and provisional hypotheses, the acceptability of which has to be decided on and has to be checked again and again.

It is important to realise, however, that the relativisation of the concept of evidence according to the above factors, just like the interpretation of the relation between the evidence and the hypotheses supported by the evidence as a plausible inference is by no means unconstrained. The insight that data are not true with certainty and that decisions based on them are not final, but fallible, that is, that they can be re-evaluated at later stages, does not mean that one loses ground and any decision whatsoever may be justified. On the one hand, the criteria for data and evidence laid down in (47) and (49)–(51) represent a serious restriction, since they require that the system of relations between the pieces of information at one's disposal are revealed and the plausibility of the latter is continuously evaluated. On the other hand, it is possible to formulate methodological rules with respect to the cyclic and prismatic argumentation that ensure the rationality of scientific theorising. For instance, the striving for the elimination of inconsistencies constitutes this type of a rule, or the requirement that one should consider the widest range of data at one's disposal even if they, at least initially, constitute an inconsistent set.[1]

The *theoretical background* to the concept of 'evidence' is summarised in Sections 13.3 and 13.4.

Relevant examples

Examples 32–34 in Section 13.3 illustrate the concepts of 'weak evidence', 'relative evidence' and 'strong evidence' with the help of several linguistic examples.

Chapter 16 shows how experimental data may play the role of evidence in the evaluation of rival hypotheses in relation to metaphor processing.

19.9 Conclusions

The reader must not forget that (OQ1)–(OQ7) have been left open in the current literature we analysed in Chapter 5. It is by no means accidental that the literature could not answer these questions. As we have seen in Chapter 5, a remarkable characteristic of current debates on linguistic data and evidence is that there are considerable differences between the proposed views. There is *no* single correct characterisation of the structure, the types and the function of data immediately acceptable to every linguist, in every field. As soon as linguists scrutinise what they consider as data and evidence, a series of different, even contradictory assumptions and unsolved problems arise. This finding bears witness to the insight that *the linguist's naïve self-reflection is not enough*; rather, it is necessary to investigate linguistic data and evidence by making systematic and conscious use of the tools provided by the philosophy of science. The structure and function of linguistic data have to be made subject to scientific investigation in a similar way to society and nature or language itself. The question of what linguistic data are and what functions they have is *a scientific question*, as are, for instance, questions concerning what the language system is, what syntactic rules there are in the grammar of a given language, in which context a complex sentence preserves the presuppositions of its clauses etc.

Just as the naïve linguistic competence of the native speaker is not sufficient to describe the rules of the language at issue, but it is necessary to develop and apply the scientific methods of linguistics, *the linguist's naïve self-reflection is not sufficient*, either, to determine what can and cannot be data/evidence in linguistics. What is necessary is the systematic development and application of scientific – that is, in this case, *meta*scientific – methods. Therefore, systematic and well-founded metascientific reflection is indispensable.

The tools of linguistic theorising – linguistic theories, models, methods, concepts, and means of scientific research in general – are, according to the p-model, parts of prismatic argumentation processes. They are *prisms* allowing us to examine our research objects – 'the language', 'the language system', 'language use', 'language acquisition' etc., in whatever sense we understand these terms. A well-known characteristic of prisms is that they break up light. They change the appearance of the objects to be investigated: they enlarge some – actual or alleged – features of objects while excluding others from our field of view. Therefore, if we do not want to arrive at distorted, false information on what we call 'language', 'knowledge of language', 'grammar', 'word', 'sentence', 'language use', 'communication' etc., we have to strive to filter out the distorting effects of prisms. This is possible only if we explore the prism itself, that is, our linguistic tools. The more one knows about the structure of linguistic theories, methods, models etc., the more easily one can see their shortcomings, which must be avoided in order to judge the object of the research more accurately, with less distortion. Consequently, metascientific reflection on linguistic theorising contributes indirectly to the understanding of the *object* of linguistic theories. Thus, the more one knows about the theories with which 'language', 'language usage', 'language acquisition' etc. (in whatever sense) are investigated – that is, about our prisms – the greater are the chances of having a better understanding of the object of these theories, that is, of 'language', 'language usage', 'language acquisition' etc. In this way, metascientific reflection on linguistic theorising *also contributes to the solution of linguistic problems*.

The application of the p-model to the problem of data and evidence is a cycle of an argumentation process that re-evaluates the object-scientific problem-solving process at a metalevel. We have interpreted linguistic theorising as an argumentation process, and the application of the p-model is part of the argumentation process. From this, it follows that the p-model is, as one of the cyclic re-evaluations, an integral part of the process of linguistic problem solving.[2]

Our considerations have revealed that the self-image of linguists who accept and echo (SVAPS) in an unreflected manner is intrinsically mistaken, since, as we have seen, the structure of linguistic theories does not meet the norms of (SVLD). This false self-image is destructive because it discredits problem-solving techniques based on plausible argumentation, and propagates often destructive norms legitimised by an incorrect – or at least, deficient – account of scientific theorising.[3] This anachronistic attitude is one of the *unreflected* and *outdated* methodological background assumptions that, as we have shown in Chapter 3, are accepted by several linguistic theories. These linguistic theories presuppose the rationality-concept of (SVAPS), while, in practice, they are based on plausible argumentation. Since they declare that they accept the norms of (SVAPS), one should deem them *irrational* on the basis of their own criteria. This is a contradiction that cannot be resolved with the help of the tools at their disposal within their own theoretical framework.

It is important to remark that we called into question neither the rationality nor the scientificness, nor the prestige of linguistics. We only want to contribute to the *reduction of the gap between the accepted norms and the actual problem-solving practice in linguistics*. Narrowing this gap is one of the most fundamental tasks of metascientific reflection according to the post-analytic philosophy of science:

> The question is now: what should be done about this chronic discrepancy between actual and ideal science? (Fehér 1990: 231f.)

20 The solution to $(P)_V$

On the basis of what we have said in Chapters 12–19, the p-model yields the following solution to $(P)_V$:

$(SP)_V$ As an immediate consequence of $(SP)_{III}$, the p-model provides the answers to (OQ1)–(OQ7) discussed in Chapter 19.

Nevertheless, our answers to (OQ1)–(OQ7) are not the termination of our investigations into the nature of linguistic data and evidence. Rather, they should be regarded as *starting points* which a new, unprejudiced metatheoretical attitude as proclaimed in Chapter 1 can be based on.

If we realise that linguistic theories are not built up along the lines of the prescriptions of (SVAPS) but with the help of plausible argumentation, cyclically and prismatically, then it becomes clear that it makes no sense to seek for the only correct answers to our questions which should be defended to the hilt. What we are looking for are not theses true with certainty (nor solely valid theories) from which the process of deduction would conduct the truth to more and more complex statements. Rather, we strive for the successive – cyclic and prismatic – correction of our knowledge by starting from the greatest number of plausible assumptions possible.[1] We should realise that whatever prism one chooses, the perspective it gives is nothing more than uncertain information needing continuous revision during the retrospective re-evaluations.

The perspective emerging from the p-model is incompatible with the unreflected absolutism of given theories, standpoints, methods or theses and with the unreflected rejection of other standpoints. On the basis of the prismatic character of the argumentation process, it is perfectly legitimate and natural to examine the object of our investigations through the prism of different theories, methods and models – that is, plausible argumentation processes. Every prism may show the object of linguistic theorising differently and may provide us with new insights. There can be considerable differences between the particular perspectives; they may even contradict each other. Therefore, we cannot expect them to merge into a unique theory, model or approach. Instead, we should accept the *pluralism* of diverse and incompatible standpoints in linguistics. In contrast to both (SVAPS) and Kuhn's model of scientific change, this pluralism cannot be interpreted as a symptom of the immaturity of linguistics. Rather, from the p-model it follows that it is a constitutive and natural characteristic of linguistic theorising.[2] The p-model acknowledges and tolerates this pluralistic stance in linguistics and strives to exploit the potential emerging from the coexistence of a wide range of views, norms and heuristics.

21 Summary

The solution to the Main Problem (MP)

In the last chapter of the book we summarise our findings and draw the final conclusions from them.

Our starting point was the *Central Problem* of the current discussion on data and evidence:

(CP) (a) What types of data/evidence can be used,
and
(b) how do data/evidence work in linguistic theories?

We argued that (CP) cannot be solved in this form, because its solution presupposes the clarification of a series of further problems, considering the argumentation structure of linguistic theories and the elaboration of an appropriate metatheoretical framework. Therefore, we reformulated (CP) as the *Main Problem* of our investigations as follows:

(MP) (a) What is the *structure* of linguistic data/evidence
and
(b) which *functions* do they fulfil in linguistic theories
if
(c) (a) and (b) are tackled by an argumentation-theoretic model of linguistic theorising?

The aim of the book was to solve (MP). However, due to its complexity, we did not strive to solve (MP) directly, but we subdivided it into five subproblems, the solutions to which we discussed in the corresponding five parts of the book. Accordingly, now the question emerges as to whether the solution to these subproblems indeed leads to the solution of (MP), and if so, then to which solution. In order to provide an answer to this question, we have to recall our train of thought.

As a first step, we carried out a state-of-the-art analysis of current literature. The first subproblem was:

$(P)_I$ (a) What solutions have been proposed to (CP) in the current literature?
(b) What *meta*scientific background assumptions can be revealed in the particular views?

The analysis revealed two discrepancies in the current literature. The first was summarised in $(SP)_I$(a):

$(SP)_I$

(a) (i) On the one hand, in accordance with the standard view of the analytical philosophy of science (SVAPS) and the standard view of linguistic data and evidence (SVLD), 'linguistic evidence' is still interpreted as a specific subset of data which is not revisable within the theory at issue. It is supposed to comprise statements which are true with certainty and whose main task is to test the hypotheses of the theory.

(ii) On the other hand, in opposition to the tenets summarised in the standard view of linguistic data and evidence (SVLD), the new proposals surveyed raise a series of innovative ideas. These progressive insights are, however, not shared by all authors; and even if they are accepted by several of them, this acceptance takes different forms, so that they cannot be generalised. Despite this, we can highlight the following insights which appear in one or more contributions and are – in comparison to the standard view of the analytical philosophy of science (SVAPS) and the standard view of linguistic data and evidence (SVLD) – of a clearly innovative nature in that they conform to the process of differentiation, relativisation and weakening

- The pluralism of linguistic data is acknowledged instead of preferring just one type of data. The combination of several data types within a given piece of research is considered to be a desideratum.
- The origin of data is not held to be decisive; rather, it is treated as only one of the relevant factors among others, such as the structure, the complexity, the directness, the abstractness of data etc.
- All data types are assumed to be problematic; therefore, it seems to be indispensable to clarify their structure and function.
- The relationship between data and theory is assumed to be cyclic rather than linear.
- Linguistic data are considered to be theory- and problem-dependent. It is admitted that data treated as evidence very often do not support or refute the hypotheses unanimously. They are not certain and may also generate contradictions.

In addition, we showed that the literature – as a consequence of the double-facedness of the standpoints summarised in $(SP)_I$(a) – left open the questions (OQ1)–(OQ7).

Our answer to $(P)_I$(b) unveiled the double-facedness of the metatheoretical background assumptions of the literature, too:

$(SP)_I$

(b) (i) The views we have investigated *realise* the need for metascientific reflection on the structure and function of linguistic data and evidence.

(ii) This, however, does not go beyond the linguist's naïve (self-)reflection on research practice. Although the continuous, partly implicit, partly explicit confrontation of the standard view of the analytical philosophy of science

(SVAPS) and the standard view of linguistic data and evidence (SVLD) with everyday research experience suggests the unacceptability of the former, the necessity to develop alternative metascientific tools has *not been realised.*

$(SP)_I$ (a) and $SP)_I$ (b) led to the following metatheoretical problem:

$(P)_{II}$ What kind of metatheoretical model allows us to define the notions of 'data' and 'evidence' in linguistics?

The task of Part II of the book was to solve $(P)_{II}$. We introduced the p-model of plausible argumentation and illustrated it with the help of many examples taken from a great variety of linguistic approaches. We obtained the following solution to $(P)_{II}$:

$(SP)_{II}$ The p-model is a metatheoretical model that allows for defining the concepts of 'data' and 'evidence' in linguistics.

Presupposing $(SP)_{II}$, the next task amounted to showing what exactly the p-model means by 'data' and 'evidence'. Therefore, $(P)_{III}$ presented itself as a third subproblem:

$(P)_{III}$ *How* does the p-model define the concepts of 'data' and 'evidence'?

In Part III of the book, we proposed a general definition of the concepts of 'datum' and 'evidence' gained with the help of the p-model. We arrived at hypothesis $(SP)_{III}$:

$(SP)_{III}$ The p-model defines the concepts of 'data' and 'evidence' as introduced in Chapter 13.

After we had developed the metatheoretical framework we needed and obtained a novel approach to data and evidence in linguistics, we had to show how the framework and the concepts can be put to use. Therefore, the next problem was:

$(P)_{IV}$ How can the p-model be applied to the practice of linguistic inquiry?

Part IV was devoted to a detailed case study in which all the key notions and constitutive mechanisms of the p-model were illustrated. The case study seemed to bear witness to the finding that the practice of linguistic research supported our hypothesis:

$(SP)_{IV}$ The p-model is applicable to the reconstruction of the process of linguistic theorising.

As the next step we had to show that the p-model immediately yields the answers to those relevant questions which the current literature could not capture and that in this respect it is also more effective than the approaches to linguistic data and evidence we overviewed in Part I:

$(P)_V$ How does the p-model answer (OQ1)–(OQ7)?

We systematically discussed the answers to the questions and thus obtained:

$(SP)_V$ As an immediate consequence of $(SP)_{III}$, the p-model provides the answers to (OQ1)–(OQ7) discussed in Chapter 19.

At this point we have at our disposal the solutions to all five subproblems into which we subdivided the Main Problem (MP) of the book. Therefore, in accordance with the strategy we sketched in Chapter 1, now we have to derive the solution to the Main Problem from the solutions to the five subproblems.

The following solution to (MP) presents itself, which provides *a radically new interpretation* of linguistic theorising in general and of linguistic data/evidence in particular:

(SMP) Linguistic theorising – in particular, every application of linguistic theories as well as that of the tools of linguistic theorising (models, methods, programmes etc.) in general – is a plausible argumentation process built on the cyclic and prismatic re-evaluation of information. The characteristics, the structure and the functions of linguistic data and evidence are shaped by this argumentation process and depend on the latter's peculiarities:

(a) The *structure* of linguistic *data* consists of a statement and a plausibility value which is assigned to the statement and which stems from a direct source. Linguistic *evidence* has the additional property that it is part of an indirect source on the basis of which a positive plausibility value can be assigned to some hypothesis of the theory. Thereby:
   - Some piece of evidence usually neither verifies nor refutes a hypothesis, but is an element of an indirect source that makes this hypothesis plausible or implausible.
   - If the p-context changes, that is, in a new argumentation cycle, a piece of evidence may lose its evidence status. It may lose its plausibility, or there may be changes in the premises or latent background assumptions of the plausible inference connecting it with the hypothesis at issue which make this inference an unreliable source.
   - Consequently, one cannot consider evidence to be a firm basis, which would allow for determining the truth value of the hypotheses of the theory.
   - Thus, since evidence is a datum in the above sense, it can be regarded as a theory-independent and irrevisable basis neither of linguistic theorising nor of testing of theories.

(b) Since *data* are statements obtaining a plausibility value from direct sources, one of their *functions* consists in supplying the theory with plausibility values, which can be used to determine the plausibility value of other statements with the help of plausible inferences. Data are in this sense 'given', for their reliability is judged directly, often on the basis of the conventions of the particular research field or by following the methodological rules of the preferred theory. This interpretation of data sharply rejects the standard view of linguistic data and evidence (SVLD) at several points:

- Data are not objective, observable facts but plausible (in the extreme case, certainly true) statements whose acceptability can be revised on the basis of new information.
- The role of data is not reduced to securing the empiricalness of theories, since (47) covers not only 'linguistic data' capturing observable manifestations of linguistic behaviour but also those hypotheses of the theory which have not been inferred from other hypotheses but received a plausibility value on the basis of the reliability of their source.[1] Data are 'starting points' only in the sense that plausibility values enter the argumentation process through them.
- In addition to this, the special function of *evidence* is that it contributes to the evaluation and the comparison of the plausibility of rival hypotheses. Therefore, data playing the role of evidence may be tools for eliminating informational overdetermination (p-inconsistency).

Accordingly, the basic insights the p-model led to are that

(a) the argumentation structure of linguistic theories is relevant to the efficiency of linguistic research;
(b) there is a complex relationship between the argumentation structure of linguistic theories and linguistic data/evidence;
(c) therefore, linguistic data/evidence have to be interpreted in a radically new way; and
(d) the peculiarities of the argumentation process can account for, among other things, the uncertainty, the variety and the combinability of linguistic data and evidence as well as for the emergence and (provisional) existence of inconsistencies triggered by data – that is, for those characteristics of data that could not be explained with the help of other metatheoretical frameworks.

Nevertheless, it is not beside the point to examine briefly *how* we have obtained (MP). Obviously, if we accept the p-model, then it has to hold for *our own* argumentation as well, irrespective of the circumstance that it is not an object- but a metascientific argumentation process. From the constitutive reflexivity of the p-model it follows that our metascientific considerations, too, have to be regarded as a plausible argumentation process along the lines of the general characterisation of plausible argumentation as presented in Chapter 10.

First, our own premises were not true with certainty but only plausible on the basis of sources that we considered reliable – for example, conclusions drawn from the analysis of the current literature presented in Chapter 5, current theories of evidence surveyed in Chapter 8, or certain theses of Rescher and Polya on plausible argumentation. On these premises we built plausible inferences, which yielded $(SP)_I$–$(SP)_V$ as temporary, heuristic and fallible conclusions. Consequently, also (SMP) may be only a temporary, fallible and heuristic solution (and yet not the resolution) to (MP).

Second, our argumentation was cyclic – but not circular! – since at certain points, we fed back to earlier informational states and extended and modified them along the lines of the model presented in Chapter 10. For example, $(SP)_{II}$ states only hypothetically that $(P)_{II}$ can be solved with the help of the p-model; the solution was obtained as $(SP)_{III}$. Thus, the hypothesis that the p-model is capable of solving $(P)_{II}$ can be regarded as plausible only subsequently – and temporarily – by feeding back from $(SP)_{III}$ to this problem.

Third, our starting point was (CP), which grasped the problems raised in general. Then, it was explicated as (MP)(a)–(b) and by adding a condition (see (MP)(c)), we reduced it to (MP), which was regarded as the fundamental problem of this book. According to the terminology of the p-model, this reduction was nothing else but the retrospective re-evaluation of (CP) from the perspective of the peculiarities of the process of plausible argumentation insofar as we motivated (MP) with three considerations in Chapter 1. As we have seen, the retrospective re-evaluation is accomplished prismatically. The prism is the tool of the investigation: a theory, a model, a method, a concept or a system of concepts, an unexplicated background assumption, etc. All these tools are interpreted by the p-model as argumentation processes or parts of them. Which prism did indeed transform the central problem of the current literature on data and evidence into (MP)? Of course, it was (MP)(c) which was then in Part II explicated as the p-model. Since – as we have already mentioned in Section 19.9 in another context – prisms narrow down and distort our view, it is obvious that it is not problems in general that we solve but problems which are shown by our prism. From the peculiarities of the p-model it follows that (MP)(c) narrows down the perspective from which (MP)(a) and (b) can be viewed to the relationship of linguistic data/evidence and linguistic argumentation.

Fourth, the p-model does not provide us with general methodological rules which could be applied to all theories mechanically. Rather, the methodological principles and heuristics provided by the p-model place certain limits and give certain directions, which, however, can be revised during the theorising process. Methodological principles and their applications are integral parts of the argumentation process. Metatheoretical reflection is not a theory-independent level of (or above) the analysis of the theories investigated, but *part* of them. There is a cyclic relationship between metascientific reflection and object-scientific processes; the former is continuously weaving through and influencing the latter, and it may undergo changes as well.

Finally, we want to emphasise that the provisional result of our argumentation, that is, the hypothesis (SMP), will meet a fate similar to other plausible statements obtained by plausible argumentation: it has to compete with its rivals in further argumentation cycles. This competition will decide whether (SMP) can be maintained or whether it will be defeated by rivals enjoying higher plausibility in the debate about linguistic data and evidence.

Notes

1 INTRODUCTION

1 By 'linguistic data/evidence', we mean data/evidence relating to linguistics and not to language. Linguistic theories often make use of data which are not related to language directly, but which are relevant to the given linguistic theory.

2 THE PROBLEM $(P)_I$

1 See the papers listed in (a)–(j) in Section 3.3.

3 HISTORICAL BACKGROUND

1 See e.g. Bach (1965) and Allan (2003) on the relationship between these two trends of the standard view of the analytical philosophy of science and the development of linguistics in the twentieth century.

2 A concise formulation of this idea is, for example, as follows:

> all statements of *empirical science* be capable of test by reference to *evidence* which is *public*, i.e., evidence which can be secured by different observers and does not depend essentially on the observer. (Hempel 1952: 22; emphasis added)

3 For example, Kelly (2006) includes a concise overview of these aspects and their explications from logical positivism to contemporary views. The classical work presenting a detailed analysis of the standpoints concerning empirical evidence within the standard view of the analytical philosophy of science is Stegmüller (1970).

4 For instance, Russell traces back evidence to sense data, the logical positivist branch of the standard view to protocol sentences and Popper to basic statements (see also note 7), while all these terms were the subject of heated controversies. For overviews, see e.g. Kelly (2006) and Stegmüller (1970).

5 Objectivity was interpreted predominantly as intersubjective testability (see e.g. Popper 1959: 44).

6 Confirmation theory is very complex and controversial. Therefore, it would be beside the point to discuss it here. To give the reader an idea of the relationship between evidence and the confirmation of hypotheses, let it be sufficient to quote the following passage:

> To say that a body of information is evidence in favour of a hypothesis is to say that the hypothesis receives some degree of *support or confirmation* from that information. What sorts of information confirm what hypotheses is a question which has long been controversial; it was

discussed as avidly three centuries ago as it is today, when, under the heading of 'confirmation theory', it is one of the central topics in contemporary philosophy of science. Its profound interest to philosophers is due to its intimate connection with the *philosophical problem of induction*, concerning what grounds, if any, observational data can give us for accepting as a basis for action and belief hypotheses whose content logically transcends the observational data. Presumably, if it could be shown that any such hypothesis is sufficiently well confirmed by the evidence, then that would be grounds for accepting it. (Howson 2000: 108; emphasis as in the original)

7 A hypothesis can be falsified by 'basic statements' describing observable events occurring in space and time (see Popper 1959: 86, 103).

8 There is, of course, a distinction between (factual) *falsification* and (potential) *falsifiability*.

9 The relevance of the axiomatic organisation of scientific theories to linguistic theorising will be illustrated with the help of two quotations. First, Ringen gives the following brief characterisation of the criterion of deductivity:

On the standard view, the *structure* of an ideally explicit empirical theory is that of a set of abstract principles relating the hypothetical constructs of the theory to each other and to descriptions of observed phenomena. It is suggested that such a system can be construed as an *axiomatic system*. [Footnote 5 in the original: 'Sometimes (see Braithwaite, 1953; Carnap, 1956; Hempel, 1952, 1958) but not always, the structure of an ideally explicit empirical theory is represented as that of *a partially interpreted formal system*.'] The basic general principles (the axioms) of such a system and their consequences (the theorems of the system) constitute the general laws alleged to be true of the entities constituting the domain of the theory. In a correct scientific theory, the general laws must be true. (Ringen 1975: 3; emphasis added)

Newmeyer (1980), referring to Hempel, summarises some tenets of the standard view in connection with deductivity which are relevant for generative linguistics as follows:

Science is more in the business of comparing theories than in evaluating statements. A theory is simply an axiomatised system which as a whole has an empirical interpretation. We can compare competing theoretical systems in regard to such characteristics as these:

a. the clarity and precision with which the theories are formulated, and with which the logical relationships of their elements to each other and to expressions couched in observational terms have been made explicit;
b. the systematic, i.e., explanatory and predictive, power of the systems in regard to observable phenomena;
c. the formal simplicity of the theoretical system with which a certain systematic power is attained;
d. the extent to which the theories have been confirmed by experimental evidence. (Newmeyer 1980: 14)

10 See e.g. Bach (1965) and Allan (2003). Ringen applies the term 'standard view' to theoretical linguistics:

While the assumption is not always explicit, linguists apparently take for granted the standard view of the structure, function, and methods for the evaluation of explanatory theories in empirical science. [footnote 4: 'For elaborations and defense of the standard view of scientific theories see Braithwaite 1953, Hempel 1952, 1965, 1966, Nagel 1961, Popper 1959']. (Ringen 1975: 3)

Although the developments of the philosophy of science in the last thirty years have made the standard view's claims long since obsolete, its norms – as we will see later on – constitute the standard for the evaluation of linguistic theories up to the present day (see Kertész 2004a; Kertész & Rákosi 2006, 2008a, b, c).

11 There are two macro-paradigms within linguistic metatheory: phenomenological inductivism and hypothetico-deductivism . . . In the middle of the twentieth century there was a shift from a phenomenological inductivist paradigm in American linguistics to a hypothetico-deductivist paradigm, a shift known as 'the Chomskyan revolution' because it came about through Chomsky's work. (Allan 2003: 538)

See also Bach's (1965) detailed analysis.

12 Chomsky has assumed from his early works on (see e.g. Chomsky 1975 [1957]: 13ff.) that introspective data – although they do not possess spatiotemporal coordinates – fulfil the function which hypothetico-deductivism requires from data. A recent formulation of this view is as follows:

An experiment is called work with an informant, in which you design questions that you ask the informant to elicit data that will bear on the questions that you're investigating, and will seek *to provide evidence* that will help you answer these questions that are arising within a theoretical framework. Well, that's *the same kind of thing* they do in the physics department or the chemistry department or the biology department. To say that it's not empirical is to use the word 'empirical' in an extremely odd way. (Andor 2004: 98; emphasis added)

13 As already mentioned, we cannot draw a comprehensive picture of the empiricalness problem in linguistics comprising all the tendencies, theories, methods and fields of research, but we confine our discussion to only those elements which seem to motivate specifically that trend of the debate we have mentioned. For example, it is by no means only generative linguists who use introspective data, just as it is not only corpus linguists who use corpus data. However, as we will see, it is these two trends whose antagonism underlies the new problem this chapter centres around.

14 There are many remarks on this subject in Chomsky's work. For example:

Knowledge of language, like most facts of interest and importance, is neither presented for direct observation nor extractable from data by inductive procedures of any known sort. (Chomsky 1965: 18)

The gathering of data is informal; there has been *very little use of experimental approaches* (outside of phonetics) *or of complex techniques of data collection and data analysis* of a sort that can easily be devised, and that are widely used in behavioral sciences. . . . for the theoretical problems that seem most critical today, it is not at all difficult to obtain a mass of crucial data without use of such techniques. (Chomsky 1969: 56; emphasis added)

15 For example, Sampson wrote the following in the mid 1970s:

If linguistics is indeed based on intuition, then it is not a science . . . Science relies exclusively on the empirical. (Sampson 1975: 60)

16 The classic paper on the contrast between these two perspectives is, of course, Fillmore (1992). The present antagonism of the two standpoints is well illustrated

by extreme declarations in the most recent literature as well. For example, on the one hand, Chomsky still declares in an unsophisticated manner that 'corpus linguistics doesn't mean anything' (Andor 2004: 97). On the other hand, in a current discussion in the journal *Corpus Linguistics and Linguistic Theory* (Stefanowitsch & Gries 2007) Sampson maintains in an equally unsophisticated way that 'linguistics will not move forward healthily until the generative approach is bypassed as the pseudoscience it is, with its remaining practitioners retiring from academic life and new recruits to the discipline ignoring its ethos, assumptions, and alleged results' (Sampson 2007: 122).

Nevertheless, with respect to the stance of generative grammar it is important to distinguish between Chomsky's declarations and the practice of linguistic theorising. Predominantly – but not exclusively – the latter relies on introspective data. This is the main issue which the current debates on the treatment of data in generative grammar centre around (see Schütze 1996; Sternefeld 2007; Kertész & Rákosi 2008a). Chomsky's rhetoric, however, includes declarations such as:

> [I]n principle, evidence concerning the character of the I-language and initial state could come from many different sources apart from judgments concerning the form and meaning of expressions: perceptual experiments, the study of acquisition and deficit or of partially invented languages such as creoles, or of literary usage or language change, neurology, biochemistry, and so on. (Chomsky 1986: 36; for further examples, see e.g. Chomsky 1980a: 56, 192)

In an important paper, Fodor (1985) evaluates the data-handling methodology of generative linguistics in this way:

> it is probably a historical accident that, so far, the best field of data for the confirmation of grammars has been the well-formedness intuitions of speaker/hearers. It is to be hoped that new fields of data will become increasingly available as we learn more about how to use facts about the interactions between internally represented grammars and other psychological mechanisms to constrain both the theory of grammar and the theory of the interactions. (Fodor 1985: 157)

17 It is important to remark that it is not only generative grammar that takes sides for introspective data but also other, very different trends such as, for example, certain approaches to cognitive linguistics.

18 As the previous historical overview indicates, in linguistics 'inductivism' was interpreted in a somewhat different sense than in the philosophy of science.

19 Several authors do not consider the explication of the notion of 'empiricalness' and the terminological controversies related to it as relevant (see Penke & Rosenbach 2004a; Kepser & Reis 2005a). Instead, they presuppose a very broad and loose definition of this notion:

> If conceiving of 'empirical' very broadly as 'dealing with data', we can include any type of data-oriented research here. In this sense, probably every linguist works necessarily empirically – or how could one probably [*sic*] do linguistics without any type of linguistic data (defined loosely as any piece of language)? (Penke & Rosenbach 2004a: 514f.)

Others (Lehmann 2004, Geeraerts 2006) consider it as relevant and interpret it in terms of the inductivist or falsificationist version of (SVAPS).

20 The papers were re-published in Penke & Rosenbach (2007b). We refer to their first publication.

21 Above all it is clear that questions about data are *more important* than is sometimes assumed. (Borsley 2005a: 1479; emphasis added)

In short, linguistic evidence is an *extremely important* topic as well as a challenging problem for linguists of all persuasions. (Kepser & Reis 2005a: 1f.; emphasis added)

22 It seems likely, however, that questions about data will loom somewhat *larger* in linguistics in the future than they have in the past. (Borsley 2005a: 1475; emphasis added)

Given the fundamental nature of the problem, linguistic evidence is *a remarkably new topic* of linguistic discussion. (Kepser & Reis 2005a: 2; emphasis added)

23 The question 'What kind of inquiry is linguistics?' is the central problem of Kertész (1991).

4 THE PARTIAL REJECTION OF (SVLD) IN THE PRACTICE OF *OBJECT*-SCIENTIFIC RESEARCH

1 See the following characterisation of experiments in science:

In experiments, natural or artificial systems are studied in artificial settings designed to enable the investigators to manipulate, monitor, and record their workings, shielded, as much as possible from extraneous influences which would interfere with the production of epistemically useful data. (Bogen 2002: 129)

2 It does not make any sense to speak of grammaticality judgments given Chomsky's definitions, because people are incapable of judging grammaticality – it is not accessible to their intuitions . . . Linguists might construct arguments about the grammaticality of a sentence, but all that a linguistically naïve subject can do is judge its acceptability. Nevertheless, in the remainder of this book I will follow the existing literature in treating *grammaticality judgment* and *acceptability judgment* as synonyms, with the understanding that the former is unquestionably a misnomer, and only the later is a sensible notion. I do so because this usage occurs in many of the passages I quote, and because *acceptability judgment* can have misleading connotations of its own in certain contexts. For instance, the term can indicate that one is discussing contextual appropriateness rather than structural well-formedness. (Schütze 1996: 26f.; emphasis as in the original)

3 This methodological principle has already been raised in Chomsky's earlier works. For example:

Apparent counterexamples and unexplained phenomena should be carefully noted, but it is often rational to put them aside pending further study when principles of a certain degree of explanatory power are at stake. (Chomsky 1980b: 2)

5 THE PARTIAL REJECTION OF (SVLD) IN *META*SCIENTIFIC REFLECTION

1 For example:

there is no *a priori* evaluative distinction between these different types of data used in linguistics in the sense that one constitutes better evidence for the study of our language faculty than others. (Penke & Rosenbach 2004a: 493)

2 Here is an example to illustrate this:

Human beings, including linguists, are not genetically equipped to focus on linguistic data that have a certain structure, and are fallible in this task. Even researchers of good will are not immune to uncontrolled distortion of their data . . . That is, people, including linguists, subconsciously change their perceptional input. It is also well-known both to anthropologists and to linguists that the kind of participating observation that is typical of much fieldwork inevitably distorts the data; and even if the fieldworker is aware of it, he cannot eliminate the bias altogether. (Lehmann 2004: 200)

3 It is not really clear when informally gathered intuitions provide a satisfactory basis for research and when more formal methods of data gathering are necessary. It is also not really clear exactly how valuable corpora of various kinds are. (Borsley 2005a: 1479)

4 empirical research is not about restricting the investigation to one kind of method or technique: rather, it is about using experimental, and corpus-based, and other empirical approaches in combination to achieve maximally reliable results. (Geeraerts 2006: 45)

5 The theory-ladenness of observation has been generally acknowledged in the philosophy of science since the 1960s. The classical works raising this issue are Hanson (1958), Duhem (1974 [1906]) and Kuhn (1962/1970).

6 In processing linguistic data, two rules must therefore be observed: first, the editing must be transparent; second, derived versions must not replace, but accompany the original version. (Lehmann 2004: 207)

7 The papers discussed here do not raise the question of what is meant by the notions 'truth' and 'fact'. They do not go into the question, either, of which of the familiar theories of truth should be applied to which linguistic theory and under what conditions. We assume therefore that they presuppose the naïve correspondence theory of truth.

8 Eliminating and controlling for confounding factors requires us to have some idea of what those factors might be, and such an understanding can only be gained by systematic study of the judgment process. (Schütze 1996: 9)

9 To summarize, many of the worries about possible distorting factors in Schütze (1996) and elsewhere are less problematic than was feared; additionally various contributions (e.g. Weskott & Fanselow in press [2009], Bader & Häussler 2008 [2010]) have shown convincingly that the differences between methodologies gathering judgements are in practice fairly small, since all give satisfactory results in simple cases. (Featherston 2009a: 129)

10 A good model of word order variations in the middle field requires about 100–200 data points (estimated on the basis of the average number of the examples in related papers). In a single acceptability experiment, however, one can test only 4–6 of them. As a rule, however, one should compare data points gained from different experiments only qualitatively but not quantitatively. This makes an exhaustive securing of data in syntactic papers through controlled acceptability experiments practically impossible. (Fanselow 2009: 135; our translation)

11 empirical research necessarily combines inductive and deductive reasoning: on the one hand, you work in a bottom-up way from data to hypotheses, but on the other hand, those hypotheses will also be derived top-down from the theoretical perspective you adopt in thinking about your data. (Geeraerts 2006: 24)

If linguistics is an empirical science, then it depends on data, both in inductive work that analyzes and generalises over the data and in deductive work which tests hypotheses on the data. (Lehmann 2004: 187)

12 See also this chapter, note 5.

13 it is *the scientist's epistemic interest* that triggers the research, including the supply of data. (Lehmann 2004: 191; emphasis added)

In linguistics as in any other field, what sort of data one requires depends on *what questions one is investigating*. (Borsley 2005a: 1476; emphasis added)

Of course, the question of evidence itself is closely connected to the question: what for? This again crucially hinges on . . . *which aspect of language we focus on* in our research program. (Penke & Rosenbach 2004a: 480; emphasis added)

14 something is not in and of itself a datum, but it is a datum *relative to some particular empirical research*. (Lehmann 2004: 181; emphasis added)

gaining relevant linguistic evidence from the mass of potentially available data is neither a trivial matter *nor a purely methodical one that can be pursued in isolation from concrete linguistic enquiry and their theoretical concerns*. (Kepser & Reis 2005a: 1; emphasis added)

the question of *what* counts as evidence in linguistics crucially *rests on the respective approach taken to the study of language and the underlying conception of language*. (Penke & Rosenbach 2004a: 493; emphasis added)

15 Therefore, he sharply rejects introspection and – as the quotation in Section 5.2 has witnessed – attributes only a heuristic role to it. In his view, introspective data are not capable of testing hypotheses:

the procedure in which a linguist produces data on which he constructs a theory which he then tests by these data is, of course, *circular*. The data *do not actually fulfill any control function*, and the procedure has nothing to do with scientific method. (Lehmann 2004: 196; emphasis added)

16 as long as the raw data are available, one can always fall back on them *to distill better secondary representations* from them. (Lehmann 2004: 205; emphasis added)

17 a datum must have a basis outside of and independent of the researcher. (Lehmann 2004: 181)

18 functional linguists often consider Chomsky a theoretical and essentially 'unempirical' or 'axiomatic' linguist. (Penke & Rosenbach 2004a: 485)

(For the sake of clarity, let us remark that Penke & Rosenbach's (2004a: 495) definition of functional linguistics includes corpus linguistics.)

19 Evidence involving different domains of data will shed different, but altogether more, light on the issues under investigation, be it that the various findings support each other, help with correct interpretation, or by contradicting each other, lead to factors of influence so far overlooked. (Kepser & Reis 2005a: 3)

20 comparison between studies of the same issue based on different data types is possible, and potential conflicts in result can in principle be resolved. (Kepser & Reis 2005a: 1)

21 When a theory predicts a phenomenon, the corpus presence of the phenomenon is taken as a confirmation of the theory. When a theory excludes a phenomenon, the corpus presence of the phenomenon is taken as a falsification of the theory. In both cases, however, a problem arises when the frequency of the selected corpus data is low: what if the confirming or falsifying data are marginal with regard to the alternatives? Because corpus evidence is seldom a question of black or white (of one hundred percent versus zero percent of occurrences), a proper analysis of corpus materials requires that alternative patterns are systematically explored and that their frequencies are statistically evaluated. (Geeraerts 2006: 37)

22 I think that one of the main points to keep in mind about drawing conclusions from data is that it is all guessing. Really. But what we are trying to do with statistical summaries and hypothesis testing is to quantify just how reliable our guesses are. (Johnson 2008: 3)

23 Given a number of conditions, experimental results decide between competing analyses . . . (Geeraerts 2006: 26).

24 Which of these data types is then invoked to provide evidence for a linguistic statement depends on a number of factors . . . (Penke & Rosenbach 2004a: 485).

25 Data in linguistics comes in a variety of types . . . Which of these data types is then invoked to provide evidence for a linguistic statement depends on a number of factors, such as *the field of linguistics*, *the particular topic under investigation*, or *the willingness to consider data collected outside one's own field of research*. (Penke & Rosenbach 2004a: 485; emphasis added)

26 This view corresponds to the second function of data in Lehmann's view as we discussed in Section 5.6.

7 THE PROBLEM $(P)_{II}$

1 For more on this, see Kertész (2004a: 21).

8 HISTORICAL BACKGROUND

1 For more on the concept of evidence, see, for instance Achinstein (2001: 3ff.), Kelly (2006), as well as the literature cited by them.

2 A datum is *unlike the protocol truths* of the positivists not only . . . in its potential failure to be true, but also in that it . . . *need not be cognitively primitive*. (Rescher 1973: 64; emphasis added)

3 The core of the present conception of plausibility is the notion of the extent of our cognitive inclination towards a proposition – of the extent of its epistemic hold upon us in the light of the credentials represented by sources from which it derives. (Rescher 1976: 14)

4 See Rescher (1976: 118, 1977a: 122, 1979: 96).

5 The plausibility of a thesis . . . reflects the prospects of its being fitted into our cognitive scheme of things in view of the standing of the sources or principles that vouch for its inclusion herein . . . In general, the more plausible a thesis the more smoothly it is consistent and consonant with the rest of our knowledge of the matters at issue. . . . the cardinal rule governing the operation of our concept of plausibility is – in cases of conflict, never make the more plausible give way to what is less so; by all means, retain the more highly plausible theses. (Rescher 1976: 14; emphasis as in the original)

6 *'Data'*: theses that can serve as acceptance-candidates in the context of the inquiry, contentions, which, at the best, are merely *presumptively* true . . . They are *prima facie* truths in the sense that we would incline to grant them acceptance-as-true *if* (and this is a very big IF) there were no countervailing considerations upon the scene . . .

Plausibility ratings: comparative evaluations of our initial assessment (in the context of issue) of the relative acceptability of the 'data'. (Rescher 1979: 69; emphasis as in the original)

7 Because of the utmost importance of Goodman's views it is worth quoting his basic idea at length:

> How do we justify deduction? Plainly, by showing that it conforms to the general rules of deductive inference... But how is the validity of rules to be determined?... Principles of deductive inference are justified by their conformity with accepted deductive practice...
>
> **This looks flagrantly circular**. I have said that deductive inferences are justified by their conformity to valid general rules, and that general rules are justified by their conformity to valid inferences. **But this circle is a virtuous one**. The point is that rules and particular inferences alike are justified by being brought into **agreement with each other**. *A rule is amended if it yields an inference we are unwilling to accept; an inference is rejected if it violates a rule we are willing to amend.* The process of justification is the delicate one of making **mutual adjustments** between rules and accepted inferences; and in the agreement achieved lies the only justification needed for either.
>
> All this applies equally to induction. An inductive inference, too, is justified by conformity to general rules, and a general rule by conformity to accepted inductive inferences. Predictions are justified if they conform to valid canons of induction; and the canons are valid if they accurately codify accepted inductive practice. (Goodman 1983 [1955]: 64; bold emphasis added, italics as in the original)

8 It is important to note that Rescher focuses solely on the concept of 'datum', while Williamson deals with the concept of 'evidence'.

9 According to the literature, deductively invalid inferences include, for instance, inductive, analogical, abductive, defeasible, presumptive and plausible inferences as well as fallacies. However, these terms sometimes overlap and they do not have a generally accepted definition. Thus, for example, according to one of the approaches, the term 'plausible inference' is treated as the genus proximum of the formerly mentioned categories and it excludes only fallacies. Another approach considers plausible inferences to be a special class within non-demonstrative inferences. There also exists an approach which subsumes the deductively invalid inferences (excluding fallacies) under inductive inferences. Since the present book is not concerned with the history of logic, an overview of the interrelated approaches in connection with the above mentioned notions is not relevant from the point of view of the main issues here.

10 The idea of applying plausible argumentation and heuristics to the strategies of problem solving in linguistics goes back to Kertész (1993).

11 'Linguistic theorising' also covers applications of theoretical tools used in linguistics such as models, programmes, methods etc.

12 For a concise overview of this distinction, see Kertész & Rákosi (2005b, 2009c). For example, Chomsky mechanically adopts this requirement of the standard view of the analytical philosophy of science formulated by Reichenbach and applies it to his own theory without citing his sources (see Sections 3.2–3.3):

> we shall never consider the question of how one might have arrived at the grammar whose simplicity is being determined... Question[s] of this sort are *not relevant* to the program of research that we have outlined above. One may arrive at a grammar by intuition, guess-work, all sorts of partial methodological hints, reliance on past experience, etc. It is no doubt possible to give an organised account of many useful procedures of analysis, but it is questionable whether these can be *formulated rigorously, exhaustively and simply enough* to qualify as a *practical and mechanical discovery procedure*... Our ultimate aim is to provide an *objective*,

> *non-intuitive* way to *evaluate a grammar* once presented, and to compare it with other proposed grammars. We are thus interested in describing the form of grammars (equivalently, the nature of linguistic structure) and investigating the *empirical consequences* of adopting a certain model for linguistic structure, rather than in showing how, in principle, one might have arrived at the grammar of a language. (Chomsky 1975 [1957]: 56; emphasis added)

9 PLAUSIBLE INFERENCES

1 For a formal definition of deductive inference, see e.g. MacFarlane (2000), Beall & Restall (2000), Basin & Matthews (2002).

2 Different logical systems determine the logical structure of statements differently. There are differences as to which components of the statements' meaning are relevant from a logical point of view (i.e. modality, temporality), the depth of the analysis of the structure of the statements, and the 'translation' of the relevant meaning components into the language of logic (that is, for example, which characteristics are attributed to the logical constant '&' etc.).

3 There are differences in the way logical systems formalise, 'translate' natural language expressions. For example, conditionals, that is, statements of the type 'if *A* then *B*' are interpreted by classical logic as '$A \supset B$'. Relevance logic sets stricter criteria by introducing 'strict implication'. Intuitionistic (constructivist) logic spells out conditionals as 'the construction of *B*'s solution can be traced back to the construction of *A*'s solution' – and the list could be continued.

4 This means that it takes our cognitive and practical limits into consideration.

5 In Section 9.8, this statement will be made more precise with the help of notions introduced later.

6 For a thorough comparison of the concepts 'plausibility' and 'probability', see chapter IV of Rescher (1976).

7 Of course, one may attempt to reveal the sources against a given conjecture and judge their reliability. With this, however, new sources are included in the judgement process, and some of them might provide information for the conjecture. Thus, the plausibility of this conjecture will change. See also Chapter 10.

8 This concept of plausibility is traced back by Rescher to Aristotle's *Topica*:

> He took the basis of plausibility to lie in the probity of sources: the opinions held 'by all or the majority or the experts or the best and most reputable among them'. But his approach was broad, and encompassed not only the opinions of authorities as such, but also the cognitive principles on which they are generally founded . . . (Rescher 1976: 6)

Rescher interprets 'reliability' as solidness, trustworthiness which may be, in the case of personal sources, based on past performance, informedness, training, experience etc. (see Rescher 1976: 7).

9 For this distinction, see also Sections 19.3, 19.4 and 19.6.

10 Comparing (10)(a) and (10)(b), we can see that there is a difference in the meaning of the statements '*p* has a plausibility value' and '*p* is a plausible statement'. Statements which are true with certainty possess a plausibility value, but they are not plausible statements.

11 See Section 10.4.

12 For more on this, see Sections 19.3 and 19.6.

13 See Gooding (2000: 117ff.), Arabatzis (2008: 159ff.).
14 In such situations, one can narrow down *S* to a set of sources *S′* containing only sources that allow for assigning a plausibility value to *p*. Thus, one of the cases in (11)(a)–(c) can be applied to *S′*.
15 The reconstruction of inferences (a) and (b) is fragmentary; for the missing theoretical tools, see Section 9.4. Of course, the relationship of the third premise and the structural rule mentioned can be reconstructed as an indirect source (inference), too.
16 For detailed case studies on this, see Kertész & Rákosi (2006, 2009a).
17 Plank (2008: 1158). We will refer to the Universals Archive as Plank (2008). The number after the colon indicates the number of the universal in question.
18 For the statement on Coptic see Plank (2008: 1158).
19 Besides the term 'demonstrative', the term 'sound' is also used in the literature in English (see e.g. Copi & Cohen 1990: 52).
20 This means that demonstrative inferences meet (2)(a) and (b) as well.
21 As we have emphasised earlier, plausibility/plausibility values do not belong to the logical structure of statements.
22 The notions of 'context' and 'argumentation' are used here pre-explicatively. For their detailed interpretation, see Chapter 10.
23 This does not mean that demonstrative inferences are capable of securing the certainty of the conclusion once and for all and in every context. On the one hand, other sources may show the conclusion to be implausible or false. On the other hand, the plausibility value of the premises may change (for example, if the reliability of the sources supporting them is questioned). Despite this, demonstrative inferences cannot be considered to be formal in the same sense as deductive ones can, because they take into account the truth value of the premises not only hypothetically but also rely on their plausibility value at a given moment. To put it otherwise, while deductive inferences are *hypothetical*, demonstrative ones are *relative*.
24 One must not forget that demonstrative inferences assign – as we have already mentioned – a truth value to the premises not in an absolute sense and once and for all, but only relative to a perfectly reliable set of sources.
25 Truth values are interpreted here as extreme cases of plausibility values.
26 This means that it is implausible that the *wh*-transformation cannot apply twice to a given string.
27 It would be beside the point to discuss the importance of this pattern. Therefore, a few brief remarks will be sufficient. First of all, Polya calls it 'the fundamental inductive pattern' (Polya 1954: 4), 'the simplest and most widespread pattern of plausible reasoning' (Polya 1948: 222). Although it is considered to be *a paradigmatic example of plausible inferences* in the literature, it does not have a generally accepted name. However, it has long been known in other contexts. For centuries, it was referred to as 'affirming the consequence' and classified as a fallacious inference. Peirce broke with this tradition and called this pattern 'abduction', and considered it to be one of the basic tools of scientific inquiry. Walton calls it 'argument from evidence to a hypothesis' (Walton 1996: 67). Łukasiewicz (1970 [1912]: 7) uses the term 'reduction' to name inferences going in the 'opposite direction' than deduction:

> Reasoning which starts from reasons and looks for consequences is called *deduction*; that which starts from consequences and looks for reasons is called *reduction*.

We consider Polya's stance to be the most general one. Therefore, we will follow his interpretation. We will adopt Łukasiewicz's term, without, however, taking over the conceptual system applied by him.

28 See note 31.

29 For analogical inferences, see e.g. Yan, Forbus & Gentner (2003); Falkenhainer, Forbus & Gentner (1989), Itkonen (2005).

30 The concept of 'context' will be defined in Section 9.8; until then, it will be used pre-explicatively.

31 We cannot 'detach' the conclusion of our pattern of plausible reasoning. '*A* is rendered more credible' is meaningless without reference to the premises that explain by which circumstances it was rendered so. Referred to the premises, the plausible conclusion makes perfectly good sense and is perfectly reasonable, but it may diminish in value as time goes by, although the premises remain intact . . . It would be foolish to deplore that in several respects our pattern of plausible reasoning falls short of the perfection of demonstrative reasoning. On the contrary, we should feel a little satisfaction that we succeeded in clarifying somewhat a difference that we may have suspected from the beginning. From the outset it was clear that *the two kinds of reasoning have different tasks*. From the outset they appeared very different: *demonstrative reasoning as definite, final, 'machinelike'; and plausible reasoning as vague, provisional, specifically 'human'* . . . In opposition to demonstrative inference, *plausible inference leaves indeterminate a highly relevant point: the 'strength' or the 'weight' of the conclusion*. This weight may depend not only on clarified grounds such as those expressed in the premises, but also on unclarified unexpressed grounds somewhere in the background of the person who draws the conclusion. A person has a background, a machine has not. (Polya 1954: 115f.; emphasis added)

See also e.g. Rescher (1976: 111), Walton (2001: 164).

32 Inferences in the second group may be called 'strong' plausible inferences, since their premises are true with certainty. In contrast, inferences belonging to the first and third group can be termed 'weak' plausible inferences, since at least one of their premises is only plausible.

33 See also Section 9.7.

34 More exactly: if there is a consequence relation between the premises and the conclusion, then the conclusion will be a plausible statement; if there is no consequence relation, then the conclusion may be of neutral plausibility when at least one of the latent background assumptions possesses the plausibility value 0.

35 This modification can be found in Rescher's work, too; see Rescher (1976: 61).

36 That is, $d(A, B) \geq d(C, D)$.

37 Of course, one has to judge only those latent background assumptions to be of neutral plausibility about which one does not possess a sufficient amount of information.

38 Truth values are regarded here as extreme cases of plausibility values. That is, we deem them source-dependent.

39 Many of the so-called fallacies, on closer inspection, turn out to be instances of argumentation that are defeasible, or opinion-based cases of presumptive reasoning, but inherently reasonable. (Walton 1991: 216)

40 See Walton, Reed & Macagno (2008: 329).

41 See Walton, Reed & Macagno (2008: 331f.).

42 it can happen that we receive some new information that leaves our belief in both premises completely intact, but influences the trust we put in *A* in a way just opposite to that expressed

in the conclusion. To find A more plausible on the ground of the premises of our heuristic syllogism is only reasonable. Yet tomorrow I may find grounds, not interfering at all with these premises, that make A appear less plausible, or even *definitively refute it*. The conclusion may be shaken and even overturned completely by commotions *in the invisible parts of its foundation*, although the premises, *the visible part, stand quite firm*. (Polya 1948: 223f.; emphasis added)

43 See the quotation in note 42.

44 By LONG-DISTANCE BINDING we mean a reflexive occurring in a lower clause being coindexed with an antecedent in a higher clause which is a violation of Principle A of the Binding Theory. (See Plank 2008: 1319)

45 Testing of U requires the selection of relevant Marathi sentences, the judgement of their grammaticality as well as their linguistic analysis. Therefore, the negative outcome of the test does not mean that this premise could be deemed false with certainty.

46 For the notion of 'relevant characteristic' see (2) and (3).

47 Plausible inferences belonging to the first group as well as demonstrative inferences may also be tools of problem solving, because they can make implicit information explicit. Since all inferences in the sense of (2) assign a new characteristic depending on the characteristics of the premises to the conclusion, they extend the information given. However, see also (4) and the subsequent comments.

10 PLAUSIBLE ARGUMENTATION

1 Inconsistency – similarly to the logical consequence relation – is a *formal feature*, that is, it does not depend on whether the statements in question are only plausible or true with certainty. As we have argued in Section 9.3, it is possible that the plausibility of a statement is indefinite in such a way that both the statement and another statement that is incompatible with it are supported by certain sources, that is, they are plausible in a given situation. For more on this, see, for instance, Rescher (1977b: 63), Rescher & Brandom (1980: 160).

2 The sets of sources assigning a plausibility value to p and $\sim p$, respectively, have to be distinct, since a source can be regarded as suitable only if it judges p unequivocally; see Section 9.3.

3 P-inconsistency means *explicit* inconsistency among plausible statements. The plausibility value is, of course, only one of the possible characteristics that can be taken into consideration with respect to inferences in the sense of (2). For example, there are contexts where the provability of statements counts as a relevant characteristic. In such situations, plausibility may be completely irrelevant.

4 In such cases – in contrast to instances along the lines of (40)(a), which might be called *consistent solutions* – we speak of a *paraconsistent solution* that can be established as a superposition of two solutions in the sense of (a). For the paraconsistent representation of p-inconsistency, see Sections 10.5–6.

5 On the role of inconsistencies in scientific theorising, see e.g. Kuhn (1962/1970), Lakatos (1976, 1970), Laudan (1977). See also Sections 10.4–10.6.

6 The root idea of such reasoning is that of *multistage process* where we repeatedly reexamine one selfsame issue from different and mutually inconsistent points of view . . We proceed in circles or *cycles* where we return to a certain issue now in this light and now in that . . . We have here a *process of successive approximation* as it were, where at each stage we assert things that

are . . . in need of eventual *correction*. When things go smoothly, however, these successive corrections appertain to increasingly minor and insignificant respects. (Rescher 1987: 304; emphasis added)

7 This is usually characteristic of the first cycle(s).

8 A search of 1994 New York Times newswire yields no examples – is this just because they have better copy editors? (Manning 2003: 293)

9 It already appears less likely that this was just a typo. (Manning 2003: 293)

10 *as least as* seems to have robust support. (Manning 2003: 293)

11 which perhaps provides a pathway for the development of *this apparently new form*. (Manning 2003: 293; emphasis added)

12 A search of 1994 New York Times newswire yields no examples – is this just because they have better copy editors? (Manning 2003: 293)

13 If these were typos, they would be easy to explain . . . This anticipatory substitution is thus a highly plausible typo. (Schütze 2009: 155)

Nevertheless, we should not forget that this inference relies on latent background assumptions as well, since it belongs to Type 3 of plausible inferences, more exactly, it is an instance of weak reduction (see Section 9.5.4).

14 See also Sections 10.5–7.

15 If we are engaged in inquiries where we do not simply reason *deductively from preassured premises*, or if *the course of argumentation is . . . not deductively conclusive*, then it may make perfectly good sense to . . . consider an issue *prismatically*, by proceeding in the variable light of not merely different but even *inconsistent perspectives*. (Rescher 1987: 306f.; emphasis added)

Similarly, Polya also highlights the prismatic character of problem solving (Polya 1981, vol. II: 68).

16 In contrast, the standard view of linguistic data and evidence, namely, (SVLD)(e), as we have seen in Section 3.2, applies this strategy, because it requires the abandonment of a hypothesis if it leads to false predictions. Thus, according to this principle, in a conflict between a hypothesis and a (certainly true) datum, the former should be rejected; see also Section 3.1 on the falsificatory function of evidence.

17 Of course, the p-context versions may be organised around the members of the p-inconsistency as well.

18 *Z* stands for Zubizarreta's text as a direct source; I_a for inference (a) as an indirect source.

19 There is a strong connection between plausible argumentation and *paraconsistent logic*, which models contradictions with a non-contradictory metalanguage. For a detailed account of this relationship, see e.g. Rescher & Brandom (1980), Priest (2002), Meheus (2002), Priest *et al.* (2004) etc. We have examined the relationship between plausible argumentation and contradictions in linguistics in several case studies; see, for example, Kertész & Rákosi (2006, 2009a).

20 These procedures cannot be implemented completely but only partially in most cases. The steps of the cycles are executed not as applications of a thorough rule system but as applications of heuristics.

21 See also Sections 19.3 and 19.6 concerning this.

22 The process of scientific knowledge-acquisition itself can – and, I think, should – be conceived of as an *ongoing process of problem-solving*, i.e., of *inconsistency-elimination*. These inconsistencies can be internal (intra-theoretical, or to use Laudan's technical term, 'conceptual') or external (empirical) ones; the latter turn up where the task is to fit the so called theoretical and empirical part of science together. And thus, in my view, the turning up of inconsistencies in actual science is *inevitable* and *essential*, but so are *the constant efforts at their elimination*. That is what keeps science going. Because the resolution of each specific inconsistency, the solving of a given problem, generates a new one. (Fehér 1990: 238; emphasis added)

23 For the concept of 'superposition', see Rescher & Brandom (1980: 10ff.), Kertész & Rákosi (2009a: 249f.).

24 The sort of 'self-criticism' at issue does not reflect any vicious or vitiating circularity, but in effect amounts simply to a *feedback* process that uses later, more refined stages of the analysis to effect revisionary sophistications in the materials from which earlier stages proceeded. One indeed returns to 'the same point' but does so *at a different cognitive level*. (Rescher 1976: 119; emphasis as in the original)

For the distinction between cyclic and circular argumentation, see Kertész & Rákosi (2009b), Rescher 1987, (1977a).

11 THE SOLUTION TO $(P)_{II}$

1 The quotation below is fairly instructive. It manifests that although the advocates of the standard view of the philosophy of science realised the necessity of providing a solution to certain problems, their attempt to achieve this had to face difficulties that they could not overcome in the metascientific framework at their disposal:

Inductively sound reasoning based on a consistent, and thus possibly true, set of 'premises' may lead to contradictory 'conclusions' . . . When two sound inductive arguments thus conflict, which conclusion, if any, is it reasonable to accept, and perhaps to act on? . . . the credence given to any contemplated hypothesis should always be determined by the support it receives from the *total* evidence available at the time . . . This is what Carnap has called the *requirement of total evidence*. . . . the requirement presupposes a quantitative concept of the degree, $c(h, e)$, to which the evidence e confirms or supports the hypothesis h. This raises the question how such a concept might be defined and whether it can be characterized so generally that $c(h, e)$ is determined for *any* hypothesis h that might be proposed, relative to *any* body of evidence e that might be available . . . The requirement is concerned rather with the rational use, or application, of inductive reasoning in the formation of empirical beliefs . . . The distinction between rules of inference and rules of application can be made also in reference to deductive reasoning. The rules of inference . . . provide criteria of deductive validity; but they qualify as deductively valid many particular arguments whose conclusions are false, and they do not concern the conditions under which it is reasonable to believe, or to accept, the conclusion of a deductively valid argument. To do so would be the task of rules for the rational application of deductive inference. (Hempel 1966: 128f.; emphasis as in the original)

2 we should regard consistency as one important constraint among others rather than as a non-negotiable prerequisite for productive inquiry. This means that it may be fruitful (and hence permissible and 'rational') in the heat of research to violate the consistency constraint, just as it may be fruitful to violate another constraint. (Nickles 2002: 21)

3 although in theory we *can* always save the ideal of consistency . . . , the crucial fact remains that beyond a certain point it would – in practice – be *unreasonable*, nay Quixotic, to do so. . . . consistency too is a matter of degree. Like the other parameters of systematicity (coherence, simplicity, and the rest), consistency is not a matter of yes-or-no but one of more-or-less. It too emerges as a degree-admitting desideratum rather than an absolute requirement. Like the other facts of systematicity, consistency may defensibly be sacrificed on a limited basis, in return for sufficient gains within the overall framework of systematic desiderata. (Rescher & Brandom 1980: 51ff.; emphasis as in the original)

4 For more on this, see Kertész (2004a), Kertész & Rákosi (2006, 2009a).

12 THE PROBLEM $(P)_{III}$

1 See Chapter 5 note 5.

13 THE CONCEPT OF 'DATUM' AND 'EVIDENCE'

1 This is a real possibility, since as Schütze remarks,

> it was apparent that behavioral evidence was not *always* the last word. Theoretical considerations could also dictate that some sentences *must* be grammatical, regardless of how speakers might react to them. With regard to sentences containing embedded *if-then* and *either-or* pairs, Chomsky states, 'Note that many of the sentences . . . will be quite strange and unusual . . . But they are all grammatical sentences, formed by process of sentence construction so simple and elementary that even the most rudimentary English grammar would contain them' (SS, p. 23). The reasoning seems to be this: given that certain sentences are uncontroversially part of the language, our intuitions about what grammars can look like tell us that certain other sentences must also be part of it, although our judgments of these latter sentences are not so clear-cut. (Schütze 1996: 22)

2 For the interpretation of the concept of 'evidence' and for further analysis of this example, see Section 13.3.

3 This means only, as we have already mentioned in Chapter 10, that they belong to the factors on which a well-grounded decision among rival p-context-versions can be based.

4 See Hoffmann (2007: 95).

16 A CASE STUDY: A RECONSTRUCTION OF GENTNER & WOLFF (1997)

1 See Gentner & Wolff (1997: 331ff.).

2 See Gentner & Wolff (1997: 331).

3 Gentner & Wolff (1997: 333).

4 See Gentner & Wolff (1997: 334).

5 For the details of the relevant publications, see Gentner & Wolff (1997: 331f.).

6 See Gentner & Wolff (1997: 333f.).

7 See Gentner & Wolff (1997: 334ff.).

8 This hypothesis is not shared by all theories of metaphor. For example, Lakoff & Johnson's conceptual metaphor theory supposes that metaphors are mappings of one *conceptual domain* into another conceptual domain.

9 For the source of the plausibility of these statements, that is, the publications, see Gentner & Wolff (1997: 332ff.).
10 Gentner & Wolff (1997: 332).
11 Of course, papers by adherents of abstraction-first models not referred to in Gentner & Wolff (1997) and further works by Gentner may contain information which makes it possible to decide whether the explanatory power of models based on h_2 and h_3, respectively, is strong enough to explain the data in (55).
12 For the sources, see Gentner & Wolff (1997: 332f.).
13 Gentner & Wolff (1997: 332f.; emphasis as in the original).
14 (56) cannot be interpreted as strong evidence for h_2 or h_3, since it makes both of them equally plausible. Therefore, the criteria laid down in (50)(a)(ii) or (51)(a)(ii) are met neither by h_2 nor by h_3.
15 The list of sources can be found in Gentner & Wolff (1997: 333f.).
16 Gentner & Wolff (1997: 333f.).
17 Gentner & Wolff (1997: 334).
18 The list of sources for the assignment of a plausibility value to these statements can be found in Gentner & Wolff (1997: 334ff.).
19 Gentner & Wolff (1997: 334ff.; emphasis as in the original).
20 Double thin arrows indicate that the two p-context variants are rivals; simple thick arrows indicate weak evidence for the central hypothesis of the given p-context version, while double thick arrows mean weak evidence against it.

The source of the plausibility of the statements in (55), (57) and (59) could be the models at issue. In fact, these arguments stem from authors working within the models concerned; Gentner and Wolff, however, re-evaluate the plausibility value of these statements insofar as they present them as hypotheses which can be deemed plausible from an external, (theory-)neutral point of view as well.
21 Gentner & Wolff (1997: 336).
22 For explanations of the highlighted notions see the passages in *Motivation and background*. For more details and discussion, see Rákosi (forthcoming) and Rákosi (in preparation).
23 See Gentner & Wolff (1997: 336).
24 See Gentner & Wolff (1997: 336f.).
25 See Gentner & Wolff (1997: 338).
26 See Gentner & Wolff (1997: 337f.).
27 The simplest way is to reverse the two clauses of the first premise, that is, to interpret the hypothesis in the second clause as a possible explanation of the finding captured in the first clause:

$$\frac{\begin{array}{l}[0 < |\text{If no prime leads to the longest processing time, then } h_2.|_S < 1] \\ 0 < |\text{No prime leads to the longest processing time.}|_S < 1\end{array}}{0 < |h_2|_I < 1}$$

28 See Gentner & Wolff (1997: 338).
29 See Gentner & Wolff (1997: 338).
30 See Gentner & Wolff (1997: 338f.).
31 See Gentner & Wolff (1997: 339).
32 Gentner & Wolff (1997: 333, 339).
33 See Gentner & Wolff (1997: 340).
34 For the details, see Gentner & Wolff (1997: 340f.).

35 Gentner & Wolff (1997: 341).
36 See Gentner & Wolff (1997: 341).
37 See Gentner & Wolff (1997: 342).
38 Of course, at the very moment when one raises these two statements as conjectures supported by more or less vague considerations, the informational underdetermination turns into *informational overdetermination (p-inconsistency)*, since in this case, a statement and its negation possess a relatively low, but positive, plausibility value.
39 This also means that p-context version 4 can be represented as a compound of two p-context-versions built around (72) & (73) and (72) & (74), respectively. Rescher and Brandom call this operation 'schematisation' which is intended to capture situations in which the law of excluded middle is not valid; see Rescher & Brandom (1980: 9–14).
40 Dotted thick arrows indicate that the pieces of evidence listed provide only a weak support for h_4 because Experiments 1–3 did not test this hypothesis. Therefore, the plausible inferences linking the statements summarising the results of Experiments 1–3 make use of some latent background assumptions whose plausibility is neutral or low. For example, it is only supposed that the stimulus material in Experiments 1 and 2 included mainly non-stock (novel, or novel, as well as conventional and high-similarity) metaphors. Nevertheless, Gentner and Wolff carried out subsequent analyses which yielded that the mean conventionality ratings in Experiments 1–2 are comparable to those of the low-conventionality condition of Experiment 4, while the mean conventionality ratings in Experiment 3 were comparable to those of the high-conventionality conditions in Experiment 4; similar findings were found in relation to the mean similarity ratings.
41 For example: *That argument is a war* (high base conventionality × high similarity) vs *That conversation is a war* (high base conventionality × low similarity); *That genius is an eagle* (low base conventionality × high similarity) vs *That student is an eagle* (low base conventionality × low similarity).
42 For the details, see Gentner & Wolff (1997: 343).
43 For the description of the experimental design, see Gentner & Wolff (1997: 342ff.).
44 See Gentner & Wolff (1997: 344f.).
45 See Gentner & Wolff (1997: 344f.).
46 See Gentner & Wolff (1997: 346).
47 See Gentner & Wolff (1997: 346).
48 See Sections 10.5–6 and 16.3.
49 See Gentner & Wolff (1997: 342, 346).
50 See Gentner & Wolff (1997: 346).
51 See Gentner & Wolff (1997: 348f.).
52 Gentner & Wolff (1997: 348).
53 Moreover, Gentner and Wolff make a critical remark according to which 'one drawback of this proposed model is that it is difficult to separate from a comparison model' (Gentner & Wolff 1997: 348). Although they make it clear that this model supposes a processing mode different from comparison, it is not clear whether h_6 is a rival of h_4 & (79) and h_5 within the model type 'assignment-first', or whether it still belongs to the abstraction-first type together with its predecessor h_2.

54 More exactly: on the basis of the sources within this set which allow us to assign a plausibility value to it. It is important to remark, however, that this method cannot be generalised, because it may be the case that the plausibility values stemming from different sources are so different that only one or two sources are capable of making a hypothesis more plausible than five other sources in the case of its rival. Further, the circumstance that h_4 & (79) and h_5 receive a plausibility value from almost every indirect source built on the data listed ensures the tenability of a comparison of the plausibilities of the hypotheses on the basis of all sources mentioned.

55 Again: on the basis of the sources within this set which assign a plausibility value to it.

56 In order to reconstruct the plausible inference connecting the datum (70)(e) with hypothesis h_2 we will reformulate (70)(e) as follows:

> Base primes lead to significantly faster interpretation times than do blanks, while targets do not with high-conventional and low-similarity metaphors.

Thus, we obtain the following inference after conducting Experiment 3:

> $0 <$ |If an abstraction-guided process may apply to conventional metaphors in accord with h_2, then base primes lead to significantly faster interpretation times than do blanks, while targets do not with high-conventional and low-similarity metaphors.$|_{E_3} < 1$
> $0 <$ |Base primes led to significantly faster interpretation times than did blanks, while targets did not with high-conventional and low-similarity metaphors.$|_{E_3} < 1$
> ---
> |An abstraction-guided process may apply to conventional metaphors in accord with h_2.$|_{I_1} = ?$

This inference seems to belong to Type 3 of plausible inferences (see Section 9.5.4). Therefore, we can assign a plausibility value to the conclusion if we transform this inference into another one where there is a logical consequence relation between the premises and the conclusion. This can be achieved in the following way:

> [$0 <$ |If base primes lead to significantly faster interpretation times than do blanks, while targets do not with high-conventional and low-similarity metaphors as well as with high-conventional and high-similarity metaphors, then an abstraction-guided process may apply to conventional metaphors in accord with h_2.$|_{E_3} < 1$]
> $0 <$ |Base primes led to significantly faster interpretation times than did blanks, while targets did not with high-conventional and low-similarity metaphors.$|_{E_3} < 1$
> [|Base primes lead to significantly faster interpretation times than do blanks, while targets do not with high-conventional and high-similarity metaphors.$|_{E_3} = 0$]
> ---
> $0 <$ |An abstraction-guided process may apply to conventional metaphors in accord with h_2.$|_{I_1} < 1$

For us, the third statement (put into [,]) is of primary importance. This latent background assumption is of neutral plausibility on the basis of Experiment 3, since the experimental setting is not capable of providing any information about the behaviour of high-conventional but high-similarity metaphors.

In possession of the results of Experiment 4, however, the situation changes considerably. According to (76)(f), this latent background assumption is implausible. From this it follows, however, that the resulting inference-candidate does not fulfil the criteria for plausible inferences as laid down in (27) in Section 9.5.5, and the conclusion cannot be assigned a plausibility value. Thus, in the p-context extended by data from Experiment 4, the datum (70)(e) is no longer capable of providing support for the hypothesis (73).

57 See Wolff & Gentner (1992: Experiment 2).

19 THE ANSWERS TO (OQ1)–(OQ7)

1 Nevertheless, at this point the question emerges whether the function which can be fulfilled by data playing the role of evidence in the sense of (49)–(51) (see (SMP)(b) in Chapter 21) can also be accomplished by statements that cannot be regarded as data but receive their initial plausibility value from an indirect source. This problem has to be left open in this book. We will be content with remarking that one can also build indirect sources partially supporting a given hypothesis on hypotheses that have been gained by inference and possess a plausibility value. The integration of this possibility into the p-model is, nevertheless, beyond the scope of the present work.

2 This, of course, does not lead to a mixture of object- and metalanguage, and does not pose the danger of the emergence of semantic paradoxes, either. It simply means that in linguistic theorising, the retrospective re-evaluation involves object- and metascientific cycles as well. The plausibility of this hypothesis can be easily supported with the help of the example of generative linguistics, since in the elaboration of generative grammars, metascientific considerations aimed at the evaluation and comparison of grammars played a constitutive role right from the outset.

3 See e.g. Walton (2001: 151), R. Lakoff (1989: 966, footnote 8).

20 THE SOLUTION TO $(P)_V$

1 See Rescher (1987).

2 In another context, Lakoff (1989: 985f.) puts forward a similar stance.

21 SUMMARY: THE SOLUTION TO THE MAIN PROBLEM (MP)

1 Thus, for example, a conjecture may count as a datum as well, provided the (inductive) inferences with the help of which it has been gained are not included in the theory, but one has automatically assigned that low plausibility value to it which is

usually given to conjectures. Similarly, a generally accepted hypothesis may play the role of data in a theory if one simply adopts it from the literature without deriving it from other statements. This does not mean that data are theory-independent or that they are primary to theories. On the contrary: the methodological principles of the theory stipulate which source can be regarded as reliable and to what extent.

References

Achinstein, P. (2001). *The book of evidence*. Oxford University Press.

Allan, K. (2003). Linguistic metatheory. *Language Sciences* 25, 533–60.

(2007). *The Western classical tradition in linguistics*. London and Oakville: Equinox.

Andor, J. (2004). The master and his performance: an interview with Noam Chomsky. *Intercultural Pragmatics* 1, 93–111.

Andrews, A. D. (1990). Case structures and control in Modern Icelandic. In J. Maling & A. Zaenen (eds.), *Modern Icelandic syntax*. Syntax and Semantics 24. San Diego: Academic Press, 187–234.

Aoun, J., Hornstein, N., Lightfoot, D. & Weinberg, A. (1987). Two types of locality. *Linguistic Inquiry* 18(4), 537–77.

Arabatzis, T. (2008). Experiment. In S. Psillos & M. Curd (eds.), *The Routledge companion to philosophy of science*. London and New York: Routledge, 159–70.

Arppe, A. (2009). Linguistic choices vs probabilities – how much and what can linguistic theory explain? In Featherston & Winkler (eds.), 1–24.

Arppe, A. & Järvikivi, J. (2007). Take empiricism seriously! In support of methodological diversity in linguistics. *Corpus Linguistics and Linguistic Theory* 3, 99–109.

Bach, E. (1965). Structural linguistics and the philosophy of science. *Diogenes* 51, 11–28.

Bader, M. & Häussler, J. (2010). Toward a model of grammaticality judgments. *Journal of Linguistics* 46(2), 273–330.

Basin, D. & Matthews, S. (2002). Logical frameworks. In D. M. Gabbay & F. Guenther (eds.), *Handbook of philosophical logic*, vol. 9. Dordrecht: Kluwer, 89–164.

Beall, J. C. & Restall, G. (2000). Logical pluralism. *Australasian Journal of Philosophy* 78, 475–93.

Benoit, W. L., Hample, D. & Benoit, P. J. (eds.) (1992). *Readings in argumentation*. Berlin and New York: Foris Publications.

Bierwisch, M. & Lang, E. (1989a). Somewhat longer – much deeper – further and further: epilogue to the Dimensional Adjective Project. In Bierwisch & Lang (eds.), 471–514.

(eds.) (1989b). *Dimensional adjectives: grammatical structure and conceptual interpretation*. Berlin: Springer.

Blank, G. D. (1988). Metaphors in the lexicon. *Metaphor and Symbolic Activity* 3, 21–36.

Blasko, D. G. & Connine, C. M. (1993). Effects of familiarity and aptness on metaphor processing. *Journal of Experimental Psychology: Learning, Memory and Cognition* 12, 295–308.

Bogen, J. (2002). Experiment and observation. In P. Machamer & M. Silberstein (eds.), *The Blackwell guide to the philosophy of science*. Malden, MA, and Oxford: Blackwell, 128–48.

Borsley, R. D. (2005a). Introduction. In Borsley (ed.), 1475–80.

(ed.) (2005b). Data in theoretical linguistics. Special issue of *Lingua*.

Bowdle, B. F. & Gentner, D. (1999). Metaphor comprehension: from comparison to categorization. *Proceedings of the Twenty-First Annual Conference of the Cognitive Science Society*, 90–5.

(2005). The career of metaphor. *Psychological Review* 112(1), 193–216.

Braithwaite, R. (1953). *Scientific explanation*. Cambridge University Press.

Cantor, G. (1989). The rhetoric of experiment. In D. Gooding, T. Pinch & S. Schaffer (eds.), *The uses of experiment: studies in the natural sciences*. Cambridge University Press, 159–80.

Carnap, R. (1956). The methodological character of theoretical concepts. In H. Feigl & M. Scriven (eds.), *The foundations of science and the concepts of psychology and psychoanalysis*. Minnesota Studies in the Philosophy of Science 1. Minneapolis: University of Minnesota Press, 38–76.

Chomsky, N. (1975 [1957]). *Syntactic structures*. The Hague and Paris: Mouton.

(1965). *Aspects of the theory of syntax*. Cambridge, MA: MIT Press.

(1966 [1964]). *Current issues in linguistic theory*. London, The Hague and Paris: Mouton & Co.

(1969). Language and philosophy. In S. Hook (ed.), *Language and philosophy: a symposium*. New York University Press, 51–94.

(1980a). *Rules and representations*. Oxford: Blackwell.

(1980b). On binding. *Linguistic Inquiry* 11, 1–46.

(1986). *Knowledge of language*. New York: Praeger.

(2002). *On nature and language*. Cambridge University Press.

Cole, P. & Sung, L-M. (1994). Head movement and long distance reflexives. *Linguistic Inquiry* 25, 355–406.

Comrie, B. (1981). *Language universals and linguistic typology: syntax and morphology*. Oxford: Blackwell.

Copi, I. M. & Cohen, C. (1990 [1953]). *Introduction to logic*. New York and London: Macmillan.

Daniels, N. (2003). Reflective equilibrium. In *Stanford Encyclopedia of Philosophy*. http://plato.stanford.edu/archives/sum2003/entries/reflective-equilibrium./

Dodge, E. & Lakoff, G. (2005). Image schemas: from linguistic analysis to neural grounding. In B. Hampe (ed.), *From perception to meaning: image schemas in cognitive linguistics*. Berlin and New York: Mouton de Gruyter, 57–89.

Duhem, P. (1974 [1906]). *The aim and structure of physical theory*. New York: Atheneum.

Falkenhainer, B., Forbus, K. D. & Gentner, D. (1989). The structure-mapping engine: algorithm and examples. *Artificial Intelligence* 41, 1–63.

Faltz, L. M. (1985). Reflexivisation: a study in universal syntax. PhD dissertation, University of California, Berkeley.

Fanselow, G. (1987). *Konfigurationalität: Untersuchungen zur Universalgrammatik am Beispiel des Deutschen*. Tübingen: Narr.

(2009). Die (generative) Syntax in den Zeiten der Empiriediskussion. *Zeitschrift für Sprachwissenschaft* 28, 133–9.
Featherston, S. (2005). The decathlon model: design features for an empirical syntax. In Kepser & Reis (eds.), 187–208.
(2007). Data in generative grammar: the stick and the carrot. In Sternefeld (ed.), 269–318.
(2009a). Relax, lean back, and be a linguist. *Zeitschrift für Sprachwissenschaft* 28, 127–32.
(2009b). A scale for measuring well-formedness: why syntax needs boiling and freezing points. In Featherston & Winkler (eds.), 47–73.
Featherston, S. & Winkler, S. (eds.) (2009). *The fruits of empirical linguistics*, vol. 1: *Process*. Berlin and New York: Mouton de Gruyter.
Fehér, M. (1990). The essential tension. (On the role of inconsistencies in science.) *Studies in Soviet Thought* 39, 231–9.
Fillmore, C. J. (1992). 'Corpus linguistics' vs 'computer-aided armchair linguistics'. In *Directions in corpus linguistics. Proceedings from a 1992 Nobel Symposium on Corpus Linguistics, Stockholm*. Berlin and New York: Mouton de Gruyter, 35–60.
Fodor, J. A. (1985). Some notes on what linguistics is about. In J. J. Katz (ed.), *Philosophy of linguistics*. Oxford University Press, 146–60.
Foster, J. (2007). Real bad grammar: realistic grammatical description with grammaticality. *Corpus Linguistics and Linguistic Theory* 3, 73–86.
Gabbay, D. M., Johnson, R. H., Ohlbach, H. J. & Woods, J. (eds.) (2002). *Handbook of the logic of argument and inference*. Amsterdam, Boston and London: Elsevier.
Geeraerts, D. (2006). Methodology in cognitive linguistics. In Kristiansen, Achard, Dirven & Mendoza Ibáñez (eds.), 21–49.
Gehweiler, E. (2006). Review of Kepser and Reis (2005). *Linguist List* 17, 1540.
Gentner, D. & Bowdle, B. (2008). Metaphor as structure-mapping. In R. W. Gibbs (ed.), *The Cambridge handbook of metaphor and thought*. Cambridge University Press, 109–28.
Gentner, D. & Wolff, P. (1997). Alignment in the processing of metaphor. *Journal of Memory and Language* 37, 331–55.
Gibbs, R. W. (2006). *Embodiment and cognitive science*. Cambridge University Press.
Gibbs, R. W. & Perlman, M. (2006). The contested impact of cognitive linguistic research on the psycholinguistics of metaphor understanding. In Kristiansen, Achard, Dirven & Mendoza Ibáñez (eds.), 211–28.
Glucksberg, S. (2003). The psycholinguistics of metaphor. *Trends in Cognitive Science* 7(2), 92–6.
Glucksberg, S. & McGlone, M. (2001). *Understanding figurative language: from metaphors to idioms*. Oxford University Press.
Glucksberg, S., McGlone, M. S. & Manfredi, D. (1997). Property attribution in metaphor comprehension. *Journal of Memory and Language* 36(1), 50–67.
Goldman, A. (1986). *Epistemology and cognition*. Cambridge, MA: Harvard University Press.
Gooding, D. C. (2000). *Experiment*. In W. H. Newton-Smith (ed.). *A companion to the philosophy of science*. Malden, MA and Oxford: Blackwell, 117–26.
Goodman, N. (1983 [1955]). *Fact, fiction, and forecast*. Cambridge, MA: Harvard University Press.

Greenberg, J. H. (ed.) (1978). *Universals of human language*, 4 vols. Stanford University Press.

Grewendorf, G. (1995). German: a grammatical sketch. In J. Jakobs, A. von Stechow, W. Sternefeld & T. Vennemann (eds.), *Syntax: an international handbook of contemporary research*. Berlin: Mouton de Gruyter, 1288–319.

Hample, D. (1992 [1985]). *A third perspective on argument*. In Benoit, Hample & Benoit (eds.), 91–116.

Hanson, N. R. (1958). *Patterns of discovery*. Cambridge University Press.

Harman, G. (2002). Internal critique: a logic is not a theory of reasoning and a theory of reasoning is not a logic. In Gabbay, Johnson, Ohlbach & Woods (eds.), 171–86.

Haspelmath, M. (2009). Welche Fragen können wir mit herkömmlichen Daten beantworten? *Zeitschrift für Sprachwissenschaft* 28, 157–62.

Head, B. F. (1978). Respect degrees in pronominal reference. In Greenberg (ed.), vol. 3, 151–212.

Hempel, C. G. (1952). *Fundamentals of concept formation in empirical science*. University of Chicago Press.

(1958). The theoretician's dilemma. In M. Feigl, M. Scriven & G. Maxwell (eds.), *Concepts, theories, and the mind–body problem*. Minnesota Studies in the Philosophy of Science 2. Minneapolis: University of Minnesota Press, 37–98.

(1965). *Aspects of scientific explanation and other essays*. New York: Free Press.

(1966a). *Philosophy of natural science*. Englewood Cliffs, NJ: Prentice Hall.

(1966b). Recent problems of induction. In R. G. Colodny (ed.), *Mind and cosmos: essays in contemporary science and philosophy*. University of Pittsburgh Press, 112–34.

Hoffmann, T. (2007). 'Good is good and bad is bad': but how do we know which one we had? *Corpus Linguistics and Linguistic Theory* 3, 87–98.

Householder, F. W. Jr (1973). On arguments from asterisks. *Foundations of Language* 10(3), 365–76.

Howson, C. (2000). Evidence and confirmation. In W. H. Newton-Smith (ed.), *A companion to the philosophy of science*. Oxford: Blackwell, 108–16.

Itkonen, E. (2005). *Analogy as structure and process: approaches in linguistics, cognitive psychology and philosophy of science*. Amsterdam: Benjamins.

Johnson, K. (2008). *Quantitative methods in linguistics*. Malden, MA, Oxford and Carlton: Blackwell.

Kallmeyer, W. & Zifonun, G. (eds.) (2007). *Sprachkorpora – Datenmengen und Erkenntnisfortschritt*. Berlin and New York: Mouton de Gruyter (Institut für Deutsche Sprache – Jahrbuch 2006).

Kelly, Th. (2006). Evidence. In *Stanford Encyclopedia of Philosophy*. http://plato.stanford.edu/entries/evidence./

Kepser, S. & Reis, M. (2005a). Evidence in linguistics. In Kepser & Reis (eds.), 1–6.

(eds.) (2005b). *Linguistic evidence: empirical, theoretical and computational perspectives*. Berlin and New York: Mouton de Gruyter.

Kertész, A. (1991). *Die Modularität der Wissenschaft: Konzeptuelle und soziale Prinzipien linguistischer Erkenntnis*. Braunschweig and Wiesbaden: Vieweg.

(1993). *Heuristik der deutschen Phonologie: eine elementare Einführung in Strategien der Problemlösung*. Budapest: Akadémiai Kiadó.

(2004a). *Philosophie der Linguistik: Studien zur naturalisierten Wissenschaftstheorie*. Tübingen: Narr.

(2004b). *Cognitive semantics and scientific knowledge: case studies in the cognitive science of science*. Amsterdam and Philadelphia: Benjamins.

Kertész, A. & Rákosi, Cs. (2005a). Remarks on the cognitive base of pragmatic principles. *Acta Linguistica Hungarica* 52, 5–40.

(2005b). Whole–part and part–whole inferences in generative and cognitive linguistics. *Acta Linguistica Hungarica* 52, 221–80.

(2006). Inconsistency and plausible reasoning in an analysis of German affricates: a case study in the philosophy of linguistics. *Language Sciences* 28, 386–423.

(2008a). Daten und Evidenz in linguistischen Theorien: ein Forschungsüberblick. In Kertész & Rákosi (eds.), 21–60.

(2008b). Conservatism vs. innovation in the debate on data in generative grammar. In Kertész & Rákosi (eds.), 85–108.

(2008c). Conservatism vs. innovation in the (un)grammaticality debate. In Kertész & Rákosi (eds.), 61–84.

(eds.) (2008d). *New approaches to linguistic evidence: pilot studies*. Frankfurt am Main etc.: Lang.

(2009a). On the metascientific representation of inconsistency in linguistic theories. In B. van Heusden & W. Wildgen (eds.), *Meta-representation, self-organization and art*. Frankfurt am Main etc.: Lang, 233–64.

(2009b). Cyclic vs circular argumentation in the Conceptual Metaphor Theory. *Cognitive Linguistics* 20(4), 703–32.

(2009c). On current approaches to linguistic data and evidence. *Sprachtheorie und germanistische Linguistik* 19, 125–70.

Kiefer, F. (2007). *Jelentéselmélet. [The theory of meaning]*. 2nd, revised edition. Budapest: Corvina.

Kienpointner, M. (1992). *Alltagslogik. Struktur und Funktion von Argumentationsmustern*. Stuttgart-Bad Canstatt: frommann-holzboog.

Kristiansen, G., Achard, M., Dirven, R. & de Mendoza Ibáñez, F. J. R. (eds.) (2006). *Cognitive linguistics: current applications and future perspectives*. Berlin and New York: Mouton de Gruyter.

Kuhn, Th. S. (1962/1970). *The structure of scientific revolutions*. University of Chicago Press.

Lakatos, I. (1970). Falsification and the methodology of scientific research programmes. In I. Lakatos & A. Musgrave (eds.), *Criticism and the growth of knowledge*. Cambridge University Press, 91–196.

(1976). *Proofs and refutations*. Cambridge University Press.

Lakoff, G. & Johnson, M. (1980). *Metaphors we live by*. University of Chicago Press.

Lakoff, R. (1989). The way we were; or; the real truth about generative semantics: a memoir. *Journal of Pragmatics* 13, 939–88.

Lang, E. (1989). The semantics of dimensional designation. In Bierwisch & Lang (eds.), 263–458.

Lasnik, H. & Saito, M. (1984). On the nature of proper government. *Linguistic Inquiry* 15(2), 235–89.

Laudan, L. (1977). *Progress and its problems: toward a theory of scientific growth*. Berkeley, Los Angeles and London: University of California Press.

Lehmann, C. (2004). Data in linguistics. *The Linguistic Review* 21, 175–210.
(2007). Daten – Korpora – Dokumentation. In Kallmeyer & Zifonun (eds.), 9–27.
Lemnitzer, L. & Zinsmeister, H. (2006). *Korpuslinguistik: eine Einführung*. Tübingen: Narr.
Levinson, S. C. (2000). *Presumptive meanings: the theory of generalised conversational implicature*. Cambridge, MA, and London: MIT Press.
Linguistic Evidence Conference 11-13 Feb. 2010, Tübingen. www.sfb833.uni-tuebingen.de/wb/pages/de/veranstaltungen/linguistic-evidence-2010.php
Łukasiewicz, J. (1970 [1912]). Creative elements in science. In J. Łukasiewicz, *Selected works*. Amsterdam: North Holland, 12–44.
MacFarlane, J. G. (2000). What does it mean to say that logic is formal? PhD dissertation, University of Pittsburgh.
Manning, C. D. (2003). Probabilistic syntax. In J. Bod, J. Hay & S. Jannedy (eds.), *Probabilistic linguistics*. Cambridge, MA: MIT Press, 289–341.
McEnery, T. & Wilson, A. (1996). *Corpus linguistics: an introduction*. Edinburgh University Press.
Meheus, J. (ed.) (2002). *Inconsistency in science*. Dordrecht: Kluwer.
Mereu, L. (2004). Linguistic data as complex items. *The Linguistic Review* 21, 211–33.
Meurers, W. D. (2007). Advancing linguistics between the extremes: some thoughts on Geoffrey R. Sampson's 'Grammar without grammaticality'. *Corpus Linguistics and Linguistic Theory* 3, 49–55.
Moravcsik, E. (1969). Determination. *Working papers on language universals* 1, 63–98a.
(1993). Why is syntax complicated? In M. Eid & G. Iverson (eds.), *Principles and prediction: the analysis of natural language*. Amsterdam and Philadelphia: Benjamins, 73–92.
(2006). *An introduction to syntactic theory*. London and New York: Continuum.
(2010). Conflict resolution in syntactic theory. *Studies in Language* 34(3), 636–69.
Murphy, G. L. (1996). On metaphoric representation. *Cognition* 60, 173–204.
Nagel, E. (1961). *The structure of science*. New York: Harcourt, Brace & World.
Newmeyer, F. J. (1980). *Linguistic theory in America: the first quarter-century of transformational generative grammar*. New York: Academic Press.
Nickles, T. (2002). From Copernicus to Ptolemy: inconsistency and method. In Meheus (ed.), 1–33.
(1980). Scientific discovery, logic and rationality. In T. Nickles (ed.), *Scientific discovery, logic, and rationality*. Dordrecht: Reidel, 1–59.
Onishi, K. H. & Murphy, G. L. (1993). Metaphoric reference: when metaphors are not understood as easily as literal expressions. *Memory and Cognition* 21, 763–72.
Penke, M. & Rosenbach, A. (2004a). What counts as evidence in linguistics? In Penke & Rosenbach (eds.), 480–526.
(eds.) (2004b). *What counts as evidence in linguistics?* Special issue of *Studies in Language*. [= *Studies in Language* 28(3): 481–747]
(2007a). Preface. In Penke & Rosenbach (eds.), vii–ix.
(eds.) (2007b). *What counts as evidence in linguistics?* Amsterdam and Philadelphia: Benjamins.
Perry, Th. A. (ed.) (1980). *Evidence and argumentation in linguistics*. Berlin and New York: Mouton de Gruyter.

Plank, F. (ed.) (2008). *The universals archive*. http://typo.uni-konstanz.de/archive/

Politzer, G. & Bourmaud, G. (2002). Deductive reasoning from uncertain conditionals. *British Journal of Psychology* 93, 345–81.

Pollock, J. L. (2001). Defeasible reasoning with variable degrees of justification. *Artificial Intelligence* 133, 233–82.

Polya, G. (1948). *How to solve it*. Princeton University Press.

(1954). *Patterns of plausible inference*. London: Oxford University Press.

(1981). *Mathematical discovery*. New York: John Wiley & Sons.

Popper, K. (1959). *The logic of scientific discovery*. London: Hutchinson.

Priest, G. (2002). Paraconsistent Logic. In D. Gabbay & F. Guenthner (eds.), *Handbook of paraconsistent logic*. Dordrecht: Kluwer, 287–393.

Priest, G., Beall, J. C. & Armour-Garb, B. (eds.) (2004). *The law of non-contradiction*. Oxford: Clarendon Press.

Prince, A. & Smolenksy, P. (2004). *Optimality theory: constraint interaction in generative grammar*. Oxford: Blackwell.

Pullum, G. K. (2007). Ungrammaticality, rarity, and corpus use. *Corpus Linguistics and Linguistic Theory* 3, 33–47.

Rákosi, Cs. (2005). *Nyelvészet és argumentációelmélet. [Linguistics and argumentation theory]*. Debrecen: DE Kossuth Egyetemi Kiadó.

(forthcoming). The fabulous engine: strengths and flaws of psycholinguistic experiments. *Language Sciences*.

(in preparation). *On the rhetoric of psycholinguistic experiments*.

Rawls, J. (1971). *A theory of justice*. Cambridge, MA: Harvard University Press.

Reichenbach, H. (1938). *Experience and prediction: an analysis of the foundations and the structure of knowledge*. University of Chicago Press.

Reis, M. *et al.* (1998). *Linguistische Datenstrukturen: theoretische und empirische Grundlagen der Grammatikforschung*. Universität Tübingen.

Rescher, N. (1973). *The coherence theory of truth*. Oxford: Clarendon Press.

(1976). *Plausible reasoning*. Assen and Amsterdam: Van Gorcum.

(1977a). *Methodological pragmatism*. Oxford: Blackwell.

(1977b). *Dialectics: a controversy-oriented approach to the theory of knowledge*. Albany: State University of New York Press.

(1979). *Cognitive systematisation*. Oxford: Blackwell.

(1980). *Induction: an essay on the justification of inductive reasoning*. Oxford: Blackwell.

(1987). How serious a fallacy is inconsistency? *Argumentation* 1, 303–16.

Rescher, N. & Brandom, R. (1980). *The logic of inconsistency*. Oxford: Blackwell.

Rigotti, E. (2007a). Relevance of context bound loci to topical potential in the argumentation stage. *Argumentation* 22, 519–40.

(2007b). Can classical topics be revived within the contemporary theory of argumentation? In A. Blair, Ch. A. Willard & B. Garssen (eds.), *Proceedings of the Sixth Conference of the International Society for the Study of Argumentation*. Amsterdam: Sic Sat, 1155–63.

Ringen, J. D. (1975). Linguistic facts: a study of the empirical scientific status of transformational generative grammars. In D. Cohen & J. R. Wirth (eds.), *Testing linguistic hypotheses*. Washington, DC: Hemisphere, 1–41.

Rizzi, L. (1978). A restructuring rule in Italian syntax. In S. J. Keyser (ed.), *Recent transformational studies in European languages*. Cambridge, MA: MIT Press.
Rohrer, T. (2006). Three dogmas of embodiment: cognitive linguistics as a cognitive science. In Kristiansen, Achard, Dirven & Mendoza Ibáñez (eds.), 119–46.
Ross, J. R. (1967). *Constraints on variables in syntax*. Indiana University Linguistics Club.
Sampson, G. R. (1975). *The form of language*. London: Weidenfeld & Nicholson.
(2007). Reply. *Corpus Linguistics and Linguistic Theory* 3, 111–29.
Schlesewsky, M. (2009). Linguistische Daten aus experimentellen Umgebungen: eine multiexperimentelle und multimodale Perspektive. *Zeitschrift für Sprachwissenschaft* 28, 169–78.
Schütze, C. T. (1996). *The empirical base of linguistics: Grammaticality judgments and linguistic methodology*. University of Chicago Press.
(2009). Web searches should supplement judgements, not supplant them. *Zeitschrift für Sprachwissenschaft* 28, 151–6.
Simon, H. J. (1997). Die Diachronie der deutschen Anredepronomina aus Sicht der Universalienforschung. *Sprachtypologie und Universalienforschung* 50, 267–81.
Simone, R. (2004). The object, the method, and the ghosts: remarks on a terra incognita. *The Linguistic Review* 21, 235–56.
Sorace, A. & Keller, F. (2005). Gradience in linguistic data. *Lingua* 115(11), 1497–525.
Stefanowitsch, A. & Gries, S. Th. (eds.) (2007). *Grammar without grammaticality*. (*Corpus Linguistics and Linguistic Theory* 3(1)).
Stegmüller, W. (1970). *Theorie und Erfahrung*. Berlin, Heidelberg and New York: Springer.
Sternefeld, W. (ed.) (2007). *Data in generative grammar* (= *Theoretical Linguistics* 33(3)).
Subbarao, K. V. (1998). Linguistic theory and syntactic typology: a proposal for a symbiotic relationship. In L. V. Khokhlova & A. Sawani (eds.), *Vaagbhaarati: Proceedings of the International Conference on South Asian Languages. 5–23*. Moscow: Institute of Asian and African Languages, Moscow State University.
Swinney, D. & Cutler, A. (1979). The access and processing of idiomatic expressions. *Journal of Verbal Learning and Verbal Behavior* 18, 523–34.
Walton, D. (1991). *Begging the question: circular reasoning as a tactic of argumentation*. New York, Westport and London: Greenwood Press.
(1992). Rules for plausible reasoning. *Informal Logic* 1992 (1), 33–51.
(1995). *A pragmatic theory of fallacy*. Tuscaloosa: University of Alabama Press.
(1996). *Argumentation schemes for presumptive reasoning*. Mahwah: Erlbaum.
(2001). Abductive, presumptive and plausible arguments. *Informal Logic* 21, 141–69.
Walton, D. & Reed, C. (2005). Argumentation schemes and enthymemes. *Synthese* 145, 339–70.
Walton, D., Reed, C. & Macagno, F. (2008). *Argumentation schemes*. Cambridge University Press.
Weskott, T. & Fanselow, G. (2009). Scaling issues in the measurement of linguistic acceptability. In Featherston & Winkler (eds.), 229–46.
Williamson, T. (2000). *Knowledge and its limits*. Oxford University Press.
Winkler, S. & Featherston, S. (eds.) (2009). *The fruits of empirical linguistics*, vol. 2: *Product*. Berlin and New York: Mouton de Gruyter.

Wolff, P. & Gentner, D. (1992). The time course of metaphor comprehension. *Proceedings of the 14th Annual Conference of the Cognitive Science Society*. Hillsdale: Erlbaum.

Wunderlich, D. (ed.) (1976). *Wissenschaftstheorie der Linguistik*. Kronberg: Scriptor.

Wurzel, W. U. (1981). Phonologie: Segmentale Struktur. In K. E. Heidolph *et al.* (eds.), *Grundzüge einer deutschen Grammatik*. Berlin: Akademie-Verlag, 898–990.

Yan, J., Forbus, K. & Gentner, D. (2003). A theory of rerepresentation in analogical matching. In *Proceedings of the 25th Annual Conference of the Cognitive Science Society*. Wheat Ridge: Cognitive Science Society.

Zubizarreta, M. L. (1982). On the relationship of the lexicon to syntax. PhD dissertation, MIT.

Index